PRAISE FOR

God, Faith & Identity from the Ashes

"Critically important and compelling, especially at a time when there are people out there who deny or question the Holocaust. These powerful reflections of the survivors' children and grand-children are must reading for a new generation."

—**Wolf Blitzer**, anchor, CNN's *The Situation Room*

"A moving, unforgettable book on the generational impact of the Holocaust. My perspective on what it means to be human has been enriched immeasurably by reading it. Through contemporary voices, it also shows us how the Holocaust continues to impact us today."

—**Susan Eisenhower**, author; president, The Eisenhower Group, Inc.; chairman emeritus, The Eisenhower Institute

"Brilliant ... shows that there were many more than six million victims of the Shoah. It also gives us a glimpse into how much the world lost.... Most importantly, it demonstrates the tenacity of the survivors and their enormous contributions to repairing a world broken by those who perpetrated the Holocaust and those who stood idly by. Reading this book will make you sad, angry and revitalized. A great addition to the literature of history's most brutal genocide." —**Alan M. Dershowitz**, author, *Terror Tunnels: The Case for Israel's Just War Against Hamas*

"A monumental and deeply moving achievement. It is essential read-ing for those interested in assuring that the memory of the Holocaust does not fade with the passing of the generation of victims."

—**Ambassador Stuart E. Eizenstat**, former Special Representative of the President and Secretary of State for Holocaust Issues in the Clinton Administration while also holding four senior positions, and an official in three other U.S. administrations

"The children and grandchildren of survivors of the Shoah have a scarred yet sacred memory. [This book] allows them to share that memory and its important lessons with the world in a tender and moving way." —**Cardinal Timothy Dolan**, archbishop of New York

"Belongs in every home and in every library, a unique contribution.... An affirmation of the sanctity of human life and the eternity of the Jewish People."
—**Rabbi Marvin Hier,** founder and dean, Simon Wiesenthal Center

"In a world still ravaged by murderous hatred ... this powerful new set of testimonies from children and grandchildren of survivors could not come at a more fateful time. A moving and necessary book."
—**Rabbi Lord Jonathan Sacks,** chief rabbi emeritus, United Hebrew Congregations of the British Commonwealth

"This rich collection of thoughts and reflections ... is yet another link in the chain of memory. They demonstrate the multi-faceted and diverse ways in which Holocaust survivors transmitted the 'legacy' of their experience from generation to generation. It is an important collection, one that is of educational and spiritual value."
—**Deborah E. Lipstadt,** Dorot Professor of Modern Jewish and Holocaust Studies, Emory University

"It is rare that a book overwhelms emotionally while also teaching indelibly. [This] luminous collection of essays does both. These stories will both captivate and stay with you. I plan to share this with everyone who matters to me."   —**Abigail Pogrebin,** author, *Stars of David: Prominent Jews Talk about Being Jewish*

"*God, Faith and Identity from the Ashes* not only fills an important gap in modern Jewish history, but it also will serve as a guide to future generations of Jews and non-Jews who will struggle with these same issues."   —**Fred Zeidman,** former chairman, United States Holocaust Memorial Council

"A major and articulate advocate of meaningful Holocaust remembrance has addressed a compelling facet of the vital legacy of survivors' families." —**Avner Shalev,** chairman, Yad Vashem Directorate

"Writing with their hearts and minds, these [contributors] remember the horrors experienced by their parents and grandparents, and reflect on the understandings of God that animate their own lives. A truly interesting book!"   —**Susannah Heschel,** Eli Black Professor of Jewish Studies, Dartmouth College

"Prepare yourself to be touched, amazed and inspired by one of the best volumes on the consequences of the Holocaust for a long time which may just change how we understand Jewish identity after the Holocaust—and not only for the descendants of the survivors themselves. A volume of remarkable poignancy and power, it redefines the second and third generations. These remarkable authors have collectively struggled to make sense of the senseless, turning the story around from despair to hope and becoming our new guides to the future."   —**Stephen D. Smith, PhD**, executive director,
USC Shoah Foundation; UNESCO chair on Genocide Education

"An overwhelmingly affecting book!... The [contributors'] words bear consecrated witness ... and testify to the enduring power of the Jewish and human spirit. Remarkably powerful."
                    —**Rabbi David Ellenson**, chancellor,
Hebrew Union College–Jewish Institute of Religion

"The faith in humankind, intellectual depth and remarkable eloquence of the contributors are a tribute to the resilience of the human spirit. Menachem Rosensaft's magnificent book must become required reading for all who would contemplate the aftermath and consequences of hatred, bigotry and genocide."
     —**Helena Bonham Carter**, award-winning actress; member of UK
Commission on the Holocaust; granddaughter of Spanish diplomat
honored by Yad Vashem as a Righteous Among the Nations

"Truly an enriching book—an insightful read brimming with life-changing and timeless wisdom."
                    —**Richard Joel**, president, Yeshiva University

"Unique and original in its depth and range. It's worth the attention of Jews and non-Jews alike."
          —**Rabbi Neil Gillman, PhD**, professor emeritus of Jewish thought,
The Jewish Theological Seminary of America

"This great book ... is a powerful compendium of responses to the Holocaust from members of the second and third generations. As Rosensaft understands, the experience carries forward into each succeeding generation, influencing how a family lives, with what messages and what world view."
          —**Ruth Messinger**, president, American Jewish World Service

"Will be read by generations of Jews and by generations of the survivors of other genocides to learn how one can arise from the ashes, how one embraces life and enhances life in the aftermath of destruction." —**Michael Berenbaum**, author; project director, United States Holocaust Memorial Museum (1988–1993), and former director of its Research Institute

"An important book…. The range of [the contributors'] work in the world is amazing (an extraordinary compliment to the survivors). The range they offer of how to respond to life in light of the Shoah is no less amazing. You must read this." —**Rabbi Irving (Yitz) Greenberg**, director, President's Commission on the Holocaust (1979–1980); former chairman, United States Holocaust Memorial Museum

"A powerful and most important addition to the narrative of the Holocaust for this and future generations. Extraordinary and compelling essays describe how the legacy of family members' Holocaust experiences have impacted, in fact shaped, the lives of the children and grandchildren of survivors. Each essay is unique, enlightening and captivating." —**Harvey Schulweis**, chairman, Board of Trustees, The Jewish Foundation for the Righteous

"Before the loss of my son Daniel, I never considered myself a Holocaust survivor, not even a child of a survivor. The brutal murder of Danny taught me that the Holocaust, and man's inhumanity to man, did not end in May 1945. This incredible book has taught me another lesson: that I was actually there, that I took that horrible last journey with my grandparents, from Kielce to Treblinka, and with six million other brothers and sisters, not asking why, just witnessing and knowing, with the greatest certitude, that history and planet earth and cosmic consciousness will all be different from now on. Will they?" —**Judea Pearl**, president, Daniel Pearl Foundation; co-editor, *I Am Jewish: Personal Reflections Inspired by the Last Words of Daniel Pearl*

God, Faith
& Identity
from the Ashes

God, Faith & Identity from the Ashes

Reflections of Children and Grandchildren of Holocaust Survivors

Edited by Menachem Z. Rosensaft

Prologue by Elie Wiesel

For People of All Faiths, All Backgrounds

JEWISH LIGHTS Publishing

Nashville, Tennessee

God, Faith & Identity from the Ashes:
Reflections of Children and Grandchildren of Holocaust Survivors

© 2015 by Menachem Z. Rosensaft
Prologue © 2015 by Elie Wiesel

Copyright in each essay in this collection is reserved by its author, each of whom has graciously granted permission for its use in this collection.

Library of Congress Cataloging-in-Publication Data
God, faith & identity from the ashes : reflections of children and grandchildren of Holo-caust survivors / edited by Menachem Z. Rosensaft ; prologue by Elie Wiesel.
  pages cm
  Includes bibliographical references and index.
  ISBN 978-1-58023-805-2 (hardcover : alk. paper) — ISBN 978-1-58023-824-3 (ebook : alk. paper) 1. Children of Holocaust survivors—Attitudes. 2. Children of Holocaust survivors—United States—Attitudes. 3. Children of Holocaust survivors—Intellectual life. 4. Children of Holocaust survivors—United States—Intellectual life. 5. Children of Holocaust survivors—Biography. 6. Children of Holocaust survivors—United States—Biography. 7. Holocaust, Jewish (1939-1945)—Influence. I. Rosensaft, Menachem Z., 1948– editor. II. Title: God, faith, and identity from the ashes.
  D804.3.G618 2014
  940.53'1809253—dc23
  2014036075

10 9 8 7 6 5 4 3 2

Manufactured in the United States of America
Cover and Interior Design: Tim Holtz
Cover Art: *Spilt on Another Map*, etching-aquatint-mezzotint, Mirta Kupferminc, Buenos Aires, Argentina; www.mirtakupferminc.net

For People of All Faiths, All Backgrounds
Published by Jewish Lights Publishing
An Imprint of Turner Publishing Company
4507 Charlotte Avenue, Suite 100
Nashville, TN 37209
Tel: (615) 255-2665
www.jewishlights.com

For Hallie and Jacob

Contents

Part I
God and Faith   1

Part II
Identity   77

Part III
A Legacy of Memory   149

Part IV
Tikkun Olam: Changing the World for the Better 227

To Our Children

Elie Wiesel
Nobel Peace Prize Laureate, Author, Teacher

Nobel Peace Prize laureate Elie Wiesel, who survived Auschwitz and Buchenwald, has been the preeminent voice of conscience and Holocaust memory throughout the seven decades since the end of World War II. In 1984, Professor Wiesel delivered the keynote address at the First International Conference of Children of Holocaust Survivors in New York City, and he has graciously allowed us to publish the following excerpts from that address as his charge to the post-Holocaust generations as we explore who we are, what we believe, and what we stand for in the pages of this book.[1]

And it came to pass that the great Talmudic scholar Rabbi Shimon ben Yohai and his son Rabbi Eleazar opposed Roman occupation of Judea with such courage that they were sentenced to death. Rejecting martyrdom as an option, they hid in a cave for twelve years. When they emerged, they were shocked. The outside world had not changed. The same people were doing the same things they had done before. It was business as usual. Life went on with its games, temptations, illusions, dangers, and silly victories. Father and son could not believe their eyes. How was all that possible? Had they gone through ultimate trials and burning experiences only to leave no imprint on other people? In their anger, says the Talmud, "whatever they looked upon was turned to ashes." And then a heavenly voice was heard: "Have you left your hiding place only to destroy my Creation? Go back to your cave." And back they went for another year. When they came out again, Rabbi Eleazar was still angry, but not his father. Comments the Talmud: "Whatever the young Rabbi Eleazar's eyes wounded, the old rabbi Shimon's eyes healed."

I like this ancient legend for it illustrates the extraordinary challenges which you and we—your older brothers or parents—had to confront and still confront. When the war years were over—with the nightmare lifted in the mist of dawn—we too discovered the outside world with disbelief. It had not changed. History had not altered its course. Human beings were still inhuman, society still cruel, Jews still hated, others jailed, victimized. That your parents were not seized by an irrepressible anger, that they did not yield to impulses to commit violence—and reduce everything to ashes, at least in their minds—remains a source of astonishment to me. Had they set fire to the entire planet, it would not have surprised anyone.

Strange as it may sound, you are angrier than we were. And your anger is healthier than ours might have been. Like Rabbi Shimon bar Yohai, we tried to heal, maybe too soon. But we did so for your sake. Since we chose to have you, we sought to improve the world for you. That your response has been to receive the message and to pass it on has been a source of gratification to us. In other words: your anger—your right to let anger explode—has also been transformed into something else. You, too, have chosen to heal.

Menachem Rosensaft, you and your colleagues belong to a privileged generation. It was you that the enemy sought to destroy. We were only the instruments. You were the enemy's obsession. In murdering living Jews, he wished to prevent you from being born. He knew how vulnerable we Jews are with regard to children. Our history began with a Jewish child, Isaac, being threatened, but then saved....

I am convinced that it would have been natural and logical for your parents to have turned their back on culture and history, to have opted for nihilism, and to have done what Rabbi Shimon bar Yohai and Rabbi Eleazar did, to reduce history to ashes or at least to give it a taste of ashes.

And yet we have chosen you. And now we are making you responsible for a world you did not create, a world we have created for you with words, a world others destroyed against you and against us. And now you are being summoned to do something with pieces of words, with fragments of our vision, with remnants of our broken, dispersed memories.

We are always telling you that civilization betrayed itself by betraying us, that culture ended in moral bankruptcy, and yet we want you to improve both, not one at the expense of the other.

What have we learned in our adult lives? Let me tell you what I have learned. I have learned that human experiences, whatever their nature, must be shared. I have learned that suffering itself must be conceived as vehicle, not as prison. And I have learned that suffering does not confer privileges; it is what we do with suffering that matters. We will never invoke our suffering simply to create more suffering. Quite the opposite. We invoke it to limit suffering, to curtail it, to eliminate it....

And so, my friends, I cannot tell you how grateful I am to all of you for being here yesterday, today, and tomorrow. When I speak to others, surely you know that I mean you, all the time. You are my audience, because it is you who matter. Until now, whenever we would meet alone, we listened to each other, sad, proud, but we listened. We listened because we were alone. But now, at last, we can talk freely about our obsessions and share memories and hopes. We have become partners now, united by the same lofty and urgent goal. We are no longer afraid of unshed tears or of unspoken words. Until now you have been our students, perhaps even our disciples. At times, to some of us, you have been our children, troubled and exalted in our desire to see in you more than our children. We saw in you our parents. You became our parents. But now we are closer than ever before because we have spoken and because you have spoken to one another.

We look at one another with pride and gratitude and we think that whatever happened to Abraham and Isaac has happened to us too. The *Akedah*, after all, was not consummated. The testimony of our life and death will not vanish. Our memories will not die with us.

Do you know what we see in you, in all of you? We see in you our heirs, our allies, our younger brothers and sisters. But in a strange way to all of us all of you are our children.

Living with Ghosts

> night fragments created
> in fire shadows
> we are the last and the first:
> the last to taste ashes
> from the cursed century's valley
> of unwilling passers through
> where God revealed His face
> to them alone;
> and the first
> transfixed by still burning yesterdays
> to reach beyond heaven and its clouds
> beyond crimson ghost illusions
> into ourselves
> imploding
> in search of memory
> (MZR)

Many if not most children and grandchildren of Holocaust survivors live with ghosts.

We are haunted much in the way a cemetery is haunted. We bear within us the shadows and echoes of an anguished dying we never experienced or witnessed.

One of my ghosts is a little boy named Benjamin who arrived at the Auschwitz-Birkenau death camp with his parents on the night of August 3–4, 1943. In her posthumously published memoirs, my mother, Dr. Hadassah Rosensaft, recalled her final moments with her son, my brother:

We were guarded by SS men and women. One SS man was standing in front of the people and he started the selection. With a single movement of his finger, he was sending some people to the right and some to the left.... Men were separated from women. People with children were sent to one side, and young people were separated from older-looking ones. No one was allowed to go from one group to the other. Our five-and-a-half-year-old son went with his father. Something that will haunt me to the end of my days occurred during those first moments. As we were separated, our son turned to me and asked, "Mommy, are we going to live or die?" I didn't answer this question.[1]

Benjamin is one of between one million and one and a half million Jewish children who were murdered in the Holocaust. Since my mother's death in 1997, he has existed inside of me. I see his face in my mind, try to imagine his voice, his fear as the gas chamber doors slammed shut, his final tears. If I were to forget him, he would disappear.

The preservation and transfer of memory is the most critical mission that children and grandchildren of survivors must undertake so as to ensure meaningful and authentic Holocaust remembrance in future generations. As the ranks of survivors steadily dwindle, this task becomes ever more urgent.

I have been in awe of many Holocaust survivors throughout my life, but none as much as my parents, Josef and Hadassah Rosensaft, my wife Jeanie's parents, Sam and Lilly Bloch, and my teacher and mentor, Professor Elie Wiesel. They have been and continue to be my role models, and this book is meant in large part to be a continuation of and response to their work over the course of decades to ensure and perpetuate a genuine remembrance of not just the annihilation of millions of European Jews at the hands of the Third Reich and its accomplices but also the lives, culture, and spirit of thousands upon thousands of devastated and destroyed Jewish communities.

Growing up, we whose parents had come out of the Shoah believed that they were indestructible. After all, they overcame the German efforts to murder them, survived ghettos and death camps, and rebuilt their lives after the war. They also had a special appreciation and zest for life. In our eyes, they were truly the "greatest generation." It seemed to us that our parents would be here forever and that they would always protect us, their children.

But age and the frailties of the human body are proving to be inexorable. All too soon, the voices of those who suffered alongside the murdered victims of the Holocaust will no longer be heard. Many sons and daughters of survivors have already lost one or both of their parents. My father, the fiery leader of the survivors of Bergen-Belsen, died in 1975 at the age of sixty-four. My mother, one of the founders of the United States Holocaust Memorial Museum in Washington, DC, died twenty-two years later. Most survivors today are in their eighties, and many are in failing health.

The principal responsibility for transmitting the survivors' legacy of remembrance into the future has shifted to their children and grandchildren. In his keynote address at the First International Conference of Children of Holocaust Survivors, Elie Wiesel mandated us to do what the survivors "have tried to do—and more: to keep our tale alive—and sacred."[2] Over the course of the past seventy years, many sons, daughters, and grandchildren of survivors and of refugees from pre-war Nazi persecution have absorbed and integrated our parents' and grandparents' memories, spirit, and perseverance into our collective consciousness. Our task now is to convey this birthright to our children and grandchildren, to the Jewish community as a whole, and to the world.

There is no one form, or even no one prevailing form, of this multifaceted inheritance with which each of us has been idiosyncratically endowed. Some survivors spoke about their experiences in the ghettos and camps; others enveloped themselves and their families in a cloud of silence, shrouding their past in an aura of mystery and secrecy. Some refugees from Nazi Germany and Austria talked eloquently about the rise of Nazism and the persecution they had endured; others cloaked themselves in denial at their erstwhile neighbors' perfidious betrayal. Some survivors emerged from the Shoah with their faith, whether in God or in humankind, shattered; others were able to maintain an intimate bond with their Creator. Some who had been atheists became cynics, while others taught their children that human and civil rights for all, not just for Jews, is a paramount value.

I do not mean to imply that the transmission into the future of our legacy—the transference, if you will, of memory—should be our only priority. Our identity imposes other obligations on us as well. We must do everything in our power to enable all survivors to live out their remaining days in dignity. Tens of thousands of them live a precarious existence. Large numbers of survivors around the world, especially in Eastern Europe but also in the United States and Israel, live in dire financial straits. Often forced to decide whether to use their meager resources to buy food or medicine, whether to heat their homes or get their glasses fixed, they urgently need far more assistance than the meager monthly payments many but by no means all of them have been accorded under the German reparations law.

We also have a moral responsibility not to stand idly by, in the words of Mordechai Gebirtig's famous song "Es Brent" (It Is Burning), "with folded arms" (*mit ferleygte hent*), while human beings anywhere in the world are oppressed or persecuted. We have no right to criticize the world for not coming to the aid of our parents and grandparents during the 1930s and 1940s unless we do everything in our power to fight all forms of contemporary racial, religious, or ethnic hatred and to prevent contemporary genocides, whether in Darfur, Rwanda, the former Yugoslavia, or elsewhere. If we learn only one lesson from the cataclysm known as the Holocaust, it must be that the ultimate consequence of silence and indifference to the dire plight of others was embodied forever in the fires of Auschwitz and the mass graves of Bergen-Belsen.

No one response to our simultaneously collective yet by definition individually unique heritage is more valid than any other. The reality is that we are no more homogeneous than our parents or grandparents. The European Jews swept up in the whirlwind of the Holocaust ranged from the fervently observant to the defiantly secular, from Yiddishists and Hebraists to those who were so thoroughly assimilated that they barely acknowledged their Jewish roots. In the crowded barracks of Auschwitz, Treblinka, and Bergen-Belsen, the formerly wealthy slept alongside Jews who had been destitute and others from all economic strata in between. The SS doctors who carried out the selections for the gas chambers did not differentiate between Jewish intellectuals and laborers, or rabbis and businessmen, or lawyers and pickpockets.

The children and grandchildren of survivors whose views and perspectives are included in this book span a broad range of occupations and professions—from theologians, scholars, rabbis, and cantors to authors, artists, political and community leaders, physicians, psychologists, and media personalities.

Some of us have focused on the religious and spiritual aspect of Judaism. Some have devoted themselves to Holocaust remembrance. Some are historians, sociologists, or philosophers. Some dedicate themselves to healing bodies, or minds, or souls. Some are novelists, or poets, or artists, or filmmakers. Others are committed to political and social action in Israel, or within a broader Jewish and Zionist context, or, more broadly still, on behalf of humankind as a whole.

It is also important to bear in mind that even within our self-designations as the so-called second and third generations we subdivide ourselves.

Those of us born in Displaced Persons camps shortly after the end of World War II have an intuitive affinity with one another. Like our parents and grandparents, we communicate in our own shorthand. Several years ago, I met the president of a prestigious New Jersey golf club and discovered that we shared a similar past. "I was born in Foehrenwald," a DP camp in the American zone, Solomon Greenspan told me. "Bergen-Belsen," I replied. There was no need for lengthy explanations. We knew each other's histories without having to exchange any additional words.

Then there are the children and grandchildren of partisans, whose homes were different from those of camp survivors, or those of Jews who had spent the war years in Siberia or who had emigrated from Nazi Germany during the 1930s. It goes without saying that Polish Jews are culturally distinct from German Jews, who in turn often have little in common with Hungarian or Romanian survivors, or with Sephardi Jewish survivors, whether from Thessaloniki, Yugoslavia, or elsewhere in Europe. When a former camp inmate married a hidden child, or a Jew who survived on forged papers, or a pre-war refugee, the dynamics changed yet again. And then, of course, there are all those families with a parent or one or more grandparents who did not experience the Holocaust at all.

One further note of caution is essential here. Children of survivors are frequently the subject of psychological studies dissecting our supposed pathology, trauma, guilt complexes, collective idiosyncrasies, and other alleged common characteristics. Such theses are often skewed and must be read (or lectures heard) with an enormous grain of salt. Their conclusions are generally rooted in control groups consisting of individuals who have sought counseling or treatment from a therapist or other mental health professional. It is as if one were

to extrapolate the drinking habits of all adult Americans from interviews with members of Alcoholics Anonymous.

I do not mean to suggest that all children of survivors are free
of emotional issues. There are those who have been unable to cope
with their parents' experiences, or who have grown up in homes in
which the dark imagery of the Holocaust was overwhelming. At the
same time, I firmly believe that most of us look upon our parents
and grandparents as role models and a source of strength. As Elie
Wiesel told us at the First International Conference of Children of
Holocaust Survivors, "The great majority of you remain healthy and
generous, with a sense of humor, with a sense of literature and culture
and humanity. That you are so well-adjusted seems almost abnormal.
Logically, most of you should have ended up on the analyst's couch,
if not elsewhere. The fact is that you have managed to rechannel your
sadness, your anger, your inherited memories into such humanistic
endeavors as medicine, law, social action, education, philanthropy.
In other words, you are really the worthy children of your parents."[3]

This is not the first collection of writings by children of survivors.
Fifty years ago, I edited the *Bergen-Belsen Youth Magazine*, consisting
of essays, short stories, and poems by then teenagers who had been born
between 1946 and 1950 in the Bergen-Belsen DP camp. "We, who call
ourselves the children of Belsen," I wrote in the introduction to that
publication, "believe that we are a part of Belsen. We may not have lived
through the horrors of the Holocaust, but we can and do feel its tragedy." Those sentiments remain true half a century later. As it happens,
four of us whose words appeared in that initial endeavor by members of
the post-Holocaust generation to put our own mark on the process of
remembrance have also contributed essays to the present volume.

Since then, other anthologies have included *Daughters of
Absence: Transforming a Legacy of Loss*, edited by Mindy Weisel;
*Second Generation Voices: Reflections by Children of Holocaust Sur-
vivors and Perpetrators*, edited by Alan L. Berger and Naomi Berger;
and *Nothing Makes You Free: Writings by Descendants of Jewish
Holocaust Survivors*, edited by Melvin Jules Bukiet. These volumes
were published, respectively, in 2000, 2001, and 2002. More than
a decade has passed since these books appeared, and our priorities
have, to a large extent, changed. We no longer feel the need to come to
terms with the imperatives of our unique identity—to a considerable
extent we have done so. Instead, the essays in the present volume—by

eighty-eight contributors who live in sixteen countries on six continents—are intended to reflect what *we* believe, who *we* are, and how that informs what *we* have done and are doing with our lives.

Contributions range from major religious or intellectual exploration to shorter encapsulations of views, experiences, quandaries, and cultural, political, and/or personal affirmations. Almost all the contributions were written especially for this book. Only a few were previously published or written but were carefully selected by their contributors and the editor because of their uniqueness and originality. All represent the contributors' individual responses to the question each was asked— namely, how their parents' or grandparents' experiences and examples helped shape their own identities and their attitudes toward God, faith, Judaism, the Jewish people, and society as a whole.

While many of the contributions address or reflect more than one theme, they are organized into four broad, largely self-explanatory yet often overlapping categories:

- **God and Faith**—How do we, how can we, whose families were persecuted and subjected to unspeakable suffering during the Shoah, with many—often most—of our relatives brutally murdered, relate to God, and are there unique dimensions to our understanding of and attitudes toward Jewish or universal religious and/or spiritual values?
- **Identity**—How do we define ourselves, collectively or individually, in light of and in relation to our parents' or grandparents' experiences and memories, and does this inheritance set us apart from others whose families did not go through the Holocaust?
- **A Legacy of Memory**—How has memory been transmitted to us from our parents or grandparents, how are we integrating those memories into our own consciousness, and what are we doing to share this precious inheritance with the Jewish people and the world?
- *Tikkun Olam*: **Changing the World for the Better**—What are we doing and what should we be doing to prevent future genocides and similar atrocities, to fight persecution, discrimination, and injustice, or to just repair and improve even a small corner of our world? As Mathew S. Nosanchuk writes in his contribution to this book, "What does it mean

to proclaim, 'Never Forget' and 'Never Again'? How do we make those admonitions more than mere words?"

This book came about as a result of a series of almost random occurrences. On the Shabbat between Rosh Hashanah and Yom Kippur of 2013, I delivered a guest sermon at New York City's Park Avenue Synagogue in which I discussed my personal search for God in the horrors of the Shoah. Specifically, I concluded that contrary to that day's Torah reading in which God declares that "I will hide My countenance" from the Israelites during the moments of their greatest distress (Deuteronomy 32:20), God was in fact present during the Holocaust within those women and men who, even at Auschwitz and Treblinka, sought to save the lives of their fellow prisoners or to somehow alleviate their suffering.

Several weeks later, after my sermon had been published on the *Washington Post*'s religion blog, *On Faith*, it was brought to the attention of Pope Francis by my friend and colleague Claudio Epelman, the executive director of the Latin American Jewish Congress. On October 6, 2013, I was deeply moved and honored to receive a reaction to my words from Pope Francis in the form of a personal email, in which he wrote:

> When you, with humility, are telling us where God was in that moment, I felt within me that you had transcended all possible explanations and that, after a long pilgrimage—sometimes sad, tedious or dull—you came to discover a certain logic and it is from there that you were speaking to us; the logic of First Kings 19:12, the logic of that "gentle breeze" (I know that it is a very poor translation of the rich Hebrew expression) that constitutes the only possible hermeneutic interpretation.
>
> Thank you from my heart. And, please, do not forget to pray for me. May the Lord bless you.

The very fact that Pope Francis took the time to write to me, the son of two survivors of Auschwitz and Bergen-Belsen, to express his empathetic understanding of my attempt to reconcile the existence of God with the nightmarish realities of the Holocaust was remarkable. His biblical citation to First Kings was even more so.

He referred to the Prophet Elijah's encounter with God in which Elijah is told that God was not in a mountain-shattering wind, nor in an earthquake, nor in a fire, but only in a still, small sound or voice, which Pope Francis beautifully and poetically translated as "a gentle breeze."

Viewing the Shoah through a decidedly Jewish theological prism, Pope Francis effectively affirmed that God was not in the horrors, in the gas chambers and crematoria, and that He did not cause the mass murder of millions. Nor did God reside within the perpetrators of the Holocaust or other genocides, whether in Bosnia, Rwanda, Darfur, or elsewhere. Rather, the divine presence can only be found in the unfathomable inner strength of those who do not allow themselves to be dehumanized by evil.

Stuart M. Matlins, the publisher and editor in chief of Jewish Lights Publishing, read both my sermon and the Pope's response to it. In early November 2013, Stuart, with his wife, Antoinette, invited my wife Jeanie and me to dinner, in the course of which he told us of the anguish-filled spiritual crisis he had experienced upon visiting Auschwitz and noted that there was a need for a book by contemporary theologians and other scholars of religion that explored issues of faith in the aftermath of the Holocaust. He then asked whether I would be interested in compiling and editing such a book, with my sermon as a starting point. After giving this gratifying suggestion considerable thought, I suggested to Stuart that a more broad-based compilation of not just theological but also historical, sociological, cultural, and, yes, political reflections by a broad range of prominent and accomplished children and grandchildren of survivors on the impact their respective parents' or grandparents' experiences had on their lives and careers would be of far greater value and significance.

Stuart enthusiastically agreed, and so this book was born.

One final explanatory observation: Almost all the authors who have contributed to this book were born after the end of the Holocaust. The very few exceptions were less than two years old when the war ended in their respective parts of Europe. Thus, none of us has an actual memory of the war. And yet we, together, have a better understanding of and sensitivity to our parents' and grandparents' collective wartime experiences than anyone else. Because we lived with them, listened to them, observed them as they confronted their nightmares, we have in effect become their attestors.

My mother died hours after the end of Rosh Hashanah in 1997. Six months later, I took our daughter, Jodi, then a college sophomore, to Poland for the first time. She and my mother had been very close and had spent a great deal of time together as Jodi was growing up. We went to Warsaw and Krakow and then to Auschwitz. It was a gray day, with a constant drizzle. I showed Jodi Block 11 at Auschwitz, the death block where my father was tortured for months, and then we went to Birkenau. We walked in silence past the decaying wooden barracks. After fifteen or twenty minutes, Jodi turned to me and said, "You know, it looks exactly the way Dassah [which is what she called my mother, Hadassah] described it." I realized that a transfer of memory had taken place. My daughter, born thirty-three years after the Holocaust, had recognized Birkenau through my mother's eyes, through my mother's memories, which Jodi had absorbed into her consciousness.

At the Passover seder we recite, *Be-chol dor vador chayav adam lir'ot et atzmo ke-ilu hu yatza mi-Mitzrayim*—"In each generation, it is incumbent on each of us to see ourselves as if we had come out of Egypt."

We have been entrusted with a precious and fragile inheritance. In the aftermath of the Holocaust, each of us, and our children and our children's children, must also see ourselves as if *we* had emerged from Auschwitz, Bergen-Belsen, and all the other ghettos and camps, the forests and secret hiding places of Nazi Europe.

We are indeed the bridge between two worlds. Our twin grandchildren Jacob and Hallie were born in the latter part of the first decade of the twenty-first century. Someday soon, I hope to tell them about my older brother Benjamin, my mother's first child, who was murdered at Auschwitz-Birkenau, so that he may become a lasting presence in their lives. And my wife, Jeanie, will tell them about her grandfather, Joshua Bloch, who was shot by the Germans on August 2, 1941, together with other leaders of the Jewish community in the Belarusian town of Ivie.

Others will do likewise for grandparents, great-grandparents, siblings, uncles, and aunts who were gassed, or starved in a ghetto, or succumbed to typhus in a concentration camp, or were betrayed by their Christian neighbors. And so we will transmit to our children and grandchildren, and beyond, this sacrosanct body of lore that has been entrusted to us.

We who are haunted by the past must now pass on our legacy of ghosts.

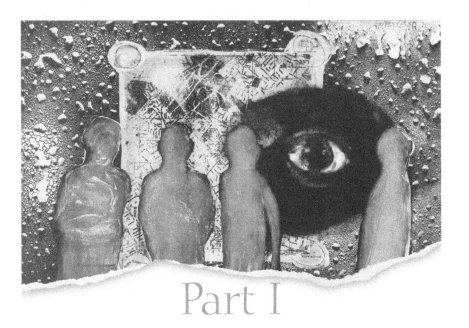

Part I
God and Faith

"And God? Where was He during those dark years? The Holocaust has had a great impact on religion. It does not really matter whether God is the impersonal God of the Reconstructionist or the personal God of the Hasid. We all speak about God in our hearts. We speak about the unknown, about that inner poetry which elevates certain moments of our existence. Where was this God then?"

—Elie Wiesel[1]

Yossi Klein Halevi

Yossi Klein Halevi is a senior fellow of the Shalom Hartman Institute in Jerusalem. He is the author of *Memoirs of a Jewish Extremist: An American Story* and *At the Entrance of the Garden of Eden: A Jew's Search for Hope with Christians and Muslims in the Holy Land*. His book *Like Dreamers: The Story of the Israeli Paratroopers Who Reunited Jerusalem and Divided a Nation* won the Jewish Book Council's Jewish Book of the Year Everett Family Foundation Award.

"The Nazis, then, seemed to reinforce the claim we had always made about ourselves: We were chosen to represent the presence of God in history. Being chosen by God for a redemptive mission made being chosen by His enemies for extinction a little more understandable, perhaps a little more bearable."

As a young man I encountered the Shoah as a kind of revelation. The anti-Sinai revelation of perfect evil, of a meaningless world. Here was no mere outburst of primal hatred but the usurpation of civilization by barbarism. Order, bureaucracy, corporate profit: The Shoah was the routinization of murder, the ultimate premeditated crime. A crime of dispassion.

But why the Jews? And why the obsession with erasing them from history?

Those questions took on an added urgency for me because of the fate of my family's community, the Jews of Hungary. When the Nazis invaded Hungary in March 1944, they were well on their way to losing the war. Yet they diverted men and resources from the front to quicken the deportation of Hungarian Jews.

Reading *Mein Kampf* as a teenager, I discovered the Nazis' philosophical rationale. The Final Solution was intended to solve not only the Jewish problem but the God problem. The Nazis, social Darwinists, were trying to free humanity from a religiously induced conscience, which only inhibited the ability of human beings to survive in brute nature. In destroying the Jews, the Nazis would banish God.

A photograph taken in Poland offered confirmation of the Shoah as spiritual war. It is a well-known image: A Jew, wearing *tallit* and *t'fillin,* is about to be shot by the jeering Nazi soldiers who surround him. The ultimate disputation: The Jew insists on the existence of a Creator and the primacy of soul over body, while the Nazis, by exposing Jewish helplessness and the absence of an invisible Protector, insist on an empty cosmos.

The Nazis, then, seemed to reinforce the claim we had always made about ourselves: We were chosen to represent the presence of God in history. Being chosen by God for a redemptive mission made being chosen by His enemies for extinction a little more understandable, perhaps a little more bearable.

My father had no use for Jewish chosenness. "Let God choose someone else for a change," he'd say, unconsciously echoing Tevye.

I honor the rejection of any attempt to discern spiritual meaning in Jewish fate—even as I do precisely that. This is where I find myself: one part of my being inconsolable, another part praising God, "who chooses His people Israel with love."

I believe that the Jews were created as a people to be a test case for divine intimacy with all of humanity. An experiment: Take a random group of people—emphatically not a community of saints—subject them in their formative years to the intensity of an unmediated encounter with the Divine, and dispatch them into history. Ultimately all of humanity will experience what the Jews experienced at Sinai. That is the promise of what is called the messianic era: the transformation of human consciousness, enabling perception of the reality of God, now obscured by material density.

Recognizing ourselves as a messianic avant-garde affirms the spiritual significance of the Jewish people. But not as a goal in itself: Jewish particularism is a means to a universal end.

A healthy Jewish people embraces its particularist and universalist commitments. Yet we are critically out of balance in our relationship to means and end. One part of the Jewish people, reinforced by the wounds of the Shoah, is barricaded in the most constricted and triumphalist aspects of our tradition, while another part of the Jewish people is so open to the rest of the world that it risks fading out of the Jewish story.

The universalists among us need to better appreciate the role of a distinct Jewish people, acting as a messianic avant-garde, in the spiritual evolution of humanity. Particularism is an essential part of a healthy Jewish universalism.

The particularists, for their part, need more humility. Growing up in the Orthodox survivor community of Borough Park, Brooklyn, heart of Jewish particularism, I imagined a Judeo-centric universe. We were the purpose, the starting point, and the end point of creation itself.

That grandiose notion has yielded to a more modest idea of chosenness. Not *the* chosen people but *a* chosen people, along with other nations and religions, each chosen by God for a specific purpose in the fitful evolution of humanity. In that small linguistic shift is a realization that we are hardly alone in proclaiming God's Oneness, in attesting to God's Presence. Only now, in the era of interfaith dialogue, have we been able to truly appreciate the spiritual vitality of Christianity. (Tragically, because of the Middle East conflict, Jews are more reluctant today than in the past to appreciate the spirituality of Islam.) And it is only now that Jews have begun to encounter Hinduism; in the Vedanta system is a pure monotheism that tempers our claim to be the sole carriers of monotheism in the ancient world.

Just as our universalists need to take seriously the responsibility of nurturing and protecting the Jewish people, our particularists need to take seriously the universalist purpose implicit in Jewish survival.

My openness to the possibility of faith—of perceiving the "chosenness" of the Jews in the Shoah as the demonic shadow of a divine chosenness—owes much to the existence of Israel. The emergence of the State of Israel immediately after the Shoah reinforced my sense of awe in standing before the Jewish story. Israel is not "the answer" to the Shoah—there can be no definitive answer to the Shoah. But Israel is, for me, a counterbalance of sorts. Without the creation of Israel, the Shoah might have become the most powerful event in Jewish history. As Jacob Glatstein, the Yiddish poet, put it, "We accepted the Torah on Sinai / And in Lublin we gave it back."[1] The existence of Israel means that the redemptive capacity of history remains open, means that Auschwitz hasn't negated Sinai. Redemption is still as potent as apocalypse.

That is why I recite the prayer affirming the State of Israel as the "first flowering of redemption." Regardless of the result of Israel's struggles to survive and to define itself, its founding after the Shoah redeemed the idea of redemption.

It is of course risky to invest religious significance in any nation-state, especially one whose existence is under permanent challenge. And as the nationalist excesses of religious Zionism in recent decades prove, the spiritual dangers of sanctifying historical processes are considerable.

Still, the possibility of religious meaning to Israel's existence continues to challenge us. A people that carried for two thousand years an irrational, even absurd messianic dream of return to its lost homeland, only to see that dream fulfilled under the most inconceivable circumstances, cannot avoid grappling with its religious implications. I have always been perplexed by those ultra-Orthodox Jews who see the hand of Providence in the smallest coincidences—but who remain agnostics toward the restoration of Jewish sovereignty after the Shoah and the ingathering of the exiles.

I believe that the return to Zion, the Jewish ability to challenge apocalypse with an approximation of redemption, has significance for the world. At a time of growing fear and despair, when we can no longer take human existence for granted, humanity needs our wisdom of survival.

I see Israel as a testing ground for trying to manage if not solve some of the world's acute dilemmas—security versus morality, religion and state, east and west. These are problems that threaten the world's most basic stability. They are worthy challenges for a people that has emerged from its own death sentence with a vitality reminiscent of its ancient youth.

Rabbi Moshe Waldoks

Rabbi Moshe Waldoks, a graduate of the Hebrew University (BA) and Brandeis University (MA, PhD), serves as rabbi of Temple Beth Zion (TBZ), an independent, non-denominational congregation in Brookline, Massachusetts. Committed to bridge building and interfaith cooperation, he sits on the board of the Interreligious Committee for Public Life; participates in Jewish-Christian, Jewish-Buddhist, and Jewish-Muslim dialogue; and teaches and lectures widely throughout the United States. In 1996, Reb Moshe was ordained as a non-denominational rabbi, by Rabbis Zalman Schachter-Shalomi (z"l), Everett Gendler, and Arthur Green.

"Both the God of consolation and the accusation against God live within me."

In his lyrical eulogy for Eastern European Jewish civilization *The Earth Is the Lord's*, Rabbi Abraham Joshua Heschel beseeched his generation and mine to take in deeply that

> a world has vanished. All that remains is sanctuary hidden in the realm of the spirit. We of this generation are still holding the key. Unless we remember, unless we unlock it, the holiness of the ages will remain a secret of God. We of this generation are still holding the key—the key to the sanctuary which is also the shelter of our own deserted souls. If we mislay the key, we shall elude ourselves.[1]

I have spent my life searching for this key.

This exploration has led me to a deep, rich association and appreciation of the life of Polish Jewry before the Shoah. My mother, from Sosnowiec, Poland, survived a forced labor camp, and my father, from Lutzk—then in Poland, now in Ukraine—survived by deserting from the Russian army into which he had been drafted and fleeing to Uzbekistan. He lost a wife and child and was the sole survivor of a large, extended family. My mother, too, lost a large portion of her immediate and extended family.

My parents met in the Displaced Persons camps near Munich in the American zone of defeated Germany. There I was conceived, and two weeks after their arrival in the United States, on July 4, 1949, I was born. Yiddish was my *mameloshn*, my mother tongue, and I received a traditional yeshiva education.

Like many children of survivors, I have been haunted by face-less phantoms of dozens and dozens of aunts, uncles, and cousins. In the only crumpled photo of a small part of the family that remained, hidden by my mother in the camp, my *zayde* (grandfather) Leibush Lipnicki sports the same potbelly I do. I jest and say I'm carrying the "Holocaust paunch."

I bear the name of two grandfathers, and my life's vocation and avocation has been to recapture their images through my work as an academic and, in most recent years, as a rabbi. This is more than a personal quest. It is my commitment to memory and hope.

At the same time, to make the dictum of the Ba'al Shem Tov taken from Psalm 100 "to serve God with joy" a reality, I edited (with William Novak) *The Big Book of Jewish Humor*, now in print for over thirty years.

I relate all this as a preface to the formation of my response to the Shoah. Undoubtedly, my family background and history, in addition to determining my deep connection to Jewish continuity, have informed and formed the rudimentary scaffolding of my theological worldview. Like many survivor families, particularly those who emerged from observant homes, we were traditional but not Orthodox, certainly not in the sense of contemporary Orthodoxy. Orthodoxy in the late fifties and early sixties was not triumphalist. Unlike its present-day descendants, pre-1967 American Orthodoxy remained inner-directed. My primary school, the Yeshiva of Eastern Parkway in the Crown Heights section of Brooklyn, had been established after the war as a refuge for many survivor rabbis and for many children of survivors. Yiddish was the primary language of study. For many survivors, these institutions offered insulation from non-Jews as well as ties to the traditions they had inherited and observed in their countries of origin.

The Orthodox rabbis of my early adolescence did not see the Shoah as a caesura, a break, in the covenantal relationship to God. In fact, according to my teacher, Reb Zalman Schachter-Shalomi (*z"l*), the founder of Jewish Renewal, their approach can be called "restorationist." The way to deal with the Shoah, they believed, was to continue the mode of traditional Judaism that had existed before the

Catastrophe, with traditional rabbinic theology seeing the Catastrophe as a result of the sins of Jewish deviance from traditional observance and belief. While this point was rarely explicitly emphasized, a clear anti-Zionism and ambivalence to modernity was evident. In contrast to current Haredi institutions, however, survivor parents insisted on intensive general studies. Later, when I attended one of Yeshiva University's high schools, religious Zionism was embraced together with rigorous secular studies.

Over the last seventy years, no Jewish ideology, of either the left or the right, has emerged that has not relied on the Shoah as its basis and justification. Ultimately the Shoah has become a projection of our own inclinations and political tendencies. The fact, however, is that the Shoah has no intrinsic meaning. We can only trace the circumstances that brought about the Catastrophe, but there is nothing in the Shoah event itself that adds anything new to the timeless questions about evil in the world. Despite its enormity, it does not alter the basic questions of theodicy and/or our skepticism about the human capacity for brutality. On its most basic level, the singularity of the Shoah can be seen in the success of the perpetrators in galvanizing a multinational mechanized killing operation that would simply not have been possible in previous eras.

The Holocaust created an extremely low bar for Jewish unity: the Jew as victim. Both Zionism and "restorationist" Orthodoxy tried to raise that bar with varying degrees of success. The former created "muscle" Jews by redefining the Jews as victims into Jews as victors, while the latter offered a premodern exit out of the failure of Western Enlightenment. Both of these "solutions" to the future of the Jewish people proved lacking. While the trauma of this most monumental destruction of Jews remains a subterranean feature of Jewish existence, it is not an adequate source of Jewish meaning. All that said, it is probably this trauma that most ties us together as a people. We are amputees suffering from the phantom pain of the loss of one-third of our body. According to the 2013 Pew Study, almost seventy years after the end of the Second World War, close to three-quarters of American Jews feel that remembering the Holocaust is an essential part of Jewish identity. This number is much larger than those who see attachment to Jewish law and observance as a marker for Jewish identity.

The destruction of European Jewry left us with a legacy that both stimulates and stunts us as a people. On the one hand, children of survivors have overcompensated for their families' losses; and on the other hand, we have yet to discover a way to assimilate this destruction into our deepest psychology.

My own particular theological stance stems from a number of sources.

My mother's God was not the God of salvation, the *deus ex machina* god, who appears in the third act to save the day. It was not the *rebono shel olam*, the traditional master of the universe—except in a deep sense of the Divine found in natural events. Upon hearing thunder and lightning, my grandmother and mother uttered, "*Gott, debarem zikh*," "God have mercy," a pagan-like plea that these natural occurrences pass in safety. "*Gottenyu*," the God of consolation, was my mother's God. The miniscule *gottenyu*, that Jiminy Cricket–like god who accompanies you into the mire and muck, into the mechanisms of destruction, sat on my mother's shoulder. So my mother wasn't a "believer" but rather a person of faith. She exhibited that faith in her deeply empathetic interactions with other human beings.

My father's response to his experiences, meanwhile, was primarily anger and frustration. This, too, without sophisticated articulation, is a theological stance. Channeling anger into the power to take God to task is a time-honored tradition: "You could not possibly do such a thing: to kill the righteous with the wicked, treating the righteous and the wicked alike. You could not possibly do that! Won't the Judge of all the earth do what is just?" (Genesis 18:25).

As their child, both the God of consolation and the accusation against God live within me. The latter binds me to God. As Elie Wiesel once observed, "I have not lost faith in God. I have moments of anger and protest. Sometimes I've been closer to him for that reason."[2]

My embrace of my mother's immanent God, one found in the world rather than beyond it, may explain my attraction to Hillel Zeitlin (1871–1942), the subject of my doctoral dissertation. Zeitlin, a Polish-Jewish journalist, public intellectual, and in the latter part of his life, a mystic, perished during a deportation from the Warsaw Ghetto to Treblinka in 1942. His "positive pessimism" was a critique of traditional Jewish theology on the one hand, and a rejection of the promise of Western Enlightenment on the other.

Influenced by Henry James and the phenomenology of religion, Zeitlin declared that the religious experience of what Heschel would later articulate as "radical amazement" is the key to accessing the Divine. This immanent pantheism, which needs little or no transcendence, supports my perception of the world. Later, my introduction to Buddhist practices, through my participation in the opening of the Jewish-Tibetan Buddhist Dialogue with the Dalai Lama in 1989–90, further strengthened my search for God "within" rather than "without."

All too often the question "Where was God?" is asked of rabbis by so many to justify their loss of faith. This is a red herring. In effect, you want to know why the God you didn't believe in didn't reveal itself during the Shoah. The tragedy of the Holocaust is precisely not in the Divine realm, but rather in the failure of human beings to behave in the image of God. In the first decades following the end of the war, we feared examining the failure of European cultural advancement; we did not challenge the premises of the Western curriculum, its aesthetics, its promise of ongoing progress through our accession of arts and *Kultur,* of *Bildung,* the cultivation of the truly human. Only in the last decades have we struggled to relate a history not only of victors but of victims. It is this failure of Western Enlightenment that has led me and others to the Eastern teachings, in which true enlightenment is not the product of a social regime but a result of individual practice.

There is no way to encounter Jewish life, secular or religious, orthodox or unorthodox, traditionally observant or mitzvah free, without coming up against the place of God in our tradition. To reject God demands a commitment to struggle to understand how God has been perceived throughout Jewish history. Deep within monotheism lies *monism,* a sense of the interconnectedness of all things. This is still the essential credo of a Jew and the path to our renewal.

I have been blessed with remarkable teachers throughout my life. They have come from all the different parts of the post-Shoah experience: rabbis and rebels, scholars and teachers, secular and religious, artists and poets.

What I have derived from their gifts to me is a deep attachment to the notion of *Netzach Yisrael lo yishaker,* "The Eternity of Israel is no lie." Our remarkable response to the devastation of the Shoah exhibited itself in the very ashes out of which a few of the saving remnant emerged. The psychic tenacity of the generation of survivors has permitted me to pursue the key to both their existence and mine. It has permitted me to see the beauty in their lives and the lives of their—and my—forebearers in Eastern Europe. It has allowed me to transcend the fascination with the details of destruction to recover a source of energy and vitality that will continue to fuel our Jewish passions for generations to come. Being a seeker of the life before the Shoah has released in me the courage to forge a relationship to the world and to the Divine that is based on the potential of human beings to become fully conscious. It is this consciousness that needs to be directed to the Other and to our planet.

Photo: Marcie Stein

Rabbi Lilly Kaufman

Rabbi Lilly Kaufman is executive director of Torah Fund, an international fund-raising campaign of Women's League of Conservative Judaism, which supports The Jewish Theological Seminary of America (New York), the Ziegler School of Rabbinic Studies (Los Angeles), the Schechter Institute for Jewish Studies (Jerusalem), and the Seminario Rabinico Latinoamericano (Buenos Aires). Ordained a cantor and rabbi, she has served as pulpit clergy at Congregation Tikvoh Chadoshoh in Bloomfield, Connecticut, and as director of Jewish learning at Adath Jeshurun Congregation in Minneapolis, Minnesota. She serves on the Editorial Advisory Committee for *Siddur Lev Shalem for Shabbat and Festivals* and on the Ethics Committees of the Rabbinical Assembly and the Cantors Assembly.

"I like to believe that I would not have easily relinquished the journey of the soul toward holiness, that I would fight for it."

It is important to learn the prayers by heart
because if you are caught by the Nazis
and put in a concentration camp
you will still be able to say
your morning blessings.

It is important to learn the prayers by heart
because if you are caught by the Nazis
and put in a concentration camp

you will be able to write the prayers down
on whatever scraps of paper you can find,
and pray them.

It is important to learn the Haggadah by heart
because if you are caught by the Nazis
and put in a concentration camp
you will still be able to hold
a Pesach Seder
with the other prisoners.

It is important to learn the Shema by heart
because if you are caught by the Nazis
and put in a concentration camp
you will still be able to say the Shema
with your last breath.

It is important to learn the prayers by heart
because unlike everything else
your prayers
can never
be taken
away from you.

I wrote these words in the voice of a child in the mid-1990s, while studying to be a cantor at The Jewish Theological Seminary. I didn't have to try to learn the prayers by heart; it seems as though I always knew them, because, very simply, I loved them. I had a vital attachment to our prayer book and a secure and happy childhood.

The child's voice in this poem is anxious, even obsessive, methodical, and near hysterics, until the ending, when her perseveration resolves into defiance and matter-of-fact resilience *in extremis*. It is dutiful, determined to be of help to others, determined to create order out of chaos, and assumes the possibility of a leadership role as if this were reasonable under the circumstances—as if anything would have been reasonable under the circumstances. It is a voice that accepts a brutal reality and rebels against it. So Jewish. So naive, and not at all naive. Pure in its conviction that we exist to praise, which, in the circumstances, is slightly mad, and is also the entire point.

Could I have preserved my instinct to praise? Could I have preserved any aspect of my humanity had I been in a concentration camp? Lesser horrors have weakened me since; it is impossible to know what I would have done.

Ma'aseh shehayah, a true incident: A few months or perhaps a year after I wrote this poem and recited it publicly at JTS, I visited the newly opened Museum of Jewish Heritage in New York City. On the top floor are war artifacts that were brought to the United States by refugees. I stopped before one display case. In it is a copybook, in which an imprisoned woman had written down whole pages of the siddur. It is open to the morning blessings.

It *had been* important to learn the prayers by heart—to a real person! To someone I had imagined myself to be, who, remarkably, had been. It was the reverse of a novelist's experience, a tiny wrinkle in the space-time continuum. My poem expressed a reality that was far beyond my comprehension, and yet one with which I empathized so entirely as to have anticipated it, fifty years after it happened. *Baruch shekivanti.*[1] I had formed a sacred wish, one that was previously formed by a fine intellect facing horror. She preserved her own humanity and her relationship with God in a living hell.

Like her, I have always lived deeply in the words of the prayer book. If I woke up very early in the morning, when the sky's shifting pinks and oranges chased away the navy, inky blues, and the deep lavenders resolved into the pale white blues, I would wait with mild pleasure for the rooster to crow, so that I might express gratitude for being alive with the words of the traditional first Jewish morning blessing, thanking God for the ability to distinguish between day and night. In a bad year of grief, when I said this blessing, I wondered whether I would ever regain my ability to tell day from night. Waking up is important. I thank God for it.

What did she pray for, who hand-wrote this blessing in a concentration camp? For an end to torture? For dirty potato peel soup? Not to be raped? To find her mother and father alive? Her little sister? Her big brother? Her aging grandparents? For liberation? For daybreak? Did she ever have the chance to say the morning blessings she wrote down? Did she ever stop? Did she never stop? Did she die before she could use her book?

What does it mean to praise and to thank God after people, weaned from human breasts, whose life had been breathed into them as their first inspiration, systematically tore words of praise from mouths poised to offer them? Tore teeth from those mouths? Tore skin from those limbs?

I am still a girl who wants to sing her prayers to an attentive God. I still reach out toward holiness, as my tradition teaches. *Kadosh, kadosh, kadosh*, rise up, rise up, rise up three times, to mimic the angels arrayed alongside the heavenly Throne. I teach the texts of Isaiah, who imagined orderly angels, and Ezekiel, who imagined strange ones. Static polyphony or a roaring wind, which is true of the heavenly realm? Can God get any rest, with perfect knowledge of the Shoah in all its intimate details? Which angels still sing before God? Which stand still and silenced?

Are we allowed to turn away from the collective memory of the screams? Are we allowed to be healthy after the Shoah?

A formative experience in my childhood synagogue: Two men belonged to the shul, one older, one younger, possibly related. One of them would periodically erupt in screams on Shabbes morning. I couldn't tell which from the women's balcony. The rabbi and the hazzan, gentle men, would wait out the screams, whether during the sermon or the davening. It was whispered among us children that the two men had been in a concentration camp, and had gone mad. This madness was accepted. If they could not scream here, in shul, before the holy ark, before God and the Jewish people, where could they? If our community could not accept the inconvenient consequences of brutality and the justice of their bitter and chaotic protest against it, who could? Shabbes was to be protected, but not at the cost of our humanity, of our *hesed*, our kindness. Prayers would resume. The sermon would resume. I learned that prayers and Torah resume.

I like to believe that I would not have easily relinquished the journey of the soul toward holiness, that I would fight for it. Could I be broken? Possibly. Have I been broken? No. Through no virtue of my own, but through the stubbornness of Israel that is my legacy and my privilege.

Almost twenty years after my poem came strangely to life, I am at work with rabbinic and cantorial colleagues on a new prayer book. It is a work that will open up hearts. I believe with perfect faith that no one will have to memorize it and that no one will have to copy it out by hand, *in extremis*. I believe with perfect faith that my people will find God in it, and through it, and with each other and that they will rejoice in its beauty on their sacred days.

MK Rabbi Dov Lipman

Rabbi Dov Lipman was elected to the Knesset, the Israeli parliament, as a member of the Yesh Atid party in 2013. He holds rabbinic ordination from Ner Israel Rabbinical College and a master's in education from Johns Hopkins University. Rabbi Lipman moved to Israel with his wife and four children in July 2004 and rose to national and international prominence for his role in combating religious extremism in his hometown of Bet Shemesh.

> "In the camps ... no one defined themselves as ultra-Orthodox, secular, religious Zionist, Conservative, or Reform. They were simply all Jews, bound together by their horrific lot and suffering."

The Holocaust has had a profound impact on my life—as a Jewish child growing up in the United States, as a rabbi and teacher both in America and Israel, and, especially now, as I am honored to serve as a member of the Israeli Knesset.

May 1944 was a dark month for my family. Cattle cars filled with my relatives traversed the railways from Hungary to Poland. Upon arriving at Auschwitz, Joseph Mengele sent my grandmother's parents, many of her siblings, and all twenty-eight of her nieces and nephews straight to the gas chamber. My grandmother and her older sister were spared.

I now fast-forward to January 2014. I arrived in Poland on an El Al flight along with colleagues of mine from the Knesset. We marched upright through the gates of Auschwitz-Birkenau surrounded by the Knesset honor guard, whose members, clad in their dress uniforms, were proudly holding Israeli flags. We stopped at the exact spot on the platform alongside the railroad tracks where Mengele stood and sent most of my family to die. There I was, a citizen of Israel and a member of the Knesset, who studies the same Torah my great-grandfather studied, who performs the same commandments that my great-grandmother observed, and who is raising children in the land toward which they faced when they prayed three times a day, the land for which they hoped and yearned.

Despite all the questions regarding God and the Holocaust, questions from which I don't shy away and questions that certainly must haunt my grandmother, standing on that platform made me feel closer to God than ever before. Only God could oversee and direct our impossible national transition from Holocaust to statehood. Only God could ensure this remarkable turnaround from my ancestors' downtrodden trek to their slaughter to my upstanding march to that very same spot declaring that the Jewish people are alive and well.

Experiencing the freezing cold of an Auschwitz winter taught me an additional lesson about God and the Holocaust. I called my grandmother when I returned to Israel and asked her how she survived the cold. I explained to her that I was bundled in many layers, including gloves, thermal socks, and a hat covering my ears, and I still lost feeling in my fingers and toes after just a few hours in Auschwitz. I wanted to know how she withstood that same cold wearing far less. She replied that she had no idea and she guesses that "it was simply meant to be" that she should survive and mother her children, grandchildren, and great-grandchildren. Survival despite that cold and suffering was miraculous and superhuman and has shown me another insight regarding how one can see God and His role in the Holocaust.

There is one other angle to the theological inspiration that I gain from reflecting on the Holocaust. This lesson helped me tremendously throughout my childhood. While I certainly don't judge those who abandoned their religious practice after experiencing the horrors of the death and labor camps, I gain constant inspiration from my grandparents and other relatives who remained devout despite what they experienced. Their love for Torah study, passion for daily prayer, and commitment to mitzvah observance has helped me maintain my connection to these values in difficult and trying times.

In addition, there is a lesson that I have gleaned from the Holocaust that has guided me throughout my life and specifically in my run for the Knesset as well as in my daily activities since entering the Knesset. My grandmother related more than once that in the camps, there were no sectors. No one defined themselves as ultra-Orthodox, secular, religious Zionist, Conservative, or Reform. They were simply all Jews, bound together by their horrific lot and suffering. They helped each other as best they could and never focused on the differences that separated them. Upon moving to Israel, I began to notice polarization between Jews and the unwritten requirement that everyone define specifically what "type" of Jew they were for the rest of the world to know and then judge. We must learn from what happened during our worst of times. During our most tragic era we saw ourselves as *one* people with *one* lot and also understood the inherent benefits of unifying together. I committed myself to do all that I could to make sure that we apply that same approach as we experience the best of times with our return to our homeland and the establishment of our own state.

May the memories of those who perished in the Holocaust be a source of blessing for us all, and may we continue to find inspiration from the remarkable stories of individual survivors and our survival as a nation. *Am Yisrael Chai!*

Rabbi Michael Marmur

Rabbi Michael Marmur is the Jack, Joseph and Morton Mandel Provost of the Hebrew Union College–Jewish Institute of Religion (HUC-JIR). Born in London, he has lived in Israel since the mid-1980s, was ordained by HUC-JIR in 1992, and received his PhD from the Hebrew University of Jerusalem in 2006. An authority on the works of Abraham Joshua Heschel, he specializes in modern Jewish thought.

"We are witnesses to God and humanity, and that call to witness is not predicated on assurances of reward in this world or the next."

The Photograph

There is a photograph of three yeshiva students from Lodz in the 1930s that was preserved by a non-Jewish family during the war. Six decades later the photograph was submitted to an exhibition, and the letter that went along with it reads:

I send you a photograph which belonged to my mother, Salomea Tarczynska. During the occupation it was covered by another picture. As far as I can figure out, they were my mama's very good friends before the war. Unfortunately, I don't know anything more about this.

One of the young men is my grandfather, Izak Zonabend. To the best of my knowledge, his two friends pictured with him in the photograph perished a few years after it was taken. How do I, a second-generation Reform rabbi living in Jerusalem, relate to questions of religion and identity presented by this heritage? Am I capable of formulating a response to the Holocaust?

Impossibilities

It is relatively easy to identify the responses that I cannot accept. The notion of Divine retribution meted out by a God of strict justice in reprisal for the sins of modernity—no. The concept of a cleansing act of atonement in which the Jews are immolated on the altar of progress—no. The idea that those who survived were spared by a discriminating God who found more worth in one person than in another and then cursed the surviving remnant to live with that impossible life sentence—no.

The list of impossible theo-political responses is a long one. The attempt to base a kind of tribal survivalism on Jewish ashes is perhaps understandable, but I am convinced that as a foundation for a Jewish politics, let alone a Jewish ethics, it needs to be resisted and overcome. In the early 1980s my father, Dow Marmur, wrote *Beyond Survival*, in which he argued against the construction of a new Jewish paradigm based on the survival imperative. In the years that have intervened, his argument only seems to have become more apposite.

I am no more persuaded by a kind of pallid universalism that argues that the root cause of the inhumanity exhibited in the twentieth century is group affiliation—ethnic, religious, and ideological. Remove these affiliations, the argument goes, and we can live out a post-national, post-religious, post-ethnic utopia. I disagree with this approach on both intrinsic and pragmatic grounds. In my view, if a new humanism is to emerge in our time, it will take strong identities and heartfelt commitments to bring it about.

The standard theological literature tends to speak in terms of a response to the Holocaust, but in the lived experience of children born in its wake, response is not quite the appropriate term. Those who lived through the events may have felt called to respond to them. If you are born to parents who lived through the Holocaust, you have both nothing and everything to respond to. Nothing—because it happened to someone else. Everything—because were it not for these someone elses, you would not be who you are.

Testimony

I don't have a theological "response" to the Holocaust that is distinct from my general theological outlook. That outlook resonates with these words of philosopher Emil Fackenheim:

> *Mir zeinen do*—we are here, exist, survive, endure, witnesses to God and man even if abandoned by God and man. Jews after Auschwitz will never understand the longing, defiance, endurance of the Jews at Auschwitz. But so far as is humanly possible they must make them their own as they carry the whole Jewish past forward into a future yet unknown.[1]

We are witnesses to God and humanity, and that call to witness is not predicated on assurances of reward in this world or the next. The God in whom I believe and to whom I pray does not hand out rewards for good behavior, nor punishes those who have been lax in ritual adherence or moral probity.

But if God could not or did not save the day when the need was greatest and the situation most dire, and if God has demonstrated such disinterest or impotence throughout history and in our own days, what use is there for such a God? I am always moved by the daring reading offered in the Babylonian Talmud of a biblical phrase that means "Who is like you *ba-eilim*, among the gods?" The school of Rabbi Ishmael, relating to the destruction of the Second Temple, offered a deliberate misreading of the verse, rendering it as "Who is like you *ba-ilmim*, among the silent?" Cries of pain and defiance are as authentic a part of tradition as are pious protestations of Divine perfection.

God's presence is not subject to my sense of appropriateness or bounded my reason. This does not mean that reason is to be abandoned—some approaches to God and faith that worked for our ancestors cannot work for me. But history teaches that ours is not the first generation to seek a new articulation of God. Indeed, Jewish concepts of God have not been static through history. God is bigger than any of our formulas.

For myself, I cannot uproot the presence of God. Rather, as I testify to my faith in the commanding presence of God I am called to replant this sense of presence in the altered ground of a post-Holocaust world. In this respect, I draw some inspiration from the photograph of my grandfather and his friends with which I began these reflections. Within a few months, he had left the garb and posture of a Gerer Hasid ensconced in learning and adopted the wardrobe and perspective of a secular Polish Jew.

My grandfather Izak abandoned the strictures, doctrines, and milieu of Halakhic Judaism of his own volition. It wasn't the legacy of Hitler that caused him to eschew the satin and fur of his childhood. A certain God idea had become impossible for him, and a certain set of strictures unnecessary, before the Final Solution was enacted. For him and for countless others, tradition had been undermined by a process seen by some as heresy and others as enlightenment. For me, as for grandfather Izak, any conception of God that includes a wrathful divinity squashing the baddies and leading the goodies to redemption is impossible. It was not Hitler but modernity that made such a God impossible (for me at least).

Both my mother and father were raised in secular Jewish surroundings. It was left to them to seek for meaning and structure from the debris that was their birthright. From them I learnt that to strive to live a life of integrity and commitment is an act of witness. To engage in acts of ritual and community is also an act of witness—to the continuity of Judaism, to God, to humanity. And I suppose that my decision to make my life in Israel has been influenced by this impulse to testimony.

Humor and Love

Izak's name comes from the Hebrew word for "laughter." If the command to testify is one major part of my theological "response," the need for humor is no less urgent. I have in mind humor born of encounter, not escape. This humor is not about entertainment. Rather, it is a theological category, described by sociologist Peter Berger as "redeeming laughter."[2] I was brought up in a household in which a mixture of voracious intellectual curiosity, a developed sense of irony, a love of life, and a certain skepticism of human motivations prevailed. This skepticism certainly extends to my own motivations. Anything too self-important should be deflated. By all accounts Izak had sad eyes that twinkled nonetheless with humor and *joie de vivre*. Such an approach has political implications, because it is inimical to pomposities and totalities. I believe that just as we are called to take life and culture and values seriously, any person demanding special privileges and claiming mysterious powers should be debunked. That includes ourselves.

After testimony and laughter, love. I have always felt an overflowing love of Judaism and the Jewish people, a love that I hope serves to deepen my sense of solidarity and sympathy with all people and many cultures. Love is also a more private and intimate category. I think it would be fair to say that my parents were saved from a broken past by their love for each other. Living life in relationship is for me an act of faith as well as a joy.

Izak survived the ghetto and the camp and later was reunited with his wife and daughter. I was two years old when he died in the 1960s. He is buried in Stockholm and lives in his daughter's sad eyes and in occasional moments of sweet reminiscence. He also lives in his grandchildren and great-grandchildren, one of whom—Nadav Yitzchak—bears his name. Nadav Yitzchak and the children of his generation inhabit a very different world from that of their great-grandparents, and yet I believe that much is similar. Their world is "disenchanted" in the sense that old orthodoxies are impossible for them, and yet in their deeds and thoughts they live lives of testimony, humor and love.

Hope

I cannot claim a simple happy ending to this story. To suggest a neat conclusion in which all is resolved would be to dishonor the other two young men in the old photograph and the millions of others they represent. It would imply that there was some rhyme or reason in what happened to them and, for that matter, in what happens to millions around the world as I write these words. My sense of blessing and fulfillment cannot excuse or explain so many inequities and so much cruelty.

Furthermore, there is much to be concerned about. The Israel I live in is endangered by missiles and upheavals from outside and by major threats from within. A thin line separates love for the Jewish people from tawdry chauvinism and bigotry, which should have been removed from our vocabulary but which have returned to threaten all of us. The Jewish world outside Israel is struggling to deal with the same processes of modernity and change that Izak and his generation strove to navigate. And the world as a whole is bleeding and reeling from a set of challenges that often seem overwhelming.

And yet, decades after the faded photograph of my grandfather and his friends was taken, there is so much to be thankful for. Izak's grandson lives a comfortable life, striving to witness to a God who has to be rearticulated in every generation and a Judaism in the process of change; I study the books my grandfather was raised on and set aside, and I feel empowered to take my place at the table of Jewish discourse; I dream in Hebrew; I take core principles and ideas—but not myself—seriously; I am surrounded by love and friendship. How can I not give thanks for all this? It is not only luck, or karma, or my gene pool, which I thank. It is God, even the God most excellent in silence.

Abraham Joshua Heschel wrote:

> As parts of Israel we ... remember where we came from. We are summoned and cannot forget it, as we wind the clock of eternal history. We remember the beginning and believe in an end. We live between two historic poles: Sinai and the Kingdom of God.[3]

My focus is more modest. I live between two realities, two poles, symbolized by one Pole and one Israeli—between Izak and Nadav Yitzchak. Perhaps one day I will seek out the granddaughter of Salomea Tarczynska, the woman who saved the photograph, and see how she is doing, living—as all human beings are fated and blessed to do—between the past and a future yet unknown.

Aliza Olmert

Aliza Olmert is an Israeli artist, author, photographer, playwright, and child welfare advocate. Her 2005 play *Piano Fantasy*, about a Holocaust survivor who returns to her village in Poland, has been performed at the Cameri Theatre in Tel Aviv; the Heilbronn Theater in Heilbronn, Germany; and the Podol Theater in Kiev, Ukraine. Her photography and paintings have been exhibited at galleries and museums in Israel and abroad.

> "In the house in which I grew up,
> the missing niche of faith was
> filled by a socialist worldview
> and uplifting patriotism."

God was not present in the survivors' home in which I grew up.

Although my parents at times faced desperate situations, I cannot recall anyone praying for help or blurting out spontaneously, "Please, God...."

My father was proud to announce that in our house one served the God of atheism, and any expression that might be construed as recognition of the existence of supernatural forces was answered with a dismissive gesture.

We used to whisper, "If only ..." when we wanted something good to happen.

When my mother was asked about her relationship with God, she would reply that it was entirely mutual: He—who didn't exist—abandoned her in the cattle car that led to the work camp at Iaia Station in western Siberia and showed no interest in her for three full years, despite her frozen legs. She, in return, broke off the last loose connection there had somehow been between them, long ago, in her parents' home in Lodz.

When she lit memorial candles on Holocaust Memorial Day or leafed through the album of photographs of "the family that was," she used to tell about the circumstances of people's disappearance or death, whichever it was, without involving divine providence. God had not punished those who were killed for the sins of assimilation, nor had He constructed gas chambers to subject them to a test. People, and people alone, were the agents of cause and effect.

She thought of the Holocaust as a collective psychotic attack that swept over Europe, hated Hitler, continued for some time to admire Stalin, and had clear criticisms against human nature and what happens to it when it gets the OK to manifest itself in its natural state.

Rehov Ha-margoa ("Serenity Street") in Ramat Gan, where I spent most of the years of my youth, was free of any indications of faith or religion. I don't recall meeting, in our neighborhood, Jews in traditional garb. I am also having trouble remembering where the synagogue was located.

The building in which we lived on that street—no. 4—was populated, at the beginning of the 1950s, by families of survivors who had been through the Holocaust in Eastern Europe. Most of the residents were still groping for the codes to a new identity and licked their wounds secretly, in the confines of a private sphere, in Yiddish.

"Rescue," "salvation," and "miracle," the words closest in their essence to a religious context, were linked in a natural way to the sighs heard around me, issued by people who had accumulated experiences of misfortune, impossible junctions, situations that normal people do not survive—and through some miracle had succeeded in extricating themselves from the horrors that did in many other members of their families.

But in these instances of being "saved" that relatives and neighbors had themselves experienced, God played no part and no credit was given to Him for what had happened.

"Rescue" or "salvation," in the terms of Rehov Ha-margoa 4, referred to the stories, which circulated orally, about amazing coincidences, honed instincts, and above all—luck: the non-Jew who appeared out of nowhere at the very second that the Gestapo came knocking at the door, the young man who jumped from a train window a minute before it passed through the gate of the camp, the preschool teacher who managed to spirit away the children shortly before the beginning of a roundup "action," and many other stories of that sort. All of these took on a visual dimension every time a man carrying a suitcase appeared at the door and fell into my father's arms or when the name of a *landsman* was mentioned on the Kol Israel radio program *In Search of Relatives*, filling the house with tears of joy.

The Bible lessons at the Yahalom School were what was supposed to introduce me, finally, to the existence of God. Here too,
though, an unexpected blockage appeared, in the form of a substitute teacher, a graduate of one of the kibbutz teachers seminaries,
who announced dryly, during the very first lesson, that we would not
be seduced into believing it was possible to create an entire world
in seven days. She insisted that the Bible was a collection of folktales printed in Hebrew letters in the language of "olden days." That
belief in God was a need felt by those who were squirming out of
taking responsibility for their lives and pinning it on some supernatural force.

Apparently, though, it was not enough that you survived and
found a country in which to take shelter.

The exalted saga of a people returning to its historical homeland after two thousand years of exile could not be taken in without
an accompanying text that would also be a unifying social contract.
In the absence of religious belief, the need grew for an alternative document that would give these words content, meaning, and
explanation.

In the house in which I grew up, the missing niche of faith was
filled by a socialist worldview and uplifting patriotism. Those two
concepts, which lived in our home in complete harmony, offered
a world of articulated content, a *Shulchan Aruch* of the permitted
and the forbidden, clothing that bespoke commitment, sanctions on
deviation from accepted norms, spiritual leaders and guides—components like those one finds in religious establishments, but so different from them in essence.

The secular social contract was shaped by the fathers of secular Zionism, with the kibbutz and the youth movements providing
inspiration. We lived by a code of positive and negative mitzvot that
was broadcast from the centers of that secular Zionist ethos.

Positive commandments, according to that new covenant, educated for activism, pride, bravery, efficiency, responsibility, and
modesty. Prohibited were weakness, paleness, readiness to knuckle
under, passivity, self-pity, distance from nature, and belief in God.

That ethos was delivered to the door each morning in the newspaper *Al Ha-mishmar* and in the Communist propaganda magazine *Ogoniok*. My parents crowded into the community center to
hear the poet Avraham Shlonsky speak about his new translation of

Quiet Flows the Don, marched in the May Day parade, and engaged in heated debates about the German reparations agreement at the local branch of the socialist party Mapam.

They established for themselves secular pseudo-synagogues that provided a spiritual response to the needs of the hour.

While traditionally observant families maintained a cultural continuity that was transmitted to future generations on the basis of traditions, in families that turned their back on religion, various types of lifestyle came into being—ephemeral styles, fluid priorities, hodgepodge patterns of behavior.

Despite the differences, though, whenever I meet people of the generation who grew up in that transitional space, in the homes of secular survivors of a socialist bent, it becomes clear once again just how broad is our common denominator, just how similar were our parents' uncertainties and vacillations in the search for a new kind of "spiritual home."

The fact that we were shaped according to the models of the secular ethos and became free, insolent children, liberated from concerns about identity and speaking Hebrew, served our parents as decisive proof of their victory over Hitler. We could read it in the sparkle in their eyes. They gave us reasons to believe that we were select and special and different from anything that had ever existed before—a native version of the traditional formula of Jewish chosenness—and we believed them.

We celebrated belonging to the demographic majority that established the secular nationalist ethos. We were joined together in a "collective ego" that was solid and free of contradictions. We spoke in terms of "we" rather than "I." We rested on our laurels without identity crises or any need to find ourselves an alternative covenant or God.

But those salad days passed, and life's complexion changed beyond recognition.

Ideals wore thin. The socialist establishment lost both its political and spiritual hegemony. The Land of Israel grew broader and became messianic, on one hand, and pseudo-Western on the other. The behavior of Israel's religious establishment engendered revulsion against religion on the part of a significant portion of Israelis. Patriotism isn't what it once was either.

All this left behind a kind of vacuum.

Today, the search for meaning and a source of authority, whether secular or religious, is a privatized mission undertaken by choice, through a variety of channels and without an established consensus. The search is apparently inevitable in the face of an accelerated pace of events both within and outside our protected Zionist bubble.

I keep an open channel of communication with the girl who was born in a DP camp in Germany to a pair of survivors who didn't know which way to turn after everything around them came crashing down. That biographical fact shapes my consciousness. It is difficult to escape from its implications.

The absence of God from my life does not contradict my personal "prayer of thanksgiving" for having been born at the right time—in parallel with the birth of a state that enabled me to grow up as a free person with a taken-for-granted sense of belonging. That thanksgiving comes with an appended wish as well—a "prayer of supplication," if you will—that my children and grandchildren continue to live here, in Hebrew, in a worthy and safe place.

An anecdote that I heard recently does a good job of articulating the inner command that is the corollary of this map of the soul.

Two elite paratroopers, one secular and one religious, are on the verge of collapse during a long, backbreaking exercise of running while carrying fellow soldiers on stretchers.

The secular soldier: "Tell me, where do you get the strength to keep running?"

The religious soldier: "From God in heaven. How about you?"

The secular soldier: "From Auschwitz."

[*Translated from the Hebrew by Rabbi Peretz Rodman*]

Rabbi Chaim Zev Citron

Rabbi Chaim Zev Citron is a professor of Talmud at the West Coast Theological Seminary (Ohr Elchonon Chabad) and the rabbi of Ahavas Yisrael Synagogue in Los Angeles. He previously worked doing outreach on the Berkeley campus of the University of California and served as rabbi of the Young Israel of Santa Monica. He currently resides with his wife in Los Angeles.

"When I think of my mother, when I think of the Holocaust, I cry."

I suppose I acquired the way I look at the Holocaust from my mother.

My mother, Esther Ackerman, was taken from her home in Beregsaz (Berehovo), Czechoslovakia (now Ukraine), in 1944 and deported to Auschwitz. Her married sister Gella was murdered at Auschwitz along with her infant son Shalom.

Her younger brother Chaim Volf, after whom I am named, was shot during a death march. My mother's parents had made it to America before the war, but she never saw her mother again, since my grandmother died in the early 1940s in McKeesport, Pennsylvania, of a "broken heart," as my mother put it.

My mother used to speak of her sister and her brother, both of whom she loved dearly, and start crying. She would speak of her home and the life that her family had lived before the war and would start crying. She spoke of her experiences in the death camp and of actually being in the gas chamber when the Nazis' plans somehow changed and she survived. She told how if she ever found an extra scrap of food, she would share it with her friend. She told other stories. But she never cried when telling them, for she had survived. She cried for what she had lost: her family and a peaceful and beautiful life that was gone forever.

She never complained or asked why. She was a woman of great faith, a simple faith, a modest faith. A faith without philosophy or even theology. A faith that needed no answers. And yet she would cry.

When I was a teenager and I was by myself, I would think of the pure innocents who had died, and I, too, would cry. I would cry silently sometimes, sobbing for the men, the women, the children who had been mercilessly murdered. Then I would go back to my life as a student not much different from that of any of my fellows. But a week or a month or two later, in a solitary moment, I would cry for the pain of my people. It was my people, my family, my friends, my pain. I asked no questions. I believed in the A-lmighty. Yet I cried.

Somewhere in those years, I came up with an answer, although no question had ever been posed. The answer was that if I could do anything to bring Jews a little bit closer to G-d, a little bit closer to Judaism, I would somehow fill the terrible void that the Holocaust had created. European Jewry was no more and could not be replicated. But American Jewry could grow and could blossom. To help in that effort was the least I could do. I considered it a holy obligation.

I have spent my life as a teacher in different circumstances: in elementary school, on college campuses, in rabbinic seminaries, in outreach programs. I do not know how many people I have affected. I have tried to help, and, please G-d, I will continue to do so to my dying breath.

And still, when I think of my mother, when I think of the Holocaust, I cry.

Joseph Berger

Joseph Berger has been a reporter and editor with the *New York Times* for over thirty years and received the 2011 Peter Kihss Award for a career's work from the Society of Silurians, New York City's leading association of journalists. He is the author of *Displaced Persons: Growing Up American After the Holocaust,* chosen by the *New York Times Book Review* as a notable book of 2001 and praised by Elie Wiesel as a "powerful and sweetly melancholic memoir, brilliantly written." His latest book is *The Pious Ones: The World of Hasidim and Their Battles with America.*

"What God's culpability or at least responsibility was remains a mystery that I'll never resolve."

When I reflect on the Jewish legacy my parents left me, my mind inevitably wanders back to my father in his yellowing *tallis* sitting in shul murmuring Hebrew prayers amid the hubbub of Jewish men doing much the same. I also remember my mother standing over flickering Friday night candles murmuring what seemed like a magical incantation, drawing circles in the air in some timeless gesture that for all I know goes back to Sarah, Rebecca, Leah, and Rachel.

These were people whose brothers and sisters and parents were slaughtered in cruel fashion, whose Jewish village communities were wiped out, whose lives were upended in terrifying ways, and who were forced to rebuild in a strange country with little to go on. Yet they never lost their faith in a Jewish God. Perhaps it was their lack of education or stubborn willfulness. But they kept on believing. After a reunion of Shoah survivors in Jerusalem in 1981, I asked my father what he was thinking about as he sat with the crowd of seven thousand other survivors for a moving ceremony at the Western Wall. "I was angry at God," he said, "that he took away my sisters." It was the first time I had heard him express such thoughts—and he had six sisters who were killed—yet when I think about that conversation now, what stands out is not his anger but that he still maintained his relationship with God, like a child fleetingly furious at a parent but knowing the bond will never be broken.

Murky as it is, my parents bequeathed faith to me, together with a Jewish identity and soul. Unlike some people struggling for belief after the Holocaust, I cannot rationalize my faith by telling myself that God stood by the victims in the gas chambers or offered merciful consolation to the survivors in the children they had after the war or the success they found. That six million Jews were murdered is an outrage and an ignominy. What God's culpability or at least responsibility was remains a mystery that I'll never resolve. But *Ani Ma'amin*, I believe. Because my father draped himself in that *tallis*, that prayer shawl, and my mother whispered blessings over the candles.

Ultimately, after wrestling with these supreme questions I can't give a cogent explanation as to why I pray to a God whose existence I would not try to argue for or whose management I often question. Except to say that it was absorbed from my parents by osmosis like the priceless Yiddish phrases that reverberate in my brain or a taste for schmaltz herring and jellied calves' feet or the emotional power of a nostalgic Yiddish melody or what Saul Bellow called "potato love" for my brother and sister, no matter what they do to cross me.

My parents also transmitted a love for Jews, Jewishness, and Jewish culture and language. They did it partly by sending me to a yeshiva for nine years, whatever their own misgivings about the divine failures during the war. That has translated into a soulful response to the Torah scroll and parchment and the power and poignancy of communal Jewish prayer. Donning a *tallis* wraps me in a spiritual embrace, divine or otherwise.

Toward Jews, the love I absorbed is not blind love, but it is a kind of chauvinism, an affection that is there to be given unless the evidence shows me otherwise. Again, the reasons are often ineffable and may have something to do with my sense of Jewish suffering and all it took to rebound. When I was in my early twenties, I made plans for a summer-long ramble through Europe, and my parents kept goading me to include Israel, since it was in the neighborhood. I refused. I was in a phase of young adulthood where I fancied myself a cool adventurous contrarian American, and Israel smacked of a provincial world of parents and yeshivas. But when circumstances led to my changing my itinerary and landing at Lod Airport anyway, I found myself weeping when I stepped off the plane. I was in the land of the Jews, and it was a land they fought so hard to acquire and sustain. How else to explain an emotional outburst I could not have anticipated? That Jewish consciousness has extended into a curiosity about the worlds of Sholem Aleichem and George Gershwin and Irving Berlin, an unflagging interest in the news out of Israel, a deep pleasure in hearing Yiddish spoken or sung, and a camaraderie with people who share those enthusiasms.

I developed my social consciousness on my own, but my parents left me with a strong sense of responsibility to those I loved and a strong work ethic—sometimes too strong, but there it is. They did not do so by preaching, but by the way they went about their daily lives. They had three children to feed, clothe, and house, and it did not matter that their work was not intellectually or emotionally fulfilling. My father managed a floor of Spanish-speaking sewing machine operators who stitched asbestos ironing board covers, and with his mechanical skills, he kept the machines in running order. My mother did the intricate stitching on straw hats in a downtown Manhattan factory. They got up early each day to make sure they arrived at work on time—my father traveling an hour and a half from the Bronx to Newark—and were exhausted by day's end. But they came home to prepare dinner for their children, wash up, and tend to bills and other household chores. They complained about their work, but they knew this was something they had to do unless a better opportunity came along, and given their shortcomings of language, education, and connections, it almost never did.

But that spirit of responsibility to the work you're called to do has always animated my siblings and me. Sure, we have chosen careers that fulfill us, but we would have been as diligent with work that simply paid the bills. We feel the same responsibility to our children and spouses, that we must work at keeping our families thriving and together. It has been an outlook that has given us productive, satisfying lives. Obviously, people who have not had parents who suffered through the Shoah display the same diligence. But it would be unfair to the refugees not to state clearly that their diligence came from a sense that the lives they had prepared to live had been truncated by supposedly cultured barbarians and that they had to recover their footing or wither.

To be sure, my parents bequeathed my siblings and myself a sense of fun—at the absurdity and irony of so much of life and the need to respond with a deep belly laugh, even sometimes at the pain around us. But finally, I would have to thank my parents for leaving me with the sense of acceptance of life as a struggle. I get unhinged as easily as the next person by the slings and arrows of daily life, but my parents' bitter experience and their resilience have given me some perspective and taught me to keep trying for what I need—to knock on a door more than once—or find a worthwhile alternative. They never succumbed to defeat or despair, yet who could have blamed them if they did?

Peter Singer

Peter Singer is professor of bioethics in the University Center for Human Values at Princeton University and laureate professor in the School of Historical and Philosophical Studies at the University of Melbourne. His books include *Animal Liberation, Practical Ethics, Rethinking Life and Death, One World, Pushing Time Away,* and *The Life You Can Save.*

"'If God takes such a good man as my husband, I'm not going to follow his laws.'"

I grew up, in Melbourne, Australia, in the years after the end of the Second World War. What the Nazis had done to my family and the communities in which they lived was the single most significant aspect of being Jewish. Because we were not an observant or religious family, it sometimes seemed like the only aspect.

My parents had lived rich and stimulating lives in Vienna until 1938, when the Nazis took over. My mother had graduated in medicine from the University of Vienna. My father was selling coffee. In summer they went to one of Austria's beautiful lakes, and in winter they skied—they met in a gondola. They had been aware of anti-Semitism but had not really suffered from it. Their response had been to assimilate as much as possible with the culture of Austria. Neither of them came from observant families. My father's family celebrated Christmas, as other Austrians did. My mother's home was divided: her father was an agnostic who ate what he liked, while her mother kept kosher and went to synagogue on Saturdays. The children chose to follow their father's practices.

When the Nazis took over Austria, my parents found out that their assimilation did not help them. They left as soon as they could and went to Australia because by chance they had a non-Jewish acquaintance there who provided them with a visa. In Melbourne, most of their close friends were other Jewish refugees from Central Europe, but my parents were always looking for opportunities to blend into the wider Australian society and especially keen for their children to do so.

Judaism was not present in our daily life. We ate whatever we liked. When I was young, my father went to synagogue twice a year, on Rosh Hashanah and Yom Kippur. Later, he stopped doing even that. My mother never went. When I was twelve, I was asked if I wanted to have a bar mitzvah. The gifts that I knew I would get tempted me, but not enough for me to be willing to spend time on Sundays learning Hebrew. I declined.

In primary school, I attended Preshil, a progressive secular school, and when it was time for me to go to secondary school, my parents sent me to Scotch College, an elite Presbyterian school that educated the sons of many of Melbourne's business leaders. Of my circle of school friends, only one was Jewish, and his family had been in New Zealand for generations.

It was the past that made being Jewish important. The knowledge that the Nazis had forced my parents to flee what had been a beautiful, progressive, cultured city; that they had murdered my father's parents and brought about the death of my mother's father—inevitably, these facts weighed on me as a child.

After my parents left Austria, all four of my grandparents planned to join their children in Australia. Tragically, they did not realize the urgency of doing so, and the outbreak of war left them trapped in Vienna. My father's elderly parents were sent to the Lodz Ghetto and from there taken to Chelmno and murdered with exhaust gases in the back of a truck. My mother's parents, perhaps because her father had medals for his bravery in fighting for Austria-Hungary in the First World War, received the relatively privileged treatment of being sent to Theresienstadt. There the overcrowding and lack of sanitation, coupled with insufficient food, caused many to die of dysentery and other diseases. My grandfather was one of them. My grandmother tended him as best she could during his final illness and then went on with her work in the administration of the ghetto. She survived to be liberated by the Russians. Returning to a Vienna from which her large extended family had fled or been deported to the east and murdered, she went to a friend in Switzerland to recuperate and then, around the time of my birth, in 1946, joined us in Australia, where she lived another nine years.

My grandmother lived for part of each week with my family and for the other days with my aunt, her only other child, who had also managed to come to Melbourne. Neither family kept kosher, and I'm told that when my grandmother arrived, there was some discussion about providing her with the kosher food that she had eaten in Vienna. She brushed it aside, my mother later told me, with a line that has always stayed with me: "If God takes such a good man as my husband, I'm not going to follow his laws."

Whether my grandmother's personal experience of the Holocaust had in fact persuaded her that there is no God—or that if there is a God, he was not worthy of being obeyed—I do not know. I was only nine when she died, too young to discuss it with her. She continued to fast on Yom Kippur. Perhaps she simply did not want to trouble her daughters and their families as they struggled to establish themselves in a new country and a different culture.

If, however, my grandmother's rejection of the more observant Jewish life she had led in Vienna was a response to the systematic murder of more than six million people, it seems to me entirely reasonable. The problem of evil has always loomed as a powerful objection to belief in a God who is omnipotent, omniscient, and good. The usual defense, when the evil in question is human crimes like the Holocaust, is to say that God gave us free will, which is so great a good that it outweighs the appalling uses we have made of it. In the face of the Holocaust, that defense is morally dubious. Is free will really *so* great a good? I would rather have had less free will and less suffering and murder. Or—since we know that if we do have free will at all, it starts from the base of a human nature over which we have no control, because we inherit it from our ancestors—couldn't God have shaped human nature so that repugnance at cruelty and compassion for the sufferings of others would be strong enough to stop free human beings rounding up men, women, and children and herding them to their deaths?

The Holocaust gives us sufficient reason to reject the possibility of the existence of God, or at least of a God worthy of our prayers and worship. Suppose, however, that free will is such a great good that God was right to provide us with it, even while foreseeing—as an omniscient being must have foreseen—that it would lead to the Holocaust. That would still not overcome the problem of evil. Droughts, hurricanes, floods, and earthquakes cause a huge amount of suffering, and they have nothing to do with free will. And in case you think we sinful humans deserve to suffer and die prematurely in such natural disasters, remember that infants and nonhuman animals are also among the victims. What has a kangaroo done to deserve to suffer for days and then die when the creeks and waterholes dry up in one of Australia's periodic droughts? Why would a just God allow that to happen?

Perhaps I would have become an atheist even if I had not grown up as the child and grandchild of Holocaust survivors. I certainly hope so, because atheism seems to me the most rational response to the world we observe. It is hard to say what other impact growing up in the shadow of the Holocaust has had on my work and my philosophical outlook. Obviously, I grew up opposing racism and nationalism and supporting freedom of thought and expression as an important barrier to the kind of authoritarianism that was exemplified by fascist leaders in Europe in the inter-war period.

My family's past gave me an interest in history, especially the history of Europe in the first half of the twentieth century, which I studied, along with philosophy, for my undergraduate degree at the University of Melbourne. I wanted to understand how the Nazis could come to power and carry out their plan to murder all the Jews of Europe. Though I then went on with philosophy rather than history, my interest in history persisted and led me eventually to write *Pushing Time Away: My Grandfather and the Tragedy of Jewish Vienna*, in which I got to know as much as I could about my family and their fate.

The other possible outcome of my family's fate is the direction of my work in ethics. When other Holocaust survivors and their children say, "Never again," and are scathing about those who, while not perpetrators of the Holocaust, stood by and allowed it to happen, I see us all standing by and doing nothing to prevent other atrocities that, if not exactly comparable with the Holocaust, are still causing immense amounts of unnecessary suffering and death. If there is a single dominant thread in that work, it is the priority I give to preventing unnecessary suffering.

In biomedical ethics, I advocate the legalization of voluntary euthanasia and physician-assisted suicide, because I cannot see why people with incurable illnesses who do not consider their quality of life satisfactory should have to suffer longer than they wish. But the amount of suffering that reform in this area would prevent is minor compared with the suffering we allow to continue because of global poverty. Here those of us living comfortable lives in affluent countries truly are standing by while more than six million children die every year from preventable poverty-related deaths like diarrhea, malaria, measles, and pneumonia. Millions more go blind because they lack a simple treatment that prevents trachoma, or cannot afford cataract surgery. To allow this to happen while we spend money on trivial luxuries seems to me indefensible.

The same concern for preventing unnecessary suffering—and perhaps, a Holocaust-related awareness of what humans will do to those who are absolutely within their power—lies behind my arguments for including all sentient beings within the sphere of moral concern. Turning animals into mere things and rearing tens of billions of them each year in factory farms that ignore cruelty unless it interferes with profitability is one of the great atrocities of the past fifty years.

Photo: © Shlomo Photography

Judge Karen "Chaya" Friedman

Judge Karen "Chaya" Friedman is an associate judge of the Circuit Court of Maryland for Baltimore City and was previously an associate judge of the District Court of Maryland. In 2010, President Obama appointed her to the United States Holocaust Memorial Council. Judge Friedman was chosen three times as one of "Maryland's Top 100 Women" by the *Daily Record* newspaper.

> "My observance and my transmittal of the heritage—including the 'particulars'—is my gift to my grandfather and to his generation."

Growing up in Borough Park, New York, the heart of the Orthodox Jewish community in America, in the 1980s, nearly every family I knew had been touched by the Holocaust. The few girls in my grade whose grandparents were not survivors seemed different. Their family dynamics and experiences were just different from the rest of ours. I was always very aware of why my mother never knew what it was like to have grandparents. My grandfather rarely spoke about his pre-war life and almost never discussed the war itself. My grandmother thankfully did.

To me, my grandparents and their generation were unbeliev-able heroes. The strength of spirit that it took to emerge from utter desolation, to arrive in a strange new land, and to rebuild is unimagi-nable. They started families and built communities. They amassed wealth and prestige. Remarkable. With all that being said, what truly amazed me is that although they had lost everything—literally—the one thing they never lost is their faith in G-d.

Every year on Passover, at the seder, my grandfather would recite the Haggadah with a fervor that would literally light up his face. To me he always looked like an angel. There were always a few tears streaming down his face as each word was precisely recited. I learned that the last time my grandfather saw his family was the first night of Passover. He had been drafted into the Hungarian army and went AWOL to see his family. He celebrated the first seder with them and then returned to the army. His family was taken shortly after. Knowing this, the tears on Passover made sense to me, but the fervor of the recitation did not. This G-d he was praising for taking the Jewish people out of Egypt was the same G-d who allowed Hitler to kill his family. If anything, for him Passover should be a reminder of G-d's betrayal, not an occasion to wholeheartedly celebrate His glory. Every year it amazed me.

My grandfather served in the Hungarian army's kitchen, cook-ing and preparing food for the troops. He was surrounded by and had access to food all day, and yet he would not eat. Why? The food was not kosher. He ate raw potatoes to survive as opposed to eating non-kosher. To me, as a teenager and even as an adult, this seemed like madness. In times of emergency, the Jewish dietary laws, the laws of kashrut, were surely meant to be suspended. And why even bother? All the devotion to G-d and His laws did not prevent this human tragedy.

To my grandfather, keeping the mitzvot and belief in the Torah were so integral to who he was that not even the Holocaust could cause him to question his belief or waiver from his observance. He, and so many others like him, went back to their homes after the war only to discover that no one was left. They picked themselves up, went to America, and continued to live their observant lives. They started synagogues, yeshivas, and kosher supermarkets and rebuilt religious communities. The depth of their belief in G-d and His just nature allowed them to move on, with G-d still being the central focus in their lives. Truly extraordinary.

I have carried that feeling of amazement with me all my life. My life has been easy and blessed. Certainly I have faced no challenges in my life even worth mentioning in comparison to my grandparents' lives. Yet, there are times when I doubt and when I question. I don't question the presence of G-d. I truly and innately have a deep belief in G-d and His total control of the universe. It's the particulars—the details—I have an issue with. Would G-d really be offended by my eating a non-kosher tuna sandwich? Does not opening a light on Sabbath really demonstrate one's commitment to G-d? As a more liberal, intellectual Jew, I have grappled with these questions. The one thing I always come back to is neither liberal nor intellectual. It is my vision of my grandfather willing to starve to death during the war, rather than break G-d's commandments.

The man I admire and respect most in this world was willing to die for the "particulars." His steadfast belief in G-d translated into a strict observance of the details—before the war, during the war, and after the war. No change. No divergence. No distractions. That knowledge has always made a deep impression on me. For him, the tradition is a living, breathing entity to be passed from him to his children, to his grandchildren, and so on. Knowing that it has been successfully passed on was the ultimate victory over the Nazis for him and his generation. How dare I rob him of that? How can I turn my back on that kind of dedication? I cannot and I have not. My observance and my transmittal of the heritage—including the "particulars"—is my gift to him and to his generation. My grandparents have taught me that it is not the devil that is in the details, but G-d himself.

Rabbi Elie Kaplan Spitz

Rabbi Elie Kaplan Spitz has served as the spiritual leader of Congregation B'nai Israel in Tustin, California, since 1988. A graduate of The Jewish Theological Seminary of America and Boston University School of Law, Rabbi Spitz has authored two books for Jewish Lights Publishing: *Does the Soul Survive? A Jewish Journey to Belief in Afterlife, Past Lives & Living with Purpose* and *Healing from Despair: Choosing Wholeness in a Broken World.* He and his wife, Linda, are the parents of Joseph, Jonathan, and Anna.

"Despite their encounter with life-destroying evil during the dark days of the Holocaust, my parents affirmed the goodness of life. More than what they lost, how they lived informed my worldview."

Why would a man honor another fifty years later for a song? In this case the man honored was my grandfather, who perished days before the liberation from the death camps. I grew up with tales of my grandfather, Mordechai Shmuel Smilovic, tales that profoundly shaped my own aspiration for living with goodness and piety. My grandfather lived in Munkacs, then Czechoslovakia. The small city was nestled in the Carpathian Mountains, the area of the Ba'al Shem Tov, where Hasidism emerged and which remained immersed in a longing for piety. My grandfather was a Hasid, a disciple of a local rabbinic sage. I grew up with a visual image of my grandfather through a single photo that remained of him.

The family photo was taken in the 1930s. It hung in my parents' home, and a copy is now in my hallway, a photo displayed by grandchildren in countries around the world. He has a long dark-gray beard; side curls; a double-breasted, long black coat; and a serious face. His wife and nine of his eleven children are also pictured. My grandmother wears a wig made by her daughter the wig maker's apprentice, my mother. My teenage mother, who wears a sailor dress matching those worn by three of her sisters, stands directly behind her father. When I was growing up, my mother described how her father studied the Talmud late into the night and how even non-Jewish lawyers would come to consult with him. She would tear up when recalling the heartfelt beauty of her father's singing at the Shabbat table or in synagogue on the High Holy Days, joined by his three sons as a backup choir.

Mordechai Shmuel used his melodic voice and outgoing personality to raise money for *hachnasat kallah*, the charity he headed in his town that provided dowry funds for poor brides. An important day for such fund-raising was Purim afternoon. Each year, along with two musician friends, my grandfather would travel from house to house in a wagon decorated with bells and colorful streamers, visiting the town's leading families. My grandfather, so I was told, would literally get up on the dining table after the dishes were cleared to sing and dance.

In 1943, the Hungarians, who had occupied their region, arrested my grandfather. At that time and place, it was a crime to aid Jews fleeing Nazi-controlled areas. My grandparents, who owned a grocery store and a saloon, had violated that law. After my grandmother learned the location of her husband's prison, she visited as often as possible. As Purim drew near, she brought a bowl of borscht. On Purim day, the family story continues, my grandfather took the sweet soup, added water to increase its volume, and placed it on a table with a spoon for others to taste. He stood on a nearby table and began to sing and dance. Uplifted by his performance, the other Jewish inmates joined in the traditional revelry as if inebriated. The guards looked on in amazement.

The next day, a prison official took my grandfather from his cell to the warden's office. "I am told that you were quite entertaining yesterday. Sing me the Hungarian song that you sang," the warden demanded. And my grandfather sang "Szól a kakas már," a Hasidic song based on a Hungarian folk melody, which describes the crowing of a rooster and an observer at the start of day longing for a colorful bird to wait for him. More than a hundred years previously, Rabbi Yitzhak Isaac Taub of Kalev had tacked on words of yearning for redemption and a return to Jerusalem. When my grandfather finished singing, the warden said, "For what crime were you arrested?"

"In my nine months in prison, I have never had a trial and have never formally been charged. So, I am unsure."

"Where do you come from?" the warden asked.

"From Munkacs."

"Okay," the warden announced, "you are free to go home."

My grandfather returned home shortly before Passover of 1944. At the seder table, he sang familiar melodies, but without his familiar joy. He told his family that they would be taken away soon and it was unclear who would return alive. And so it was, within seven weeks the Nazis who had recently occupied their area of Carpathia rounded up the Jews and put them on trains to death camps. My grandfather and his teenage son, Shiku (later Sam), would find themselves in Buchenwald in the same barracks that would house Elie Wiesel and his father.

Fast-forward to San Diego and fifty years after the war. Marking his liberation from Buchenwald, a survivor sponsored *Kiddush* in his synagogue. As congregants gathered around, he announced that he wished to dedicate his celebration to the memory of Mordechai Shmuel Smilovic. A visitor from Toronto knew that name. It belonged to the father of his friend, Sam Smiley. Although he had never met Mordechai Shmuel, his friend had told him many stories of his beloved, saintly father. After returning to Toronto and telling Sam of the *Kiddush*, Sam telephoned the *Kiddush* host. "Was it my father that you were honoring and if so, why?"

"Yes, it was your father. He would stand in front of the barracks and sing 'Ani Ma'amin,' a traditional song that proclaims faith in the coming of the Messiah even though he may tarry. When I felt like throwing myself against the electrified barbed wire, your father's faith sustained me. His heartfelt singing kept me alive."

Learning of this tribute to my grandfather validated the stories that I had heard since infancy. His singing conveyed an ability to celebrate life, to do good, and even to yearn for God's redemption amid despair.

Despite an idealization of my grandfather, however, I see us as quite different. I do not literally await the coming of the Messiah, but see the possibility of a world of harmony as a human achievement that we must collectively work to attain. Rather than viewing the Bible as dictated by God letter by letter, I am persuaded by modern scholarship that the Bible is a human document woven of oral traditions, and yet, holy as our people's most inspired imagining of God's will. Rather than living in a closed religious community, I have the privilege of interfaith dialogue and experiences that both reveal neglected insights in my own tradition and offer resources to incorporate into daily spiritual practice, such as meditation techniques.

And yet, like my grandfather, when I turn to God in prayer, I let go of analysis and allow myself to imagine God before me. I do so by both making the words of liturgy my own and on occasion using my own words to express my deepest yearnings to a caring Presence. For me, God is an abiding Consciousness intertwined with all that exists and who flows through the deepest parts of my core. When I listen intently within, I can hear God's voice beckoning me to fulfill my potential as God's partner, a beckoning infused with love. I do not believe that God willed the Holocaust.

When I was in my twenties, I visited the *Kotel*, the remnant of the Western Wall built as part of the courtyard of the ancient Holy Temple in Jerusalem. Just behind me a group of young men dressed in white shirts and black pants were celebrating their pilgrimage with song and a circle dance. I grabbed hands and joined their celebration. Abruptly, their religious teacher declared, "Please stop. I have an important story to share."

Once upon a time, the man said, there was a young artist. He climbed a steep mountain with a friend to paint the beautiful landscape. He set up an easel and grew more and more focused on his art. After painting for a while, he started to walk backward, with his thumb extended to survey the perspective displayed on his canvas. Behind him was a cliff. His friend shouted, "Stop," but the artist was oblivious. Desperate, his friend picked up a rock and heaved it. As the stone burst through the canvas, the painter leaped forward. In doing so, the artist's life was saved in the nick of time.

So it was, the man went on, before the Second World War, when the Jews were assimilating quickly. God needed to grab their attention to prevent a total loss. The Holocaust, the young men's teacher concluded, was God's drastic effort to save the Jewish people.

The story knocked the air out of me. I was revolted by this justification of the murder of a million and a half children and a total of six million Jews. Later, I would read Elie Wiesel, who emphasized that it was blasphemy to explain God's role in the Holocaust. There are no answers to God's place in tragedy or willful human cruelty that satisfy me. Faith requires critical thought if we are to avoid falling into the trap of accepting colorful stories as wisdom.

My parents, Heddy and Arthur Spitz, raised four children, who each felt deeply loved. They helped found a Jewish day school in Phoenix, where my father served as president for close to a decade.

They succeeded in the wig business and gave generously both to communal needs and quietly to individuals. Despite their encounter with life-destroying evil during the dark days of the Holocaust, my parents affirmed the goodness of life. More than what they lost, how they lived informed my worldview. Their love of Jewish ritual, their appreciation for the miracle of Israel, and their compassion for others nurtured my spiritual identity and guides my service as a rabbi.

Although I never met my grandfather, his presence has also shaped me. From him I learned that a legacy can endure through stories and abiding love. His ability to yearn for a better day touched by God's presence in each moment remains, for me, a constant aspiration. From him I learned that a song can save a life.

Rabbi Lody B. van de Kamp

Rabbi Lody B. van de Kamp, a member of the Strategic Network on Countering Radicalization and Polarization of the City of Amsterdam, has served as rabbi in The Hague, Amsterdam, and Rotterdam and as a member of the Chief Rabbinate of Holland and the European Conference of Rabbis. He received his rabbinic ordination from the Talmudical College Chaye Olam in London after studying at the Talmudical College in Montreux, Switzerland; served for twelve years as a member of the city council in Amsterdam; and is a founding member of the "Seven-Member Council" of the city of Amsterdam, a municipal think tank that deals with matters of integration, participation, and interfaith and interracial relations, including in particular anti-Semitism and Islamophobia. His most recent book is *De Joodse Slaaf* (The Jewish Slave), a historical novel about the Jewish role in the Dutch slave trade of the eighteenth century.

"'What would we have done?' To this day I wonder what my father would have answered to this question."

Together with father we walk to shul. On the way, right in the center of town, we meet a few Germans who crossed the nearby border to do their weekly shopping at the Saturday market. One of them gets pushed in a wheelchair. Another one walks on crutches. "They must have been soldiers in the war," father tells us. Mumbling under his breath, he wishes them a long suffering and adds the ancient Jewish expression *kol yemey chayecha*—"all the days of your life." This takes place only a few years after father had left his wife and his two little children behind in Auschwitz. He himself came back, alone, after miraculously surviving two and a half years in that camp.

In the summer, mother often takes us to the nearby forest. She bends down with us and spells out the names of the flowers and the plants. She helps us to collect chestnuts, acorns, and beechnuts. In the winter, she sits with us next to the stove and tells us stories. Stories about lost tribes in Tibet, about the gold rush in California, about the discovery of Antarctica. She never tells us her own story. That is the story of spending the war years in Holland in hiding. All on her own, at twelve different addresses. They were years of terrible fear. Every footstep, every knock on the door, every stranger she came across, awakened in her the fear of "What is next?" Sometimes she was lucky and the family she was staying with was nice. Other times she had no other choice but to pick up her meager belongings after spending one night with people who treated her badly and to try to find another roof over her head for the coming evening. On the run for years, she discovered only after the liberation that her parents had perished in the extermination camp of Sobibor in Poland, and her brother in the concentration camp of Mauthausen in Austria.

Mother reads to us from the book *Uncle Tom's Cabin*, about the slave trade in America. She explains how the French Revolution started. She never tells us her own story. "My story? That is not worth telling. I was only in hiding. Papa, his story you will have to know. After all, he was in the camps."

The fourth of May is the Dutch National Remembrance Day for the dead of the Second World War. In the evening just before eight o'clock, two minutes of silence are observed throughout the entire country.

My sister and I sit closely together on the sofa. There is no sound. Outside the cars have stopped; nobody speaks a word. We believe that even the birds stop chirping.

Father and mother stand next to each other in front of the window. Father has his hands in his pockets. Mother leans against his shoulder. One can hear a pin drop. At that time we were too young to realize what went through their minds. Now, many years later, we do know. There they are, a young father and a young mother with two little children. All on their own. No parents, no uncles, no aunts. My father had been left with only two of his brothers and one sister, my mother with one sister. Standing there, with just memories of the cattle train, of Auschwitz, of murdered children, of hiding places, of being on the run, and of loneliness. Just loneliness. They see and sense all this during those two minutes on the evening of the fourth of May.

Full of fear, my sister and I look at each other. We are waiting for the inevitable moment, every year. The moment when we hear father and mother sobbing. There is nothing worse for a child than to hear parents cry.

Our parents could not cope with the Shoah, the destruction of Jewish life in Europe. Mother died too young to be able to distance herself from the indescribable tragedies in her personal life. Father, at a very advanced age, tried to understand what made me take my yearly trips to Auschwitz, Majdanek, Sobibor, Treblinka, Bergen-Belsen, Mauthausen, Belzec, and all the other places of hell on earth. Every time after I returned from my journeys, he wanted me to tell him my stories. But he asked no questions, he never commented. He always ended with a vague smile and the same sentence: "I have been there as well."

Years have gone by.

I am listening to Dr. Eli Cohen. He, an inmate of many concentration camps, tells me about his meeting, more than twenty years after the war, with former Sobibor camp guard Hubert Gomerski. Dr. Cohen forces himself to meet Gomerski. He is determined to experience what "inspired" a man like Gomerski to act as such a cruel beast toward fellow human beings, there in the middle of the forests at the Polish eastern border.

Gomerski sits in an armchair and hears Cohen's story about his journeys from the Dutch transit camp of Westerbork to Auschwitz, to Mauthausen, and to other camps. Gomerski shows no emotion. In his blue jacket, his dark red vest, and his suede shoes, he looks a lot smarter than in his uniform with his boots. Gomerski offers Dr. Cohen a cup of tea and a cigarette, and he starts talking. "That's how it was. Over there I was the boss and you were the prisoner. I was the Nazi and you the dirty Jew."

"It all started in the thirties," he continues. "An article in the paper against the Jews. A joke about the Jews. But we still greeted our Jewish neighbors. Only a few years later I spat on the ground whenever I met a Jew. Slowly but surely, every Jew became in our eyes not worth more than a fly, a parasite. That's what the system taught us." Gomerski gets up from his chair. "Until the moment," he says, "after the Führer had been in power for enough years, when the Jew became *vernichtbar*—destructible." While Gomerski uses this word, he lifts his heel from the floor and makes a turning movement with the front part of his shoe. *Vernichtbar*, "destructible." Dr. Cohen completes his story, he stares ahead and repeats once more, almost whispering, "*Vernichtbar*." But then he sits up straight and stares at me. "Rabbi Van de Kamp," he asks, "but what would we have done? If we would have been subjected to the system of declaring others 'destructible,' what would we have done?" Dr. Cohen doesn't wait for my answer. He gets up and walks away. His words are ringing in my ears. "What would we have done?" To this day I wonder what my father would have answered to this question. Not long after our meeting, Dr. Cohen passed away.

More years have gone by.

The man, a retired preacher, is sitting opposite me in the lunchroom of the railway station. He tells me about his father, an SS officer in the German army. That father got killed somewhere in Lithuania at the end of the war. Long after the war the son discovered a letter that the father wrote to a family member. "Now I am in Kaunus, in Lithuania. Down the road is the entrance of the Ghetto. Not far from here is the 'Fort' where the Jews are going to be killed."

The preacher sighs. I, the rabbi sitting across from him, also sigh.

That afternoon in that lunchroom we spoke about his father. We spoke about my father.

That afternoon the man told me that his mother was a great admirer of the Führer, right until her last breath. I told the man that my mother was a victim of the Führer, right until her last breath.

We spoke and we were silent. We shared our views about guilt and about forgiveness. We spoke about Christianity and the Shoah. We spoke about Judaism and the Shoah. We exchanged our views about faith during and after the Shoah.

And finally we spoke about G-d. The man bends forward, toward me. "G-d. Did your father, honestly, after all that my people, the German nation, had done to him, still believe in G-d? Your mother, after she lost almost her entire family, did she still have faith in G-d, in the Almighty?" I was thinking of asking him in response, "Did your father, honestly, after all that he and his people, the German nation, had done, still believe in G-d? Your mother, who admired Adolf Hitler her entire life, did she have faith in G-d?" I did not ask him this question. Instead, I just answered the preacher, "I don't know about the faith of my father and my mother after the war. They hardly spoke about their suffering. They didn't speak about their inner feelings. I presume that they couldn't. One thing I do know. They made sure that my sister and I, small Jewish children born after the war, went to synagogue. They made sure that we attended religion classes twice a week. They made sure that the Jewish holidays were observed in our home. They made sure that after the destruction of almost their entire family, a new generation of Jewish children were formed to establish their own Jewish homes."

The preacher, the son of an SS soldier and of a fierce believer in the Nazi ideology, bowed his head in shame. I think my father would have smiled, vaguely.

Rabbi Mordechai Liebling

Rabbi Mordechai Liebling is the founder and director of the Social Justice Organizing Program at the Reconstructionist Rabbinical College, of which he is a graduate. He was previously the executive vice president of Jewish Funds for Justice, and before that he was the executive director of the Jewish Reconstructionist Federation. He is married to Lynne Iser, they have five children, and their family was the subject of the award-winning documentary *Praying with Lior*.

"In order for there to be a healthy Jewish community, we must begin to explore what healthy Holocaust remembrance could and should be. We don't really know, and it is high time for us to find out."

I am in the men's barracks at Auschwitz-Birkenau dancing to a Shlomo Carlebach *niggun* being played by Ohed, an Israeli rabbi, with my right arm on the shoulders of a Zen abbot and my left on the shoulders of Krishna Das, the leading US singer of Hindu devotional music. The faded German sign on the wall commands "Silence." My brain is flashing: "This does not compute, must rewire." It is November 2013 and I am on a meditation retreat.

I had decided that for my sixty-fifth birthday I would participate in the Zen Peace Making Order's eighteenth annual weeklong retreat to Auschwitz-Birkenau. It was time to go another level deeper into my emotional, intellectual, and spiritual legacies.

My father Joel and my mother Zelda were each the sole survivor of their respective immediate families. Before the war they lived in Chortkov. When my father was born in 1913, it was still within the Austria-Hungarian Empire; when they grew up, it was Poland; by the time they left, it had become part of the Soviet Union; and today it is in Ukraine. This part of Poland had one of the lowest Jewish survival rates during the Holocaust.

We were approximately one hundred people, a little more than half from Germany, Austria, Poland, and a smattering of other European countries; about thirty-five to forty were Americans, plus several Israelis and two Palestinians. There about fifteen Jews in the group, of whom seven or so were children or grandchildren of survivors. Most are Zen practitioners. Many had been here before. It was my first trip to Poland.

We began at Auschwitz-1, the original camp, much of which is now a museum. The first gas chamber with Zyklon-B was actually developed there. It still exists. We entered, barely fitting; the door and the lights were shut. I wept. Curiously, I felt no fear, only sadness. We then went through the museum filled with all that the dead had left behind—luggage, spectacles, shoes, hair ... I sobbed, deep, gut-wrenching sobs. Evy, a German woman, gave me a hug and apologized for what her people had done.

I felt as if I were in a vortex of evil. I was there to bear witness to evil, to squarely look at it without turning away. Since childhood I have been unable to believe in an omnipotent, omniscient God. No such God could exist and allow this to happen. I felt confirmed in my Reconstructionist theology. God was in the deeds of resistance, in the ability to unflinchingly look at the pain and to feel compassion for both the victim and perpetrator.

It was a rainy, gray day, and suddenly as we walked I saw a flash of color. Israeli teenagers wrapped in large Israeli flags. Most

Israeli high school seniors who will enter the army are brought to Auschwitz. My first thought was how proud and pleased my father would have felt seeing this. My next thought, how inappropriate, no one else carries flags. They are brought here to be re-traumatized, I thought. I spoke with the Israelis on our trip who had done this as teenagers. The students are told that this could easily happen again, that only the strength of the Israeli army prevents this from happening again, that "Never Again" means that Israel must have a powerful army. I worried that they are taught fear, that they are taught to live from a place of potential catastrophe, from inside trauma.

For Americans, the Holocaust has become the symbol for universal evil. For Israelis, the Holocaust epitomizes the fate of Jews without an army. Caught in the middle, we need to find a way to hold both the universal message of "Never Again" to any people anywhere and the particular message of the need to protect the safety of all Jews in all countries.

The next day we entered Auschwitz-2, or Birkenau, the death camp. We began at the "sauna" where people were brought, stripped of their identities, heads shorn, tattooed. I sobbed as deeply as I ever have in my life. I stayed with the pain and sadness. From there we went to the sites of the gas chambers and crematoria. I remained there for the longest time, crying and stroking the moss as if it were a child's hair, knowing that human ash had been the fertilizer.

That day we began our formal meditation. For four days, we sat outside on the ground or in folding chairs, surrounded by barbed wire, alongside the railroad tracks where the cattle cars stopped, disgorging their prisoners, and Mengele made his selection—who would be sent to death immediately and who would work in the brutal conditions of slave labor.

The third day, we divided by gender into two groups and went to the men's and women's barracks. That is when I found myself dancing at Auschwitz. The next event was even more stunning. As we left the barracks there was some confusion over where we were supposed to go next. A few of the men walked over to the women's barracks to find the other half of our group, Rabbi Ohed among them. As he arrived, Marushka, whose mother was a survivor of Auschwitz, spontaneously asked him if he would on the spot perform the marriage with her fiancé, who was on the trip and happened to walk over with Ohed. He agreed.

I must admit that my first response was shock and a slight feeling that this was perhaps not quite appropriate. The more I thought about it, however, the more it grew on me. Marushka's mother didn't expect to survive, let alone have a daughter.

That afternoon we divided into faith groups for a service. We Jews walked over to where the crematoria had been. It was late afternoon, the sun had come out, the light had a magical quality, the grass was green, and it was beautiful. Ohed began a lovely song; we looked up, and there was a rainbow in the sky and the sun was shining on the wedding couple. Again, my brain flashed, "This does not compute, must rewire." There was so much love and beauty in this moment, and I was standing next to the crematoria at Auschwitz, the epicenter of human degradation.

That night after dinner we returned to the men's barracks for our only evening sit of the week. After two meditation periods, about half the group returned to our lodgings, and the remainder elected to stay until midnight. We sat for a while longer and then began sharing. As it had been the day of a wedding, I decided to tell the story of my parents' "wedding day."

Joel and Zelda met in 1941 during the Soviet occupation of Poland. She was a college student, he a dentist. They kept up their romantic relationship first in a ghetto, then in a labor camp. One day in early spring of 1943, the *Lagerführer*, the camp commandant, rounded up all the Jews who were still alive, trained machine guns on everyone, and told them to lie down. He then called out about a dozen people whose labor was still deemed valuable. Among them was my father. It was clear that everyone else was to be killed. Lying there were my mother, her sister, and my father's sister. My father approached the *Lagerführer* and asked, "Can my wife get up?"

He replied, "That was a sudden marriage," and told my mother to get up.

Everyone else was killed. That evening my parents escaped from the camp and lived in hiding for a year until their liberation by the Soviets.

My father wrestled the rest of his life with guilt; it was the pain of that decision that was communicated to me. Only when I was in my twenties was I able to reframe it and see it as the act of heroism that it was. He had risked his life to save the woman he loved. And that evening, telling their story on that wedding day in Auschwitz,

I was able for the first time to speak of my father's rescue of my mother as my parents' wedding day.

By providing me with the structure and the safety to delve into my deepest places of sadness and pain, the retreat empowered me. It was my path to healthy remembering.

After seeking safety for the last seventy years, it is time for the Jewish people as a whole to embark on a similar journey. I returned from the retreat with the realization that in order for there to be a healthy Jewish community, we must begin to explore what healthy Holocaust remembrance could and should be. We don't really know, and it is high time for us to find out.

Eric Nelson

Eric Nelson is professor of government at Harvard University. He received his PhD from the University of Cambridge and is the author of *The Hebrew Republic: Jewish Sources and the Transformation of European Political Thought*, which received the Erwin Stein Prize from the Justus-Liebig University in Germany and the Laura Shannon Prize in Contemporary European Studies from the Nanovic Institute for European Studies at the University of Notre Dame. His most recent book is *The Royalist Revolution: Monarchy and the American Founding*.

> "It strikes me that, for all of my doubts and questions, if my grandfather can go on thanking the God of Israel for the gift of dew, then surely I ought to consider doing so as well."

My grandfather, Jack Sarna, recently had emergency surgery to address a serious case of intracranial bleeding. In the aftermath of the procedure, he predictably experienced terrible pain, as well as a good deal of restlessness and disorientation. As I sat with him in the intensive care unit, I tried to offer him relief in any way that I could— changing the position of the bed, holding his hand, speaking to him, and so on—but without apparent success. Finally, it occurred to me that I had downloaded some old recordings of cantorial music to my iPhone, and I wondered whether he might like to listen to them. I put my earphones in his ears and selected the first track, which happened to be Yossele Rosenblatt chanting the *Tal* prayer from the *Musaf* service on the first day of Passover. Upon hearing the melody, my grandfather suddenly closed his eyes, smiled, and began to move his right hand, as if conducting. A moment later, this man who had been unable to speak and who had no discernable idea of where he was, began to sing along, chanting the words with some fervor.

My grandfather is now ninety-one years old. He lost his parents and two of his brothers to the crematoria and survived the war in a series of Nazi concentration and labor camps—including, most notoriously, the Płaszów camp outside of Krakow. Yet, despite these horrors and the dramatic questions of theodicy that they raise, he has attended synagogue on every Shabbat and *Yom Tov* since he was liberated in January 1945. There are, of course, several possible explanations for this fact, and they are not mutually exclusive. Attending synagogue surely reminds him of the shtetl in southern Poland where he grew up and, in particular, of his beloved father, who sat beside him during services each week. My grandfather also has a strong and beautiful tenor voice and plainly relishes the opportunity to sing along, loudly and boisterously, as the liturgy is chanted. He has also undoubtedly treasured the community of survivors, now sadly depleted, in whose company he has prayed for decades. But I have no doubt that there is at least one additional reason for his punctilious observance of Jewish ritual: strange to say, he believes in the God of Israel.

I found myself thinking about this apparently remarkable fact in the ICU as my grandfather mouthed the words to the *Tal* prayer. It has always been one of his favorites (and mine as well). Yet it is an extraordinary prayer for a Holocaust survivor to delight in. *Tal* is, after all, a prayer for dew, which, in the rabbinic imagination, is a token of God's sustaining love of the earth. The central feature of dew is its regularity, the fact that it falls without any fuss. We might be inclined to suppose that God intervenes in nature only through spectacular acts of extravagant power—the thunder and lightning on Sinai, the parting of the Red Sea. But *Tal* gives the rabbis an opportunity to insist that this is not so. The earth, we are told, requires God's sustaining, generative love each and every day, made manifest in the dew that comes down unbidden.[1] The God of Israel may not be *of* the world, but he is somehow radically present within it all the same. And if he intervenes in nature with such regimented grace, then surely he will intervene in history as well, rebuilding "the city now deserted ... with dew."

Now this, one might think, is not the sort of God for which a Holocaust survivor should have any patience. A "clockmaker" God who simply sets the world in motion and then withdraws is one thing; but a God who is present in the world would seem to have a great deal to answer for. Why does he allow the world to be as it is? A standard reply on behalf of those who, like Milton, wish to "justify the ways of God to men" seeks to acquit God of complicity in human evil by emphasizing our essential freedom. What is of true value about human beings, to use Kant's formulation, is that we are capable of morality. But to be capable of morality, we must be free to choose, from which it follows that God must allow us to choose badly—even calamitously badly. God did not cause the Nazis to commit their outrages against human dignity; rather, the possibility of there being Nazis who commit such outrages is the price we pay for freedom.

Yet the God of Israel is evidently willing from time to time to intervene in history, redeeming slaves from Egyptian bondage, and so on, without obviously compromising the order of human freedom. Why, then, does he routinely refuse to intervene in order to prevent catastrophic suffering? When we consider human morality, we are inclined to give some weight to the distinction between "doing" and "allowing." We may say, for example, that we have a "perfect" duty to avoid committing injustice, but only an "imperfect" one to aid those who are suffering for reasons independent of our own actions. But this notion derives much of its plausibility from the fact that our capacities for agency are extremely limited: I can't dive in to rescue the man who is drowning off the shore of Cape Cod while at the same time delivering a vaccine to a child in the Congo and coming to the aid of a battered woman in Nepal. I am constrained by the laws of physics; it is perfectly fair to demand that I should "do my bit" to help my fellow man, but it would be unreasonable to hold me personally responsible for alleviating human suffering in each and every instance. God, however, presumably has infinite capacities of agency. Why, then, should he not have a perfect duty to aid victims of terrible injustice?

But these may, alas, be the easy questions. The more difficult ones return us to the world of *Tal*. If God creates and sustains the natural world, why is it so seemingly awful? Before Auschwitz, the great challenge to theodicy was the horrific Lisbon earthquake of

1755, which elicited Voltaire's famous assault on theistic belief. Why does God allow earthquakes? The question seems to leave a religious believer impaled on the horns of a dilemma: either God caused the earthquake (or allowed it to happen despite being able to prevent it), in which case he is not good, or else God has no control over earthquakes, in which case he is not God (because God is meant to be omnipotent). One line of reply returns us again to the value of freedom: perhaps in order for there to be creatures like us who are capable of morality, there must be earthquakes. God, on this view, is free to decide whether or not to create a world with creatures like us in it, but having decided to create such a world, he must, as it were, "follow the recipe"—and among the indispensable ingredients are the set of natural forces that jointly have the effect of producing earthquakes (and perhaps subdural hematomas in the heads of ninety-one-year-old Holocaust survivors). Perhaps. But I confess that this is not an answer from which I myself derive much comfort.

I am therefore left, like countless others, without any firm ground upon which to stand. Yet it strikes me that, for all of my doubts and questions, if my grandfather can go on thanking the God of Israel for the gift of dew, then surely I ought to consider doing so as well.

Chaim Reiss

Chaim Reiss, the chief financial officer of the World Jewish Congress (WJC), is a certified public accountant, a member of the American Institute of Certified Public Accountants, and serves on the Not-for-Profit Committee of the New York State Society of CPAs. A graduate of Brooklyn College, he also received rabbinical ordination from the world-renowned Mirrer Yeshiva and has published articles in the areas of finance and taxation. Prior to joining the WJC, he served for eighteen years as the vice president of finance and administration of the American Associates of Ben-Gurion University of the Negev.

"One should never criticize or look down on anyone who went through the Shoah and lost faith in G-d."

Probably because the parents of most of my friends in elementary school were Holocaust survivors, growing up in the Brownsville section of Brooklyn as a child of survivors did not seem different or unusual. As we grew older, I came to realize that there were differences between the way our parents acted and how the American-born parents (*Americahners*, as we called them) of other children acted. Most survivors who were fortunate enough to have children were and continue to be very protective of their children. My parents were similarly overprotective of my siblings and me. My mother always insisted that we eat every bite of food on our plates and was always careful about not wasting food or throwing things away. However, the most important aspect of our lives was faith in G-d and keeping our Jewish traditions.

As I grew older, I often wondered how my parents, who had survived the cruelties of Nazi persecution and the horrors of war, had been able to maintain their belief in G-d and insist that their children continue this tradition.

My father once told me that his revenge on Hitler and the Nazis was seeing a new generation of Jewish children being raised as Jews. My parents were always proud of the fact that my siblings and I remained true to our faith and traditions. The *mashgiach ruchni* (the dean, or spiritual mentor) of the Mirrer Yeshiva, where I did my post–high school religious studies and received *smichah* (rabbinic ordination), once spoke to a group of students about Holocaust survivors. He said that the Holocaust was a terrible tragedy for the Jews and that one should never criticize or look down on anyone who went through the Shoah and lost faith in G-d. This was a remarkable statement coming from the person whose primary responsibility was the religious and spiritual growth of the students. I realized that he was teaching us an important lesson in life.

There is a story told about the famous Hasidic *rav* the Satmar Rebbe. As the Rav was about to leave on a trip to Israel, one of his Hasidim came to him for a *bracha*, a blessing, and expressed his concern that with the Rebbe away, there would be no one worthy of giving *brachas*. The Satmar Rebbe answered him, "Go to any Jew who has a number tattooed on his arm and ask him for a *bracha*. A Jew who has a tattoo on his arm and still puts on *t'fillin* can give you the best *bracha*. When such a person is available, you do not need the Satmar Rebbe to give you a *bracha*."

Rabbi Dr. Bernhard H. Rosenberg

Rabbi Dr. Bernhard H. Rosenberg is the spiritual leader of Congregation Beth-El in Edison, New Jersey. He received his ordination and doctorate of education from Yeshiva University and was awarded a doctor of divinity degree by The Jewish Theological Seminary of America. He is the author of numerous books on Holocaust remembrance and theology, including most recently *The Holocaust as Seen Through Film.*

"Even Auschwitz could not diminish my parents' faith."

I am the only child of Holocaust survivors, Jacob and Rachel Rosenberg of blessed memory, who were from Poland. Jacob, of Wodislav, survived Auschwitz and Buchenwald, and Rachel, of Slomnika, survived the work camp Skarzisko and Buchenwald. The Nazis murdered their entire families, including my father's first wife and two children, except for one cousin and aunt on my father's side.

I admire and honor my parents for their strength and courage in forging ahead to rebuild from the ashes and tears. Even Auschwitz could not diminish their faith. They could have rejected humanity; instead they aided others in their daily fight for existence. My entire life has been devoted to keeping their memory and their memories alive. Perhaps the Holocaust never leaves me because my parents met and married in a Displaced Persons camp in Regensburg, Germany, after the war, and it is there that I was born.

Growing up, I constantly looked at the numbers on my father's left arm, which he received in Auschwitz. Those numbers instilled in me the urge to fight for the State of Israel and against anti-Semitism, wherever it may occur. I became a rabbi because of those numbers.

I mourn for my grandparents, uncles, and aunts who perished at the hands of the Nazis, and I often weep for not having experienced their love. I cry in anguish when reminded that six million of my brethren, young and old, left this earth via gas chambers and crematoria. I feel the pain of my family and friends who saw their elders shot before their very eyes and witnessed the unthinkable: their babies hurled against brick walls and bayoneted.

I have taught Holocaust studies for most of my life on the high school and college level. When I discuss the Holocaust and God, I share many possible views. I cannot in good conscience believe that the Jewish people were punished, because if I were to believe that, I would not be a rabbi and would probably be an atheist. One and a half million priceless Jewish children were murdered. What was their sin? The answer I give myself and others is that people caused the Holocaust, not God. I blame the murderers. I blame humanity for remaining silent. I blame the leaders of countries who refused to intercede on behalf of the defenseless. We are not puppets to be controlled by our Creator. It is the only answer I can live with.

Should I then hate humanity? Should I live with anger in my heart, rebelling against the environment, rejecting those of other faiths and cultures? Perhaps I should bend in fear like a blade of grass when the winds of anti-Semitism turn toward me?

No! I will not live in a shell of neurotic chaos, and I will not reject society. I believe in hope, born from the seeds of hatred. I feel no survivor's guilt for the privilege of being alive.

Now that I am an orphaned adult, I appreciate even more the impact that my parents had upon me. All that I am and all that I ever will be I owe to them. They instilled within me pride and fortitude; their motto became my personal outcry, "Never again."

Refuse to discuss the Holocaust? Sweep these memories under the rug? No, I protest. Let the truth be known! Let others realize what the world did to an ethical, moral, and religious populace. Let them hear the testimony of valiant survivors. Contrary to what we are told, the passage of time does not ease our pain or theirs, nor does it diminish the scope of the horror that was the Holocaust.

My students ask me, "Can the Holocaust happen again?" My answer is a definite yes. A number of atomic bombs thrown at Israel by its enemies would annihilate the Israeli population. One is naive to believe that anti-Semitism does not exist throughout the world. If we have learned anything from the Shoah, it is that it is possible for a madman to arise who wants to annihilate the Jewish people. Never fool yourself into believing that you are safe anywhere. We must always be alert and fight against prejudice wherever it may exist.

In my opinion, all the museums in the world and all the books that are written are not enough to preserve the memory of the Holocaust. In time, the Holocaust may become nothing more than a date in history. If we teach the Holocaust and genocide together as one subject, we guarantee that the impact of the Holocaust will merely blend into other genocides. What then is the solution? We must incorporate into our religious services and religious traditions, memoirs, readings, and liturgy, readings concerning the Holocaust. I have, therefore, already written a Holocaust Passover Haggadah and a Holocaust siddur.

I promised my parents that one day I would fill up a station wagon with my children. Together with my wife, Charlene, we have four children, all of whom are named after family members murdered in the Holocaust, and, so far, seven grandchildren. It is to them that we must pass the torch of remembrance.

Let us therefore join hands and loudly acclaim, "We will keep the memory of the Holocaust alive." I pray that you will use this book to continue this essential conversation about our history, and the Holocaust that is our inheritance.

Shimon Koffler Fogel

Shimon Koffler Fogel serves as the president and chief executive officer of the Centre for Israel and Jewish Affairs, the advocacy arm of the Jewish Federations of Canada. He introduced the concept of the "Shared Values" approach to Israel and Jewish advocacy, which has been adopted globally by the pro-Israel community. He is an ordained rabbi and completed a doctorate in international relations and was recently appointed to the International Experts Committee of the International Holocaust Remembrance Alliance.

Photo © Jerome Scullino 2nd

> "There is an imperative for the Jewish people to foster and preserve a sense of nationhood, a quality of unity, a commitment to mutuality. For to truly love G-d, one must love His children."

Man, like the world in which he lives, is filled with contradiction and paradox. None, however, seems as deep and fundamental as the belief in the existence of a Living G-d in the wake of the unspeakable horror of the Shoah. It is tempting to duck the question by citing the profound words of the famed Chofetz Chaim,[1] who observed that "with faith, there are no questions; without faith, there are no answers."

Still, the question persisted in the mind of a young boy struggling to understand why he alone was bereft of grandparents, while all of his classmates could boast of two, three, four—or in one case, even six! The challenge loomed large as his cheeks burned with embarrassment while a sanctuary filled to overflowing waited for what seemed like an eternity for the hazzan, his father, to compose himself following the recitation of *Yizkor*—the memorial prayer—on the sacred day of Yom Kippur.

Gradually, however, over days and years—through words and deeds, the boy came to understand. His father and mother both, contained of a boundless sense of optimism, gratitude, and love, taught him about G-d and the exceedingly personal relationship one can establish with the King, who in yet another paradox, is also our Father.

"I am unworthy of all the mercy and kindness You have bestowed upon me," declared my father, quoting our Patriarch Jacob. That was the first lesson: that we dare not harbor a sense of entitlement; that our blessings be cherished as gifts from G-d, that each was a privilege, not prerogative.

At our seder table every year, immediately following the ritual consumption of the *marror*—the bitter herbs reminding us of our Egyptian enslavement—my mother would distribute strips of uncooked turnip. As we would nibble on this vegetable that easily tasted as bitter as the *marror*, she would proclaim her gratitude to the Almighty for having provided this lifesaving food that she had discovered rotting in a field adjacent to the concentration camp barracks to which she was assigned. It took some years to discern the sweetness of that root vegetable and the annual thanksgiving offering that its addition to our seder represented.

Kevodo malei olam, "His glory fills the world," served as an axiomatic belief that informed the very essence of my father's being. Everything and everybody was infused with a G-dly spark, and our challenge was to recognize the Divine in the mundane. G-d is inherently good, and all that flows from G-d is therefore good—whether in an obvious and revealed manner or one cloaked in a dark shroud.

To a child, the verity of that lesson was not always obvious. But as I grew older, the truth of that insight has become increasingly manifest. How else to understand the frequently uttered and uniquely Jewish mantra "Thank G-d ... it could have been much worse."

The Kotzker Rebbe's response to his own rhetorical question "Where can G-d be found?" was "Wherever man lets Him in." The quintessential feature of love is its unconditionality; and that holds as real regarding our love of G-d as it does in respect of His love for us.

The third, but inherently connected rudiment drawn from my parents and their experiences during the Holocaust defines my relationship with the people of Israel. With simple acceptance they saw the unadorned, raw truth of the prophetic statement "It shall dwell as a nation apart." What that means, more than anything else, is that there is an imperative for the Jewish people to foster and preserve a sense of nationhood, a quality of unity, a commitment to mutuality. For to truly love G-d, one must love His children. So strongly held a conviction was that for my parents that I have pledged my life to this purpose—transforming their experience into a living and life-affirming legacy.

Unquestioning love of G-d, unqualified commitment to His children, and unending gratitude for His blessings. Life is complete ... and it is all good.

Photo: Frida Sterenberg

Lily Brett

Lily Brett is the author of six books of fiction, four books of essays, and seven volumes of poetry. Born in Germany after World War II, she grew up in Melbourne, Australia, and now lives in New York City.

Falling in Love in Cologne

In a wildly unexpected and completely unpredictable turn of events, I fell madly in love, in Cologne. It was the sort of love that makes your heart pound. The sort of love that seeps into your arteries. The sort of love that leaves you smiling at nothing in particular.

It was May 2006. I was happily married at the time, but that didn't turn out to be a problem. My husband is a very reasonable man. And he has always believed in love.

Cologne is not the sort of city where you expect to fall head over heels in love. It is a beautiful city, but it doesn't have the drama or the romance of a city like Paris or Havana. But, it was in Cologne that I fell in love. I fell in love with a church. A Catholic church. A church called St. Agnes.

St. Agnes is the second largest church in Cologne. Only the famed Cologne Cathedral is larger. St. Agnes is a relatively plain church. Its beautiful but simple lines and its white vaulted ceiling and pink-hued stone columns give it a grandeur. Not a grandeur of superiority. St. Agnes has an embracing, inclusive, and very human grandness.

It is unadorned and unpretentious, with a minimal amount of symbolism or decoration. It also has warmth. A warmth that is palpable. A warmth that allows your spirit to float, to soar, to question, and to be challenged. A state that feels remarkably like being in love. Being headily in love. And I was.

There was, however, a problem with this love match. I am not a Catholic. I am Jewish. And it gets worse. I am an atheist. A Jewish atheist. Maybe I am not a 100 percent, wholly committed atheist. Maybe only 90 percent of me is an atheist. Even if only 90 percent of me is an atheist, falling in love with a Catholic church is pretty problematic.

I was brought up to not believe in God. Not believing in God was like a family mantra. I was born to two people who had each survived years of imprisonment in Nazi ghettos, labor camps, and death camps. My mother was seventeen when she was imprisoned in the Lodz Ghetto. She had four brothers, three sisters, a mother, father, grandparents, aunties, uncles, cousins, nephews, and nieces. When it was all over, she was the only person in the universe she was related to. Every single person in her family had been murdered. My father's mother and father and sister and three brothers were also murdered.

It took my mother and father six months to find each other after the war. They were sent to a Displaced Persons camp in Feldafing. I was born in Germany, one of the first group of children born to survivors of the Holocaust.

"There is no God," my mother said, over and over again, when I was growing up. I grew up in Australia, a country of blue skies and sunshine. It didn't seem like a place in which it was important to know that it was a God-less world. My mother said, "There is no God," at the oddest times. And always out of the blue. "There is no God," she said when she was washing the dishes or hanging out the washing or getting dressed up to go to a bar mitzvah or birthday.

Both of my parents had come from religious homes. After the war, religion was a word they both scoffed at. My father, at ninety-seven, still rails at the mostly young, religious Jews who live near him on the Lower East Side, in New York, and who frequently ask if they can accompany him to synagogue.

And he has kept up his lack of faith in God or an afterlife. I woke up one morning worried by the sudden thought that my father, who bought himself a burial plot in Queens when he moved to New York about a decade ago, might want to be buried next to my mother in Melbourne, Australia.

"I don't want you to spend thousands of dollars to fly me to Australia when I am dead," he said when I asked him about being buried next to my mother. He said it in the sort of severe tone he sometimes used when I was a fifteen-year-old beatnik.

"You won't be flying business class," I said. "It won't cost thousands."

This temporarily derailed him. "Where in the plane would I be flying?" he asked.

"Probably with the luggage," I said. He started laughing and then resumed a monologue about being completely dead when you were dead.

"Mum won't know if I am next to her or not," he said. "I do not believe in God and I am not going to change now," he added.

I have envied people who are religious for most of my life. As a child I wished I was a Methodist because they served apple pies and cream and jam-filled sponge cakes at their church fetes. I had not been inside many Catholic churches when I first stepped into St. Agnes.

It was not love at first sight. I wasn't instantly smitten. I was nervous. I felt out of place. And uneasy. The feeling reminded me of being a teenager on guard against any inadvertent infraction of the rules that might slip out of me in my overly strict, highly academic high school.

I was at St. Agnes to do a reading from my newest novel. I had never read in a church before. I waited in the sacristy for the audience to be seated. I felt cold. It was strange sitting in a room usually occupied by priests. There was a male aroma in the room. I felt like an intruder. Or an alien.

A few minutes later, I walked into the main body of the church and sat down to read. I looked around me. There was something timeless and uncluttered and unfettered about this beautiful church. Something deeply moving. I felt calm. And embraced. I looked at the audience. Row after row of people were smiling at me.

I went back to St. Agnes the next day. And I didn't want to leave. I was in love, I loved the church. I felt part of the church. I was not alone in this. St. Agnes, which sits right in the middle of the district, has a devoted community. They have over the last ten years hosted contemporary music events, art exhibitions and book readings. Last year three hundred people came to hear the writer Ulla Hahn read poems.

I have been back to St. Agnes many times since that first reading. I have read there again. The church has, in their permanent collection, one of my husband's paintings, a triptych called *Passage and Crossings*. It hangs in the nave. Each panel has soaring red and black lines that stretch upward pointing to somewhere above the earth, somewhere celestial, somewhere above the minutiae of everyday life.

My relationship with St. Agnes has changed my life. It has changed my view of religion and showed me how we can be deeply connected while holding different religious beliefs or no religious beliefs. I feel as though St. Agnes is my church. I refer to it as my church. Or our church. This sometimes makes my ninety-seven-year-old father laugh. But there is a sense of pleasure in his laughter. I suspect it is the pleasure of possibility. All possibility.

I am still in love with St. Agnes. And still in love with my husband.

Photo: Joshua A. Cuppek

Rabbi Kenneth A. Stern

Rabbi Kenneth Allan Stern, currently the spiritual leader of a Conservative, egalitarian community in Fort Lee, New Jersey, is passionate about Judaism, Israel, people and pastoral work, youth activities, interfaith collaboration, education, and inclusion (substance abuse, learning disabilities, autism, and the elderly). He participated in marking the sixtieth anniversary of the liberation of Bergen-Belsen and in 2012 visited concentration camps in Poland and Germany, ending his journey in Sweden, where his mother convalesced after liberation. He is married to Suzanne Rose, MD, and has two grown children, Zachary and Isadora.

> "My mother gave me my faith. It was mine to grow and nurture—or to question and perhaps abandon."

A formative and foundational memory is seared into my mind: It was the late 1950s and my sister and I were left in a neighbor's care for the day. My mother, Helene/Illy Stern (née Stern), dressed in a navy, stylish, form-fitting suit with a matching pillbox hat, exited our apartment clutching a small accordion file that I had never seen before. She returned hours later, a shuddering, sobbing shadow of the woman who had left in the morning. First to our neighbor, and then on the phone to my father at work, and finally to her sister, she repeated over and over through her tears, "Never again—never again. No amount of money is worth this." She had gone to give a deposition with the hope of receiving German reparations; she had not been able to complete the interview.

Never wanting to upset or trigger my mother after what I witnessed that day, I never asked her anything about her Shoah experiences. As a result, I know relatively little about the horrors she went through, except for what she would volunteer in a passing conversation or relate when speaking to others. On those occasions I listened with rapt attention.

My younger sister has no memory of that day that looms so large for me, and as a result, she would regularly pepper our mother with questions about her family, the deportation, Auschwitz, the death marches, Belsen, and liberation. And I, trying to protect my mother, would admonish my sister, "Don't ask Mommy ... Don't bother Mommy ... Leave Mommy alone."

This pattern persisted even into adulthood, when the taboo (in my mind) was broadened to include theological discussions, specifically theodicy. Yet she raised her children to believe in God, gave us an awareness of Shabbat, read Bible stories to us, sent us to Hebrew school, davened fervently on all the holidays and on the other rare occasions when she would go to shul. I can only speculate that either her faith was that strong or her faith—and her sister—were the two things that she needed to retain in order to build a new life and give life.

While the above story has had a profound influence on me, another encounter shook my mother to the core. My mother's internist was also a survivor. One day he took a letter from his desk and gave it to her to read. It was an account of how his parents had been murdered. He told her that he was raised *frum*—davened every day with *tallit* and *t'fillin*. And then he went on to say that if God could do this to his parents—if God could let this happen to his parents—then God would get nothing more from him. Her physician's words shocked her, so much so that she was unable to respond. Interestingly, she was more upset by what her doctor had told her than by the letter he had given her to read. Her only comment was that God did not instigate the Shoah; men did ... and thank God, other good men, at a huge expense of life, brought down the forces of evil.

Clearly my mother never blamed God. But because I could not bring myself to probe further, I can only surmise that if from the depths of *Sheol,* she prayed to God for her deliverance, on another level she was certain that her deliverance would come either with her death or from the military defeat of her tormentors.

My mother gave me my faith. It was mine to grow and nurture—or to question and perhaps abandon. And I do question. I will probably go to my grave vacillating between the bedrock faith with which she raised me and the doubts that constantly creep into my mind—all this despite not having my faith tested in any way comparable to what she endured.

When my mother was diagnosed with inoperable lung cancer, my wife, with tears in her eyes, told me, "Your mother doesn't deserve this." And I responded with resignation, "It's not a matter of what we deserve, Suzi; that's not how it works." And then, with tears in my eyes, I sought refuge in God, davening the afternoon *Mincha* service and including a prayer for recovery, a *Mi Sheberakh*, in the appropriate section of the *Amidah*, the silent standing prayer that is central to the Jewish liturgy.

In retrospect, perhaps that moment was the culmination of a series of life/faith lessons taught to me by my mother.

Menachem Z. Rosensaft

Menachem Z. Rosensaft, who was born in the Displaced Persons camp of Bergen-Belsen, is general counsel of the World Jewish Congress, and teaches about the law of genocide and war crimes trials at the law schools of Columbia and Cornell Universities. Appointed to the United States Holocaust Memorial Council by Presidents Bill Clinton and Barack Obama, he is founding chairman of the International Network of Children of Jewish Holocaust Survivors, senior vice president of the American Gathering of Jewish Holocaust Survivors and Their Descendants, a member of the advisory council of the Lower Saxony Memorials Foundation in Germany, and a past president of Park Avenue Synagogue in New York City. He is the editor of *Life Reborn, Jewish Displaced Persons 1945–1951* and co-author (with Jodi Rosensaft) of "A Measure of Justice: The Early History of German-Jewish Reparations," published in the *Fordham International Law Journal* and as an occasional paper by the Leo Baeck Institute.

"If God was at Treblinka, I want to believe that He was within Janusz Korczak as he accompanied his children to their death. I feel certain that the mystical divine spark that characterizes Jewish faith, the *Shekhina*, was within my mother as she and the other women in her group rescued 149 Jewish children from almost certain death at Bergen-Belsen."

On October 4, 1997, on Shabbat Shuva, the Saturday between Rosh Hashanah and Yom Kippur, I sat in the sanctuary of Park Avenue

Synagogue in New York City together with our daughter Jodi. My mother had died the previous evening, only a few hours after the end of Rosh Hashanah, the Jewish New Year. After being increasingly ill for months, she had finally succumbed to the hepatitis she had contracted at Auschwitz-Birkenau. Her funeral would take place two days later.

In the hospital, my mother had been upset that she would not be able to go to the cemetery where my father is buried. He had died twenty-two years earlier midway between Rosh Hashanah and Yom Kippur. We had gone to his graveside every year on the day after Shabbat Shuva. I had tried to reassure her that my wife Jeanie, Jodi, and I would represent her. As it turned out, my mother was indeed with us at Mt. Carmel Cemetery that year—she was laid to rest beside my father on his *yahrzeit*, the anniversary of his death.

Since my father's death, I have been listening to the Torah reading for Shabbat Shuva while thinking first of him and then of both my parents. It is a deeply unsettling text.

In his final substantive address to the Israelites, Moses prophesies a future of misery and despair for the people he has led for forty years. Emphasizing in Deuteronomy 32:4 that God is "faithful ... never false, true and upright," Moses tells the Israelites that they and their descendants would be responsible for all the manifold misfortunes and disasters that would befall them over the course of generations, and he describes in graphic detail how their God would wreak destruction on them for their apparently inevitable collective treachery and sins. "I will sweep misfortunes on them, use up My arrows on them: Wasting famine, ravaging plague, deadly pestilence, and fanged beasts will I let loose against them.... The sword shall deal death without, as shall the terror within" (Deuteronomy 32:23–25).

And, as Moses takes great pains to make clear, this divine devastation would not be unleashed only on those who had committed transgressions, but on the entire people, young and old, women, children, and infants alike, the innocent as well as the guilty.

Even more disturbing to me is God's declaration that "I will hide My countenance" from the Israelites in the moments of their greatest distress, their greatest need (Deuteronomy 32:20).

This is not a new image. "Then My anger will flare up against them on that day, and I will abandon them and hide My countenance from them," we read in the previous week's Torah reading, followed by "And I will keep My countenance hidden on that day because of all the evil they have committed by turning to other gods" (Deuteronomy 31:17–18).

Both my parents survived Auschwitz-Birkenau and Bergen-Belsen. My mother described her fifteen months at Birkenau as "a time of humiliation, torture, starvation, disease, fear, hopelessness, and despair."[1] After managing to escape and being recaptured, my father was imprisoned and tortured for months at Auschwitz in Block 11, the so-called Death Block. What sins could they have committed to deserve such punishment?

My parents' entire immediate families were murdered in the Shoah. My mother's five-and-a-half-year-old son, my brother, was one of more than one million Jewish children who were killed by the Germans and their accomplices only and exclusively because they were Jewish. Again, what possible transgressions could any of them have committed to cause God to turn away from them?

Every year, I am forced to remember my parents in the context of a Torah reading that challenges my ability to relate to God. How, we ask ourselves, can we believe in God in the aftermath of the Shoah? Shouldn't an omniscient God have had to know that the cataclysm was being perpetrated? And shouldn't an omnipotent God have been able to prevent it?

But then again, isn't any attempt on our part to want to understand the very essence of divinity presumptive in the extreme? Any exploration of this formidable if not utterly impenetrable topic must, in my opinion at least, be approached with tremendous reticence and humility. In the introduction to his book *Faith after the Holocaust*, Rabbi Eliezer Berkovits observes, "Those who were not there and, yet, readily accept the Holocaust as the will of God that must not be questioned, desecrate the holy disbelief of those whose faith was murdered. And those who were not there, and yet join with self-assurance the rank of the disbelievers, desecrate the holy faith of the believers."[2]

There are those who believe that the brutal annihilation of millions was God's wish and had a divine purpose. Rabbi Joel Teitelbaum, the leader of the ultra-Orthodox, rabidly anti-Zionist Satmar Hasidim—whose own life, incidentally, was saved by a Zionist—blamed the Holocaust on Zionists who had refused to wait for the messianic redemption and instead sought to implement a secular

Jewish national agenda. Others went even further. Rabbi Eliezer Schach, a spiritual leader of the non-Hasidic Ashkenazi ultra-Orthodox in Israel, declared that the Holocaust was God's divine punishment for all the perceived heresies committed by Jews under the influence of Zionism, socialism, and the Enlightenment.[3]

My friend Rabbi David Ellenson, the chancellor of Hebrew Union College–Jewish Institute of Religion, has called my attention to a manuscript written after the Holocaust by Rabbi Yechiel Yaakov Weinberg, the last head of the Hildesheimer Rabbinical Seminary in Berlin and a giant of pre–World War II modern Orthodoxy, in which Weinberg wrote, "The *Rabbinerseminar* was destroyed on account of our many sins." The troubling corollary that follows from this one simple sentence is that the Germans who were responsible for murdering the institutions' teachers and students were somehow the instruments of a divine vengeance.

To his credit, Rabbi Menachem Mendel Schneerson, the Lubavitcher Rebbe, categorically rejected this approach. "The destruction of six million Jews in such a horrific manner that surpassed the cruelty of all previous generations," he declared, "could not possibly be because of a punishment for sins. Even the Satan himself could not possibly find a sufficient number of sins that would warrant such genocide!"[4]

In a similar vein, the Talmudist David Weiss Halivni, who survived several Nazi death and concentration camps, has dismissed as "obscene" any suggestion that the Holocaust was "a divine response to the spread of the German culture of Haskalah [the Enlightenment], or secularism, among the Jews." Any such rationalizations, he wrote in his memoirs, "are theologically offensive.... A justification, by definition, means: it should have happened, it's justice, it's the fitting course of events. People who make such statements suggest, in effect, that had it not happened, they would have worked to bring it about."[5]

Nevertheless, the Lubavitcher Rebbe insisted that the Holocaust had to have been part of a divine plan, even if human beings could not comprehend God's reasons. Holocaust historian Yehuda Bauer has quoted Schneerson as writing, "It is clear that 'no evil descends from Above' and buried within torment and suffering is a core of exalted spiritual good.... So it is not impossible for the physical destruction of the Holocaust to be spiritually beneficial."[6]

In mid-October 1943, during Sukkot, my father smuggled a tiny apple into the Birkenau barrack where the inmates had gathered to pray so that the highly respected rabbi of the Polish city of Zawiercie, known as the Zawiercier Rov, could recite the *Kiddush* blessings. Throughout the prayers, my father recalled, the aged Rov stared at the apple, obviously conflicted. At the end of the clandestine service, he picked up the apple and said, in Yiddish, almost to himself, *"Un iber dem zol ikh itzt zogn, 'Ve-akhalta ve-savata u-verakhta et Hashem Elohekha ...'"*—"And over this, I should now say, 'And you will eat, and you will be satisfied, and you will bless your God....'" *"Kh'vel nisht essen"*—"I will not eat," he said, *"veil ikh vel nisht zat sein"*—"because I will not be satisfied"—*"un ikh vill nisht bentchn"*—"and I refuse to *bentch* [to sanctify God]." And with that, the Zawiercier Rov put down the apple and turned away.

The Zawiercier Rov never lost his faith in God. Like the Hasidic master, Levi Itzhak of Berditchev, however, he was profoundly, desperately angry with Him, and this anger caused him to confront God from the innermost depths of his being.

One evening around the same time, my father and a group of Jews from Zawiercie were sitting in their barrack when the Zawiercier Rov suddenly said, again in Yiddish, "You know, *der Rebboine shel-oilem ken zein a ligner"*—the "Master of the universe can be a liar." Asked how this could possibly be, the rabbi explained, "If God were to open His window now and look down and see us here, He would immediately look away and say, '*Ikh hob dos nisht geton,'"*—"I did not do this"—"and that," the Zawiercier Rov said, "would be the lie."

The following year, the Jewish *kapo*—an inmate assigned supervisory tasks by the Germans—in charge of Block 11, where my father had been an inmate for more than five months, wanted my father to conduct the Yom Kippur service. Emaciated, starved, my father chanted *Kol Nidre* from memory in the Death Block of Auschwitz and then led the prayers there that evening and the following day for his fellow prisoners. As a reward, the *kapo* gave my father and the other inmates of Block 11 an extra bowl of soup to break the fast.

"You have screened Yourself off with a cloud, so that no prayer can pass through," we read in the book of Lamentations. And yet it is told that Reb Azriel David Fastag, a disciple of the Hasidic Rebbe of Modzhitz, spontaneously composed and began to sing what has become the best-known melody to Maimonides's Twelfth Principle of Jewish Faith while in a cattle car from the Warsaw Ghetto to the Treblinka death camp: "I believe with perfect faith in the coming of the Messiah; and even though he may tarry, nevertheless I will wait every day for him to come."

A young Jew managed to escape from the Treblinka-bound train, taking with him the *niggun*, the melody of Reb Azriel David Fastag's "Ani Ma'amin." Eventually the melody reached the Modzhitzer Rebbe, who is said to have exclaimed, "With this *niggun* the Jewish people went to the gas chambers, and with this *niggun*, the Jews will march to greet the Messiah."

Very much in the spirit of the Shabbat Shuva Torah reading, Professor David Weiss Halivni has written, "There were two major theological events in Jewish history: Revelation at Sinai and revelation at Auschwitz.... At Sinai, God appeared before Israel, addressed us, and gave us instructions; at Auschwitz, God absented Himself from Israel, abandoned us, and handed us over to the enemy."[7]

Which raises a fundamental question: How can we pray to or have any relationship with God if we believe, in Weiss Halivni's words, that He abandoned us and handed us over to the enemy?

But maybe, just maybe, Professor David Weiss Halivni, the Lubavitcher Rebbe, and Rabbi Yechiel Yaakov Weinberg all looked for God's presence and power in the wrong place. What if God was very much there during the Holocaust, but not with the killers, with the forces that inflicted the Holocaust on humankind? What if He was in fact alongside and within the victims, those who perished and those who survived?

Could it be that God, the true God, did not hide His face from Reb Azriel David Fastag in the cattle car to Treblinka but instead gave him the inspiration and strength to compose his *niggun*? And could it also be that God was praying alongside my father in Block 11 on Yom Kippur in 1943?

On the façade above the main entrance of Park Avenue Synagogue is a relief sculpture of the Polish-Jewish educator Janusz Korczak surrounded by children who are desperately holding on to him. Born Henryk Goldschmidt, Korczak, a secular Jew, founded and directed an orphanage in Warsaw. After the German occupation of Poland, Korczak declined numerous offers to save himself, refusing to leave his children behind in the Warsaw Ghetto. On August 5, 1942, Korczak led the children through the streets of the Ghetto to the *Umschlagsplatz*, the deportation square, from which they were taken by train to the gas chambers of Treblinka. Abandoned by the world, seemingly abandoned by God, Korczak did not want his children to feel that he, too, had abandoned them.

My mother was sent from Auschwitz-Birkenau to the concentration camp of Bergen-Belsen in November of 1944. By that time, her parents, her first husband, her child, her brother, and her sister had all been murdered. She was utterly alone and by all rights should have succumbed to despair. Instead, she had used her medical skills at Birkenau to enable countless women to survive, more often than not at the risk of her own life. Assigned to that camp's infirmary, she had performed rudimentary surgery, camouflaging women's wounds, sending them out of the barrack on work detail in advance of selections and thus keeping many of them out of the gas chambers.

At Bergen-Belsen in late December 1944, my mother and several other Jewish women inmates took a group of Dutch Jewish children into their barrack. My mother then proceeded to organize what became known as a *Kinderheim*, a children's home, within the concentration camp. One of my mother's fellow inmates subsequently recalled that my mother "walked from block to block, found the children, took them, lived with them, and took care of them.... Most of them were orphans, and she was like a mother to them."[8] Among them were children from Poland, Czechoslovakia, and elsewhere. Some had been brought to Bergen-Belsen from Buchenwald, others from Theresienstadt.

My mother wrote in her memoirs that she and the other women in her group "had been given the opportunity to take care of these abandoned Jewish children, and we gave them all our love and whatever strength was left within us."[9]

Despite the horrific conditions at Bergen-Belsen in the winter and spring of 1945, despite a raging typhus epidemic and other virulent diseases, despite the lack of food and medicine, my mother and her fellow prisoners kept 149 Jewish children alive until the day of their liberation on April 15, 1945.

If God was at Treblinka, I want to believe that He was within Janusz Korczak as he accompanied his children to their death. I feel certain that the mystical divine spark that characterizes Jewish faith, the *Shekhina*, was within my mother as she and the other women in her group rescued 149 Jewish children from almost certain death at Bergen-Belsen.

Perhaps God was also within every Jewish parent who comforted a child on the way to a gas chamber and within every Jew who told a story or a joke or sang a melody in a death camp barrack to alleviate another Jew's agony. Perhaps it was the *Shekhina* that enabled young Jews like Jeanie's father to take up arms against the Germans in ghettos and forests. Perhaps God was within the Ukrainian farmer who hid Jeanie's mother and grandparents and within all the other non-Jews who defied the forces of evil by saving Jews in Nazi-occupied Europe.

And so it is, as I remember my parents on their *yahrzeit*, that I have come to the conclusion that perhaps God did not hide His face from them after all during the years of the Shoah. Perhaps it was a divine spirit within them that enabled them to survive with their humanity intact. And perhaps it is to that God that we should be addressing our prayers during these Days of Awe and throughout the year.

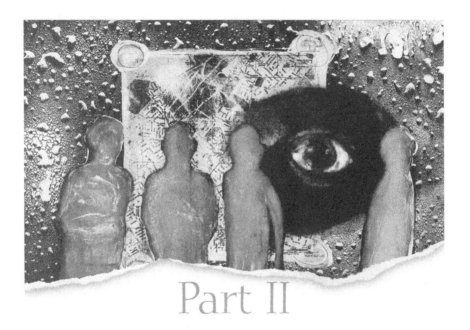

Part II
Identity

"'Somewhere,' said Rebbe Nahman of Bratzlav,
'there lives a man who asks a question to which
there is no answer; a generation later, in another
place, there lives another man who asks another
question to which there is no answer either—and
he doesn't know, he cannot know, that his question
is actually an answer to the first.'"
—Elie Wiesel[1]

Thane Rosenbaum

Thane Rosenbaum, a novelist, essayist, and law professor, is the author of the critically acclaimed novels *The Stranger Within Sarah Stein*, *The Golems of Gotham*, and *Second Hand Smoke*; the novel-in-stories *Elijah Visible*; as well as the nonfiction *Payback: The Case for Revenge* and *The Myth of Moral Justice: Why Our Legal System Fails to Do What's Right*. His articles, reviews, and essays appear frequently in the *New York Times*, *Wall Street Journal*, *Washington Post*, *Huffington Post*, *Haaretz*, and the *Daily Beast*, among other national publications. He is a senior fellow at New York University School of Law, where he directs the Forum on Law, Culture & Society.

"We are all, to some degree, answering the call of the concentration camps, not as eyewitness, but as dutiful sons and daughters."

Much has been made of the seeming paradox, if not perversity, of children of Holocaust survivors ending up as practitioners of the healing arts—especially in the field of mental health. The second generation, as they have come to be known, have surely produced their share of psychiatrists and psychologists. Whether they are statistically overrepresented in these fields is not definitively known. There is, however, the rich sense of triumph in thinking about how those who emerged from the ashes of Auschwitz—in the most unnaturally life-defying of environments—had somehow produced offspring that took as their life's mission the task of helping others cope with their own quite ordinary lives.

Surviving a death camp was surely a testament to personal fortitude, but it was also an invitation to madness. The monstrousness of the Nazis was not easily forgotten. For many, survival was paid for in the devalued currency of insanity—legal tender minus the tenderness. Nightmares came at night and appeared nightly. Moods darkened faster than cloud cover. Glances froze into blank stares from all those memories recalled and deaths un-mourned. There was no way to successfully disguise the symptoms of a traumatized people. They were survivors, of course, but in body alone. Indeed, Hollywood would become particularly enamored of the survivor as psycho with such examples as *The Man in the Glass Booth*, *The Juggler*, *Sophie's Choice*, *Shine*, and even *X-Men*.

It should come as no surprise that the children of those survivors, by accident of birth and sheer proximity to those who narrowly escaped death, ended up all too familiar with emotional pain. And so they put that knowledge to good use in the service of others.

It could have been worse. There were surely other career choices that may, in fact, have made more logical sense. Given the lessons of the Nazis and its imprint on the survivors (for some, it was forever branded on their forearms), the children of these victims might have just as readily become serial killers, Mafia hit men (or women), or even morticians. Humanity should not have been their calling cards; the repertoire they inherited should have been stocked with more gruesome fare. After all, regardless of their pre-war occupations, the Jews of Europe who had survived the Third Reich would forever be in the death business—no matter how they actually earned their livings. Damage was their trademark; survival, by any means necessary, their tradecraft. Many were as ruthless in their business dealings as they were silent in their parenting. These survivors were in no condition to make their children feel safe. What worthwhile skill set could these children have reasonably developed?

The Nazis created the ideal conditions for a generation of Jewish psychotics and psychopaths—lawless, faithless, and incorrigible to the core. And yet, the children of survivors, for the most part, were measured and disciplined in their pursuits, buying into all the romance and possibilities of civilization like Black Friday consumers on the hunt for bargains. The children, improbably, managed to have faith in humanity even though their relatives—both alive and dead—had fallen victim to the annihilating fury of a twisted society that was at the time the most civilized nation on earth.

Rebuilding lives was for most survivors a singular priority. Dwelling on all that death was unhealthy. Many children of survivors would go off and enter the workforce and create a home life with little thought to their legacy. It was as if it could be tossed aside or, worse, forgotten. Inheritance would be measured in money and other tangible possessions, not history. There were, to be sure, occasional intimations of where their parents had come from. But it was compartmentalized, set apart like a firewall erected to keep away the simmering embers of crematoria flames. Nonetheless, the burden was always there, easily activated, dormant but not dead. This kind of legacy is relentless and demanding. It can't be quelled or neglected forever. The damage from which its existence depends expects nothing less than absolute obedience.

Whether openly avowed or clumsily suppressed, the one theme common to most children of survivors is that of rescue. The aftermath of the Holocaust produced the greatest rescue fantasy of all, largely because the Holocaust itself was the debased archetype of a failed rescue—the definitive tutorial on what *not* to do if humankind wished to make any further claims on its own humanity. The indifference of the world to the inhumanity of man would become the signature slogan of the twentieth century. Healing the survivors was never a realistic possibility. And applying the lessons of the Holocaust to ordinary life was both a futile exercise and a trivializing insult. When it came to the evil of the Nazis, nothing applied. There were no meaningful analogies, legal precedents, or sanguine explanations. There was no way to make restitution or repair. The chasm of the rupture—the depth of loss and the reach of its generational impact—was unspeakably and unknowably vast.

What united so many children of survivors was the impulse to rescue—if not their parents, for whom rescue was far too late, then perhaps the world.

More than two decades ago, I left a job as a Wall Street lawyer in order to write novels about post-Holocaust themes, teach human rights to students who were otherwise committed to corporate law, and lecture publicly on matters of human dignity, moral justice, and issues central to the Jewish world. Along the way I've represented clients on a pro bono basis on matters dealing with immigration and housing, and governmental benefits.

There is little doubt that those career choices—how I spend my day and why—are traceable directly to what happened to my parents, who were both concentration camp survivors—in a family where very few actually survived. My parents died long before I set this career in motion (indeed, they died before I reached manhood), and I'm quite certain that the path I took would have shocked them. After all, they never discussed their wartime experiences in our home. The war years were forbidden ground, like haunted cemetery plots. And at the time I displayed a shocking lack of curiosity—or was it perhaps an anticipatory defense mechanism? Nonetheless I lived an idyllic childhood free from prejudice and bigotry, but not from loss.

I understood that my parents were among Hitler's victims, and that's why there were no grandparents or much in the way of uncles and aunts. Cousins were a luxury denied to us—once or twice removed had an altogether different meaning in Holocaust households. The black sheep of our decimated family could have easily risen to the ranks of pious elders had we managed to locate any such black sheep. Hitler had killed them, too.

I have no delusions that the legacy that curls within my sentences and stands beside me at the lectern makes what I do special in any way. What was unique, what *was* miraculous, was that *anyone* had survived. The fact that the children of survivors built lives of their own based on the contorted architecture of their parents' suffering is neither surprising nor in any way exceptional. The children were not actually *there*; they are merely the artifacts of the aftermath, witnesses not to the event itself but to the absurdity of an afterlife at all. Their knowledge is limited inasmuch as their legacy is nontransferable. It is the gift that keeps on giving. And in many ways it is a curse.

My parents would have no doubt preferred that I remain a buttoned-up, emotionally detached, conscience-deprived attorney. The world is already too wicked. There are no reasons to be haunted by someone else's dreams or to fantasize about daring rescues that will never produce a happy end. One might as well just make money and watch plenty of cable TV.

With the Holocaust as familial backdrop, it is a challenge teaching human rights in a world where such rights are so demonstrably lacking. It's not my job to sugarcoat. The life-affirming message is neither in my nature nor in my arsenal of quick-fix remedies. The vanished life of my parents left me a realist, if not a fatalist. The world's problems are largely unsolvable—but that doesn't mean that we mustn't try, that we shouldn't be expected to direct our family truths for the purpose of rebutting another's lie. A new round of rescue becomes a moral imperative—even if it, too, results in failure. After all, these latest injustices, at least this time, are happening on our watch.

Of course, I'm also a novelist, and writers of such dark arts are ultimately professional dreamers. The human condition is a canvas, and leaving it blank is not an option. Something must be said. Some things must be written. Some outrages must produce a scream of a deafening frequency. A legacy that goes ignored eventually limps back. We are all, to some degree, answering the call of the concentration camps, not as eyewitness, but as dutiful sons and daughters.

Eva Hoffman

Eva Hoffman is the author of seven books, including *Lost in Translation: A Life in a New Language; Shtetl: The Life and Death of a Small Town and the World of Polish Jews;* and *After Such Knowledge: Memory, History and the Legacy of the Holocaust.* She has worked as an editor at the *New York Times* and has lectured and broadcast widely on a range of topics, including issues of exile, memory, Polish-Jewish history, psychoanalysis, and human rights. Born in Krakow, Poland, she received her PhD in literature from Harvard University and currently teaches writing at Kingston University near London.

"I do not believe that the spiritual lesson of the Holocaust is to live in mourning forever."

A little while ago, during a conversation at a London dinner party, a psychoanalyst who is interested in such issues asked me what defines my Jewish identity. I found myself answering—although I didn't know I would do so—that my sense of Jewishness began with mourning; and that this constitutes a powerful and deep bond with Jewishness.

In a sense, I was answering a question I have often asked myself. My sense of Jewish identity is strong but does not fall into easily available categories. I am not an ethnically or religiously defined Jew; indeed, I did not have a religious upbringing. My parents, who had grown up in a tiny shtetl in what was then the Polish part of the Ukraine, came from Orthodox families; but they were of the modernizing generation (insofar as this was possible in the village of Zalosce) and were becoming less observant even before the war. During the Holocaust—as they saw the horror unfold and all of their relatives murdered—they lost the remainder of their faith. They therefore did not give my sister or me any religious instruction; indeed, they were, in their ostensible philosophy, determinedly secular. They both knew Hebrew and spoke Yiddish to each other, but they did not pass either language on to my sister or me.

But there were other strains of history, and of feeling, which informed my sense of what could perhaps be called spirituality—of what were in any case quite foundational strata of thought and emotion. Once a year, we attended Yom Kippur services in one of Krakow's atmospheric old synagogues; for my parents, the need to honor the dead—and to do so through the rituals they would have understood—was clearly unequivocal, no matter what their more explicit religious feelings. In the synagogue's darkened interior, with its candles and swaying silhouettes, I knew I was encountering a whole community in mourning; and the prayers and chants conveyed a profound sense of lamentation. I think I understood then—or I felt—that the dead and those mourning for them cannot be betrayed; that there was a kind of absolute obligation to keep faith with them.

My bond with the past was partly cemented there.

But of course the most powerful transmission of the Holocaust experience came through my parents—not so much through what they told us about it as through their persons, their eruptive fragments of memory, and most of all, through their palpable and pervasive personal suffering. Even as a child, I understood that such suffering has a kind of sacredness; that there is a moral imperative to respond to it and respect it; that it needs to be treated with delicacy and delicately honored. I also felt the obverse of this: a kind of helpless, powerful rage at the violence and injustices my parents and others suffered, and the need to reject the perpetrators of such cruelty absolutely. This was a basis of what became an intense need for justice altogether; a need for a moral understanding.

In my adult development, I was very much a person of my generation: a kind of secular, cosmopolitan universalist and an aesthetic modernist. In other words, I didn't want to be defined by my past. I still don't—or at least, I don't want to be determined by it. But it was a revealing surprise to discover how much weight the parental Holocaust legacy, and those first, formative feelings I experienced in relation to it, continued to have in my psyche. A lot of my work has emerged from trying to understand the Holocaust as history, as well as family story; and further, to grapple with themes and problems which were enacted in the Holocaust in a paradigmatic way, but that which themselves in other situations, other histories: the roots of prejudice and the causes of mass violence—especially among neighborly groups—of which we have seen so many examples in our own times; the role of ideology in fomenting hatred; the terrible toll of injustice. But the other driving impulse in my work—springing from the other side of that early moral universe—has been what the psychoanalysts might call a reparative urge. My (sometimes controversial) book *Shtetl* came out of an urgently felt need to show that the history of Polish-Jewish relations wasn't exclusively—or even largely—a history of anti-Semitism and to acknowledge the instances of Poles' generosity and compassion toward Jews during the Holocaust. My own parents, after all, were saved by their Polish and Ukrainian neighbors, who were coming to their rescue at the risk of their own lives.

I do not believe that the spiritual lesson of the Holocaust is to live in mourning forever; indeed, I think the task for us literal children of survivors is to learn how to separate ourselves from the past, after fully acknowledging it, so that we can live and act in our own, sufficiently complicated present. But my responses to that present—my interpretation of political events, for example—are often informed by the internalized legacy of the Shoah. I find that my sense of justice is offended when Israel is the target of exceptionalist political hostility (as opposed to well-founded criticism), and I have occasionally registered my objections in writing. I also find myself deeply dismayed when the international community does not come to the aid of those who need help—currently, for example, in Syria. Whatever the difficulties of intervention, I think the duty to protect, or the instinct of normal human compassion, is the greater imperative (and, it seems to me, the better part of political wisdom) than purely pragmatic interest. Such, at least, are my feelings, and their intensity is undoubtedly stoked by what I know of the most terrible instances of human helplessness and of unjust prejudice.

In the last few years, it has been my privilege to meet with people in various countries—South Africa, Japan, Rwanda—who have inherited their own histories of collective trauma. It turns out that the affinities of response and feeling among these very different second generations are surprisingly strong. I could talk to the now elderly "children" of Hiroshima survivors with mutual empathy and communicative ease—barriers of language notwithstanding. There has been a great expansion of consciousness in this, and great reparative value. To be able to sense a commonality of feeling across such historical gulfs, and to sense such shared human truths, is a great consolation. Insofar as the Holocaust has led me to contemplate some of those most fundamental truths and aspects of *the* human condition, it has been an ethical legacy—and perhaps, a spiritual one as well.

Avi Dichter

Abraham (Avi) Dichter served in the Israel Defense Forces' most elite commando unit, *Sayeret Matkal*, before joining the Israeli Security Agency (ISA), better known as "Shin Bet," in 1974. As director of the ISA from 2000 to 2005, a period of significant Palestinian terrorist activity against Israel (known as the Al-Aqsa Intifada), he is credited with restructuring the agency to effectively deal with this challenge, leading to a dramatic reduction in the number of terrorist attacks and to a restoration of public morale and safety. He is a former Israel minister of public security (2006–2009) and minister of home front defense (2012–2013) and now serves in a voluntary capacity as chairman of the Foundation for the Welfare of Holocaust Survivors in Israel.

"While I understood the significance of the Holocaust for the Jewish people on the national level, I still did not fully comprehend its meaning for our family. I had to become the father of three children and a grandfather of four for the full dimensions of the Holocaust to become evident."

I was eight years old when I was first confronted personally with the Holocaust. The experience was a particularly painful one.

Ever since my early childhood, my parents had always combed my hair from left to right, as I continued to do after I was old enough to comb my own hair. One morning before leaving for school, I decided to comb it instead from right to left. When my mother saw this, she became angrier with me than I had ever seen her. I didn't know what I had done to upset her and asked, "*Imma*, is something wrong?" In response, she slapped me hard across my face—the first time one of my parents had ever hit me—and roared at me in a tear-filled voice, "Don't you ever dare to comb your hair that way. The only one who combed it that way was Hitler."

"Who's Hitler?" I asked naively. "Who is Hitler?!" my mother repeated in a pained voice, with question mark and exclamation point hopelessly interwoven, and then uttered words that have shaped the course of my life: "Hitler was responsible for the fact that you have no grandfather and grandmother, that you have no aunts and uncles, and that you have no family like other children."

I was left with many questions that I was unable to ask and that my parents, who rarely spoke about the Holocaust, were not to answer.

I subsequently learned that my paternal grandfather, Avraham Moshe, whose name I bear with pride and a sense of sacred awe, was murdered in the Holocaust, as were my father's four brothers and sisters and all but one of my mother's seven siblings.

My parents were born in the Polish-Ukrainian town of Rozhishche. My father, who enlisted in the Polish army at the outset of the war and then fought in the Soviet army, never spoke about the annihilation of his entire family. My mother escaped from the ghetto of their town, but not before she saw the Gestapo shoot her ten-year-old brother after Polish neighbors informed the German authorities that the boy had been slipping out of the ghetto through a hole in the wall to play with his Polish friends. It was only decades later that I discovered some details about her experiences during the Shoah from testimony she gave to Yad Vashem.

Growing up, I knew that my entire family had been slaughtered, together with six million other Jews, only because they were Jews. That is why, when I became head of Israel's General Security Services ("Shin Bet") and a minister in the government of the State of Israel, I declared proudly time and again, in Israel and abroad, that "the era in which Jews are murdered just for being Jews is over!"

My parents were incredibly proud of the family they built after the war. They brought two children into the world. My sister Yael (also known as Henia, in memory of our maternal grandmother) was born in Austria in a Displaced Persons camp while they were awaiting aliyah to Israel. I was born in Israel in 1952, in the southern city of Ashkelon, where my parents settled and lived until their last days. My father passed away in March of 1992. The two of them lived to see and hug six grandchildren, and my mother got to know and love eight great-grandchildren before her recent passing.

It is difficult to describe in words how critical the reestablishment of their family was for my parents; or their sense of pride when I joined the Israel Defense Forces; or the extent of their anxiety when they found out that I had volunteered to serve in the General Staff's elite commando reconnaissance unit known as the *Sayyeret Matkal*. For three weeks during the Yom Kippur War, I was unable to contact them to let them know that I was all right. My friend and downstairs neighbor, himself the son of Holocaust survivors, was killed on the Golan Heights at the beginning of the war. My sister's brother-in-law, who had enlisted in the army with me, was killed in his tank near the Suez Canal on the third day of the war. I did not realize at the time that my parents were sick with worry until they finally heard from me.

What a lack of sensitivity it was on my part not to try harder, regardless of the difficulties involved, to get word to them that I was OK! I was unaware back then how much any parent worries about a child, especially when the parents had survived the Holocaust but were left with no family. Of course they would be frantic with fear over the fate of their son. I simply did not understand then what they were really going through.

Much later, when my father was battling cancer and I was driving him to treatments, it was clear to both of us that the end was near. I asked him to tell me a bit more about his family's fate in the Holocaust. At that point, he surprised me by insisting that I, too, had to share with him the things I had done in the army and was doing in my security work. Under that reciprocal agreement, he told me about the last days of the war, when he was a soldier in the Red Army.

His battalion had returned to Poland and was camped not far from his hometown. He requested permission to go into Rozhishche to see if anyone was left there. Together with a friend who was also from that town, my father got to the end of the street on which he and his family had lived. Polish neighbors saw my father carrying a rifle, recognized him, and fled into their homes, afraid for their lives because they had moved into the houses of the Jews who had been killed or had fled, including my father's family's house.

And then, my father saw Polish children playing on that same street, wearing the clothes of his murdered brothers. Seeing my father's agitated demeanor, his friend grabbed him by the shoulder and pulled him out of the town. That was the last time my father saw the place where he had been born and raised. He vowed never to return—and in fact he absolutely refused to travel there with me. "Poland for me is a black hole, and I don't want to go back there," he said, leaving no room for further consideration of the idea.

Only two of my father's relatives, two brothers, Anszel and Jack Gun, survived the Holocaust. They immigrated to the United States after the war, but our families have remained close to this day. Once, when Anszel Gun had come for a visit to Israel, I came home from the army for Shabbat. On my way from the Ashkelon bus station to our house, dressed in a uniform decorated with paratroopers' wings, wearing red boots and a red beret and with a Kalashnikov over my shoulder, I saw my father and Anszel standing on the street near our house. When they saw me approaching, they hugged each other, and when I reached them, they stood in each other's arms, crying.

I didn't know how to react, wondering why two grown men, one of them my father, were crying in the middle of the street. When I told my father, maybe even a bit aggressively, to stop crying because it was embarrassing, he gave me a look full of love without the slightest shred of anger and said, "You don't understand what it means for us to see an Israeli soldier—a paratrooper, no less—and above all to know that he's a son of the Dichter family." No, I did not understand. I was a fighter who took part in improbable missions that were beyond most people's imagination. I did not want to believe that the millions of slaughtered Jews had been powerless to prevent their fate. I had never encountered powerlessness in my life.

While I understood the significance of the Holocaust for the Jewish people on the national level, I still did not fully comprehend its meaning for our family. I had to become the father of three children and a grandfather of four for the full dimensions of the Holocaust to become evident.

Recently, I was appointed chairman of the Foundation for the Benefit of Holocaust Victims in Israel. I see Holocaust survivors up close and hear them tell the story of their lives, and their near-death experiences, with the utmost candor. As a member of the second generation of Holocaust survivors, I have a sense of pride and satisfaction at having been entrusted with this sacred task. I am convinced that somewhere on high, in Paradise, my mother is sitting with her friends and each one is telling the others about her children.

I am sure that when my mother, Malka (née Koniach), and my father, Yehoshua (Shaike) Dichter, are asked to look back on the various positions I have held over the course of my career, they might mention, without much elaboration, my service as a commando fighter, my roles in the Israel Security Agency, and my terms as minister of internal security and minister of home front defense. However I am quite certain that when they talk about their son's role as chairman of the Foundation for the Benefit of Holocaust Victims, my mother swells with pride and probably says, most probably in Yiddish, "*Nu*, we're finally getting some *nakhes* from the boy ..."
[*Translated from the Hebrew by Rabbi Peretz Rodman*]

Vivian Glaser Bernstein

Vivian Glaser Bernstein, the daughter of Czech Holocaust survivors, recently retired from the United Nations, where she worked for over thirty-five years, initially in human resources and for her last fifteen years in education outreach in the Department of Public Information. Happily married to Daniel, she is the proud mother of Michelle, Peter, and Jen, and the delighted grandmother of Benjamin.

"Our parents gave us wings; and what a span they had!"

After surviving Theresienstadt, Auschwitz, and other camps, my mother with my maternal grandmother and my father independently emigrated from Prague, Czechoslovakia, to Caracas, Venezuela, where I was born and raised. All three of them, although very different in their reactions to their personal experiences, had a deep impact on me, defining who I am and shaping the choices I have made and continue to make in my life.

My grandmother, my primary caretaker for the first few years of my life, was the most scarred and adversely affected by her experiences and immense losses. In spite of that, I have many wonderful recollections of her varied passions. Her deep love of classical music—a love that she shared with and transmitted to me—is something that keeps her ever-present in my life.

My mother, who had also survived Bergen-Belsen, was twenty when she returned to Prague after liberation with a fervent wish to have children. She quickly married and had twin boys in June of 1946. In 1948, when the Communists took over Prague, she obtained visas to Venezuela for the entire family. This first marriage did not endure, and sadly my mother experienced another unimaginable loss when one of the twins died in a playground accident at the age of five. I was born three years later.

My parents, who re-met and married in Venezuela, were complete opposites when it came to speaking about their experiences. My mother spoke about her experiences with ease, while my father resorted mostly to silence and we just knew not to ask. Yet, they both emerged from the Shoah with faith in humankind, a tremendous joie de vivre, optimism—the glass was always half-full—and a noticeable absence of bitterness or anger. They both possessed the ability to live dignified, meaningful lives and to focus on what they had rather than on what was lost—although my father remained haunted by his inability to save his younger sister.

Even more remarkable is that they gave us wings; and what a span they had! We were sent to summer camp in the United States from ages nine to eleven in order to learn English, a skill they wanted us to master, as they were determined to send us to college in the United States. They were overjoyed when after graduating from Tufts University, I married an American and had the opportunity to make a life in the United States, the country where they had initially hoped to settle after the war but to which access was denied.

"I am a child of survivors"—I utter these six words as frequently as "I was born in Caracas" or "my family was from Prague." It is an integral part of how I define myself, of who I am. *It* is part of my DNA, as are my hazel eyes and brown hair. These words are always said with a tremendous sense of pride and gratitude for my parents' ability to radiate such positive energy and provide a home filled with a deep, unconditional love for each other and their children.

Through the lives they led following survival, they transmitted humanity, compassion, courage, and the ability to be open to and care for the other. This openness served me well as I grew up in a Catholic country, attended a Lutheran elementary school, and had mostly non-Jewish childhood friends. It also was an asset in my work at the United Nations, where I worked harmoniously and forged many friendships with individuals of different faiths and nationalities.

I started at the United Nations, the only place I could legally work while still on a student visa, following my college graduation. Once there, it felt like the perfect fit. Not only is it the world's only universal organization born out of the ashes of the Second World War, but it is committed to the betterment of humankind. For more than three decades, until I recently reached mandatory retirement age, I worked in human resources and public information and, whenever possible, contributed to Holocaust remembrance activities.

"Our children are our best revenge" are words my mother often uttered and that will always resonate within me. Although raised in a mostly secular Jewish home, I always felt very Jewish and knew unequivocally that I would have a Jewish home in order to continue rebuilding that which was lost. We have recently added another link to the chain with the birth of our grandson, named in memory of my mother, to whom I hope to convey the legacy of memories I received from my grandmother and my parents.

Photo: Vera Tammen

Josef Joffe

Josef Joffe was born in Lodz, Poland, in 1944 and grew up in post-war Berlin. He is publisher-editor of *Die Zeit* in Hamburg and, after teaching at Munich University, Johns Hopkins, and Harvard, is visiting professor of political science at Stanford University and Distinguished Fellow at the Freeman-Spogli Institute for International Studies as well as Abramowitz Fellow at the Hoover Institution. His most recent book is *The Myth of America's Decline*.

"Mercurians" and "Appollonians" in Germany

A forbidding dark school building in bombed-out West Berlin, September 1950—the backdrop for a classic immigrant experience. This six-year-old was the only Jewish kid. He had a perfect command of Berlin argot, and blond and blue-eyed, he looked like a poster boy for the SS. And yet he was an alien, as he found when his first school day began with a prayer, Jesus and all. Refusing to join in, he felt a quick slap on the back of his head, coupled with the teacher's rebuke: "You can pray, too, you know; it's the same God." Tell that to a kid who had soaked up centuries of Christian anti-Judaism with his mother's milk.

Having survived the Vilna Ghetto and almost two years in the primeval forests of what is today Belarus, my parents and other Jews who had remained alive there, in Poland, and in other parts of Eastern Europe had drifted into Western Germany after 1945. Of course, these survivors, perhaps a quarter-million, hadn't gone to "Germany," but to "America." The United States, with Britain and France in tow, was running the western half of the occupied country, offering safety and succor on the way to a new home. One-tenth or so stayed in the "accursed land," usually because they couldn't snag a visa to the United States or Canada. Alas, my mother's x-rays had betrayed an earlier bout with tuberculosis.

Thus began a typical immigrant's tale. You are in, and you are out. You are about to master the cultural tools of the "new country," but your parents—Yiddish, Polish, and Russian speakers—never quite did. By the age of twelve, their son was their cultural superior, interpreting their new surroundings for them and typing out grammatically correct letters to officialdom over their signature. He looked and acted like a native, and yet his was a split personality, with one foot planted in the old world, and one in the new.

This has been the fate of millions in the twentieth century, and it continues in the twenty-first. So does the classic pattern whereby immigrants turn into locals and eventually into citizens. Tightly knit families dissolve. Religion loses its hold, as does the authority of fathers and clerics. Exogamy creeps in. Kosher yields to *traif*, and *halal* to *haram*. Children understand but no longer speak the language of their elders. In Hollywood's vernacular, this tale is called "Hester Street" and "Avalon."

How is the Jewish experience different? At the risk of committing crimes against post-modernity by asserting the cultural advantages of some groups, this author believes that Jews stand out on two counts. One is the obsessive pursuit of learning. My parents never made it past the eighth grade, but they hired a tutor to teach me to read and write by age four. The other is "mobility," both horizontal and vertical, the very essence of modernity.

In his dazzlingly original book *The Jewish Century*, Yuri Slezkine divides the historical world into "Appollonians" and "Mercurians." The former, he argues, lived in and off the land as peasants—herders and craftsmen, their unchanging lives beholden to hierarchies both feudal and ecclesiastical. The "Mercurians," in contrast, were fleet-footed service nomads, exploiting "arbitrage" between various cultures by disseminating novel techniques and sources of knowledge. The Jews, excluded from land ownership and the trades, were the classic Mercurians: "urban, mobile, literate, articulate ... and occupationally flexible."[1] No wonder, when they knew that they might have to migrate or to run tomorrow.

Naturally, the Mercurian advantage required a special role: the outsider-as-insider. To thrive or even survive, Jews needed to understand the host culture at least as well as, if not better than the embedded Appolonians. In fact, *any* newcomer has to do better than the locals in order to overcome a myriad of obstacles: insider networks, market barriers, religious resentment, xenophobia, and outright discrimination. "I must beat them at their own game" is the classic shibboleth of the Intruder who wants to make it. Either that, or he must invent a new game, as did those Jews who could not break into banking and industry and so went off to build Hollywood a hundred years ago.

Nor is this necessarily a conscious choice. Given the exigencies of the Diaspora, Jews only had one "country" from which they could not be driven: literacy, doggedness, and learning—at first grounded in Torah and Talmud, then in knowledge-based careers from law and medicine via literature and journalism to the sciences both social and hard. Jewish children used to grow up with two commandments: "*Ess, ess, mein kind*" ("Eat, eat, my child," because there may be no food tomorrow) and "What you have in your head, nobody can take away from you."

All his life in post-war Germany, my father was an obsessive hoarder of canned foods and durables like sugar. With his eighth-grade schooling, he instilled in me a no less obsessive quest for learning: "You will go to the *Gymnasium* and then to university." Naturally, nothing but A's counted; naturally, this kid ran for class, then student council president, making it all the way into the Berlin

Student Parliament. Unlike your typical ghetto kid, he also joined a boxing club (until nearsightedness got the better of him) and then applied himself to swimming and track-and-field. Naturally, he put on his *t'fillin* only a few times after his bar mitzvah. His motorbike was more interesting than the shul.

"You must do better than them" is familiar immigrant lore. Not so standard in my case is the chapter titled "America"—after curiosity, teenage rebellion, and a nasty battle with an unregenerate Nazi teacher segued into sheer serendipity. I was chosen to be an exchange student in Grand Rapids, Michigan, where I first encountered a strange new faith called Reform Judaism. More good luck: a scholarship at Swarthmore, thence to Johns Hopkins (MA) and Harvard (PhD in government).

Then another twist of fate, just right for a twenty-something who wasn't exactly passionate about a strictly academic career. While at Harvard, I was lured to *Die Zeit*, the prestigious Hamburg news weekly. An apprenticeship at my high school newspaper now blossomed into a journalistic career, moving from staff member at *Die Zeit* to op-ed editor at the *Süddeutsche Zeitung* in Munich (1985–2000), then back to *Die Zeit* as executive editor and now as its co-*Herausgeber* (publisher-editor) with Helmut Schmidt, the former West German chancellor, with a German Order of Merit and a bunch of journalism awards in between. As they say when listening to such flattering accolades, "My father would have been very proud of me, and my mother would have believed it."

The "Mercurian" train did not stop there. It has chugged along between the United States and Germany, between journalism and academia. I have taught political science at Munich University, Johns Hopkins, Harvard, and Stanford. I spent longish stints at the Wilson Center and the Carnegie Endowment in Washington, DC, think tanks both. At Stanford, I have been a Fellow at the Institute for International Studies and the Hoover Institution since 2004 and have written for most of the major papers in the United States and Britain—from the *New York Times* to the London *Times* and *Financial Times*, from the *Guardian* to the *Wall Street Journal*, from the *New York Review of Books* to *Commentary*.

What is the gist of this immigrant's progress that leads from Svir (today Belarus) some fifty miles from Vilna, where his parents were born, via Berlin to Cambridge, Massachusetts, Hamburg, Munich,

and Palo Alto? It is above all a micro-chronicle of the twentieth century, the bloodiest of them all, which has claimed the lives of tens of
millions and driven as many others into exile. It is the blessing and
curse of one man's "Mercurian" life.

Such a life is a blessing because it sharpens wit, fuels achievement, and builds a unique perch for the outsider-as-insider, where
he learns to fathom two or more cultures, their habits, and their
histories. Or put it thus: a vantage point in culture A hones the
understanding of culture B, and then sharpens the sensitivity for C,
D, etc., which an "Apollonic" perspective, for lack of comparison,
cannot do. It is a life of intellectual arbitrage.

The "Mercurian" existence is a curse for the same reason.
Once you learn how to compare and contrast, to savor the unique
strengths of two cultures, and to "think" in both, you can never be
completely content in either.

According to a wonderful Jewish joke, a Russian Jew emigrates
from the USSR to Israel in the 1970s. After half a year in Tel Aviv, he
returns to Moscow. Half a year later, back to Israel. And so it continues, back and forth. Finally, the KGB calls him in for interroga-
tion. "Listen, you keep coming back; so don't you like it in Israel?"
The Jew: "No, not really." The KGB man: "But you won't stay in
Moscow. So where do you like it?" The Jew: "To be honest, com-
rade, I like it best on the go."

Mercurians move because they *can*—because they are at home
in many places. And they move because they *want* to, which is no
longer just a Jewish trait, but also true for "Davos Man," as Samuel
Huntington has called the maestros of globalization. Nor are Jews
forced to move these days. Yesterday's precarious homelands are
gone. Central and Eastern Europe as well as Russia were emptied out
thanks to the Holocaust, then by dint of mass emigration. Ethnic
cleansing and flight spelled the end of two thousand years of Jewish
history in the Islamic world. In Europe and in the English-speaking
world, Jews have become fully empowered citizens, latter-day
"Appolonians," so to speak.

And yet you wonder when looking at Europe and especially
its German-speaking hub. Before America, the German *Kulturkreis*
(cultural sphere), circa 1870–1933, used to be the "Promised Land"
centered on Berlin and Vienna, Prague and Budapest. This is where
aspiration, ability, and opportunity combined to unleash a "Golden

Jewish Age." Indeed, one can't think of Central Europe's breathtaking triumphs in the arts and sciences without the Jews who intruded from everywhere—from Vilna and St. Petersburg, from Lemberg and Odessa.

Today, the paltry twenty thousand German Jews of my parents' generation have multiplied into one hundred thousand, plus perhaps another hundred thousand who are unaffiliated. For a while, German Jewry was the fastest-growing Jewish community in Europe; it is still the third largest after Britain's and France's. Germany's Jews are well-off, but hardly visible—a far cry from the pre-Nazi era.

The dearth of German Jews in this book testifies to this lackluster rebound. "Hitler" can't quite explain it, not three generations later. On the other hand, this author recalls that most of his professors at Harvard would have taught in Riga, Vienna, Prague, and Berlin had the Nazi nightmare never descended. Those who are dead cannot train the next generation. And those who fled sowed their seed elsewhere, mainly in the United States.

Still, better not to overdo "biologism" and to stress instead society and economics. Maybe the expanding European welfare state—regulated, munificent, and inclusive—does not deliver the best playing field for talent and desire. Strangely, the "Mercurians" have flourished best in a setting where they were both in and out, unwelcome for who they were and wanted for what they had. Paradoxically, ambition and ingenuity demand both barriers and opportunity, neither of which is the strong suit of the modern welfare state.

As this state tears down the barriers of exclusion and discrimination, it erects new ones of regulation as brakes on initiative, and so do generous social support systems. Yesterday's fences spurred achievement; today's compress opportunity—the freedom to turn dreams into realities. At this point, New York, Cambridge, and Palo Alto embody mightier magnets for the "Mercurians" of all colors and faiths than do Berlin, Vienna, or Heidelberg.

Though the Jews' love affair with the Germans was not really reciprocated, both wrote a story of magnificent accomplishment during the "Golden Age." One-third of Germany's Nobel Prizes until 1932 went to Jews. That story ended the following year, when German Jews, including much of the country's intellectual, cultural, and scientific elite, began to flee their homeland. That was eighty years ago. So far, the story has not resumed.

Dr. Eva Fogelman

Dr. Eva Fogelman is a psychologist who pioneered groups for generations of the Holocaust. She is the co-founding director of Psychotherapy With Generations of the Holocaust and Related Traumas, co-founder of the Jewish Foundation for Christian Rescuers (now the Jewish Foundation for the Righteous), and co-director of Child Development Research and its International Study of Organized Persecution of Children project. Dr. Fogelman, who earned her PhD from the Graduate Center of The City University of New York, is the author of the Pulitzer Prize nominee *Conscience and Courage: Rescuers of Jews During the Holocaust*, writer and co-producer of the award-winning *Breaking the Silence: The Generation After the Holocaust,* and contributing producer of *Liberators: Fighting World War II on Two Fronts.*

> "There has always been a tension between my identity as a child of survivors who knows what my family and my people suffered and the joy I derive from Judaism and being part of the Jewish community."

On July 20, 1969, everyone at Camp Ramah stayed up all night to watch the historic moon landing. That day, we had traversed a long distance back in time and place, studying Torah and praying the same prayers as our ancestors. I was a counselor for ten-year-old girls, and though we had fun learning Israeli dances, swimming, knitting *kippot,* and hiking in nearby woods, I also took seriously my job of transmitting a sense of Jewish pride and Jewish history to the girls.

I had attended *Talmud Torah* and Marshalia High School in Brooklyn, and as a child I hid under my father's prayer shawl at an Orthodox shul on the High Holy Days. Judaism was a joy and fascination for me, and I hoped to transmit that same feeling to the girls. When the campers fell asleep, the other college students and I stayed up in the night's stillness until one a.m., grappling with questions about God, pondering I-thou experiences in our lives, and questioning the merits of living in Israel versus America. After all, it was two years after the Six-Day War, we Jews felt a pride in Israel, and we wanted to be a part of Jewish history.

Ten days after Neil Armstrong spoke his historic words "That's one small step for a man, one giant leap for mankind," we leapt back into Jewish history on Tishah B'Av. Sitting on the floor in a dark room with candles lit and chanting *Eicha*, the book of Lamentations, we remembered the destruction of the First and Second Temples and of European Jewry. That night, many of the girls crawled into my bed, distraught over the graphic and gruesome Holocaust movie *Night and Fog*, which had been shown that day. They were too young for this, I thought, nowhere near mature enough to understand the complexity of being Jewish. Indeed, it was something I was still grappling with myself, the mixture of joy and sorrow I felt at being Jewish.

The following morning, we were instructed to hold our morning prayers in the cramped quarters of the library foyer as a simulation of a concentration camp. More than sixty of us stood on top of each other and shared one prayer book. One counselor was assigned to be a guard, and the campers were inmates, as if incarcerated with no exit. Within minutes, the "guard" lost control and physically hit a few campers for talking. The exercise was halted, the counselor was humiliated, and we were in a state of shock. As we walked to the dining hall for breakfast, I was angry that the campers' Jewish identity might be forever defined by the state of victimhood to which they had suddenly been exposed, and I reassured the girls that they had not done anything wrong. I wanted them to hold on to the memories of the Friday nights when the entire camp, dressed in white, would welcome the Sabbath queen with song and prayer in the wooded surroundings.

I have often looked back on that summer as seminal to my urge, both professionally, as a psychologist, and personally, as a child of survivors, to struggle with understanding human behavior in extreme situations. On one hand, we humans can soar to the moon; on the other, we all too often descend to a place of destruction, depravity, and inhumanity.

A few months later, I heard Rabbi Irving ("Yitz") Greenberg chillingly describe the use of Zyklon B gas in the Nazi death camps and how the Germans calculated precisely how much to use so as not to waste an ounce while using enough to kill all the men, women, and children who were packed into a gas chamber.

Even though my father was a partisan in the forests of Belarus and my mother fled Poland with her immediate family and was incarcerated in a Soviet labor camp on an island off the Arctic Ocean, and even though I was born in a Displaced Persons camp in Germany and had overheard my parents' conversations with their fellow survivors, I had never put together a real narrative about what had happened to Jews during the Shoah. The stories I had eavesdropped on were supplemented by a horrific picture book about the persecution of Jews I saw on a relative's coffee table.

In high school, our world history book summarized the Holocaust in one sentence: "Six million Jews were murdered in concentration camps." When I heard Rabbi Greenberg speak, it was the first time that I understood how little I knew about the Jews' plight under the German occupation.

I remember sitting with my father on Cape Cod staring at the rose hip bushes when he said, "These remind me of the berries we used to eat when I hid in the woods," followed by, "I felt like an animal." The thought that my father had felt that way haunts me to this day. His revelation opened a conversation between us that continued for many years about what he had endured during the Holocaust and how that had resulted in his lack of faith in God.

Together with Bella Savran, a fellow second-generation mental health professional whom I had met in my Jewish feminist consciousness-raising group in Boston, we organized the first awareness groups for children of Holocaust survivors. Perceiving ourselves and our cohorts as diverse, complex individuals, rather than simply as victims, we facilitated working through negative images of being Jewish, shame at having survivor parents, fears of being openly Jewish, and discovering the joy of being a Jew and finding community. We discovered that if our core identity is strengthened, all the other issues of communicating with our parents about their past could be worked out. These included how to forgive them for keeping secrets; how to overcome a myriad of feelings about the persecutors, such as rage and desiring revenge; how to cope with feelings about our parents' victimization, sadness, and guilt; wanting to undo their suffering; and identifying with their strength and courage. Children of survivors in our groups who were proud of their parents and identified with their resilience had a constructive influence on the others and got them to see their "survivor" family members as something other than broken vessels.

Coincidentally, Elie Wiesel started teaching at Boston University shortly before we launched our awareness groups there, and he promoted them in his class. Students who were afraid to ask their survivor parents questions would often ask Wiesel, and when that was not sufficient, many of them joined the groups.

Our local children of survivor support groups received national attention when, in 1977, Helen Epstein published her watershed article "Heirs of the Holocaust" in the *New York Times Magazine*. The children of survivors she interviewed articulated what many of us had felt but had not put into words—that we were different and saw the world through a different lens, that we needed to mourn relatives we never knew, and that we felt a moral responsibility to make the world a safer place for all oppressed people.

Word of a second-generation identity had ripple effects across the ocean. I was invited to lead second-generation groups at the Hebrew University in Jerusalem and to do research on the Holocaust's psychological impact on children of survivors and their families. Lucy Dawidowicz's book *The War Against the Jews* became my bible. Before I interviewed a survivor, I read the chapter on the country he or she had lived in during the war to have a cognitive map of the persecution the interviewee had endured. Some of my interviews felt surreal; survivors who could not speak to their own children found it easier to give testimony to me, a total stranger.

In conversations with mental health professionals, I was told that I was bringing an American phenomenon to Israel and that the post-Holocaust generation there was not challenged by having survivor parents. It took another ten years, after the Demjanjuk Trial and the showing of Claude Lanzmann's film *Shoah*, before Israelis started to grapple with issues of communication, identity, and worldviews in the context of being children of Holocaust survivors.

During the summer of 1978, light bulbs went on as I heard the social psychologist Stanley Milgram explain how ordinary people can decide to harm others. His obedience-to-authority studies showed me how the discipline of social psychology could help me study human behavior during the Holocaust, and so I enrolled in a program with him in social and personality psychology. Psychoanalysis and family systems therapy, which I had studied earlier, now seemed too limited because they ignored situational variables that affect how individuals behave toward a group of people deemed "unworthy of life."

When I studied family therapy and we explored our own families, my professor pointed out to me that "your father is a survivor."

This comment set in motion a different consciousness of my identity as a child of survivors. I also found myself wondering how human beings decided, under conditions of extreme terror, whether to be perpetrators, bystanders, resisters, or rescuers. In particular, I wanted to understand why non-Jews risked their lives to save Jews during the Holocaust. Before joining the partisans, my father hid in the woods, where he depended on the generosity of farmers and their children, who brought him food and washed his lice-infested clothes. An altruistic Christian, Ivan Safanov of Illya, Belarus, defied the Germans and courageously introduced my father to the Belarusian partisans. Those mostly nameless, faceless people have always fascinated me. I wanted to know who they were and what had motivated them to help Jews at great personal peril. And I will be forever grateful that my father was able to honor Safanov as a Righteous Among the Nations at Yad Vashem.

Academic pursuits were not enough for me. Like many children of survivors who confront their families' persecution, I felt a need "to do something." Thus, in May 1985, I was part of a delegation of the International Network for Jewish Children of Holocaust Survivors, organized and led by Menachem Rosensaft, that traveled to Bergen-Belsen to protest against President Ronald Reagan's degrading equation of that Nazi concentration camp and the German military cemetery at Bitburg where members of Hitler's Waffen-SS are buried.

At the Graduate Center of the City University of New York, I was drawn to another scholar, Stephen P. Cohen, who supervised some of the early groups for children of Holocaust survivors. Cohen embodied a wholeness to being Jewish; he was immersed in a religious community and was an ardent Zionist who was also empathetic to the Palestinians' plight. He showed me the possibility of applying academic disciplines to the vibrancy of Jewish life and was a true mentor who understood the tools I needed to keep making a difference. Like him, I have been sustained by the rhythms of Jewish life and the Jewish community and their traditions, culture, texts, songs, prayer, and study that sustain my soul.

I have carried that personal involvement into my professional work. There has always been a tension between my identity as a child of survivors who knows what my family and my people suffered and the joy I derive from Judaism and being part of the Jewish community. I have never wanted my spiritual side to get lost in the lachrymose facets of Jewish history. While the intrapsychic work I do is helpful to patients, it is not a panacea. I feel helpless in my consulting room if I do not encourage clients to search for community. Like all other Jews, but perhaps more so, survivors and their descendants need a sense of belonging in order to mourn and to heal.

Rabbi Benny Lau

Rabbi Benjamin (Benny) Lau received his rabbinic ordination from the Chief Rabbinate of Israel in 1993, served as the rabbi of Kibbutz Sa'ad for ten years, and has been the spiritual leader of the Ramban Synagogue in Katamon, Jerusalem, since 2001. A graduate of the Har Etzion Hesder Yeshiva in Alon Shvut, Israel, he also has a BA in history and Talmud from the Hebrew University of Jerusalem and an MA and PhD from Bar Ilan University. In 2005, in collaboration with the Ma'aglei Tzedek social justice NGO, he founded the Beit Midrash for Social Justice at Beit Morasha of Jerusalem and as of 2013 heads the Human Rights and Judaism in Action Project at the Israel Democracy Institute.

"The establishment of the State of Israel is the Jewish people's resurrection."

"Your home will be in Eretz Yisrael, even if you have to acquire it through suffering...." My father, Naphtali Lau-Lavie recalls that his father, Rabbi Moshe Chaim Lau, spoke these words to him when they saw each other for the last time on the night of October 13, 1942. My grandfather was murdered at Treblinka the following week.

Two and a half years later, on April 3, 1945, in the middle of Passover, my father was separated from his little brother Lulek (known today as Rabbi Yisrael Meir Lau, chief rabbi of Tel Aviv and former chief rabbi of the State of Israel) next to Block 8 at Buchenwald. Thinking that their parting would be final, my father told his brother that "there is a place in the world called Eretz Yisrael. Say 'Eretz Israel'—the Land of Israel. Again. Repeat after me." In his memoirs, my uncle wrote, "I knew not one word of Hebrew, but I repeated those two words—Eretz Israel—without understanding their meaning."

These two stories have been with me for years. Only recently have I begun to wonder what climate enabled that profound connection to Eretz Yisrael to flourish in my father's and grandfather's family. This was a prominent Hasidic, rabbinic family, deeply rooted in Polish Jewry. They did not belong to the Zionist movement, just as most of the rabbinic leadership of their day chose to forgo any involvement in Zionist activity.

I, on the other hand, grew up in Israel in a home that identified deeply with the Zionist movement. All my grandfather's descendants—dozens of grandchildren and great-grandchildren—live in Israel and serve as leaders in the army, the rabbinate, education, and the financial world. It is a mystery to me why my grandfather, who was such a lover of Zion, did not make aliyah. He wrote about it and about Jewish self-fulfillment in the Land of Israel but did not live to fulfill his dream. We who are now raising a fourth generation of his descendants embody the promise of redemption through our presence in this country. This essay is dedicated to his memory.

For millennia, the Jewish collective was lost, unable to find its way home. Life on foreign soil, in countries not their own, changed from punishment and exile to reality and a semblance of home.

So it was, as far back as when Jacob's sons went down into Egypt. Joseph brought his father and brothers to live in Goshen during the famine. Within a few years they were supposed to return to the land that had been promised to Abraham, Isaac, and Jacob. The famine passed, but the Israelites had become well acclimated to their new surroundings: "And Israel dwelled in the land of Egypt, in the land of Goshen, and they took holdings in it, and were fruitful and multiplied greatly" (Genesis 47:27).

Despite the laconic narration, this verse speaks loudly. The words "they took holdings in it" indicate the individual's ability to become accustomed to a new place, to "take hold of it" and belong to it, even if it is not one's own. The hold that the Israelites had on the land of Goshen should not have occurred. As soon as the famine came to an end, they were to have uprooted themselves and returned home. But Egypt pulled them in deeply. Rabbi Zadok Ha-kohen of Lublin wrote, "They came to hold onto, and be absorbed by, the 'shell' [the profane outward manifestation] of Egypt ... like a fetus in its mother's womb" (*Pri Zadik, Parashat Vayyehi*).

This pattern of becoming established in a temporary refuge where one arrived under compulsion, making that place into an ideal and permanent home, has recurred many times in Jewish history.

Before the destruction of the First Temple, tens of thousands of Jews from the Land of Israel went into exile in Babylon with King Jeconiah (597 BCE). In response to activist messianic circles that sought to arouse the Israelite spirit to rebel against the Babylonian Empire, the prophet Jeremiah pleaded with the Jews living by the rivers of Babylon to settle there because their exile was to last for seventy years. The same circles nurtured the illusion that within a short time Babylon would disappear and the Jews would return to live in Jerusalem with full independence. Jeremiah proclaimed that God wanted the Israelites to establish homes in Babylon, plant gardens there, marry, have children, and "seek the welfare of the city to which I exiled you ... for in its prosperity you shall prosper" (Jeremiah 29:4–7).

It appears that Jeremiah's prophecy came true. Jewish society in Babylon, as in Goshen, "took holdings in it, and were fruitful and multiplied greatly."

In the sixth century BCE, Cyrus, king of Persia, enabled the Jewish people to return to the Land of Israel, telling them that God "has charged me with building Him a house in Jerusalem, which is in Judah. Any one of you, of all His people, may his God be with him, and let him go up to Jerusalem that is in Judah and build the house of the Lord God of Israel, the God that is in Jerusalem" (Ezra 1:1–3).

But the first group of returnees was negligible. The people sitting by the waters of Babylon and weeping while remembering Zion found it difficult to cut their ties to their new land. A new mother earth took them into her womb, and it was warm and comfortable for them there. They had no reason at all to uproot themselves and relocate to the desolate Land of Israel. Only a tiny minority heeded the call to go home. Most continued to pray for the restoration of Zion and remained in Babylon.

After the destruction of the Second Temple, there was a momentary outburst of sovereign pride, which developed into a rebellion, led by Bar Kochba. The rabbinic sages were divided about this uprising. The students of Rabbi Johanan ben Zakkai sought to preserve the Jewish spirit and made do with the study of Torah and the performance of acts of kindness. Others, led by Rabbi Akiba, fought to be an independent national entity, not subjugated to a foreign power.

The fierce anger of Hadrian, the Roman ruler, brought the Jews to destruction and desolation unlike any in Jewish history until the Holocaust. In its wake, many Jews emigrated from Israel, and the Torah academies of Babylonia grew in power until they became the spiritual center of the Jewish people—a new Jerusalem.

At the end of the eleventh century, Rabbi Yehudah Halevi saw Jews integrated into the enlightened culture of Muslim Spain and well established in the local economy. In his seminal book *The Kuzari*, Halevi describes the Land of Israel in romantic hues and expresses the exclusive connection of the people Israel to its land. The king of the Khazars then addresses a question to the rabbi, who speaks for the author: If that special land was intended for you and your people, what are you doing here, in Spain? The rabbi replies that the Jews' refusal to return to Zion was "the sin that kept the divine promise with regard to the Second Temple," deploring that while some were ready to end their exile, "the majority and the aristocracy remained in Babylon, preferring dependence and slavery, and unwilling to leave their houses and their affairs" (*Kuzari* 2:24).

Rabbi Yehudah Halevi traces a thread across a millennium and a half of Jewish history. The Edict of Cyrus had been, in his view, a divine invitation to return to Zion. For a moment there had been a chance of returning to being established on their land, accompanied by an elevating divine spirit. But most of the Jews had chosen to remain in exile.

Surviving for thousands of years, the Jews of the Diaspora succeeded in building splendid communities, educational systems serving every Jewish child, social welfare systems, and synagogues. As the years passed, the communities everywhere grew stronger, and the Land of Israel was forgotten. The lips still mouthed the prayer "May our eyes witness Your return to Zion," but the heart was no longer there. To arouse the people, a new, external power was needed, one that would remind those dwelling in darkness of their real home.

At the beginning of the Jewish awakening to a return to Zion in modern times too, this tragedy was repeated. Some Jewish leaders at the beginning of the nineteenth century heard "the voice of the turtledove" in our land (Song of Songs 2:12) and tried to arouse the hearts of Jews to aliyah—the students of the Ba'al Shem Tov and those of the Gaon of Vilna alike, Jews from Hungary and Morocco and everywhere else. They sensed the power of the moment. But the vast majority of the Jewish people did not lend a hand to the renewed project of a return to Zion.

As in the time of Cyrus, very few Jews came home. For every one Jew who was moved at the end of the nineteenth century to return to Zion, a hundred and more went to the "*goldene medine,*" the United States of America. Zionism was of almost no import.

The modern Zionist movement rebelled against the comatose state of exile, but it too received a decidedly mixed reception. Religious traditionalists sensed that nationalism had nothing in common with religion, and the nationalist movement sought to give credence to that view by disengaging from the old Jewish world.

Nearly unique in his generation was Rabbi Avraham Yitzhak Ha-Kohen Kook, who adopted the Zionists' vision of redemption and considered nationalism as part of Torah. In his view, Jewish nationalism gets its vitality from religion, and the Jewish religion comes to life with the rise of Jewish nationalism.

And still there was no large-scale Jewish immigration to Eretz Yisrael. Dribs and drabs arrived, to be sure, but the vast majority of Jews were comfortable where they were or chose not to see the warnings around them.

Only after the Holocaust was there a true national awakening. In his essay "Kol Dodi Dofek" (The Voice of My Beloved Knocks), Rabbi Joseph B. Soloveitchik wrote:

> In the midst of a night of terror filled with the horrors of Maidanek, Treblinka, and Buchenwald, in a night of gas chambers and crematoria, in a night of absolute divine self-concealment (*hester panim mukhlat*), in a night ruled by the satan of doubt and apostasy ... in a night of continuous searching ... in that very night the Beloved appeared. "God who conceals Himself in His dazzling hiddenness" suddenly manifested Himself and began to knock at the tent of His despondent and disconsolate love, twisting convulsively on her bed, suffering the pains of hell. *As a result of the knocks on the door of the maiden, wrapped in mourning, the State of Israel was born!*[1]

And so, all of a sudden, the State of Israel burst into being. Ezekiel's visions of the dry bones was made real before our eyes in all its awesome splendor: "Thus said the Lord God, I am going to open your graves and lift you out of your graves, O My people, and bring you to the land of Israel" (Ezekiel 37:12).

The State of Israel, which opened its gate to every Jew anywhere, is the fulfillment of the dreams of all the generations. Today, when the majority of the Jewish people lives in the State of Israel, most of the world of Torah is driven by scholars in the Land of Israel, and the identity of Diaspora Jews is bound up with the State of Israel, it is no longer possible to deny the unique historical shift taking place before our eyes. The establishment of the State of Israel is the Jewish people's resurrection.

[Translated from the Hebrew by Rabbi Peretz Rodman]

Sylvia Posner

Sylvia Posner is the assistant to the president and administrative executive and assistant secretary to the Board of Governors of Hebrew Union College–Jewish Institute of Religion. She has known six of the twelve presidents of HUC-JIR in the institution's almost 140-year history and has been fortunate to work with five of them.

> "The overriding principle by which I raised our children can be simply stated: I wanted them to feel the tragedy in their hearts first and learn the facts later."

After a turbulent voyage across the Atlantic in December 1949, my parents, Hena (née Ingber) and Szloma Smialy, and I were warmly embraced in this land by two women, both larger than life. The first, the Statue of Liberty, and the second, no less important, my mother's aunt, who had come to America at the turn of the century and who, together with her husband and children, set us up in our new home in the Brownsville section of Brooklyn.

My parents never forgot to instill in me their fundamental Jewish values, the traditions of *Yiddishkeit: tzedakah* (charity), *Talmud Torah* (Jewish learning), and *mishpacha* (family). They wanted me to be Jewish in America, not just a Jew in America.

My first lesson in *tzedakah* came early. When my father cashed his first paycheck, our first month in America, he made arrangements to send a portion of it to a brother in his hometown of Pabianice (in Yiddish, Pabyainitz), Poland, and another portion to a brother in Israel. When he received his first vacation paycheck, he sent it once again to them.

Ours was the ethic of the extended family, enriched by ties of history. We frequently traveled across the Canadian border to Montreal, via overnight train, to visit our Canadian relatives who had left the same Displaced Persons camp in Germany we did.

My parents guided my American education, but they guarded my Jewish education. They sent me to *Talmud Torah*, where I had no problem being a non-observant Jew in an Orthodox setting.

As a child of survivors, I always knew I was afforded the luxury of being one step removed from the nightmare. That realization has permeated my entire life. Just as we are to believe that we were all at Sinai when God gave us the Torah, I felt it my responsibility to raise our children, Rachel and Raphael, with the imprint and conviction that they, too, were witnesses to the Shoah. I believed and believe that if they, who are now a further step removed, do not and cannot shed a tear, the Holocaust will be for future generations merely another Haggadah, a tale told on a different night. Though we should be shedding tears on Passover for our ancestors who languished in Egyptian bondage, the truth is that we do not—not even at the seder table.

How, then, did I raise our children and retell the tale?

To begin with, I have never felt it my right to be critical of or to analyze how my parents communicated the Holocaust to me. I believed that they were analyzed and criticized enough and for their own child, at least, to "get off their backs."

In the privacy of their own room, our children would ask my parents, their *baba* and *zayde*, about *their* parents. They did not ask for bedtime stories or fairy tales; they wanted to know about their roots. Knowing that my parents had already laid the groundwork with careful simplicity made it much easier for me to answer any questions our children had. It now became my responsibility and that of my husband to perpetuate the truth. When our children asked how many people were killed, along with my mother's and father's parents, I answered honestly. When they asked if children were killed as well, again the answer was straightforward. To be truthful became all too easy as the media covered more wars, more genocide, and more horrors worldwide.

As they grew into adulthood our children—and then our children-in-law—recognized that the "unsaid" mattered as much in our home as the "said." There were products that I would not buy; there were airline carriers that I would not use; there were countries that I would not visit. I never demanded that our children comply with my principles, but only that they understand why I have and maintain them.

Our home was a modern Jewish-American home with a Yiddish accent. My husband, Rabbi David M. Posner, is a Reform rabbi, so ritual observances, Sabbath, and holidays were celebrated in a manner harmonious with his philosophy of Judaism. Jewishness was an everyday matter in our home; it was not something we preached, it was something we practiced and lived.

So finally, because now is the time of my life that I should be looking back, how did my children know that their mother was a child of survivors?

- I spoke Yiddish to their *baba* and *zayde*, to my relatives, and to my parents' friends.
- I sought a profession that would be as fulfilling Jewishly as it would be professionally.
- I celebrated holidays with a moment of memory.
- I condemn and am still horrified by genocide as if it were the first time it occurred because "I, too, came out of Egypt."
- And ultimately I personally suffer when I retell the history of our people during the Shoah.

On reflection, the overriding principle by which I raised our children—and by which I hope they will raise our grandchildren Chase, Simon, Felix, and Elias—can be simply stated: I wanted them to feel the tragedy in their hearts first and learn the facts later.

Dr. Mark L. Tykocinski

Mark L. Tykocinski, MD, is provost of Thomas Jefferson University and dean of its Sidney Kimmel Medical College, in Philadelphia. He previously served for a decade as chair of the Department of Pathology and Laboratory Medicine at the University of Pennsylvania. As a molecular and cellular immunologist, Dr. Tykocinski, who earned his BA degree in biology from Yale University and his MD degree from New York University, has pioneered protein pharmaceuticals for the treatment of cancer and autoimmunity, and in 2007 he founded an Israeli biotechnology company, KAHR-Medical, to develop his novel fusion protein pharmaceuticals.

"Each survivor reflects a tapestry of interwoven narrative threads, as does each child of survivors by extension."

The backdrop in my study is a wall of Holocaust books, hundreds of them. The selected ones are here in my inner sanctum. The rest spill over into unused bedrooms, alphabetically arrayed, except for the prized author-less Black Books, fragmented memories of towns erased. Each volume a resource for my own child of survivor narrative building.

The first book was Raul Hilberg's *The Destruction of the European Jews*, the original edition. This was my summer reading project as a teenager at Massad Bet, housed in the camp's cave-like digs for non-camper staff, trying to grapple with his mother's passing the previous winter. Age sixteen, and I had somehow never discussed Auschwitz with her or, for that matter, anything that came before or after. Now I would have to reach back through Hilberg. I didn't just read it. I devoured it, pen in hand, underlining and filling margins with religious fervor. When the soft-cover Hilberg was ragged on the spine, other books piled on for the decades following. More than just resources for framing narratives, it dawns upon me that these books are objects for cathexis, for unburdening gnawing histories and shelving them, to make way for being and achieving.

Books aside, stories of heroism were the foundations of my family's narratives. My father had spoken willingly of his survival experiences, my mother not at all, her stories pieced together from others. The seminal story was my father jumping from a moving train, heading to the Belzec death mill from liquidated Tarnow, delivering himself, his younger sister, and three other family members through a barbed window opening, machine gun fire as staccato background. My mother too was heroic, spotting a young frail girl at the entrance to her barrack in Auschwitz, enveloping this utter stranger in a protective cocoon as they lay sardined on the wood slats, and day after day, wheeling this fragile girl's allotment of stones in the quarry. All the saved survived and sang the praises of their saviors.

Rummaging through my file cabinet one day, I stumble across a form from the post-war immigration maze leading to America. A phrase catches my eye—beaten by a Nazi on a street in her hometown, Zawiercie. I tuck it away, reflexively, as if trying to hide it from myself—so much simpler to hold on to the strong savior narrative in unadulterated form. How dare an administrative piece of paper jar that aura of my mother as all-powerful heroine.

For Holocaust survivors, it's more meaningful to speak of a kaleidoscope of narrative threads that percolate up from a seething cauldron of overtaxed anecdotes, filtered experiences, piecemeal philosophies, stray memories, conflicted emotions, all coming together into variably structured storylines. Each survivor reflects a tapestry of interwoven narrative threads, as does each child of survivors by extension.

In piecing together the narrative tableaux, one question has loomed large. How did my parents rejoin humanity after the camps and embrace life so fully? How does one make sense of such psychological survival? How so normal?

Our memories are but a string of defining moments, so Proust and Woolf hammered home. Time is not linear and the highest-impact moments are inflated and concatenated as a stream of defining landmarks that preoccupy our memories and frame our mental lives. But what happens when the defining moment is more than five years of unimaginable hell? I puzzle over how my parents survived, mentally that is. That moment of moments should have pushed all else aside, should have left no room for the mundane, for the spiritual, for emotion itself. How did they make room for the continuation? How did they transcend the fracturing? And by extension, how did their progeny evolve as great achievers?

Survivors like my parents were masters of compartmentalization, naturally wired for sequestering impossible memories, deflating
the most horrible of moments, and thereby making room for normalcy. Coupled to a remarkable ability to live with fractured realities, they felt no pressing need to repair them. They seemed fine with
narrative threads frayed and untethered, felt no imperative to piece
things together, just sidestepped the swirl of nightmarish flashbacks.
The miracle is that most survivors were able to transcend a narrative
structure that defied coherence. This, I have come to believe, is key
to explaining the riddle of why, despite their having been victimized,
there was no abiding sense of victimization.

The ability to compartmentalize and tolerate fracture was often
passed down. It certainly was to me. I simply don't know why this
survival tool is so prevalent in the heirs of the Holocaust, as compared to others with tragic family histories, perhaps an elaboration
of a generic Jewish trait cultivated for survival over the millennia.
And maybe a part of the special bond we, the children of survivors,
subliminally sense, regardless of the differences in our narrative tap-
estries. We can tolerate the ironic and move on; we share an uncanny
ability to cope with narrative complexity and overcome a hypersen-
sitivity to the hypocrisy taunting us.

Mastery of compartmentalization sometimes manifested to the
odd point of forgiveness. "Dad, would you be offended if we bought
a Mercedes SUV?" "No," he responded, "as long as it has all the features you need." We tolerate the ironies and contradictions, partition
them off, shelve them away, and move on. My father was not consumed with bitterness against the Jewish shoe store owner in Budapest
to whom he was delivering false Christian papers but who turned him
in to the Gestapo. And soon after the liberation of Buchenwald, when
an American soldier handed him a gun and motioned to an SS guard
bound up on the ground, my father turned it away. Even after Auschwitz, even after Buchenwald, he couldn't take a life, even that life.

Compartmentalization enables us to at once be shocked by
God's world and yet to love God. Staying with my uncle during my
youth, I would marvel at the depth of his spirituality, sustaining the
traditions of Ger and Gerrer Hasidism despite all he had experienced
during the Holocaust. Perhaps this, too, was a manifestation of compartmentalization. Making room for spiritual space—for God, for
Judaism, for love of Jews, for belief in mankind.

Almost two decades ago, I videotaped my father's war experiences. In the course of the extended seven-hour interview, he broke down crying, but only once, and not where one might have expected. He was stoic as he described the horrific liquidation of Tarnow; the hiding and running; his escape, across Czechoslovakia, from Poland to Hungary; the brutality of Auschwitz; the liberation from Buchenwald. It was early in the war, and he had decided to head east to find safety. His father followed the horse-drawn cart for miles, repeating the priestly blessing, "*Yevorechecha Hashem v'yishmerecha …*"— "May the Lord bless you and watch over you"—over and over. A clearing in my father's emotional space suddenly flooded with a rush of raw emotion, the memory of his father's love channeled through an unshakeable, intuitive belief in God. For my father, this was what was unbearable, making room for the dialectic of his father's resilience versus vulnerability, within the swirl of his love and faith. For this, there could be no cathexis. This is the narrative thread that I will treasure the most.

Shulamit Reinharz

Shulamit Reinharz is the Jacob Potofsky Professor of Sociology, the founder and current director of the Hadassah-Brandeis Institute, and the founder and current director of the Women's Studies Research Center, all at Brandeis University. An advocate for the study of Hebrew, she has published thirteen books and is currently involved with major efforts to make the Hebrew language attractive to American Jews. Her book in progress is titled *A Memoir in Four-Hands: My Father's Holocaust Experiences in Germany and Holland.*

"My parents enacted the narrative of my being a symbol of the survival of the Jewish people when they gave me a Hebrew name—Shulamit."

The Facts

My father, Max M. Rothschild, spent six weeks in Buchenwald after *Kristallnacht*; my mother, Ilse H. Strauss, was terrorized but never sent to a concentration camp. Young German Jews, one from a religious Zionist background, the other from an assimilated family, my parents survived the Shoah by fleeing to Holland in 1939 and going into hiding after the German invasion. My father's parents also survived the war, as did his two sisters who were sent to England on a *Kindertransport*. My mother's father, a lawyer, died of starvation in the Gurs concentration camp in Pau, France, where my grandparents had been shipped from Germany; her mother, a German hausfrau, was deported from Gurs to Auschwitz, where she was killed. My mother's two sisters survived the war by getting into Palestine. I was born in Amsterdam, Holland, in 1946, thirteen months after the liberation.

The Assumption

Human beings are born as helpless babies and can survive only if adults nurture and protect them. Especially in the early years, the adults' influence is very great and shapes the personality and outlook of the child, even if the outcome is a rebellion against the parents. It is reasonable to assume that when Holocaust survivors became parents, they shaped their children with regard to many aspects of the Holocaust, such as whether it is good or bad to be a Jew, whether people are basically good or evil, whether the world is a safe place or not, whether one can trust authority, and more.

The Theory

Each child comes into the world with a narrative the parent(s) define in advance, whether consciously or not. Damaging narratives might include "This child is extremely vulnerable because the Shoah could happen again, or simply because the world is anti-Semitic," or "This child will never know he/she is a Jew," or "This child stands for all the children, or a specific child, who died in the Holocaust." Positive narratives might include "This child is a miracle that demonstrates that we survived and the Jewish people is still here," or "I will let this child know what happened to us so that she/he will be strong."

My Narrative

I was blessed with a positive narrative: I was evidence of the survival of the Jewish people. My parents—deliberately or not—spoke about what happened, not in long speeches but in snatches of stories here

and there. My father became a rabbi and used the theme of the Holocaust in many of his sermons. As a child, I was told stories about my
amazing appearance at ten months or so, when I arrived with my parents in the United States, where my grandparents had found refuge.
I was the first grandchild and was "adopted" by my grandparents'
friends whose ability to have children was disrupted by the war.

My Take on the Narrative

Despite the generally positive climate of my early years, my attitudes toward the Shoah as a young child were complex. First, I was
extremely proud to have been born in Amsterdam and liked seeing
the expressions on people's faces when I told them. I was not blond
or blue-eyed. How could I have been born there?

I also remember being afraid of officers, particularly police officers. Not specific individuals but police in general. The evil forces
in my "bad dreams" were not devils or "boogeymen." Rather, they
were the police, who would come and get me if I misbehaved. I also
feared corporal punishment, which I somehow deduced or heard
was practiced in the public school where I went to first grade in a
suburb of Boston. I have no idea if there really was such punishment,
but I believed that the principal carried it out in his back office with
a paddle. In other words, I had picked up that there was violence in
the world, that it was close at hand, practiced by people in authority,
and that I was vulnerable to it.

My parents enacted the narrative of my being a symbol of the
survival of the Jewish people when they gave me a Hebrew name—
Shulamit. I was never ashamed of having an uncommon name, and
as I grew older, I loved telling the story of what my name meant and
why I had been given it. To explain "Shulamit" required and enabled
me to talk about my parents surviving the Shoah and the fact that
I was Jewish. It also enabled me to tell the inquirer that it was a
Hebrew name found in the Bible. I repeated the stories my parents
had told me about my mother's sister who had died in Palestine and
for whom I had been named. I was proud of all of it. I regularly
"taught" my non-Jewish (and sometimes Jewish) friends about Judaism, the Hebrew alphabet, the Holocaust, and Israel. I put myself
out there and still do. Recently, for example, I rode in an elevator
with a woman and her adult daughter. As I exited, the older woman
said, "God bless you; Jesus loves you." Instead of just moving on, I

responded, "Does Jesus love me? I'm a Jew." She said Jesus does love me because the Jews are one of the chosen peoples. I said, "Chosen for what? We've had a pretty difficult history." She said, "You have suffered because you have not accepted Jesus as the son of God." Her evangelical anti-Semitism appalled me.

Secular Education

After moving from Boston, I attended New Jersey's excellent public schools from grades K through twelve. The towns in which I lived had few children, and I found myself proudly explaining why I did not recite the Lord's Prayer at the start of each school day. And when the school instituted one "Chanukah" song to be learned along with a plethora of Christmas carols, I was the only one who could pronounce the Hebrew words of a Zionist pioneering song that had nothing to do with Chanukah, but I let it go.

Jewish Education

To reinforce my identity and knowledge, my parents continuously educated me Jewishly. Their love for my father's parents led me to adore my grandparents, who remained strongly Jewish but rejected American synagogue life. Since we spent the major Jewish holidays with them, I internalized the ideas that family and family gatherings were unassailable, the idea of the transmission of Jewish identity from generation to generation, and the value of Jewish knowledge. In addition to this informal education, I received formal Jewish education as well. I was enrolled in Hebrew school from a very young age until I went to college.

Zionist Education

Second, and extremely important, was my parents' Zionism, especially that of my mother. My father had been eager to get to the United States after the war to reunite with his parents and two sisters. As mentioned above, my mother's two sisters had escaped to Palestine/Israel. After a short while in the United States, my father began to work for Zionist organizations, where he befriended people with similar ideas. My parents and these other couples and young families prepared to immigrate to Israel, which we did a year and a half after arriving in the United States. As my mother said, "I didn't survive Hitler in order to live in Malden, Massachusetts."

The positive valence of Israel became deeply engrained in me when my mother began telling me stories about her life as a teenage girlfriend of my father. As a way of distancing themselves from their hostile Nazi environments in Germany, they joined Zionist youth groups, particularly the socialist Zionist Habonim, which had a program to help German-Jewish teens acquire agricultural skills they could use on a kibbutz. This took the form of farms or camps to which German-Jewish youth flocked for fun, social life, and an alternative to the horror around them. My father's Zionist involvement actually saved his life, when the Zionist youth organization to which he belonged got him and others out of Buchenwald with a permit to go to Holland.

Zionism and Israel were the most positive entities imaginable, and we moved there when I was three years old, planning to spend the rest of our lives there. If Israel had only existed a decade earlier, the murder of six million Jews could not have happened, my father told me. My parents experienced endless challenges—disease, lack of food, marauding Arabs, lack of electricity—but especially for my mother, it was heaven. Israel meant sunshine, outdoors, happiness, rebirth. My sister was born there. But my father's dreams were not fulfilled, and we soon returned to the United States. Although my father loved Israel and traveled there many times, sometimes for long periods, it was my mother who passed her overwhelming love for the country—its language, its culture, its landscape, and its people—on to me. When I was twelve years old, she took me to Israel for eight weeks, and I, too, fell in love with the people and the land. My attachment was so great that I determined to marry an Israeli—which I did. He and I have continued the tradition of giving our children Hebrew names—Yael and Naomi—and inculcating an involvement with Israel, which turns out to be the core of the work that each of them does.

"Second-Generation" Membership and My Work

Given that they were refugees, a point my father reiterated frequently, my parents were unable to help me deal with selecting a college and other challenges of being a teenager. And so I learned to be self-reliant. I chose sociology as a major in order to understand the United States, my adopted home. I chose to earn a PhD in part because my father had one and we all valued education so highly.

My research as a sociologist has had many foci, including numerous studies in Israel and various historical projects. And over the last twenty-five years, I have devoted much of my time to feminist research and activism, which I define as continuing the process of self-liberation in which my parents were engaged.

After earning a full professorship, I directed the Brandeis University Women's Studies Program for a decade, using the position to create a myriad of opportunities for students and faculty. As director of the Hadassah-Brandeis Institute and the Women's Studies Research Center, two facilities that unite dozens of scholars and students in explorations of gender or of the nexus between Jews and gender, my work today consists largely of organizing, helping, promoting, and in every way joining forces to improve the world. I resonate with the motto of my university—"Justice, Justice Shall You Pursue."

Final Thoughts

Both my parents died in January 2013 at the age of ninety-two. In the years preceding their deaths I began writing a book about their lives, utilizing the hundreds of documents they had somehow saved from their youth in Germany and their rescue in Holland. But I also asked them pointed questions. My mother's dementia made it difficult for her to answer, but my father was coherent until the end. One of the last questions I posed was "If you were to give me a single idea that you derived from your Holocaust experience, what would it be?" He answered, "That there are good people in this world." He was referring to all the people—Jews and non-Jews—who had saved his and my mother's lives. Unbeknownst to me, I had completely internalized that attitude and have become a very trusting person who sees the value of each human being. Ultimately, that idea is deeply Jewish (we all are created in God's image) and a very satisfying way to live.

Alexander Soros

Alexander Soros is a PhD candidate in the Department
of History at the University of California, Berkeley
and the founder of the Alexander Soros Foundation.
He is the son of billionaire investor George Soros.

> "I only hope that had I been
> in the same position, I would
> have done the same thing."

When I was six or seven years old, my father sat me down and told
me about how when he was a child in Budapest in 1944, the Germans and Hungarians started to hunt down and then kill the Jews.
It was the first real bonding experience I ever recall having with him.
He described my grandfather's prescience in recognizing the existential nature of the threat early on: he placed the family in hiding
and helped save other Jews. As a teenager facing mortal danger and
watching his father struggle on the right side in the battle for humanity by forging fake identity papers and finding refuge with non-Jews
for many Hungarian Jews, my father came to see those terrible years
as the ultimate adventure, the experience that most defined and
shaped him as a person.

My reaction, which I would later recognize as common among
the children of survivors, was to question whether or not I, too,
could have survived those terrible times. I recall telling my third
grade teacher that if there was a war, I would sign up, in order to
have an experience like my father's. I had a sense of guilt. Instead of
danger and adventure, I was living a safe life in the lap of luxury. But
I also felt, and still do, as if I had missed out on history. Such feelings
and associations, I would later discover, are also common among
the children of survivors. What was perhaps unique in my case was
my father's age and hence the time separating me from the events.
My father was fifty-five when I was born in 1985. I grew up with
complexes and issues more suited to an earlier time, when the second
generation, now old enough to be my parents, were coming of age.

For much of my life, I felt as if I was straddling two eras. I had
one foot in the present and one foot constantly in the past. This left
me feeling alienated from contemporary society. Already set apart

from most of my peers by incredible material wealth, I felt the need to fight doubly hard to stay grounded in the present and ordinary. A fanaticism toward sports and a compulsion to stay up-to-date on current events defended me against further alienation and gave me a way to relate and communicate with (I hate the term) "ordinary people."

All these feelings were intensified when we would travel back to Budapest each year as a family. I was constantly reminded that had I been in this city four or five decades earlier I would have been hunted as prey, attacked for something I could never change. Accepting my Jewish heritage wasn't a choice; I was a Jew whether I liked it or not. As other members of my family remained in a kind of hiding, continuing to conceal their identities, I decided to get a bar mitzvah to affirm my history and heritage.

This has led some to say that I have a negative Jewish identity, since my Judaism has been defined by Nazism and the most monstrous events in history. While I see the validity in this notion, I believe that the "negativity" of this identity is outweighed by the positives that emerge from it. It has engrained in me an affinity and empathy for other minorities and victims of persecution. I feel this is an obligation because of the history of my own people. It has also made me try to recognize and rid myself of whatever fascist tendencies I may have myself.

I was forced to ask, what if during the time of the Holocaust, instead of being a Jew, I was born a German or a Hungarian? Would I have stood up and been a righteous gentile? Or would I have allowed myself to be lulled into ignorance or perhaps, even worse, participated in some of the atrocities? I would later learn that this line of questioning is not unique among Jews, especially for the descendants of Holocaust survivors. This hit home when in high school I saw a documentary called *Jewish Americans*. In the film, a woman explains why she had risked her life to fight segregation in the American South during the civil rights movement, against the pleas of her mother to come home. She refused to go home because, in her eyes, had the average German done the equivalent of what she was doing, then members of her family would still be alive. I only hope that had I been in the same position, I would have done the same thing. If feelings like this result from a negative identity, then I embrace it!

Alexis Fishman

Alexis Fishman, an actor and singer, was born and raised in Sydney, Australia, and is a graduate of the Western Australian Academy of Performing Arts. She is the co-writer and star of *Der Gelbe Stern (The Yellow Star)*, a one-woman musical about a Jewish cabaret singer performing her final show in the last days of the Weimar Republic, which she has performed at the Adelaide Cabaret Festival, in Sydney, Melbourne, and New York City. She was nominated for a Helpmann Award (Australian Tony) for her performance as the young Dusty Springfield in the hit musical *Dusty*, starred as Spiderwoman in the Australian premiere of *Kiss of the Spiderwoman*, and in 2007 sang for Australian troops in Iraq and Afghanistan.

> "I realized it wasn't victimhood that I identified with but the opposite. It is the strength with which our people go on. Our commitment to ourselves and to humanity."

A friend of mine, who is of Sephardic background and lost no immediate family in the Holocaust, recently expressed irritation at some Jews she knew whose only connection to their Jewish identity was as victims of anti-Semitism. I didn't like what she was implying. The idea that a point of communal connection could be a defensiveness against those who want to kill us seemed absurd. There are more positive things that identify us, I protested! What about food, culture, family, *Seinfeld*? I realized later that I was defensive because she had hit a nerve of truth. I was one of those Jews she was describing. My most immediate bind to my Jewish identity is as the granddaughter of Holocaust survivors.

My grandmother survived Auschwitz alongside four of her five sisters, and I use her trauma as a shield. When people question why Judaism is important to me despite my lax attitude toward religious obligations or ask why I want to marry a Jew and raise Jewish children, I play the "Auschwitz card" and effectively end the conversation. I use my grandmother's suffering to defend my assimilated, modern, unobservant Jewishness. Needless to say, this discovery was not a pleasant one.

My grandmother grew up in an Orthodox household in Czechoslovakia before the war but afterward wasn't at all devout. Despite this marked decline in ritual observance and the fact that what she had experienced could turn even the most fervent believer of God into a staunch and eternal atheist, she remained Jewish. Ardently Jewish. At her funeral the rabbi referred to her faith. A faith that wasn't necessarily a faith in God but an undeniable faith in life. A faith that allowed her to pick up the pieces, move to Australia, a strange country halfway across the world, raise a family, and most importantly continue to identify as a Jew no matter what form that identification took.

On further examination I realized it wasn't victimhood that I identified with but the opposite. It is the strength with which our people go on. Our commitment to ourselves and to humanity. Our continued pursuit of our identity even in the face of utter destruction. The joy our Jewishness continues to bring us in a world where religion is becoming less meaningful. My grandmother, who experienced unfathomable trauma in the early years of her life because she was Jewish, lived to the age of ninety never letting go of her Jewishness. She never gave up. It's that resilience I identify with. Joyful, *dafka* resilience.

Photo: Jeff Watts

Michael Brenner

Michael Brenner is professor of Jewish history and culture at the University of Munich and the Seymour and Lillian Abensohn Chair in Israel Studies at American University in Washington, DC. He received his PhD from Columbia University, is the author of *After the Holocaust: Rebuilding Jewish Lives in Postwar Germany*, and serves as international president of the Leo Baeck Institute. Among his latest books are *A Short History of the Jews* and *Prophets of the Past: Interpreters of Jewish History*.

> "Every child of the second generation knows what it means to grow up in the shadow of the Holocaust.... In Germany, this meant a constant tension between the close familiarity of, and perhaps even love for, the German language, culture, and nature on the one hand and the fact of the ever-present Nazi past on the other hand."

I share with many second-generation children of survivors the fact that the same atrocities responsible for the murders of most of our families brought our parents together. But for the Holocaust, I would not have been born. My parents would never have met. They grew up in two different countries and in two very different Jewish communities. It was their common experience as survivors that brought them together and that remained an eternal bond between them.

What was different in my case is that I grew up in the direct shadow of the past. I was born in Weiden, a small Bavarian town near the Czech border. It was twenty years after the Holocaust, but only a few miles away from the former Nazi concentration camp of Flossenbürg, 70 miles from Nuremberg, the site of the Nazi rallies with many visible remains, and 150 miles from Munich, the birthplace of the Nazi Movement. In my youth, Weiden was a quaint little town, home to thirty-five thousand Catholics, ten thousand Protestants, and fifty Jews.

Everyone in the small Jewish community was a survivor. Most of them came from Poland. I grew up listening to their stories and conversations about the *Sonderkommando* at Auschwitz, the Warsaw Ghetto, and the death marches, the lack of food, and the dreams of what could be if normalcy returned. Some had lost their religious faith before the war, some during the war; two families remained strictly observant even in the small Bavarian town. The small Bavarian Jewish community resembled a last remnant of a Polish shtetl. Almost everyone spoke Yiddish. One older lady walked for miles to get kosher milk directly from a farmer, and every Friday, the carp she put on the Shabbat table was pulled from her bathtub; the chicken for the Jewish community was slaughtered by her husband in the basement of the synagogue in accordance with kosher law. If you wanted brisket on Rosh Hashanah, it had to be ordered from Munich and brought in on the train.

Many of the Jewish survivors were broken souls in a strange environment. They found refuge among each other, when they came to pray in the synagogue during the holidays and when they met almost every morning over Yiddish newspapers and chat in *mameloshn*. Some men had married German women and worked in "red light" establishments frequented largely by the American soldiers from the base. The others, including my father, worked almost exclusively in the textile business. On Rosh Hashanah and Yom Kippur, most of the clothing stores in the town center were closed, as if nothing had changed from the year 1932, when the stores had different names and were owned by Jews who a few years later were driven out of the country or murdered. Only one Jew had returned to Weiden from the pre-war Jewish community. He opened his store again and kept quiet about his history. He knew too much about what his neighbors had done.

In my youth, the relationship between the Jewish survivors and their German surroundings was ambivalent. The Jews earned their living in Germany, many loved the surrounding nature, they appreciated the benefits of the West and a prospering economy. But some still had the urge to *give it back,* so to speak, to the Germans. There was one Holocaust survivor who when pulled over for speeding, which happened often, would say something along the lines of "After what the Germans did to my family, you dare to ask me to pay a fine!" There was the respected shop owner who would lift his hat politely when his German customers greeted him and would wish them in the most friendly way, "*a mise meshine*" (a violent death); they would smile back in the belief that this was some friendly Yiddish or Hebrew greeting.

The fact that I was born was purely accidental. So many things could have happened differently, and my parents would not have met. Had a nurse not hidden my father during an *Aktion* in the *Durchgangslager* of Sosnowiec when German SS men were pushing Jewish men out of a window and into a truck, he would have been sent to Auschwitz. His mother was not as fortunate: she was taken to Auschwitz and perished in the gas chambers. There was a guard in the concentration camp of Gross-Rosen who beat my father up, but later, when he learned that they shared the same last name, gave my father some extra bread, which kept him from starving in that bitter-cold last winter of the war. My mother spent her youth doing forced labor in Dresden, assembling weapons for the Germans. She and her mother were among the last 120 Jews there and were scheduled to be deported on February 16, 1945. Had Allied fighters not bombed Dresden to smithereens on February 13, my mother would not have been able to rip off her yellow star and go into hiding for the last months of the war. After my father was liberated in May 1945 from the Waldenburg concentration camp in Poland, like many others, he was taken by American soldiers into the American zone of Germany. Had my father, and later my mother, not have stayed there with other Polish-Jewish concentration camp survivors, but followed my father's two surviving sisters to California, my brother and I might have called Los Angeles our home, just like our cousins. It would have been a very different life.

In Weiden, I was the only Jewish kid in my school but not the only Jew in the classroom. The other one looked down from the crucifix on the wall next to the blackboard. Since the other Jew in the classroom could not speak, I was asked to report in history about the Jews in Germany, in politics about the Middle East conflict, and in religion about the Jewish holidays. At age ten, I was the default resident expert. I did not feel anti-Semitism, but I felt philo-Semitism in that I was sometimes treated specially and even better than the other kids. My old biology teacher was especially nice to me. I later learned that he had been a Nazi. In Germany, all children have required religious training in the public schools. I had my Jewish religion lessons once a week. Four or five Jewish kids, ranging from age five to eigh-teen, met in the small Weiden synagogue with a traveling rabbi, who served four or five small surrounding Jewish communities. While the rest of my class had their Catholic or Protestant instruction, I played soccer with the one student "without religion," the Muslim, and the member of the New Apostolic Church. We had fun.

The presence of the Holocaust was not in the forefront of daily life. Both my parents spoke about their different experiences in Poland and Germany. My father said less about what he went through with respect to the specifics; my mother was more open. Being that both of my father's parents and two of his siblings were murdered, this was understandable. Still, we integrated in many ways. My father's cus-tomers were Germans, our neighbors were German, my friends were German. We played basketball and went out for beer and edited the school newspaper. Unlike them, I did not have extended family. On weekends they spent time with grandparents and uncles and aunts and cousins. My family was small. I had my parents, my brother, and my grandmother, who lived with us. We had very few relatives, and they were far away, spread all over the globe: in Israel, Bolivia, the United States, Sweden, and Denmark. In this and in many ways, I knew life was different between me and my friends. I did not feel excluded, but I knew I did not quite belong either.

But we also did not belong anywhere else. When we visited Israel to see my father's cousins, I could sense how embarrassed he was that we stayed in Germany. Unlike some other German Jews, he did not claim that we came from Switzerland or Austria (which was still legitimate before Waldheim), but he felt visibly uncomfortable telling people that he lived in Germany, considered by many Jews as bloodstained soil. My aunt and uncle from Los Angeles came every year to Europe to see us, but we met in London and Paris, in Amster-dam and Zurich—everywhere but in Germany, where they refused to ever step foot again.

The heavy dark past was one constant aspect of life, but only one. My parents refused to let the Holocaust define them, and that was true for their sons. Still, staying in Weiden was something that was clearly not in my future, while staying in Germany was always, and remains, an open question. In high school, I was encouraged by a German teacher to write about the history of the Jews in Wei-den during the Nazi period. This sparked my interest in becoming a historian. I went to Heidelberg to study, then on to Jerusalem, and later to Columbia University in New York for my advanced degree. Was it because of the Holocaust that I studied Jewish history? Certainly, many other roads were open to children of Holocaust survivors. In fact, in my generation, few Jewish kids studied humanities, as opposed to business, medicine, or law.

The only book I ever wrote about the Holocaust was the one that grew out of my high school work on the Jews of Weiden. None of my other books deal explicitly with the Holocaust, but when I look closely at them, they deal with themes that relate to it: the blossoming of Jewish culture in Germany just before its destruction, the Displaced Persons after 1945, and the history of Zionism and the creation of the State of Israel. If I write about the Holocaust, I do so indirectly. Maybe this is my way of dealing with my parents' legacy.

When my wife—an American Jew, who grew up in a Chicago suburb with a Jewish population almost as high as in the whole of Germany—moved to Munich for a few years, everything that seemed so normal to me seemed so very unusual to her. It gave me a different lens to look upon my home than the one I was used to. She would ask me why there was never a dinner conversation without someone dropping the name of Hitler. She felt the philo-Semitism, often remarking on people treating her differently or taking a deeper interest in her if they learned she was Jewish. And I became more aware of how every second person would speak about their grandfathers' role in the German resistance. Germans have dealt more than any other society in history with the crimes their parents and grandparents committed. This is necessary, but it does not lend normalcy to Jewish life there.

Every child of the second generation knows what it means to grow up in the shadow of the Holocaust, and we all cope with this experience in our own unique ways. In Germany, this meant a constant tension between the close familiarity of, and perhaps even love for, the German language, culture, and nature on the one hand and the fact of the ever-present Nazi past on the other hand. The result was both an immersion in and an estrangement from the immediate surroundings in which one grew up. For those who stayed, it meant a constant questioning of living on the "bloodstained" German soil. For those who left, it often meant a longing for the familiar place of a distant childhood. To rephrase one of Kafka's most apt descriptions of German Jews in pre-Nazi Europe, the second generation of Jews after the Holocaust were glued with their back legs to their parents' experience, while their front legs were desperately looking for new ground. Not always did the ensuing despair become their inspiration.

Diana Wang

Writer and psychotherapist Diana Wang, the daughter of Shoah survivors, was born in Poland in 1945 and immigrated to Argentina in 1947. The author of numerous books about psychotherapy and about the Holocaust, she is the president of Generaciones de la Shoá en Argentina (Generations of the Shoah in Argentina). In 2006, she received the *Premio Moisés* (Moses Award) from the Sociedad Hebraica Argentina in Buenos Aires for her work in preserving and transmitting the memory of the Holocaust.

"I refuse to let myself be defined as a victim."

During the first fifty years of my life, I never thought that being Jewish differentiated me from others.

In order to be admitted as immigrants to Argentina in 1947, my family ominously arrived under the pretense of being Catholic. During those first years, we avoided speaking about Judaism or being Jewish in our daily interactions, both within and outside of our family. We did not belong to any Jewish organizations. We did not deny our identity, but we did not broadcast it either.

"Forgive me," I heard my mother's trembling voice over the telephone that Monday morning. Now decades later, it was July 18, 1994. "It's happening again, forgive me for bringing you to this country—I did not know." After catching her breath, she explained herself, referring to that day's deadly terrorist attack on the building of the Argentine Israelite Mutual Association in Buenos Aires: "AMIA was bombed! They want to kill us! Again!"

Us? ... Us? What did she mean by *us*? They wanted to kill *me*? Here, in Argentina? And what was her "again" for? My mother's "us" and "again" were the catalysts that thrust me suddenly, at age fifty, into the roles of being both an heir to the legacy of the Holocaust and a Jew. Puzzled and surprised, I had to understand. In my quest for answers, I met children of survivors, and we began to disclose to each other information about who we were. After so many years, I felt as though I had finally begun my journey home.

Our identity is not a static, monolithic condition bestowed at birth, once and for all. It is an ongoing construct, forged from our gender, ethnicity, nationality, profession or vocation, ideology, age, hobbies, skills, and the myriad other aspects of our ever-evolving lives. The Jewish identity I have cultivated for myself ever since that fateful Monday morning is intertwined with the knowledge that I am a daughter of Holocaust survivors. This merger of my previously concealed identities brought to light some lost pieces of the puzzle of who I was—or who I thought I was—based on what had been meaningful to me earlier in life. But, to my surprise, this "new" Jewish identity had, in reality, always been there. Lying dormant, waiting patiently for me, it fit as snugly as a second skin. Bewildered, I had discovered just how Jewish we were, despite the fact that we had never spoken of it growing up.

I live in Buenos Aires in a secular Jewish microcosm of people who do not base their identity on religion. For most religious Jews—as for the Israelis—there is no need to contemplate their Jewish identity. But for the secular Diaspora, the question of identity thirsts for answers. As the old joke goes, "If you have two Jews, you'll have three synagogues," and so arriving at a consensus regarding identity will always be an uphill battle. Now that the world is more welcoming to Jews than ever before, the temptations of assimilation, intermarriage, and secularism have put the feeling of a common Jewish identity at stake. If not religion, what binds us together to give us a sense of community within this heterogeneous, individualistic, and highly opinionated collective?

For many, the Holocaust seems to fill that void. The Nazis defined very specifically what it was to be a Jew—proud or self-hating, converted or not, in acceptance or denial. For them a Jew was a Jew. There was no debate. And as every Jew was targeted for extermination, Judaism equaled victimhood. Jewish identity was unambiguously imposed not only by the Nuremberg Laws, but also by the common prospect of death.

With religion no longer a common denominator among secular Diaspora Jews, identifying ourselves as heirs to the Holocaust is a tempting alternative. It was our worst suffering ever, and—in an absurd way—this low-hanging fruit is now subconsciously ready to be used to homogenize us into a common identity. But while being a victim then was not a choice, it is today.

After decades of silence, hundreds—if not thousands—of papers, dissertations, books, museums, exhibitions, films, and survivors' testimonies have sprung to life and thrust the Holocaust onto the world stage. Society has finally opened its ears, shut for so many years. For us, the Holocaust family, justice has been accomplished, and our painful past can now be recontextualized in a meaningful way.

Anti-Semitism still exists today and overlaps with anti-Zionism. Highlighting anti-Jewish attacks is important to keep us alert, our eyes open. But I sometimes find people deriving an almost perverse pleasure from hearing that there has "again" been an anti-Jewish attack—the Holocaust has become the lens, the central pillar of identity that beckons to be mentioned at every possible occasion.

This "Holocaust identity" directly links being Jewish with being a victim; so by definition there is an imperative need to be attacked regularly in order for this identity to be justified and validated. This attitude is, in my opinion, counterproductive. How can we free ourselves from the shackles of victimhood if we insist on using that very victimhood as the primary means by which we define ourselves?

I am Jewish, and I refuse to let myself be defined as a victim. As the daughter of survivors, I believe that we must place ourselves in the positive context of Jewish values and that we must continue teaching not only about not succumbing to being a perpetrator of evil, but also how to affirmatively choose not to become a victim. As historian Yehuda Bauer said in his January 27, 1998, address to the German Bundestag, we should add three new commandments to the original ten: not to be a perpetrator, not to be a bystander, and not to be a victim—again.

Photo: Scott C. Soderberg

Richard Primus

Richard Primus, professor of law at the University of Michigan, has served as law clerk to Associate Justice Ruth Bader Ginsburg at the United States Supreme Court and was awarded the first-ever Guggenheim Fellowship in Constitutional Studies for his work on the relationship between history and constitutional interpretation. Before studying law at Yale University, he earned a DPhil at Oxford University, where he was a Rhodes Scholar and the Jowett Seminar Scholar at Balliol College. His mother, Romana Strochlitz Primus, was born in the Bergen-Belsen Displaced Persons camp and immigrated with her survivor parents to the United States in 1951.

"The paradigm of the Holocaust will not last forever."

It is February, and cold. I am walking down State Street, at the end of the university campus. I pull my parka closer to my body, and my mind conjures an image. It is the image of another person on another cold day: *Saba* Sigmund, my mother's father, in the winter snow in Auschwitz. He had no parka. He could not predict whether he would survive the winter and, if he did survive it, whether he would see the next one. He was cold; I feel his cold; I know that I do not feel his cold.

The whole thought cycles through my mind in an instant, as it has on many other cold days, for as many years as I can remember. And as always, the next instant brings reproach. Why does the cold make me remember my *saba*'s pain, as if there weren't plenty of other pains to consider, many of them being felt right now? Why do I think of my *saba*, who no longer feels the cold, rather than sympathizing with nearby people in need who are cold today?

But of course, I now am thinking of those who suffer today. My *saba* is the gateway through which my mind passes on its way to them. I feel a bit of comfort at this thought. Not tremendous comfort: I have not relieved anyone's suffering, and I should not congratulate myself for merely remembering that the suffering exists. But my mindfulness of my *saba* is not dulling my concern for others. It is directing my thoughts to them, as I think first of him and then react. And I realize that my thought of my *saba* is different from my thought about those who suffer now. Toward them, I feel pity and, I hope, compassion, and some desire to help, and sadness for not helping enough. But I do not pity my *saba*, even when I think of him cold and starving. My mind does not work that way. He is a source of strength.

This, then, is how my mind does work. First, the Holocaust. Then, the reaction, the attempt to figure out what else I should be thinking about, besides the Holocaust.

In college I studied political theory. In class after class, I noticed that instructors and students alike regularly used the Holocaust as a way to test ideas. Any successful principle of political morality must show that the Nazis were wrong; any successful theory of political institutions must be structured to prevent Nazis from rising to power again. These were the implicit rules of the discipline. I preferred to argue in other ways. The Holocaust was personal, and too big to be put to use. Surely I could ground my ideas in something else, some problem or event other than the Holocaust. But that was a conscious preference, not an instinct. My instinct was to go to the Holocaust first. My conscious self intervened, moving the grounds of my articulated ideas elsewhere. And so it went: my mind goes first to the Holocaust, and then I remember that this is not the world but just my corner of it, and that sends me out into the world.

Perhaps my sense that the conversation in my academic field was filled with the Holocaust was partly a matter of confirmation bias. I sense the Holocaust even when I am just pulling on my parka, so of course I saw the Holocaust everywhere in political theory. It was there to be found. To me, it appeared to dominate the conversation. I wanted to know why. So I set out to examine the ways in which the Holocaust structured normative theory in law and politics in the decades after the war. But just as my thought of my *saba* ricochets to an uncomfortable thought about others who suffer in ways unconnected to the Holocaust, my fascination with the primacy of the Holocaust in shaping political ideas in my time and place led me to ask what other concerns had structured the field for those who came before the Holocaust. That question launched the project that became my entry into the guild of political theorists: a book about three separate historical traumas, in three centuries, that successively reshaped American conceptions of political morality, with the Holocaust as the third.

One implicit lesson of that project was that the paradigm of the Holocaust will not last forever. New historical traumas come and move new concerns to the fore. I wonder how I would feel if I lived to see a generation of scholars for whom the Holocaust had no more resonance than any of a dozen other historical phenomena. My sister once wrote that we grandchildren of survivors share two things: a void, and the fear that we will lose it.

I have two daughters and a son. They did not know my *saba*; he did not impart to them what he passed to me. They will know much of what I know, but they will not feel how I feel. My children do not think of the Holocaust when they pull their coats tight against the cold. I hope that they have the thought that follows that one.

André Singer

Dr. André Singer is adjunct research professor of anthropology at University of Southern California, Los Angeles; creative director at Spring Films, London; and president of the Royal Anthropological Institute of Great Britain and Northern Ireland. He is the director of *Night Will Fall*, a documentary about filming during the liberation of the Nazi concentration camps in 1944–1945. He received his doctorate in anthropology from Oxford University.

"Identity and religion are both a source of strength and a potential for conflict, but for many, in times of peace and prosperity, both remain quietly in the background. It takes out-of-the-ordinary events to bring them sharply into focus."

President Obama tells us in his *Dreams from My Father*, "My identity might begin with the fact of my race, but it didn't, couldn't, end there. At least that's what I would choose to believe."[1] Many of us take our identity for granted. We are born into it, grow within its cocoon, and have no need to question it. It gives us comfort, protection, and an indelible sense of recognition about where we stand in this tumultuous world and thus how we should behave, not only toward our peers but also toward others whose identity is different.

For many, this is where the trouble starts. It seems an almost universal reaction that the members of one group, one identity, are suspicious of members of another. They may look different, speak differently, eat different food—and believe in different gods. This suspicion can be neutralized by education and familiarity. But sometimes it intensifies into resentment and then hatred, and when accompanied by power and brutality, into acts of barbarism that change the course of history.

Identity and religion are both a source of strength and a potential for conflict, but for many, in times of peace and prosperity, both remain quietly in the background. It takes out-of-the-ordinary events to bring them sharply into focus.

When asked to contribute to this collection of reflections by descendants of Holocaust survivors, I initially felt uncertain. Yes, my mother's family from Czernowitz in Bukovina were a part of the Holocaust—some ghettoized; my grandfather, his sister, her husband and son all probably dying in Transnistria; my mother being sent to London from Vienna, and my uncle fleeing to Paris—but my identity, my belonging, my shared cultural and religious influences are nonetheless confused. Perhaps having a German gentile father and a secular upbringing all contribute, although he too, as a leading Communist figure in Berlin, endured persecution, imprisonment, and eventual flight to London via Prague. So when reading with humbleness and some awe the clarity of faith and understanding that Menachem Rosensaft was able to derive from the extraordinary experiences of his parents and others in the Nazi concentration camps, I felt distinctly inadequate.

I have spent the past year interviewing the most remarkable individuals I have ever met for a film called *Night Will Fall*. The documentary tells the story of film evidence of what happened in the camps, collated by the Allies in 1945, given dramatic shape by Alfred Hitchcock, and intended to be shown to the German people and perhaps the rest of the world; it was never completed and was shelved by the British government. The process of living with the filmed archive and hearing of the experience of such sustained and unthinkable suffering has been cathartic and life changing. Everyone needs to know what I have been privileged to hear. The individuals I spoke to were camp survivors on the one hand, but also soldiers and cameramen instrumental in the liberation of the camps on the other.

Without exception the experience they underwent had what can only be described as a spiritual impact. Menachem Rosensaft poetically summarizes his thoughts about how and whether God supported or abandoned his parents or other victims of that horrendous era by stating that "perhaps it was a divine spirit within them that enabled them to survive with their humanity intact." If I have learned one lesson from this intense involvement in the experiences of others during the Holocaust, it is that our species has an astonishing spiritual resilience in adversity.

So I return to Obama's words and conclude that I am profoundly grateful for an identity that incorporates the wisdom and experience of all my family, but as he wrote, it can't end there—it is an evolving identity that I hope to bequeath to my sons, grandchildren, and all those who follow; and I can only hope that within that identity lies a recognition of all the best component parts that make up the individual, divine or otherwise.

Dr. David Senesh

Dr. David Senesh, the nephew of the late Hannah Senesh (Szenes) and a former prisoner of war in the 1973 Yom Kippur War, is a clinical psychologist (PhD, University of Calgary) and a lecturer at Levinsky College of Education in Tel Aviv, Israel, and at The Jewish Theological Seminary of America in New York City. He is a member of the Public Committee Against Torture in Israel (PCATI) and other psychoactive organizations of professionals for human rights in Israel.

"I was born in Israel about ten years after Hannah Szenes had been executed in fascist Hungary. I had the extra burden of Hannah's legacy, which had become a part of Israeli and Jewish legend."

On October 6, 1973, I was thrown into a terrible battle, which almost claimed my life and left me psychologically injured. Some thirty years earlier my aunt, the Jewish national poet and hero Hannah Senesh (Szenes), had volunteered to try to save Jews in her native Hungary but was caught, tortured, and executed by the Nazis. Other members of my family were also incarcerated for various periods of time during the years of the Holocaust.

Reflecting on my own experiences as a prisoner of war, I ask myself whether and how suffering can also be inspiring and liberating. Can it boost resilience and hope? I reclaim my own freedom by linking my story to those of others in my family and thereby carve out my own conclusions and imperatives. For me, this is a liberating venue where cowardice and heroism, humiliation and pride, cruelty and humanity may be contained, contemplated, and become inspiring.

Communicating my own story as it has unfolded in my mind to my patients, my students, and my readers may also help them liberate themselves from their own imagined or actual prisons, just as it has helped me free myself. The question is whether I can further extend this approach to those individuals who currently occupy the position of my adversarial "others."

Redemption of captives is a formative Jewish obligation tracing back to the days of Moses. It takes time, however, sometimes forty years in the desert, sometimes even longer, before a person's psyche is truly liberated. In Jewish tradition there is a saying that "a prisoner cannot release himself." A spiritual leader or a healer may be needed to initiate the act of liberating oneself from bodily, mental, or spiritual restraints. The necessity for such an external lever or fulcrum to instigate an intrinsic change raises the complementary question of whether actually releasing another person may free oneself from one's own internal sense of imprisonment.

In order to demonstrate such relatedness between self and others, I merge my personal and family stories in ways that may transcend the measure of comfort and familiarity, extend the boundaries of conventional discourse, and distort the simple linearity of history. I allow my personal experience from the 1973 Arab-Israeli war to be superimposed on family narratives from World War II where experiences of survival and heroism reverberate.

To fully understand my story, it is imperative to anchor it to its broader historical context. On the morning of Yom Kippur in 1973, the Israeli soldiers were oblivious to any imminent threat. Arrogant, seemingly invincible after the swift victory of the 1967 Six-Day War, they felt confident and complacent. Up to that day I, as most Israelis, saw ourselves as the reincarnation of biblical warriors. We were also conscious of the ever-enduring threat of annihilation. We were both the defenders of and fugitives from our history. In retrospect, all of this, while seemingly a source of pride and strength, should also have been a premonition of an inescapable defeat.

A desert can be a huge and deadly prison. I was a nineteen-year-old soldier stationed at the Suez Canal. On the third day of fierce fighting, Egyptian tanks broke through our fortified position. Within minutes we were turned into humiliated, debased, and powerless captives. For some unknown reason, our lives were spared. Was it a divine intervention or sheer luck? Was there someone rolling the dice? I remembered Hannah's poem describing her struggle with the same questions while she was awaiting death in her Budapest prison cell.

We were handcuffed, blindfolded, and taken to a central prison in Cairo. The Egyptians had no respect for any convention or law pertaining to the humane treatment of captured soldiers. There was a blend of built-in neglect and oversight of basic needs, alongside a systematic, intentional, at times sadistic cruelty. At first, there were extremely aggressive interrogations accompanied by beatings and other forms of torture to elicit military information while we were still fresh from the battlefield. Fear and pain, hunger and thirst were combined with prolonged periods of solitary confinement to soften defenses and break the prisoner's body and spirit. This resulted in a sense of mental void, numbness, disorientation, and confusion.

I was constantly wary of the risk of losing my own mind. My continual conversations with myself kept me in touch with the core of my being, which I knew to be my last impenetrable stronghold. The battlefield had transformed itself from a military confrontation to a more personal domain, where psychological warfare proved to be equally cruel and dangerous. It struck me that although facing other circumstances and adversaries, I was nevertheless following my father, grandmother, and aunt in a struggle for life and sanity. I knew then that I must tough it out and that my response could make a difference.

In my cell, I contemplated my fate, my family heritage, and the history of my people at large. I was born in Israel about ten years after Hannah Szenes had been executed in fascist Hungary. I had the extra burden of Hannah's legacy, which had become a part of Israeli and Jewish legend. Born into a secular and highly assimilated Jewish family in Budapest in 1921, Hannah confronted the rising waves of anti-Semitism by becoming a Zionist and immigrating to Palestine, only to be re-summoned by an inner voice that called her to save Hungarian Jewry from extermination. Her inner conviction, writings, and mission had become a dictum for many Israelis like myself who were willing to sacrifice their lives for their country.

In October 1973 I felt myself, like Hannah, to be in the midst of a deadly vortex. There was no way of knowing who would survive that dreadful Yom Kippur and who would perish, who would die by water and who by fire, who by bullet and who by shrapnel, who by a wound and who by imprisonment.

Hannah's story ended all too prematurely and tragically. She joined a small group of youngsters in Palestine who volunteered to go on a mission conceived by the Haganah and the British army to cross enemy lines into Nazi-occupied Europe. Hannah's plan was to go back to Hungary to organize and attempt to rescue the Jews there. However, in March 1943, after Hannah and the others had parachuted into Yugoslavia, Hungary was invaded by Germany. Against all odds, Hannah nevertheless continued her mission but was immediately captured upon crossing the border. Tortured by the Gestapo, she refused to talk even when her interrogators confronted her with her mother, my grandmother, to make her cooperate and disclose classified military information.

Imprisonment and torture are inseparably weaved into my family history. Not only was Hannah's mother, Catherine, held in the same prison as her daughter, but my father, George, was incarcerated in Spain after escaping the Nazi invasion of France and crossing the Pyrenees. Unlike Hannah, Catherine and my father were both eventually released. Both made their way to Israel, and my father participated in Israel's War of Independence.

Israel was supposed to guarantee a secure place for the Jewish people. It seemed to me in my prison cell in Egypt, however, that settling in our ancient homeland had resulted in more hardship, war, and imprisonment. I wondered then and still wonder today whether we are ever able at all to determine our own destiny.

As we know, personal and collective traumas do not allow for a full range of experiences, resulting in a compromised inner discourse. Thus restricted, the mind then loses its flexibility to process and express its experiences and vitality. When trauma involves a transition from power to helplessness, a combatant soldier becoming a captive will experience a reduced sense of continuity, agency, and selfhood. In my case, I was dispossessed of my own personal narrative and compelled to proceed in a linear and predictable way. Later on, physical prison walls were replaced by repression and silence. Fear, suspicion, hatred, and revenge became the chains that could limit the psyche from exercising its autonomy and relatedness to the fullest.

When remembering and retelling a story there always exists an opportunity to repent, repair, and redeem oneself from its powerful hold. We may then need others to help us liberate ourselves from imprisonment of past impingements and insults. Are those the teachings of our ancestors' stories that may reshape the course of our own narrative? How can traumatic stories be reconstructed by attentive and supportive witnesses to become meaningful and inspirational?

Wars are never really over even when they are finally over. Psychological imprisonment may continue years past formal release. Post-traumatic symptoms outlive the most fortunate circumstances, the most generous of compensations, and the best of treatments. Doubts and questions continue to torment psychologically wounded warriors. We ask ourselves: Is it appropriate to condone surrender, or should soldiers be urged to fall on their swords? Is martyrdom a sign of strength or weakness? For me, these questions took on a personal relevance in light of my heroic ancestors. Did I qualify to follow in their footsteps? Did I fit in the line of dead heroes and glorious survivors?

When free, the haunting experience of imprisonment may still be relived and reenacted by minor transgressions and can penetrate later relationships. Innocent queries or demands may remind a former prisoner of war of former acts of cruelty in interrogations and tortures. By the same token, salutary experiences can undo previous trauma and unchain the inflicted spirit.

Over the past forty years I have practiced psychotherapy in an attempt to help other people transcend difficulties and limiting life circumstances. In my practice, teaching, and research, I attempt to acquire more freedom by expanding my knowledge and expertise. The gains for patients, students, and fellow professionals help me expand my own sense of mastery, efficacy, and freedom, pushing away the mental walls of a hidden prison. I challenge the chains of fear, distrust, hostility, and prejudice that keep us anchored to its walls. I have also specialized in the study and practice of conflict mediation, group dialogues, and restorative justice, especially along the lines of ethnic diversity and social inequality.

In recent years I have proceeded beyond the symbolic boundaries of my practice and classroom and feel summoned to help people within Israel in situations where political oppression and state laws compromise human rights and limit freedom of movement and expression.

A recent example demonstrates how a growing sense of freedom may impact another person's real-life circumstances. Abraham is a young Muslim Eritrean refugee who escaped death and torture in his native country, was then trafficked through the Sinai desert, and was caught illegally crossing the border into Israel. I had the privilege of conducting a forensic psychological assessment on his behalf, which found him to be post-traumatic to such a degree that the authorities could no longer keep him incarcerated. On the eve of Passover 2013, he was among the first and few refugee inmates in Israel to be released from prison. This was a rewarding and liberating experience for me. I felt that my own imprisonment and that of my ancestors were the impetus behind Abraham's actual release. I felt that I was part of a long Jewish tradition of warriors who fight for human freedom and dignity and that by doing so I am asserting my own.

Tali Zelkowicz

Originally from Vancouver, British Columbia, Tali Zelkowicz is a sociologist of Jewish education and received her PhD in the sociology of Jewish education at New York University in 2007, following a master's in Jewish education (2000) and rabbinical ordination (2002) from Hebrew Union College–Jewish Institute of Religion in Los Angeles. Her research focuses on ethnographic investigations of Jewish day schools, specifically exploring the role of conflict in identity formation as contemporary Jews strive to straddle multiple cultures simultaneously. She lives in Los Angeles with her husband and two children, where she teaches graduate courses in sociology of Jewish education, professional learning, and curriculum design at the Rhea Hirsch School of Jewish Education at HUC-JIR, and is working on a book titled *Teaching on Eggshells: Dissonance and Ethnic Identity Formation.*

"That same audacity it takes to claim a narrative in a family's survival legacy brings emotional freedom. Rather than more Holocaust content, today I have a new yearning: To let go without leaving. To be released without rejecting."

The film crew at the "10th Anniversary Tribute to Holocaust Survivors: Reunion of a Special Family," held in 2003 at the United States Holocaust Memorial Museum in Washington, DC, and attended by seven thousand survivors and their families, did not just want to interview my grandmother. They wanted to interview her *with me.* This broke sharply with a longstanding, deeply ingrained script in my life. In all my thirty years, she had always been the rightful interviewee, and I her devoted recorder, witness, and ambassador to the outside world. After all, it was her testimony that the world needed to hear.

I grew up with four grandparents who were Holocaust survivors. Although I was not close with my father's parents, who moved to Israel soon after the war ended, the stories they told me also factored into what seemed like the virtual impossibility of my own existence. My paternal grandmother was transported from Poland to Germany, where she survived the Bergen-Belsen concentration camp.

My paternal grandfather survived regular beatings in Siberian work camps. My maternal grandfather and his six siblings and parents escaped their shtetl in Poland because his mother walked with them across the border into Russia, where they spent the rest of the war hiding in forests. But ultimately, it was my maternal grandmother, only forty-five when I was born, and still sending her love in the form of baked goods to family around the world, who became my direct and regular conduit to the Holocaust. Helping my then twenty-three-year-old single mother, "Baba" became a second parent to me. And I became her emotional translator.

The producer explained, "We would like to know how the intergenerational experience of attending the reunion has been for you both, together and separately."

Now I was sweating. I didn't have a "Holocaust story" to tell; my job had always been to tell my grandmother's. This experience was about her and for her, not me. Thankfully, I was an *outsider*. Sure, my mother and other children of Holocaust survivors—the so-called second generation—had intergenerational stories to tell. But not me, who was twice-removed and safely born almost three decades after the war had ended. But there was no time to reflect. The spotlight and video camera crew were in our faces, and the interview had begun.

While I went to DC with my grandmother to support and help her, it turned out that this *reunion of a special family* included me. There was no doubt how significant the event was for my grandmother. "This is my last chance," she whispered to me at the registration table. "Who will still be here in ten years?" But in a wholly unexpected and liberating way, the experience was pivotal for me, too. As soon as I got home to New York and was back in the "normal" world where people don't eat at tables labeled "Auschwitz," I wrote something I had never even imagined uttering in public or to my family: "I Am a Third Generation Holocaust Survivor."

Even after decades of intense immersion as my family's Shoah intermediary, it still felt risky and dishonest to take my own place in this legacy of survival.

Eventually, I would realize that this impromptu interview was my initial step toward extrication without abandoning. After all, to extend the notion of what it means to be a Holocaust survivor requires the unqualified chutzpah of claiming one's own trials, *decades removed,* about the terror, the fears, the guilt, the shame, the nightmares, and the pressure to succeed and be generative. Moreover, to do so is to shed uncomfortable light on the differing darknesses of each of the three generations. Perhaps most psychologically dicey of all, to claim any unique survival narrative is to grant voice and legitimacy to the differences between *second-* and *third*-generation Holocaust survivor experiences, specifically. When all these risks can be taken, though, there may just be a way to avoid such a thing as a "fourth generation of Holocaust survivors."

For forty years now, I have served proudly and diligently at my grandmother's side. From my earliest memories of our sleepovers when I was no more than four or five, I was a witness. I listened, completely rapt, to all of her stories from the war, making repeat requests for favorites. "Tell me the one about running in the mud after a doctor on a bike," I would ask, referring to one of the times she saved her sister's life by seeking a prescription for her in the labor camp they were in, lest her sister grow too weak to work and get deported.

Of course there was the terrifying but captivating story of the time the Gestapo agent came to their door in Paris demanding that the family come with him immediately, but her mother begged for a half hour, saying there was no way she could otherwise pack up the seven children. Miraculously, he granted her request. Needless to say, no one was there upon his return.

And then there was the time my nine-year-old grandmother and her fourteen-year-old sister took a wrong turn as they were fleeing Nazi-occupied Vichy France on foot, and some strangers yelled to them, "*Zone Libre* is that way; you're going the wrong way!"

But through my child's eyes, the best stories were undoubtedly those about the convent near Marseille where the girls arrived in 1942. Replete with kindness, humanity, and safety, the convent became a virtual sanctuary for me, too. It was never lost upon me that were it not for Mère Antoinette, who took them in, or the one particular nun, Soeur Jeanne-Françoise, appointed to care for and supervise the girls (who totaled sixty-two by the end of the war), I would not be lying there next to my grandmother in bed on those Shabbes evenings.

But surely all the positive Jewish schooling and education I received would insulate me from the piercing terror of these stories.

Surely all the *freilich* holiday and life-cycle celebrations could inoculate me against any trauma. In many ways, I'm sure they did. Unfortunately, nothing can protect a child, or young adult for that matter, from the dual role of holder and detoxifier of her family's losses at the hands of the Nazis. Well before seeing *Night and Fog* or *Shoah*, or reading Elie Wiesel or even Anne Frank, I carried with me to bed each night and to school each day the images of human mutilation, of running for one's life throughout childhood, and of depending on the arbitrary and unpredictable kindnesses of people who—knowingly or not—had the power to save or damn.

Those were my regular bedtime stories until I became old enough to read, until I could find whole books about the Holocaust. In high school, my role as witness expanded into writing essays on the Holocaust and participating in Vancouver's first delegation of March of the Living, when I was fifteen. University introduced me to the academic study of the Holocaust, and I co-chaired Holocaust Awareness Week. Meeting historian Yehuda Bauer was like encountering a famous movie star. At the same time, I volunteered taking oral histories of local Holocaust survivors and wrote a Holocaust curriculum that I taught at our community Jewish high school. While living in Israel during my first year of rabbinical school, I ensconced myself in the research and writing of a fifty-page treatise about how the Shoah is taught in Israeli state schools.

In all, I wonder if my energy and desire to be immersed in the Holocaust had any bounds at all. For the first twenty or so years of my life, my Jewish gaze was virtually trained on the Holocaust. And one of the best ways to attend vigilantly to the memories was not out there in books, but right at home, through the endless witnessing of a frightful dance between my grandmother and her children. This is the dance between Holocaust survivors (trying to keep it together) and their second-generation children (trying to grow up without being a burden—that is, without being children).

Although it sounds utterly heretical, from my third-generation vantage point observing the dance from a slight but significant distance, it looked like this second generation grew up like orphans, at least emotionally. Although at times the dance looked almost loving, it was always strained. It was clear to me that it would take another generation—but hopefully not two—for my family to unlock that dark and surreal intergenerational stance. Thus does my third-generation version of enmeshment come into view: I have literally mediated that dance, through articles, papers, photographs, and interviews. In fact, even though I didn't realize it at the time, there was even a specific event when my grandmother's stories and my own life officially blended.

Not knowing it would be just two years before Soeur Jeanne Françoise's death, the original five girls who came to the convent (of whom my grandmother was one) realized a lifelong dream of hers. They brought her to the Holy Land. While in Israel, they honored her as a "Righteous Gentile" in a ceremony at Yad Vashem in Jerusalem. Due to illness, my grandmother couldn't travel at that time. However, I happened to be living in Jerusalem that year, went to Yad Vashem, and met the heroine of my bedtime stories.

As the ceremony was about to begin, an arm suddenly hooked my elbow, and I was being escorted to one of the empty places next to the other "girls" who had been hidden. In a split second, I went from honoring to being an honoree and was standing physically in my grandmother's place on the podium at Yad Vashem.

Paradoxically, though, that same audacity it takes to claim a narrative in a family's survival legacy brings emotional freedom. Rather than more Holocaust content, today I have a new yearning: To let go without leaving. To be released without rejecting. Remembering ceases to be a burden but can be an honor. Witnessing no longer takes place under threat but becomes an act of responsible loving-kindness. In this way, it is possible to prevent a "fourth generation of Holocaust survivors." I hope I am contributing to that new reality, which I might call "Jews of a fourth generation who know their past." There is a difference.

To my graduate students studying to become the next generation of Jewish educators and rabbis, I offer the chance to examine and cross-examine a host of both academic and communal assumptions about contemporary American Jewish identity formation that are often bound up in narratives of loss, scarcity, tragedy, and victimhood. As a social scientist, I have the opportunity to interrogate Jewish communal life at one of its most vulnerable and charged joints: education. Education represents no less than transmission. Too often, the burden of survival and continuity is placed on Jewish schools and teachers, with the ultimate assumption that one causes (or had better cause) the other. In other words, we still live in a world where Jewish education is expected to produce Jews or "Jewish identity," however conceived by whomever utters it.

To be sure, a rich Jewish future requires Jews who are steeped in knowledge of our history—all of our history. But a healthy Jewish future will also need Jews filled with chutzpah who are willing and able to walk away, once and for all, from a terrifying and stifling dance of entanglement with the pursuers in our past. May my students help Jews to navigate their ongoing Jewish identity formation knowledgeably and compassionately, without anyone needing to heal from it later. May the lives of those survivors and victims of the Holocaust after whom my children are named be recalled not as ominous warnings, but as strong links. And may I be the last generation of Holocaust survivors in my family.

Part III

A Legacy of Memory

"For in the end, it is all about memory,
its sources and its magnitude, and, of course,
its consequences."
    –Elie Wiesel[1]

Aviva Tal

Aviva Tal has been lecturer in Yiddish literature at the Rena Costa Center for Yiddish Studies of Bar Ilan University since 1989. Born in the Displaced Persons camp of Bergen-Belsen in 1947, she immigrated to Israel in 1952, served in the Israel Defense Forces with the rank of lieutenant, and received her BA in Hebrew and English literature from Hebrew University and her MA and PhD in Yiddish language and literature from Bar Ilan University. She and her husband, Yechiam, live in Tel Aviv and have two children, Shelley and Yonatan, and four grandchildren.

"One night I had a dream: I was standing by a deep pit, a mass grave. Instead of corpses, there were layers of Torah mantles.... Over them was a layer of Torah scrolls and among them many Yiddish books.... Yiddish words and Hebrew letters. I stood by the grave and felt a life rising up toward me, living letters and living words for me to read and interpret."

It all began in Tel Aviv, shortly after I made aliyah with my mother (my father had come here earlier). My mother, a tall, slim, beautiful woman, with blond hair and green eyes, exquisitely dressed and coiffed, and I, a chubby five-year-old, with braids tied with ribbons, would sit together, my eyes glued to her soft face, listening with halted breath to her melodious voice.

She would tell me stories about her school days in Lodz, her loving parents, her eight brothers and sisters, all brimming over with laughter and song. And then came the other stories, the ones I dreaded. One of them in particular, though gruesome and painful, had a special significance, which I didn't fully understand at the time:

My mother was carrying a heavy load of coal, coughing, stumbling, vomiting. All of a sudden a woman began singing, in Yiddish, "I thank you *Gottenyu*, dear God, that I am a Jew." Some women picked up the tune, and soon gales of laughter went through the lines of the emaciated, starving women. The German guards started to swing their whips, lashing at the women and screaming abuse. But the women couldn't stop laughing. On and on they sang under the brutal blows, their hands and feet bleeding in the snow of the freezing winter morning in the Ravensbrück concentration camp. Their punishment was to stand barefoot in the snow for many hours without food and water. Some fainted, others became sick. None of them thought it was too high a price to pay for the laughter. I have never told this story until now.

I was born in 1947 in the Bergen-Belsen Displaced Persons camp, an only child to my parents. I had been a pampered child, talkative and full of energy. I spent most of my time with adults, family and friends of my parents, survivors of the slaughter. One day, after a short plane ride, I landed in an Israeli sandbox with children in shorts and sandals. I did not understand a word they were saying. From shock I stopped speaking for a whole year. In kindergarten plays, I was given the role of a tree or a duck. At home I spoke German. The language I heard from my aunts and uncles and in the streets and shops was mostly Yiddish, not Hebrew. I was not allowed to speak German, then a forbidden language, in public. Once I did so on a bus, and the other passengers almost beat me and my mother. So I was mute on the streets as well. And since at that time I had no friends my own age, I would listen to my parents' stories.

I decided to make it all up to them and also to their childless survivor friends, who treated me like a daughter. I felt I had to become a model daughter, a high achiever, never show sadness, never cry. I must become a "typical" Israeli girl, seemingly uncomplicated, robust, popular. In school I very quickly learned to read and write. I memorized poems and songs and in first grade began reading voraciously, including encyclopedias and dictionaries (it became a lifelong habit). I memorized whole chapters of the Bible. I wrote for the school newspaper, went to poetry readings, and took part in public literary debates. I was not allowed to join a youth movement but learned all their songs by heart. I had a notebook filled with texts I picked up from the radio. I began writing poetry and lyrical prose in

long flowery sentences, deriving sensual pleasure from the music of
the Hebrew language. All my other languages were hushed up. But
the Yiddish newspapers at home, the Yiddish theater, songs sung by
my parents and relatives were a reminder of another culture.

After high school graduation and enlisting in the Israeli army,
I became an officer—the highest possible achievement. My parents,
my aunts and uncles, their friends, all gathered at the ceremony. They
were crying with joy and pride when the military band started playing and we, the marching cadets, walked onto the parade ground,
carrying the blue-white flags. After the officer pins were placed on
our uniforms, we threw our hats in the air. The entire audience stood
up for "Hatikva," the new officers saluting for the first time. It was
a moment of pure joy for me but I also felt that I was saluting the
whole group around my parents. I was a symbol of their personal triumph, and this became a pattern for my academic studies, my wedding, and the birth of my two children.

I played my roles with determination until it all became too
much. One evening, during a concert, I burst out in tears. I ran out,
drove home, and continued sobbing, to the fright and agony of my
husband and children. They had never seen me cry before and were
helpless at my evident distress.

I felt that I had to take an honest and harsh look at myself and
my life. I soon realized that I had been living a life of self-denial. My
Yiddish heart had been crying all these years, and I had repressed it
mercilessly. No one around me had any idea; everybody believed the
smiling mask. But once it started to crack, it was time to take it off.

The process was long and painful. The first step, which
demanded a great deal of courage on my part, was to stop expect-
ing approval. After a recess of seventeen years, I decided to resume
my academic studies, at first without any direction or real purpose.
Literally shaking, I entered once again into a classroom. I started
with a neutral subject—art history. After a year, with growing confidence in my abilities, I landed in my own territory, the civilization
of Yiddish.

I started from scratch and, as in my early childhood, began
reading voraciously: poetry and fiction, literary criticism, the Bible
in Yiddish translation, and yes, encyclopedias. Hebrew had been a
colorful bird I snatched from the clear blue skies. Yiddish I had to
dig up from my depths. One night I had a dream: I was standing by a

deep pit, a mass grave. Instead of corpses, there were layers of Torah mantles, all blue and purple velvet, the golden embroidered words darkened and almost unintelligible. Over them was a layer of Torah scrolls and among them many Yiddish books that had been printed in Warsaw, Vilna, Chernowitz, Odessa, Moscow, New York, and elsewhere. Yiddish words and Hebrew letters. I stood by the grave and felt a life rising up toward me, living letters and living words for me to read and interpret. So I began teaching the literary Yiddish language on top of the vernacular we had spoken. I remembered the Yiddish theater performances my parents used to take me to as a child and started teaching dramatic texts. I sang the songs my family had sung to me, the lullabies, the wedding songs, the holiday melodies and *niggunim*. And then there were the pre-war Yiddish films and the few survivors' films, which played in Israel for a short time and quickly disappeared, that I had once watched with my parents and now revived in my classes.

It was only after I finished my MA and my PhD (both cum laude) that I felt a wholeness in my spirit. For the first time in my life, my Hebrew identity and my Yiddish self came together. I achieved this on my own and for myself alone. I could now fulfill what has become my life's dream: to create a living Israeli-Yiddish community, truly intellectual, knowledgeable, witty, singing. I accomplished that as well.

But it was only in recent years that I felt confident enough to read and teach the literature of the Shoah. To my and my students' amazement, many of the texts that spoke of horrible losses and sorrows breathed with great energy and courage. There was defiance even in the bitterest laments. Most of them were written in Yiddish and many by writers who had written in Hebrew before the war and turned to Yiddish when faced with annihilation.

And then I remembered my mother's Ravensbrück story and for the first time understood the spirit and courage behind it.

When my mother contracted Alzheimer's, I grieved with her over the loss of her acute memory and her life skills. I came to see her a few days before she died. As I was sitting and trying to talk to her, I do not know what compelled me to sing one of her favorite Yiddish songs. All of a sudden she joined me. And I knew that it was all still inside her. I only needed to find it.

Cantor Azi Schwartz

Cantor Azi Schwartz has been the cantor at Park Avenue Synagogue in Manhattan since 2009. He earned a master's degree in music from the Mannes School of Music in New York City, where he majored in voice and conducting, is a graduate of the Tel Aviv Cantorial Institute, and studied classical music at the Jerusalem Rubin Academy of Music and Dance. Born and raised in Israel, he also graduated from the Har Etzion Hesder Yeshiva, completed his military service as a soloist in the Israel Defense Forces Rabbinical Troupe, and has performed, among other places, in the United Nations General Assembly Hall, the United States Capitol Rotunda, the Knesset, and Carnegie Hall.

> "I feel an enormous responsibility
> to perpetuate the music, the culture,
> the spiritual essence and the soul of
> pre-Holocaust European Jewry."

In June of 2000, standing outside Block 24 at Auschwitz-Birkenau, I held in my hands a letter from Grandma Irene, my mother's mother, that she had given me with instructions not to open it until I would be where she had been fifty-six years earlier.

I was an eighteen-year-old Israeli in Poland as a member of the Jerusalem Great Synagogue Choir. The previous evening we had given a concert in Krakow during that city's annual Jewish Culture Festival. That first visit to Auschwitz was one of the most difficult experiences of my life.

I am the grandson of four survivors of the Shoah. Grandma Irene was deported to Auschwitz from her hometown in Slovakia in 1944 and was liberated by American troops at the Mauthausen concentration camp in Austria in the first days of May 1945. She met my Grandpa Imbu, who had also been an inmate at Auschwitz and Mauthausen, in the transit camp of Atlit after they had both made their way to Israel, then Palestine. My father's parents, Geeza and Yoji, both came from eastern Hungary and survived, respectively, Buchenwald and Terezin, and Auschwitz and Plaszow. They married in Hungary after the war and then also came to Israel.

Grandpa Imbu was a phenomenal cantor but had to work as a farmer to make a living. He led services every year on the High Holy Days until his premature death in 1986. As a little boy, I used to sit on his lap and he would sing to me. Grandma Irene has always told me that he believed that I would be the one to continue our family's cantorial tradition. His angelic tenor voice inspires me every day of my life.

"Did you see my beautiful black braids?" Grandma Irene, to whom I have always been extremely close, asked me in the letter I read at Birkenau that June day in 2000. "My dad's *t'fillin*? Did you see my mom's wig? Did you see their shoes? We arrived to Auschwitz on the last transport. My wounds will never heal. Now you know why I often cry, especially on Friday nights and on holidays. I was fifteen years old when my life changed."

As a cantor, I am often invited to chant the *El Maleh Rachamim* prayer at Holocaust commemorations. I had the great privilege of doing so at the United Nations and in the US Capitol Rotunda in Washington, DC. Even more meaningful for me, however, was when I was invited to chant this prayer at Yad Vashem in Jerusalem on Yom Hashoah in 2013. Grandma Irene was in the audience that day, together with my parents. Their presence made me feel that I was representing my family and the entire Jewish people. My grandmother told me that for her, the pain and mourning of the commemoration were made more bearable by a sense of pride and perhaps even victory.

Given the history of my family, it is not surprising that I feel an enormous responsibility to perpetuate the music, the culture, the spiritual essence, and the soul of pre-Holocaust European Jewry. I want my cantorial students at Hebrew Union College–Jewish Institute of Religion to be able to place our prayers in a historical context. I try to relate the prayers we sing today to events that happened before and during World War II. This understanding helps them to become better cantors emotionally, intellectually, and musically. I tell them, for example, about the great hazzan Gershon Sirota, who refused to leave the Warsaw Ghetto and was killed there. We try to imagine what his chanting of the *Avinu Malkeinu* (Our Father, Our King) prayer during the 1942 Rosh Hashanah service meant to his fellow Jews in the ghetto.

At the same time, I believe that the melodies of our contemporary prayers must not merely be nostalgic relics of the past. They must be relevant and, more important, sound relevant to Jews today, in the present. My way of accomplishing this is by re-creating, composing, rearranging, or commissioning music that retains the integrity of our people's musical DNA and at the same time resonates with Jews living in the twenty-first century. I encourage the composers I work with to be creative without losing the connection to the Jewish world that was almost destroyed.

Amichai Lau-Lavie

Amichai Lau-Lavie is an Israeli-born Jewish educator, performance artist, and writer. Described by the New York *Jewish Week* as "one of the most interesting thinkers in the Jewish world," he is the founder of Storahtelling Inc. and the spiritual leader of Lab/Shul NYC.

"My grandmother is now a lake. 'The ashes,' mother says, 'were spread in the lake that was next to the camp, divided by a brick wall.' Now there is no wall, just a blue lake in green German scenery. My grandmother is now a lake."

"Even if we are all wise, all educated, all as knowledgeable as our elders, all of us familiar with the whole story, even then we are obligated to tell the story of how we were liberated from Egypt. And the more you tell—the better."

(THE PASSOVER HAGGADAH)

An Arabic woman, around the same age as my mother, is standing at the entrance to the Jerusalem Market, holding bunches of green herbs, a basket of white horseradish roots at her feet. "Bitter herbs," she quietly announces to the passersby, intent on their shopping. It is Passover Eve and the market is very busy.

"Bitter herbs."

My mother lingers at the cucumber stand, and I stop behind her and look at the fish jumping around in the fish stand. One fish jumps onto the sidewalk, onto the filthy cement, its eye piercing the arched plastic roof and through it the very gray sky. A young boy grabs it in one hand, the same way I'd pick a piece of paper off my carpet, holding a cigarette in one hand, and with the other hand tosses it back to the crowded shelf of wriggling fish.

When I was younger we'd go to the supermarket on Jerusalem Street, and I sat inside the cold metal shopping cart, my feet tucked under the handles and my mother's hands pushing the cart and me toward the food. In the fish department my mother would pause, and there we'd watch the metal pool where a man in a soiled apron would fish the fish out of the water and hit them on the head with a big piece of wood and they would stop wriggling. My mother's hands pushed mine away, inside the cart. She pushed me in a baby's pram, and then in a stroller, and in a shopping cart. Once on my back, then sitting, and now I walk next to her, her hands point the way, pushing us both forward through the crowds.

When I think of fish I think of carts, when I think of carts I think of trains, when I think of trains I think about crowds.

Crowds. "In January 1945, when she got there, they put 1,000 people in barracks that were made for 250." My mother navigates through the traffic lanes heavy with cars and honks. She turns left off King George Street and into the parking lot nearest to the market. She is telling me about Ravensbrück, the concentration camp where my grandmother, my father's mother, died. "It is a beautiful resort area in Germany," she says. The night before, my parents had come back from There. My father had gone to see the site of his mother's death, and my mother had joined him.

My grandmother is now a lake. "The ashes," mother says, "were spread in the lake that was next to the camp, divided by a brick wall." Now there is no wall, just a blue lake in green German scenery. My grandmother is now a lake.

Before that she was a corpse, open eyed and open mouthed in a mass of crowded corpses. Before that she was an identifiable corpse next to a woman skeleton, who saw and recognized and maybe gently closed the dead eyes, and then removed her to the mass of other bodies.

"It was so cold, we couldn't get out quickly enough." My mother turns off the engine, and we head out to the market. We pass by the Arabic woman selling the bitter herbs, by the cucumber stand, by the fish, by the boy. The shopping cart that I'm wheeling behind me is getting heavier. I just want to go away, to leave the cart in the middle of the crowded market alleyway, and let mother worry, be angry, get stuck with a cart full of fresh deaths and bitter herbs. But I help her until the cart is full and noisy plastic bags full of fruits bind my arms, and finally we walk back to the car.

"I've got to go," I tell her. "I'm going to the ghetto." I mean that I'm going to Mea Shearim—the ultra-Orthodox quarter of the city. She doesn't reply or maybe doesn't hear. I cross King George Street, bundled up in a leather jacket, thinking about my mother, and my father, and my father's mother.

Second, maybe third grade. I am sitting in the big cold assembly hall at school. We're here because it is the Fast of the Tenth of Tevet, and the principal explains that this is the official memorial day for all those who died in the Holocaust and whose date of death is not known, who do not have a gravestone in the field of time. On this day my father always lights a memorial candle for his mother, and only that day I understood why.

I go home and take a framed photograph off of the wall. My grandmother is looking straight at the camera. My father, Tulek, is to her right, and his younger brother, Millek, to her left. She is very beautiful. They are all wearing furs. The window is open in my room and it is cold but I don't close it. It was colder There and they didn't even have shoes.

I sit on my bed and look into her eyes. I know she died of hunger, alone. I know that by that time she already knew that her husband was dead. Did she know Millek was dead too? The last time she saw him was on the night of the deportation. He was clutched to her back, under her coat, and Lulek, her youngest son, was clutched to her front. The German soldier called her name off the list and she was allowed to leave the crowded synagogue where they were kept. The children's names were not called out so she risked it. The German at the door lifted his hands in the air and with one swift blow separated her from Millek. Lulek, whom I once saw demonstrate this moment, raised his hands up in the air clasped tight and coming down heavy. Lulek survived. Millek was left behind. I know he ended up in Treblinka with his father. But what did she know?

I knew that she was born on January 1, 1900, and died sometime in the winter or early spring of 1945, not long before the liberation. One woman who saw her die told a man who brought my uncle Lulek a piece of paper one day and he brought it to his brother Tulek, my father, who read the note and tore it up and then tore his shirt and Lulek's shirt too. They were wearing shirts that they had taken from the SS guards' uniform storage at the Buchenwald concentration camp after their liberation. I read this once in a newspaper interview with my uncle.

On April 11, 1945, the American army marched into Buchenwald and liberated my nineteen-year-old father and his eight-year-old brother, Lulek.

The eleventh of April is my father's Special Day. It has become a family holiday, a second birthday, a quiet celebration.

We are sitting around the table in the kitchen, the morning paper spread between us. The date: 11 April 1995. It is only a few days before Passover. Father is sitting across from me. He is still wearing his coat; the suitcases are still by the door, next to the duty-free bags with Swiss chocolates and foreign magazines. My mother is sorting the pile of mail. Germany is four hours and fifty years behind them.

"What was the most important moment for you on this trip?" I ask him. He thinks for a minute. "When I walked out of that camp and got into the car, with my wife, and just drove away as a free person—that was the most important moment." My parents smell nice, like perfume and airports. They smell like Europe.

The framed photograph of my grandmother hangs over my father's bed, in a simple wooden frame. Her eyes are the eyes of my father, and so are the angles of the mouth, and so are my eyes and so is my mouth.

I remember hugging the photograph tightly and crying, loudly. My sister (who was named after my grandmother) yelled at me to stop the nonsense. I yelled back that it's not nonsense. She is the oldest, I the youngest. Twelve years separate her birth and mine, her name remembering my father's mother, and my name—Amichai, "my people lives"—remembering them all.

Small fires burn in the street corners of the Jerusalem ghetto. The bread is burnt away and excited children clasp their fathers' coats as the ritual prayers are quickly chanted over the flames. The people are hurrying among the shops and I walk among them, huddled in my leather jacket, a stranger. Soon it will be evening.

Soon it will be evening and the moon will be full. We will sit around the seder table and raise our silver goblets, the ones on which our names are engraved, and we will drink the wine. My mother is now making the sweet *haroset* mix in which we will drown the bitter herbs. We will eat bitter, ground herbs bought this morning at the market. We will eat it and weep and then we will eat it and laugh.

Soon it will be evening and the moon will be full. I buy white skullcaps for myself and for my brothers and their sons. White new prayer shawls for my father and for myself. Flowers for my mother.

Compensations for everyone.

Natalie Friedman

Natalie J. Friedman is dean of studies at Barnard College. Born and raised a New Yorker, she received her PhD in literature from New York University and still resides in New York City with her husband and two children. She is the grandchild of four Holocaust survivors.

"Perhaps that is what spoke so deeply to my son ... in *The Sound of Music*. The image of the Von Trapp family climbing over the Alps to freedom, away from the dangerous Nazis, was for him a triumphant, happy, hopeful image. When I finally told him about his great-grandparents, his eyes were shining with admiration as he asked me, 'They must have been very strong to survive, right?'"

A few years ago, when he was barely four, my son began asking about ghosts. We would often crawl along the baseboards of his room, peering under the bed or opening the closet door until he was sure he was alone, and then he would get into bed and fall asleep.

I used to live in a haunted house, and sometimes I think I take the ghosts with me every time I move. After my son began asking about haunted rooms, I began worrying that he had inherited my ghosts, which was odd, considering I had yet to introduce them.

I didn't want him to meet the past in the same way I had. We lived with my maternal grandmother when I was young, and she had survived a ghetto in Hungary and three concentration camps before living through Stalin's purges and immigrating to America. Except for one sister, all of her siblings, her parents, and her extended family had gone up the chimneys in Hitler's camps. But they haunted her, and as soon as she could tell that I was a listener of stories, they began haunting me, too.

She spoke frequently of the dead; perhaps her own guilt at having survived made her push my attention away from the survivors. The stories she told me induced nightmares that persist even today, and I was determined not to pass on our family history in the same way when it came to my children. I absolutely wanted them to know about their family's relationship to the Holocaust—above all, to know they are the great-grandchildren of four survivors. But when I became a parent, I began to think that maybe I had had this intimacy with ghosts too early. I wanted to keep my children innocent a little while longer.

And so I read articles about how to prepare children for learning about the traumatic past, and I began hoarding book titles for future use. I also hoped that the Hebrew school at our synagogue might take some of the burden away from me and perhaps introduce my son, who had begun classes at the school at the age of five, to some of the nastier and more brutish bits of history, albeit in a gentler, more appropriate way.

What I didn't expect was *The Sound of Music*. My son came home from a playdate one day and told me he'd seen part of it, and he begged to see more. After viewing this gentle tale of a noble-hearted Austrian resister, the brave and resourceful ex-nun whom he married, and his singing children, my son became obsessed with finding out more about World War II and these "Not-sees" he kept hearing about. "Why are they called the 'Not-sees'?" he would ask me. "And why were they so mean?"

I realized that not only could I not shelter him from history, I had a budding historian on my hands, a child as interested in stories from the past as I had been. When he turned seven, I bought him some books that I considered as age appropriate.

I braced myself. He had learned some of the facts about the Shoah. It was time for me to tell him about our family. As I mulled over how I would introduce him to the ghosts, I recalled something a friend had told me. He is a black man who grew up in the white

Midwest, and he had heard terrible truths from his family as he was growing up, too. We were both traumatized by what we had learned in our families, and we didn't want to induce trauma in our own kids. "So maybe," he said, "we need to stop telling them we are the victims and tell them instead that we are the victors. We are here, today, because those people who came before us made it out alive."

Although I often resist the language of victory and the triumph of survival, because I believe that survivors of the Holocaust made it out alive because of a combination of luck and stamina, I embraced my friend's optimistic view. Perhaps that is what spoke so deeply to my son, after all, in *The Sound of Music*. The image of the Von Trapp family climbing over the Alps to freedom, away from the dangerous Nazis, was for him a triumphant, happy, hopeful image. When I finally told him about his great-grandparents, his eyes were shining with admiration as he asked me, "They must have been very strong to survive, right?"

I hugged him hard. Focus on the survivors for now, I thought. The ghosts can wait.

Ethan Bronner

Photo: Kevin Percival

Ethan Bronner is the deputy national editor of the *New York Times*. He has also been deputy foreign editor, Jerusalem bureau chief, and education editor for the paper. He is a graduate of Wesleyan University and the Columbia University Graduate School of Journalism.

"Jewish willingness to engage with Poles, to visit here and help Poland come to terms with what happened on its soil, is good not only for the Poles. It is good for the Jews, an act of self-exploration."

For a Jew who associated Poland with historic anti-Semitism, the scene felt unreal: a group of Polish high school students, in their jeans, jackets, and adolescent hairstyles, earnestly arranging jagged pieces of Jewish gravestones into a memorial shrine. The site was the overgrown and no longer marked Jewish cemetery in the tiny central town of Sienno (population two thousand), which until the 1930s was one-third Jewish. Guided by a Polish foundation that is trying to help the young here come to terms with the phantom limb of their society's Jewish past, these pupils were showing what they had learned from a week reimagining their town before World War II.

There stood the house of the merchant Goldberg, the students noted on a walking tour. And there was the synagogue and the slaughterhouse. And here, just down the road where a squat building stands in ruins, is where the Nazis herded the Jews of Sienno and neighboring towns into a ghetto before shipping them to the Treblinka extermination camp.

For more than nine hundred years, Poland was the epicenter of Jewish cultural life. In the 1930s, there were as many Jews in two Polish cities, Warsaw and Lodz, as in all of Germany. But as in the rest of Europe, they stood little chance against the Nazis. The Holocaust, which eliminated the Jews, was followed by Soviet occupation, which then expunged them from the collective conscience. To the Jews who left or survived, it felt like the Poles had no regrets.

The work of the foundation, the awkwardly named but serious-minded Forum for Dialogue Among Nations, is one of a number of signs that the situation was—or at least had become—more complicated. Poland—independent, stable, and growing in self-confidence—is starting to absorb what happened to the Jews on its soil, what that loss has meant, and what responsibility it must assume for their deaths. The goal is to rebuild relations, but that will only work if the Jews are interested. And so far, they are wary.

Historically, certainly in comparison with Germany, Poles have devoted little effort to examining their role in the Jews' fate. But from what I could see during a week's trip in Poland devoted to this issue, that is starting to shift. They are erecting memorials and museums, making films, restoring cemeteries, reviving once-Jewish neighborhoods, launching university Jewish studies departments, and looking inward. Auschwitz-Birkenau, where nine hundred thousand Jews were slaughtered, was visited in 2013 by 1.4 million people, six hundred thousand of whom were Polish schoolchildren.

"Everything Polish is partly Jewish," observed Agnieszka Smolen, our guide at Auschwitz-Birkenau, as she walked near the crematoria. "We owe these people a remembrance."

When she began her studies of Jewish history in preparation for becoming a guide, her brother and mother asked to join in.

As Dariusz Stola, a history professor at Collegium Civitas in Warsaw, put it, the number of anti-anti-Semites here has been growing steadily. One result has been a strong relationship with Israel. Today Poland is one of Israel's steadiest friends in Europe, an irony lost on no one. Israeli businesses are flourishing, and tens of thousands of Israelis visit annually.

But this is a fraught relationship. Israel believes it needs to exist because of anti-Semitism in places like Poland. As a result, Israeli visits—indeed most Jewish visits here—are built around the Zionist narrative of "Never again." Poland is the graveyard that Israel's creation helped Jews escape. So visits here are to death camps and cemeteries, where the tearful recitation of *Kaddish* and the proud carrying of Israeli flags help spur renewed belief in national purpose and unity.

Poles are trying gently—and so far not very successfully—to deepen that narrative. They want their own suffering under the Nazis acknowledged (the grim pictures at Auschwitz of Pole after Pole slaughtered there offer arresting testimony to this), but they also want the Jews to look at Poland as a place with a bright future, not merely an ugly past, including for Jews.

"Israeli youngsters come here in the wet weather and see two concentration camps and get a very bad impression of Poland," lamented Maciej Klimczak, undersecretary of state in the Polish president's office. His father, a Polish partisan, was a prisoner in both Birkenau and Bergen-Belsen, and as a boy Mr. Klimczak accompanied his father to meetings of former Auschwitz prisoners. One of his goals is for there to be far more encounters between Polish and Israeli schoolchildren. The Israelis have not expressed a great deal of interest in the prospect.

But Jewish willingness to engage with Poles, to visit here and help Poland come to terms with what happened on its soil is good not only for the Poles. It is good for the Jews, an act of self-exploration. It certainly was for me. Both of my paternal grandparents were born in Poland. Being here helped me know them better.

My father's parents left Poland years before World War II for Vienna, where my father was born, and then moved to Berlin, where he spent his childhood. After Hitler came to power in 1933, he was forced out of the local state school and into a Jewish school, before being sent first to Switzerland and then, at the age of fifteen, to live with cousins in Washington, DC.

My grandparents, meanwhile, also eventually made their way to the United States via the Netherlands, incarceration of my grandfather in a work camp in Vichy France, and a perilous trek over the Alps and through Spain into Portugal, where they obtained the visas that enabled them to be reunited with their son. But many of their relatives lost their lives in the Final Solution. Standing in Sienno in October 2013, I thought of what my grandparents' and my father's fate might have been if they had remained here.

And something else must be said from this vantage point. While the parallels are hardly exact, Polish-Jewish reconciliation could provide something of a model for Israeli-Palestinian dialogue. In both cases, the majority's identity is bound up with that of the minority. To become whole again means for both sides to recognize that.

One Polish site that is starting to draw Jewish visitors that is not linked to death is the stunning Museum of the History of Polish Jews on the site of the Warsaw Ghetto. Inaugurated in April 2013, the museum focuses on Polish-Jewish life through the centuries. Along with Jewish community centers in Warsaw and Krakow—and a well-established Jewish festival every summer in Krakow—the museum is helping to provide a balance to all the sites devoted to mourning.

But resetting the balance cannot move forward without some painful discussion of historic Polish anti-Semitism inside the Roman Catholic Church and especially the vicious strain that flourished during the Nazis' occupation of Poland. The description of a massacre of the Jews of Jedwabne in 1941 by their own townsfolk, chronicled by the Polish historian Jan Gross in his 2001 book *Neighbors*, has forced long-suppressed facts in the open. A recent film, *Aftermath*, is a powerful fictional version of those events and has led to vicious debates in Poland.

The film's producer, Dariusz Jablonski, said the reaction after it opened, including hate mail to the star, Maciej Stuhr—a beloved comic and character actor—showed how deep a nerve it touched.

Of course, Jews faced hatred in Poland at other moments as well. One of the most infamous was the massacre of Holocaust survivors who returned to their homes in Kielce, north of Krakow, in

July 1946. In 2007, a public monument was inaugurated to commemorate that pogrom and declare that such a thing would not happen again. The work is a menorah sinking into the earth, as if being absorbed by quicksand.

Watching the determined high school kids in Sienno restore the Jewish cemetery, joining the Krakow Jewish community for Shabbat dinner on Friday night, and speaking to a range of deeply serious non-Jewish Jewish scholars here, one couldn't help but think of that Kielce menorah and wonder: Is it sinking? Or rising?

Elaine Culbertson

Elaine Culbertson is executive director of the American Gathering of Jewish Holocaust Survivors and Their Descendants and director of the Holocaust and Jewish Resistance Teachers' Program. She has taught English methods courses at the University of Pennsylvania for Teach for America master's candidates, worked as a consultant to the Philadelphia school district on issues of high school reform, and retired in 2006 as director of curriculum and instruction in the Wallingford-Swarthmore, Pennsylvania, school district, ending a thirty-six-year career. She is the chair of the Pennsylvania Holocaust Education Council, a statewide organization of teachers, survivors, and liberators.

> "As I grow older, my emotions are more intensely triggered by something I call the 'presence of absence.' It is a feeling I have known since childhood."

I travel each summer directing a program for American high school teachers studying about the Holocaust. One would think that after many, many years, the authentic sites we visit in Poland, Germany, and the Czech Republic, the concentration and death camps, railway stations that served as departure points to hell, cemeteries and monuments, would have lost their effect on me, at least a bit. But nothing could be further from the truth. As I grow older, my emotions are more intensely triggered by something I call the "presence of absence."

It is a feeling I have known since childhood. No grandparents, one aunt, one uncle, three cousins. Where are the others—where are the people who are supposed to populate your family? That was a hard question to pose to my parents, both Holocaust survivors who suffered such tragedy in their young lives. I did not want to upset them about anything, least of all by demanding an explanation of something that I now know cannot be explained.

To be a member of the second generation is to exist in a rare space. Your very presence defies the odds. You were not supposed to be here at all. You serve as a stand-in for all those who were lost. You bear the names of your murdered grandparents, your murdered aunts and uncles, some of them small children who never reached adulthood. Though it is against Jewish tradition to name children after those who died young, our situation demanded a different response. So we carry these names that brought both heartache in the reminder of the loss and joy as we grew to adulthood, safe from the hands of the murderers.

In the summer, I follow the path my grandmother Chava Golubowicz walked at Birkenau. Her two older daughters were selected to live, but she and her younger children, a boy and a girl, were not so lucky. My heart cries out to her especially. I am a mother, and I cannot fathom what it would mean to walk with your children to certain death. At Belzec, where my other grandmother, Malka Freilich, was murdered along with her teenage daughters and son just days after giving birth to a baby girl, I light a candle and hope that she knows I am there. I bear their names, their blood runs through me, and if it is possible, I am filled with loss for those I never knew. Their absence is permanently mine to hold.

Their story deserves to be told, not only to the grandchildren and great-grandchildren they never saw, but to others for whom it might make a difference. As a teacher, while I know it is important to convey the history of the Holocaust to my students, I believe that the stories of individual lives are equally vital. This is at once a burden and my passion. My family comes alive for me in telling what happened to them. Perhaps I am standing in the exact places they stood, under the same sky. The teachers I travel with remember the stories that I relate and tell them to their students when they return home. The absent become present, if only for a moment.

Stephanie Butnick

Stephanie Butnick is a senior editor at *Tablet Magazine*. She has a bachelor's degree in religion from Duke University and a master's degree in religious studies from New York University.

"My life is the sum of many experiences, my own and those that preceded me, and I am very much a product of my family's legacy, in the best possible way."

I grew up in a Jewish home in a predominately Jewish town in a predominately Jewish suburb. I spent two hours every Monday, Wednesday, and Sunday at Hebrew school, and attended High Holy Day services with my family at our local Conservative synagogue. I was Jewish, of course, just as everyone around me seemed to be, but I could sense early on that the world of Judaism in which I existed was just a bit different from everyone else's.

None of my friends, after all, had great-aunts and great-uncles and grandparents with inky numbers scrawled on their forearms. I understood it from a young age as something that set my family apart—set me apart—and somehow marked us, too. We were a family of Holocaust survivors, and that was the lens through which, unbeknownst to me at first, every biblical account I read and every prayer I learned was filtered. From a young age, my faith was bound to my family's legacy; their stories my ritual text, their sorrows my liturgy.

We eat matzah to remember the unleavened bread our ancestors were forced to eat as they were fleeing Egypt, one of my Hebrew school teachers explained to the class before Passover one year. I remember instinctively raising my hand. We don't eat scraps of potato, I countered, to glorify what prisoners in concentration camps were forced to eat. So why would we eat matzah? I'll always remember the look on my teacher's face—a mix of perplexed surprise and resigned exhaustion that I can understand far better now than I did then.

In my early teens I devoured books like *Number the Stars* and *The Devil's Arithmetic*, unwittingly subjecting myself to nightmares about roundups and check-ins. I obsessed over the particulars of Anne Frank's hiding quarters and wondered how people knew what to grab from their homes as they were being forcefully ushered out. My adolescent peers, I was certain, were not weighed down with the same crushing existential questions.

It was on a trip to Germany in 2005 to commemorate the sixtieth anniversary of the liberation of the Bergen-Belsen concentration camp that I became distinctly aware of another set of emotions surrounding this part of my life: anger, and something I was surprised to find resembled jealousy. Also on the trip, which was sponsored by the local German government, were dozens of former inmates of the camp, plus a handful of children and grandchildren of survivors. My own grandparents, who met at the Displaced Persons camp at Bergen-Belsen, had died when I was four years old, and my sister, my cousins, and I, then a senior in high school, seemed to be the only teenagers on the trip who weren't sharing the powerful experience with their grandparents.

I realized then that I had missed out on years of questions, stories, and, more acutely, years of a real relationship with my grandparents. All I had were my pieced-together memories, grainy home-movie footage, and secondhand accounts of their experiences during the Holocaust. The lore I had been consumed by when I was younger had been largely cobbled together from what I knew about them at the time, snippets of stories of my grandmother surviving because of her skill as a seamstress, of cousins and uncles looking out for each other during the war and after. It wasn't fair, my seventeen-year-old self angrily thought. There were so many more things I needed to know.

It was on that trip that I learned about my grandparents from the friends they had made at the DP camp, who would become lifelong friends after they all immigrated to the United States. I heard stories—and saw archival photographs—of a theater troupe my grandparents were a part of, and I ate meals in the same dining hall they would have eaten in after liberation. Here, in this strange, unsettling place, I felt closer to them than I ever had. During our tour of what had been the concentration camp and the area surrounding it, I picked up a small rock from the train tracks and put it in my pocket.

When I came back home, I placed the rock on a shelf in my bedroom as a tangible reminder, a memento of sorts, of not just the trip but of my grandparents.

When I got to college that fall, I enrolled in a course about Holocaust memory and memorials. I had never studied the Holocaust in an academic setting, and I wasn't entirely sure how we were supposed to approach the topic with the same distance we afforded computer science or psychology. One of the first things I learned, thanks to the notes my professor repeatedly scribbled in the margins of my essays, was that the word "survivor" wasn't supposed to be capitalized. That semester I discovered Paul Celan, Theodor Adorno, and Primo Levi and immersed myself in discursive concepts like "laughter after" and the challenges of representation and memorialization. After nearly two decades of a rather isolating fixation on the Holocaust and its aftermath, I realized I was very much not alone.

I would ultimately become a religion major, fascinated by the study of what draws people to religion and the ways in which faith dictates our decision making and understanding of the world. I went on to get a master's degree in religious studies, with a concentration in journalism, and found a fitting home at *Tablet Magazine*, where I get to unpack these issues on a daily basis as the editor of the site's blog, *The Scroll*. I'm no longer the young girl plotting escape routes from my parent's house in case the Gestapo arrived one day, though I now understand where those impulses come from—and have figured out how to channel them in a productive direction. My life is the sum of many experiences, my own and those that preceded me, and I am very much a product of my family's legacy, in the best possible way.

I think my grandparents would be pretty proud.

Moshe Ronen

Moshe Ronen is a Toronto-based lawyer, business and strategic policy advisor, and currently vice president of the World Jewish Congress. A human rights leader and activist since his student days, as president the Canadian Jewish Congress he successfully advocated the formal legislation of Yom Hashoah in each Canadian province. He is the recipient of several distinguished public service awards and has over the years collaborated closely with Elie Wiesel, Avital Scharansky, and several Israeli and Canadian prime ministers.

> "The Nazis did not defeat my
> father in the camps, and neither
> he nor my mother allowed them
> to defeat us in our home."

Mordechai Markovits was only sixteen years old when he emerged from the sea. The bodies of other Jews killed in the explosions still floated in the water as he and his brother Shalom made it to shore. There, they found themselves surrounded by armed men with their weapons drawn.

It would be a transformative moment in his life and one that would deeply affect my own.

Markovits had been an Orthodox child born in the Hungarian town of Dej. He sang in the town choir on the High Holy Days; was sent to Auschwitz at the age of twelve; joined the Irgun, the Revisionist Zionist paramilitary organization led by Menachem Begin, at fifteen; and set sail for pre-state Israel at the age of sixteen on the ill-fated *Altalena*, a ship that would be sunk by the Haganah, the paramilitary arm of the Zionist establishment, off the coast of the Land of Israel in June 1948. He subsequently spent almost twenty years in the Israel military.

He is in one way or another all these things still, and much, much more. He is also my father.

Unquestionably, his life is reflected in my own Jewish trajectory, from my membership in the Betar youth movement as a teenager to an adulthood devoted to advocacy on behalf of the State of Israel and the Jewish people.

Like my father, I have embraced the indispensability of religious practice to Jewish peoplehood and survival, and like my father and the grandfather whose name I carry, I also sing, and have served as a hazzan on the High Holy Days for thirty-five years.

This symmetry in volition and experience between father and son is especially striking given the dearth of Holocaust dialectic in our relationship.

It was only in the sixth grade that I become aware that my father was a survivor who had arrived in Israel still carrying the striped uniform issued to him in Auschwitz. And though we discussed the war openly from then on and I accompanied him twice to Auschwitz, the trauma of those years was never insinuated into our family's inner life.

While the afflictions of memory were more of a backdrop than an active ingredient in the development of my Jewish consciousness, several key vignettes from my father's post-Holocaust experiences coalesced into an animating principle in my own life.

My father had boarded the *Altalena* following an extraordinary deliberation. Shortly after the war, he and his two brothers had met again in their hometown of Dej. They spent days pondering whether it would be safest for future generations if they were to completely abandon their Jewish identity, which had marked the Jews for death and could well do so again. Ultimately, the three chose to be chosen regardless of the consequences.

Emotion consumed my father on his trip to a new Jewish beginning aboard a ship carrying arms and a thousand souls willing to fight for Jewish statehood. But the shells shattered his anticipation. As my father and uncle set foot in the Land of Israel for the first time, they found themselves once again confronted by drawn weapons. But this time the guns were in the hands of Jews, not Germans. My father's anguish at this inversion of roles was overwhelming. But then, one of the soldiers suddenly screamed at my uncle, "Are you Shalom Markovits? Why am I doing this?" He began to weep, threw his gun aside, and embraced the two teenagers—for he too was from Dej and had survived Auschwitz. Other Haganah fighters also threw down their weapons and joined them.

It was that moment when Jewish peoplehood transcended both its oppressors and internal divisions that would become the central narrative of my Jewish development. My father's description of Menachem Begin on the *Altalena* threatening to shoot anyone who fired back at another Jew has informed my commitment to the totality of the Jewish people. And it would be my father's choice to be chosen that served as the impetus for my own Jewish choices—far more than the legacy of horror he endured as a child.

There were never any illusions in our home about the precarious nature of Jewish existence, but there were no scars imposed by its ravages either. My father changed his name from Markovits to Ronen, which means "joy" or "song" in Hebrew. It is that joy, that faith, that I inherited. The Nazis did not defeat my father in the camps, and neither he nor my mother Ilana allowed them to defeat us in our home.

I owe much to the child named Mordechai Markovits and to the father who became known as Mordechai Ronen. It is a debt I will continue to repay.

Faina Kukliansky

Photo: Milda Rukaite

Faina Kukliansky, an attorney in Vilnius, is chairperson of the Jewish Community of Lithuania. In 2013 she was awarded the Cross of the Knight of the Order for Merits to Lithuania by the president of Lithuania for bringing together the Lithuanian Jewish community and preserving the heritage of Lithuanian Jews.

"I inherited the desire to learn, to strive to achieve the unachievable, not to be part of the crowd, to make independent decisions, sometimes in opposition to the great majority, and to fight against despair."

What did I inherit from my family who survived the Lithuanian Holocaust? Surely not silver knives and forks. Nor did I inherit Sabbath candlesticks from my mother's parents. They were Ríve and Hirsh-Tsvi Taube from the Lithuanian town of Šiauliai, called Shavl in Yiddish.

My grandmother Ríve was extremely beautiful, with smooth black hair, light blue eyes, and fair skin. My children and grandchildren inherited my grandmother's eyes. They are electric blue.

It was my grandmother Ríve who saved my mother, Klara, known as Kéylke, during the operation to exterminate the children in the Šiauliai, or Shávler, Ghetto; it was she who ended up in the Stutthof concentration camp with three daughters; and it was she who pulled her gold fillings out of her own mouth and sold them to save her children. It was she who came back to Šiauliai, but with only two daughters, Kéylke and Básye—the third was buried at Stutthof. She came back because she hoped to find her only son, unaware that he had been killed fighting the Nazis as a soldier in the Soviet army.

My maternal grandparents, who died while Lithuania was still under Soviet rule, prayed to the Most High until the last day of their lives, heedless of the atheism surrounding them. They were buried in the traditional way, *mit di takhríkhim* (in shrouds). I don't know why, after all the horrors, they still believed in the Most High. Perhaps because not all of their children were murdered, they believed that the Most High had taken pity on them.

Nor did I inherit silver candlesticks from my paternal grandparents, Saulas (Shéyel) Kukliansky, a pharmacist and chemical engineer, and Zísele Kukliansky, a medical doctor, who lived and worked in the cities of Veisiejai and Alytus near the Polish-Lithuanian border. Although they were highly educated, they did not observe Jewish traditions and did not attend synagogue, but of course, they did have a set of silver candlesticks at home. In that respect, most Jewish homes were alike.

The war began for my father, Samuelis (Shmuel) Kukliansky, in 1941 when he was ten and was bombed by the Germans at his Communist youth movement camp in western Lithuania. Quickly identified as a Jewish child, he was forced to clean the homes of murdered Jews.

After a long, difficult search, my grandparents found their youngest child and returned with him to Veisiejai, but they were only together again for a brief time before my grandmother Zísele was grabbed off the street by her Lithuanian neighbors, locked up, and killed. Her murderers probably included some of her own patients. My father was guilt-ridden for the rest of his life, believing that my grandparents' extended search for him had prevented the family from leaving Lithuania in time. He somehow blamed himself for his mother's murder.

My grandfather Saulas was left with three children. Despite being physically weak and traumatized by the murder of his beloved wife, he did not break down. Late one cold, rainy night in the autumn of 1941, he led his children out of Veisiejai. The next day all of the city's Jews were shot.

The Kukliansky family's wanderings had only just begun. On foot, they managed to get to the Belarusian city of Grodno. They then fled the Grodno Ghetto just before its liquidation and survived the remainder of the Nazi occupation in a cramped pit deep in a forest. My father spent his adolescence underground, knowing that his mother, grandparents, cousins, and all of his school friends had been murdered. In that pit, my grandfather Saulas taught the children geography, mathematics, and literature and sang them opera arias every day.

From that time onward there has been no Most High in the Kukliansky family. I believe my father's brother is one of only a few Jews in all of Israel today who refuses to hang a mezuzah on his door. Their God died with the murder of their mother.

I ask myself, what have we, the children of the survivors, inherited beyond the pain?

We inherited the names of murdered family members, but they were changed so that they would not sound Jewish. The war had ended, but we still had to hide the fact that we were Jews. We competed to see whose name was less Jewish. In our family, Azriel became Azalia, Jonah became Eugenius, Feygele-Tsipóyre became Faina (me), and Zísele became Zinaida. After all, we were born in the Soviet Union, where our parents, after accidentally surviving the war, were not supposed to be Jewish any longer. We were supposed to be Soviet citizens, a kind of "ethnic" identity.

We inherited the terrifying fear of war. From our childhood onward, this fear was our identity, the expression of our Jewishness. The grown-ups didn't stop talking about their memories in our presence. They did not tell their children what had happened to them, but they spoke about it all among themselves, and we drank it all in: fear hovered everywhere around us, as if our parents' awful reminiscences had been events in our own lives. Maybe that was why we became just as traumatized as they were.

When grandmother Ríve was in her advanced years, she always used to yell to me, "Feytske [the diminutive form of my name], hide! The children's *Aktion* is beginning, hide!" (An *Aktion* meant the mass deportation and killing of Jews in the Nazi ghettos.) Before we went to sleep at night, we used to ask our parents, "Will there be war?" Only after we were told "no" could the light be extinguished and we could fall asleep.

I inherited Jewishness and pride in my people. Despite the misfortunes of war, the post-war Soviet anti-Semitism, and all the restrictions on freedom in the Soviet Union, in our family we were taught to be proud that we were Jews.

When we were children, they did not tell us that Lithuanians had murdered Jews. It is only now that I am able to fully reflect on the environment in which we grew up. Anti-Semitic propaganda was rabid before and during the war and contributed to the extermination of more than two hundred thousand Lithuanian Jews, to Lithuanians looting Jewish property, to their entering Jewish homes and dividing up and selling clothes ripped from corpses, never mind stealing jewelry and paintings. What reasons were there to make them love us more after the war?

The Soviet occupation also continued the fascist anti-Semitic propaganda, and no one told us the truth about the mass murder of Jews. The Soviets even blew up the monument that Vilna Ghetto survivors erected at their own expense at Ponár (Paneriai), outside Vilnius, one of the larger Jewish mass murder sites in Europe, and erected a different one with a Soviet star in its place.

We were proud to identify as Jews, even if that didn't help our careers. When I was seven, I had to tell a children's library employee I was a Jew in order to fill out my reader's form properly. Soviet propaganda and our parents' fate are what turned me into a Zionist. I remember clearly the Six-Day War, when the Israeli "aggressors" rapidly won the war against all the Arab states. My entire athletic team refused to talk to me because I was "one of those."

I truly inherited a folkloric type of Jewishness. There was no end to singing and jokes in my mother's family, even after all the misfortunes of war. Heedless of all the troubles and comparisons of "life before the war" versus "life after the war," my mother's family preserved authentic Jewish folklore. My mother still has a blue notebook with songs from the Shávler Ghetto. Everyone sang them regularly. As a child, I never learned any other songs. Only those.

I loved being with my grandmother. Sometimes it was tragicomic. I still hear her words ringing in my ears: "Kéylke, do you remember how she lost the key in the ghetto and we couldn't go home? Oh that was funny. And remember that sweater I knitted? It was so beautiful.

Now who gave me the old wool? That winter when we were in the Kafkaz [name of a section of the Šiauliai ghetto], it was so warm thanks to that sweater. And do you recall Avrémke, who died during the children's *Aktion*? He knew so well how to make people laugh. His mother, poor thing, she couldn't endure it, she couldn't survive his death. And remember that little joke, '*Kumt Meyshke Blékher, macht dem gelékhter*' [Yiddish semi-rhyme for, "Here comes Meyshke Blecher and makes a joke"]. That was real fun ..."

And they used to laugh, the sisters Básye and Kéylke and grandmother Ríve. But grandfather Hirsh never laughed. Instead he checked, "Is everyone home? Are we all together?" And then he'd make sure the door was latched.

I inherited the desire to learn, to strive to achieve the unachievable, not to be part of the crowd, to make independent decisions, sometimes in opposition to the great majority, and to fight against despair. Baruch (Benedictus) de Spinoza wrote that that which must take place will of necessity take place. For my parents, Spinoza, who sometimes acted and thought differently from his entire community, was a role model. Do not be cattle driven to their death, even if a spiritual leader wants to lead you there. My parents and grandparents did everything they could to stay alive and to give the gift of life to their children. That is their heroism.

So I have inherited a faith in life and the future. It could not have happened any other way.

Annette Lévy-Willard

Journalist and author Annette Lévy-Willard is a senior staff writer at the French newspaper *Libération*. She has also served as a diplomat in the French embassy in Tel Aviv. Among her numerous books is *Summer Rain: A Reporter's Diary of the 2006 War between Israel and Hezbollah*.

> "We, who believed ourselves to be French, became French Jews once again."

"Happy as a Jew in France!" goes the Yiddish proverb.
    True? Well, yes and no.

The French Revolution and Napoleon indeed got the Jews out of the ghettos and made them equal citizens of their country. Then Jews came from all over Europe to live in this country of the "Declaration of the Rights of Man and of the Citizen" where they were free.

But France was also the anti-Semitic country where, at the end of the nineteenth century, a Jewish officer, Captain Alfred Dreyfus, was wrongly accused of spying for the enemy, convicted on forged documents, and sentenced to life imprisonment on Devil's Island in French Guiana. The Dreyfus Affair divided the country into two camps. The outrage of anti-Semitism was so shocking that it inspired a young Viennese journalist, Theodor Herzl, to write his book advocating for a Jewish state. And at the same time, France was the country where Émile Zola, one of its most famous writers, launched a campaign to prove Dreyfus innocent, gathered other French intellectuals behind him, and prevailed.

This is the historical backdrop to World War II. My family was a part of that history. Old French middle class from Alsace, reformists on my mother's side—they founded the Copernic synagogue—Orthodox on my father's side—they founded the synagogue on the rue Montevideo—my grandparents and parents lived in Paris.

Yes, they all survived the war thanks to the help of Catholic farmers in the French Alps, like a great many of the 330,000 Jews living in France at the beginning of the war who were saved by a local policeman, inhabitants of a Protestant town, Catholic priests, or just a neighbor, all French "righteous" men and women who helped Jewish families to escape death. Like many Jews, my parents also took part in the underground resistance that fought the Germans.

But 77,000 Jews were deported from France to the Nazi death camps and died in the Shoah. Most of them—around two-thirds—were so-called "foreign" Jews who had immigrated to France or had fled from Nazism in Germany and elsewhere in Occupied Europe. They were not considered to be "genuinely" French like my parents, who did not speak Yiddish. These refugees were arrested by the police and the administration of the Vichy government. Maréchal Pétain and his collaborationist French government volunteered to put foreign Jews on trains to Auschwitz.

So you had a "good" France and a "bad" France.

That's the legacy I inherited, as I still live in Paris, like my two brothers, raising my daughter and my son in this country. First generation, we knew what happened, we saw films, read books, met survivors. But anti-Semitism was a taboo in post-war France. Until the Israeli-Palestinian conflict hit the shores of Europe after the Six-Day War. Then our synagogues had to be guarded by the police, anti-Semitism returned in a new packaging, now called "anti-Zionism." And in a subtle way we, who believed ourselves to be French, became French Jews once again.

Julius Meinl

Julius Meinl V is president of the Euro-Asian Jewish Congress, a member of the Steering and Executive Committees of the World Jewish Congress, and chairman of the Supervisory Board of Meinl Bank AG and Julius Meinl AG. Because his paternal grandmother was Jewish, his grandfather, Julius Meinl III, was forced to flee to England with his family after the annexation of Austria by Nazi Germany, while his mother and her parents fled from Vienna to Uruguay. After the war, his father's and mother's families returned to Austria, where he was born in 1959, and he now lives in Prague.

Photo: Meinl Bank

"Only one generation after the horrors of the Holocaust we suffered a second indignity: We were denied the right to grieve for those we had lost.... The Jewish refugees and survivors, we were told, especially those who had fled and subsequently returned to Austria, had been sitting in leather armchairs in exile and hadn't experienced the real trauma of the war."

On December 18, 1932, illegal Austrian Nazis threw tear gas grenades through the windows of the fashionable Gerngross department store in Vienna. My grandfather, Paul Gerngross, the owner of the store, believed that such attacks on Jews and Jewish property were just isolated incidents, that the growing wave of anti-Semitism would pass. So did most other Austrian Jews at the time.

My family, like so many others, was decimated in the Holocaust. At first they believed that they would be spared. The exclusion, isolation, persecution, and eventually murder of the Jewish people happened step by step, slowly enough that one could keep on believing that it would all eventually pass. Only, of course, it didn't.

I was born fourteen years after the war ended, but its legacy remained etched in every family portrait that survived the war years, in every record of both my mother's and my father's family businesses. Although it was never an active part of my childhood (history classes covered great swathes of European history, but there was never time for the years of World War II, let alone the fate of the Jews), with hindsight I can see its lingering presence in our home. Following the March 1938 annexation of Austria by Germany, the *Anschluss*, my paternal grandfather's family business, the largest food retailer in Central Europe during the first several decades of the twentieth century, was taken over by the Nazis, and my grandfather together with my grandmother, my father, and my uncle fled to London to save their lives.

It all came step by step in Austria. First the enthusiastic popular embrace of the *Anschluss*, then the application of the Nuremberg Laws, then deportation and death. I still have the letters from my paternal grandmother's lawyer and doctor, both personal "friends," that much to their regret they could not represent or treat her, a Jewess, any longer.

All this simply wasn't spoken about. Only one generation after the horrors of the Holocaust we suffered a second indignity: We were denied the right to grieve for those we had lost. The real victims of the war, we were told, were the countries that had been destroyed. The Jewish refugees and survivors, we were told, especially those who had fled and subsequently returned to Austria, had been sitting in leather armchairs in exile and hadn't experienced the real trauma of the war.

After the war, my grandfather went back to Austria and helped the Allies identify Nazis who remained in positions of power, hoping that their criminality and racism would go unnoticed and unpunished. However, in an utter inversion of logic, it was he who was portrayed as being unreasonable, as acting unjustly. Those of us who should have expected remorse, introspection, and justice from the country our totally uprooted family had called home instead were shamed out of demanding justice for the crimes inflicted on us by the Nazis and their collaborators.

An element of that attitude remains very much present to this day. We hear and read all too often in the Austrian media that Jews talk too much about anti-Semitism and the Holocaust. Artworks stolen from Jews during the war years hang in public galleries, and elderly Jews are made to feel uncomfortable about asking for them to be returned.

The guilt of surviving took its toll. A cousin of my mother's who bore the exact same name as she was murdered in Auschwitz in 1943. The abnormality of leading a normal life in Uruguay while brothers and sisters and aunts and uncles had perished proved a heavy burden on my mother's family both before and after returning to Austria in 1947.

It took decades before we really spoke about those years in my home. Over the years I learned that persecution comes in many forms, that it is often masked by the prevailing zeitgeist. I learned that no one tells you outright that they want to exclude you, to remove you from society, but that they just do it one step at a time. I learned that assimilation had proved to be an all too vulnerable armor that can easily be pierced.

There is no doubt that the lessons of the Holocaust have guided me to where I am today, but as an individual I refuse to allow those who sought the destruction of my family to define my identity. The Holocaust, immediately followed by more than forty-five years of Communist dictatorship, decimated Eastern and Central European Jewry. Many young Jews in Ukraine, Belarus, Russia, and other erstwhile Communist-ruled countries have almost no connection to their own identity, having grown up in homes where no one mentioned their Jewish lineage or their Jewish heritage. It is the stories and memories of once sprawling Jewish communities, of yeshivas full of eager young students, of Jewish theater and literature, of the great Jewish thinkers, philosophers, businessmen, and politicians who were murdered, that have led me to devote myself to strengthening and helping to rebuild Jewish life in that vital part of the world. My goal, to put it simply, is to enable the Jews there to feel more Jewish.

Esther Perel

Recognized as one of the world's most original voices on couples and sexuality across cultures, Esther Perel is the author of the globally best-selling and award-winning book *Mating in Captivity: Unlocking Erotic Intelligence*, translated into twenty-five languages. Fluent in nine of them, she is a celebrated speaker, therapist, and teacher invited around the globe for her expertise in emotional and erotic intelligence, work-life balance, cross-cultural relations, and identity of modern marriage and family. She serves on the faculty of the Family Studies Unit, Department of Psychiatry, New York University Medical Center, and the International Trauma Studies Program at Columbia University.

"For me, being able to connect my family's history of suffering and death with the erotic dimension of sex as an expression of aliveness has been an epiphany that has shaped and continues to shape who I am and what I do."

My identity was imposed on me.

I say this as the daughter of Polish Holocaust survivors who had clear ideas about my purpose on earth and about the very essence of my existence from my earliest childhood. This prefab identity instantly connected me to a larger history. I was not just a daughter of two people, nor even a daughter of a tribe; I was a symbol of survival and revival for parents who together lost two hundred people under the most horrific circumstances. As a result, from the moment of my birth in Antwerp, Belgium, my life was bigger, more important than just me. I even carried the name of someone who was no longer there. My presence affirmed that these two concentration camp survivors were still human, still able to procreate. Death and dehumanization didn't prevail because I breathed. Now there could be joy. Now there must be joy. My parents did not only want to survive, they wanted to feel alive, to reconnect with life, vibrancy, vitality.

When I was four years old, I remember asking my parents about the number on their friends' arms, the numbers I eventually learned had been tattooed at Auschwitz. And I remember asking why I didn't have grandparents. This was when I first realized that other children had grandparents, and I wanted to know where mine were.

I remember being told that they had died. And then I found out where and how they died. First I heard that they died in the war. Next came the words "concentration camp." Then they talked about how many other people—how many other members of my tribe— were sent to these camps and not just died but were killed, murdered. And then it was revealed that my parents were the sole survivors of their families, of their entire clan. This is when I began to grasp what I meant to them, and this is also when I began to connect with that larger history.

My awareness of what I am here to do came gradually until it hit me: I'm not meant merely to be a small speck. This made me feel special, but also very burdened, because now I saw that I had better accomplish big things in my life. My books had better be good books. They must not be average books. Nothing in my life could merely be ordinary, good enough. It had to be much bigger, much more, because I had learned almost by osmosis that if you were only good enough, you didn't survive. To survive you had to be really daring, really cunning, really determined, in addition to being lucky. Being average, halfway, didn't get you there.

My husband, Jack Saul, directs the International Trauma Studies Program affiliated with Columbia University, where he often works with torture survivors. When he first created it, I would wonder, "When do you know that you have reconnected with life after a traumatic experience?" The answer we came to is: When people are once again able to be creative and playful, to go back into the world and into the parts of themselves that invite discovery, exploration, and expansiveness—when they are once again able to claim the free elements of themselves and not only the security-oriented parts of themselves—that's when you have gotten through.

Among Antwerp's Holocaust survivors there were two groups: those who had not died and those who had come back to life. Those who had not died were people who often lived tethered to the ground, afraid. The world was dangerous, and pleasure was not an option. They didn't trust the world to be a safe place anymore, and they generally could not experience much joy without guilt—nor could their children. They had survived—were surviving—but they were not really alive. They were too vigilant, too scared and anxious to enter the unselfconsciousness and freedom necessary to experience playfulness and fun.

Those who had come back to life understood eroticism as an antidote to death. They knew how to maintain a sense of aliveness in the face of adversity. They were able to hope, fantasize, dream, imagine, play in their mind, make love to someone they would never touch.

When you experience eroticism and sex in their full intensity, you are defying death. You feel alive as at no other moment. And this implies playfulness; it implies taking risks, being bold and trangressive. Eroticism for me is about aliveness. It's the mystical sense of the word rather than what modernity has done with it, which is to reduce it to sex.

When people come to my office and complain about the listlessness of their sex lives, they sometimes want more sex, but they always want better sex. They want to reconnect with a quality of renewal, playfulness, and connection. It is the poetic dimension they long for. These were all qualities that I had seen among those Holocaust survivors who had come back to life. Luckily, my parents belonged to this group.

When I work with couples on sexuality, I work on desire. It's about helping them to own the wanting that requires a healthy sense of self-worth that one has permission to ask, take, receive, give, refuse—that they are entitled to experience pleasure in the existential sense of the word.

This is far from the more typical emphasis on the act of sex focused on performance and frequency. The fact is that you can have sex and feel totally numb. My work is not about that. It's just the reverse.

"Touch me without touching me" invites you into the realm of the imaginary, and imagination is the central agent of the erotic act. Eroticism is sexuality transformed by our imagination. My father used to tell me of a woman he fell in love with in the camps—I suppose he made love to her only in his head. He used to tell me that it gave him energy to work in the frozen Polish winter and feel her warmth in the subzero temperatures.

For me, being able to connect my family's history of suffering and death with the erotic dimension of sex as an expression of aliveness has been an epiphany that has shaped and continues to shape who I am and what I do.

Maram Stern

Maram Stern, associate executive vice president for diplomacy of the World Jewish Congress since May 2013, previously served as the organization's deputy secretary general from 1996 to 2013. Based in Brussels, he is also responsible for the WJC's participation in interreligious dialogue and consultations with Christian churches and other faiths. In 2004, he was decorated with the Golden Laurel Medal of the Republic of Bulgaria and appointed as honorary consul of Bulgaria in Belgium (Province de Liège).

> "I know that I simply followed in the footsteps of my family history and have chosen to confront rather than evade both my Jewish identity and the shadows of trauma."

I wrote this reflective essay during Pesach, a period that holds particular significance for my family. For my mother especially, Pesach is not commemorated as an important Jewish festival that celebrates "Jewish liberation" thousands of years ago; rather, it is traumatically remembered as the beginning of the inexorable extermination of the "people of her kind"—the liquidation in the Warsaw Ghetto started on the first day of Pesach, and she subsequently lost her parents, brothers, and sisters. This traumatic experience is so deeply rooted in her brain that the elapse of years and the gradual loss of general memory—she is in her early nineties—have only made it more vivid and prominent. In fact, one of the earliest verbal phrases I learned from my mother is *"Heute sind die Deutsche ins Ghetto und haben alle Juden liquidiert"* ("Today the Germans are in the Ghetto and have liquidated all the Jews"), as she always mentions it at this time of year without, however, going into any further details.

As the second son in the family, I was born and grew up in post-war Berlin. Given the profound mistrust of Germans, my parents' decision to live in this city was very unusual and even surprising for Jewish families immediately after the war—something we never quite understood. This mistrust was reflected in the kind of education that they chose for us, as all three brothers went to Lycée Français of Berlin and received an entirely French schooling. This intellectual development certainly added "extra foreignness" to a Jewish family living in post-war Germany, and in many ways we were encouraged to keep a critical distance from the German culture from very early on.

Despite the horrors of the Holocaust, my parents, unlike many other survivors, never extensively discussed or described the event in front of us. There seemed to be a conscious attempt to suppress the trauma on their part. Yet, it is precisely my parents' silence, the unspoken, that makes every family gathering and dinner particularly unbearable for their children and grandchildren. Far from a denial of their traumatic memories, my parents' silence leaves us with infinite meanings and creates an overwhelming emotional paradox for us. On the one hand, we're in the powerful presence of the living testimony to the most appalling human tragedy, and as the immediate descendants, we're eager to know about our family history and what exactly happened to my parents. On the other hand, what exactly happened to them is so unimaginably excruciating that it has become a knowledge forever forbidden to us. Trauma resists verbalization but constantly finds its expression in eye contact and body gestures, and it sometimes gives a sudden twist of meaning to the seemingly least significant remarks. My father, for example, is utterly unable to eat if he doesn't see a piece of bread next to a cup brimming with tea on the table.

Looking at my own life in retrospect, I can't help surmising how this complex identity as a German Jew of the second generation of Holocaust survivors might have directly or indirectly shaped my personal ambitions and influenced my ultimate career choice. As expected, I studied medicine and dentistry at universities and became a qualified surgeon. However, at heart I always knew that I was interested in and even passionate about politics, especially when it involves Jewish issues, whether historical or contemporary, which is how I came to my current position with the World Jewish Congress. It was initially very difficult for my parents to accept the fact that their son had given up his promising medical career and chosen to work *for* an international Jewish organization instead. Now approaching the end of my professional life, I never regretted my decision to change my career path. I know that I simply followed in the footsteps of my family history and have chosen to confront rather than evade both my Jewish identity and the shadows of trauma.

Clarence Schwab

Clarence Schwab is founder and managing partner of Schwab Capital Management, an investment and advisory firm focused on publicly traded and smaller privately held companies. His writings about how to handle problem financial institutions and spur additional lending to small, credit-worthy businesses have appeared in the *New York Times*, the *Financial Times*, and *The Hill*. He received a BA from Columbia University and an MBA from the Harvard Business School.

> "The circumstances of my father's survival and my grandfather's insistence on coming to the aid of others have always inspired me."

At our weekly Shabbat dinner, my wife Pam and I ask our children, Zachary and Eleonora, and ourselves two questions: "Did an opportunity present itself to you this past week to help someone or protect someone from a bully?" and "What questions did you ask or want to ask in school?"

The first question encourages ethical action; the second, thinking for oneself and speaking one's mind.

I am the son of a young Holocaust survivor and the grandson of a rescuer. The Nazis and their collaborators murdered twenty members of my immediate family. When I was about eleven years old, my parents, both born in Latvia, began sharing with me my father's and other family members' experiences during World War II. And my grandfather and mother started telling me how my grandfather helped save the lives of tens of thousands of Jews.

The circumstances of my father's survival and my grandfather's insistence on coming to the aid of others have always inspired me.

I tell my children how in late April 1945 my father, George Schwab, then thirteen years old and severely undernourished after a week on a barge with just half a loaf of bread and little drinking water, was forced on a march in Germany. During the previous four years, he had survived the Libau Ghetto and several concentration and labor camps. Utterly exhausted, he no longer cared and just wanted to lie down. One of his fellow prisoners, Jule Goldberg, himself in acute pain from an injured, swollen leg bitten by an SS guard's dog, took my father by the neck of his ragged prisoner uniform, saying, "You are coming with me." This one selfless act saved my father's life. Surreally, British troops liberated them only hours later.

What matters most, I tell my children, is not someone's appearance, or intelligence, or strength, or wealth, but whether, when presented with an opportunity to do so, that person helps another in time of need—even or especially at personal cost or risk.

My grandfather, Hillel Storch, a successful businessman in Riga, came to Stockholm in July 1940 on a six-day business visa just as the Soviets invaded Latvia. As a stateless refugee who did not speak Swedish, he nonetheless managed to bring his wife and young daughter—my mother—from Soviet-occupied Latvia to Stockholm the following year. However, he could not save other family members, and his early attempts to rescue Jews from the Nazis also failed. Realizing the enormous resources needed for large-scale rescue efforts, he established and headed the Swedish Section of the World Jewish Congress, became a representative of the Jewish Agency's Rescue Committee, and established contacts with Swedish and US government officials.

In April 1944, he and a few like-minded Swedish Jews conceived a mission to aid Hungarian Jewry. They identified a young, well-connected Swede named Raoul Wallenberg, who was prepared to go to Budapest and issue protective papers. They then persuaded US officials to support such an effort and Swedish officials to grant Wallenberg diplomatic immunity, supplied names of Hungarian Jews through early 1945, and supported the mission financially.

In an attempt to alleviate the horrendous conditions in Bergen-Belsen, Theresienstadt, and other Nazi concentration camps, and despite enormous obstacles, my grandfather arranged for about eighty thousand food parcels to be delivered to inmates in those camps starting in late 1944, thereby saving many lives.

In March 1945, he successfully negotiated with Heinrich Himmler, through Felix Kersten, Himmler's masseur, not to carry out Hitler's orders to blow up the concentration camps in Germany and kill remaining inmates. Count Folke Bernadotte of the Swedish Red Cross, Kersten, and others updated my skeptical grandfather, who wanted to make sure that Himmler kept his promise. After my grandfather's death in 1983, Swedish prime minister Olaf Palme recalled that as a seventeen-year-old boy he had witnessed my grandfather's first meeting with Kersten and that "it is a well-known fact that many Jews were saved from the concentration camps at the last minute, and that Storch played an important role in that respect."

Jule Goldberg, who saved one life, and my grandfather's actions, which helped save thousands, make me appreciate the true nature of ethical behavior. It is in order to nurture such instincts in myself and my family that I developed the two questions we discuss each Friday night.

Hariete Levy

Hariete Levy is an actuary at a French insurance company. She lives in Paris with her husband and two children.

"It is often forgotten that Sephardi Jews like my grandparents were also victims of the Shoah."

My grandparents, originally from Thessaloniki but who lived in Paris, were taken in November 1943 to the Drancy internment camp and then, at the beginning of February 1944, were deported from there to Auschwitz, where they were immediately killed. My mother and her brother and sister were able to escape down the service stairway thanks to my grandmother's remarkable composure. Being the oldest, my mother always felt herself responsible for her brothers and sisters, and later on for their children, for whom she played the role of grandmother.

My mother married an extremely observant Moroccan Jew who had come to study in Paris. She came from a traditional but not particularly religious family, but having been sent after the liberation by her uncles to a children's home run by the Oeuvre de Secours aux Enfants (Organization to Save the Children), better known as OSE, she had also become more observant. She thought that this was the way to remain true to her ancestors. Later on, when we were adolescents, she returned to being less strict in her religious practices. I don't know if she lost her faith or if, in fact, she never truly had it in the first place.

I was born on February 5, 1953, that is, precisely nine years to the day after my grandparents had been gassed. For my mother, I was therefore simultaneously her daughter and the image of her deported mother. I lived my entire childhood with the ever-present yet unarticulated sensation that death prowled around us even though we never spoke of my deported grandparents. This feeling was accentuated by the fact that we lived in my grandparents' apartment and none of the furniture had been changed.

In contrast with what had been the case during my childhood, my mother spoke a great deal to my daughter about her parents. She told her about the good things, how happy her life had been before the war, but also about the less good, especially how much she missed her own mother. Strangely, she seemed to want my daughter to protect me, perhaps because she blamed herself for not having been able to protect her mother.

It is often forgotten that Sephardi Jews like my grandparents were also victims of the Shoah. Most of the more than forty-five thousand Jews the Nazis deported from Thessaloniki to Auschwitz were murdered in the gas chambers. As Israeli president Chaim Herzog once said, "Hitler did not differentiate between Ashkenazi and Sephardi Jews as he did not between Orthodox, observant and secular Jews, or between men and women, the young and the aged." It is also often forgotten that North African Jews like my father's family were also discriminated against by the Vichy regime, although they were more fortunate and avoided deportation to the death camps.

One of my goals, therefore, together with other Sephardi Jews whose families went through the Shoah, is to preserve the Sephardi Ladino language and culture, just as many Ashkenazi children and grandchildren of survivors want to preserve their Yiddish language and culture. This is our way of remembering.

[*Translated from the French by Menachem Z. Rosensaft*]

Michael W. Grunberger

Photo: Miriam Lomaskin

Michael W. Grunberger joined the staff of the United States Holocaust Memorial Museum in 2006, after more than twenty years at the Library of Congress, where he was head of the Hebraic Section. In his role as director of collections, he leads the museum's "Rescue the Evidence" initiative, which includes acquiring, making available, and preserving the historical record of the Holocaust. He currently serves on the Advisory Board of the European Holocaust Research Infrastructure—a consortium of twenty research organizations from thirteen countries whose purpose is to encourage collaborative research on the Holocaust.

"Throughout my career, I have focused on one basic goal: to ensure, to the best of my ability, that the source materials of and about Jewish life are not only gathered and made available to all, but are also preserved as part of America's national patrimony."

Over the course of my professional life, I have worked in several of America's leading research institutions, including the Library of Congress and the United States Holocaust Memorial Museum. From the start, my focus has been on collecting, preserving, and making available the source materials of and about Jewish life, in all its diverse forms. My work has always given me great fulfillment, and the reasons for this are tied directly to my family's story.

My parents were survivors from Munkacs, a city formerly in Hungary, briefly part of Czechoslovakia, and now in Ukraine. My mother, Ruth Weinberger, spent much of the war in hiding, while my father, Nathan Grunberger, was conscripted into a Hungarian forced labor battalion in 1940. As the war was ending, he escaped and found refuge on a Ukrainian farm, whose owners kept him alive until liberation. Through it all, my father carried a small prayer book and a pair of *t'fillin*—ritual objects that he said his mother believed would protect him from harm.

In 1946, my parents were married in the Ranshofen Displaced Persons camp in Austria, and soon afterward they left for the United

States, arriving in New York City in 1947. My father's first purchase on landing in America was a bag of oranges. Years later, he told one of his grandchildren that those oranges were the most delicious he had ever eaten because they "tasted like freedom."

Our family life followed the rhythms of a traditionally observant household. We kept the Sabbath and celebrated the holidays. Jewish literacy was a core value. I remember a neighbor asking my father why he insisted on sending his children to an expensive yeshiva when there was a perfectly good public school down the block. It would not only save money, he said, but would also make the children more American. My father answered that as a survivor he had a special responsibility to make sure that his children knew what it meant to be Jewish. In a memoir from his final years, he wrote:

> I have much to thank America [for]. It took me a few years, I established myself in a trade. I became a member of Typographical Union No. 6 and managed to raise a beautiful family, gave them a Jewish education and above all made sure they knew how their forefathers died in the gas chambers.

For me, as his son, this legacy has taken on a broader meaning, one that has informed my life's work. Throughout my career, I have focused on one basic goal: to ensure, to the best of my ability, that the source materials of and about Jewish life are not only gathered and made available to all, but are also preserved as part of America's national patrimony.

Years ago, I came across a monumental nineteen-volume edition of the Talmud that touched me deeply. Known as the "Survivors' Talmud," it bears a publication date of 1948 and was printed in Germany by the United States Army. Its primary impetus was both simple and noble: to help survivors rebuild their shattered spiritual lives in the immediate aftermath of the Holocaust.

At the head of its title page is a radiant sun overlooking a Jerusalem cityscape, bearing words made familiar from the Passover Haggadah: "From slavery to redemption; from darkness to a great light." At the bottom is a depiction of a Nazi slave labor camp flanked by barbed wire, with a caption underneath from Psalm 119:97: "They have almost exterminated me from the land, but I have not forsaken your commandments."

The edition is dedicated to the United States Army,

[which] played a major role in the rescue of the Jewish people from total annihilation and after the defeat of Hitler bore the major burden of sustaining the DPs of the Jewish faith. This special edition of the Talmud published in the very land where, but a short time ago, everything Jewish and of Jewish inspiration was anathema, will remain a symbol of the indestructibility of the Torah. The Jewish DPs will never forget the generous impulses and the unprecedented humanitarianism of the American forces, to whom they owe so much.

The reasons this particular edition of the Talmud resonates so strongly for me are many. It reflects the devastating impact of the Holocaust on European Jewry, the redemptive vision of the Holy Land, the rebirth of the spiritual lives of the survivors, and the role of America—defeating Germany, liberating the camps, caring for those who survived, and more personally, its place in my own family's story, providing it with both a haven and a home that "tasted like freedom."

Jeanette Lerman-Neubauer

Jeanette Lerman-Neubauer is a corporate communications executive and a philanthropist. Her film *The Upside of Memory*, documenting her parents' remembrance activities, has been shown frequently on college campuses, on public television, and in film festivals.

"My parents taught us to remember and then showed us how to thrive.... We pray that none of us will ever be tested by chaos as virulent as they faced. But we know that resilience comes from the ability to remember human kindness and to use adversity to transform the future."

When I was a very small child, I climbed onto my mother's lap and stroked the tattoo on her forearm. "Why did you put our phone number there?"

Thus began my Holocaust education. My mother describes how she struggled to find ways to speak truthfully without terrifying me. She didn't want to teach fear or hatred. But of course, a child senses everything, even if there aren't any words.

My parents, two of the most positive people I have ever known, used the trauma of their youth to forge lives full of meaning and purpose. My father, Miles Lerman, was one of the founders and then chairman of the United States Holocaust Memorial Museum. He raised $200 million to build the museum at a time when many survivors were still loathe to speak of their experiences, Jews and Germans were highly suspicious of one another, Poland was still rife with anti-Semitism, and Americans wondered what purpose a Holocaust museum would serve on the National Mall.

Fluent in many Eastern European languages, he negotiated with crumbling Communist dictatorships to obtain Holocaust artifacts for the museum and to access records documenting the gruesome evidence of Jewish enslavement and annihilation.

My father inaugurated the museum's Committee on Conscience. Survivors felt that documenting history was imperative but that applying lessons learned was the only way to mitigate future catastrophes. The museum became not only a memorial to six million murdered Jews, but also a promise not to ignore or abandon victims caught in maelstroms yet to come.

When I was a child, my parents helped me to imagine the inconceivable. And then, they helped millions of museum visitors, the vast majority non-Jews, to imagine a world of conscience and tolerance and to speak up for human rights.

After the war, my parents were disinterested in Jewish divisiveness—the battles between factions and styles of observance. "To our enemies, we are all the same," they insisted. "Judaism has sustained us. If we are to be persecuted, at least know the value of your heritage." (This was a non-negotiable command, not a gentle recommendation.) By heritage they meant all of Jewish culture—history, philosophy, literature, humor, food, music—not just religious practice. They knew that all of it had evolved radically over the centuries. They were more interested in enriching the future than arresting the past. Jewish literacy symbolized the ultimate victory over the Nazis. But what Jewish life to live was left entirely up to us.

If anything assuaged their personal losses, it was the creation of the State of Israel. Jews would no longer be forced to depend on others for justice or defense. But it was precisely anti-Semitism that made them dream of alternatives to xenophobia, not revenge. They dreamed of a progressive, multicultural, democratic, Jewish homeland.

It is my mother, Chris Lerman, who speaks about her personal relationship to God. In 2006, she guided her grandchildren through Auschwitz-Birkenau, describing her arrival at age eighteen. "Here is where they stripped me naked and tattooed my arm; here is where they shaved my head; here is the wooden platform where I slept. You could see the chimney belching flames from this window."

The young people listened, dumbfounded—wondering what they would have done in her stead. My mother did not dwell on the suffering but, rather, on the hope. "One night, a woman risked her life to visit our barracks. She carried two wax stubs hidden in her rags. 'Tonight is *Kol Nidre*,' she told us. 'Let's light the candles and pray.'"

In the frigid desolation of Auschwitz, the notes of *Kol Nidre* re-humanized a fragile congregation. Even more than staying alive, my mother says the greatest struggle was to stay human; to believe that Auschwitz was the aberration; that humans were meant to take care of one another. Compassion is the purest form of theology. The need to take care of others kindled her desire to live. Memories of kindness stoked her resilience.

"In every generation, each of us must see ourselves as though we personally had escaped from Egypt." Each spring, extended family gathers around our seder table. We remember Egypt, and the Holocaust. We celebrate American democracy and worry how frequently anti-Semitism accompanies political turmoil. We wonder what dangers lie ahead and what our personal choices will be.

We are the last to hear about the Holocaust directly from those who experienced it. My parents taught us to remember and then showed us how to thrive. By now, their legacy is well integrated into our personal and family identities. Among us, we practice many styles of Judaism, but we are united by conscience—the need to look after our fellows, as ourselves. We pray that none of us will ever be tested by chaos as virulent as they faced. But we know that resilience comes from the ability to remember human kindness and to use adversity to transform the future.

David Silberklang

David Silberklang is senior historian at the International Institute for Holocaust Research at Yad Vashem, editor of the scholarly journal *Yad Vashem Studies,* and series editor of the Holocaust Survivors' Memoirs Project. He teaches Jewish history at the Rothberg International School of the Hebrew University of Jerusalem and at the University of Haifa MA Program in Holocaust Studies. Dr. Silberklang, who received his PhD from the Hebrew University of Jerusalem, has published widely on the Holocaust, and his book *Gates of Tears: The Holocaust in the Lublin District of Poland* appeared in March 2014.

"My parents' stories always included the human face of the events they experienced, and I, too, look for the human face in what I research, write, and teach."

The Holocaust was a presence in our home when I was growing up. My parents, Boruch and Rywka (Rivka), told my older brother Mel and me their personal stories without hesitation, but they never let the subject cast a pall over our home or lives. They lived life and looked forward, though never forgetting or letting us forget the past. Remembering the past included preserving the culture that my parents had lived in pre-war Poland—deeply Jewish, Yiddish, Hebrew, Zionist, religious, "modern," valuing education highly. And that's how my parents raised us—with both rational thinking and religious belief; both deeply Jewish and deeply "modern."

Both my parents lost dozens of relatives in the Holocaust, and both credited their survival at certain junctions to God's intervention, while also recognizing their own role in making choices in their struggle to survive. God might have helped them, but in their attitudes to their past and to life they were also clear that God helps those who help themselves. And where was God during the Shoah and ever since? They couldn't be sure of God's ways, but they were sure that God is there somehow, and that was enough. The main thing for them in their everyday life was to be a good person and a good Jew, and they taught this by example.

For my parents, two major events dramatically and irreversibly changed the world and their Jewish lives—the Holocaust and the creation of the State of Israel. The former destroyed the world they had known; the latter gave them hope for a dramatically different future.

Although they were ardent Zionists from their youth, my parents never managed to come on aliyah, as they had originally intended before they met and after they were married in a DP camp in Germany in 1949. Fate sent them to the United States, but in many ways my brother and I have lived their dreams, reinterpreted into our dreams. My father dreamed that one son would be a famous scientist, while the other would be a rabbi or active in Jewish leadership. Neither of us is quite what he imagined, but my brother is a successful scientist, while I am a Holocaust historian at Yad Vashem and a respected teacher and speaker on the subject.

My life and work are clearly informed by them, as is my approach to life, God, and Jewish identity. I came to the study of the Holocaust through two unrelated channels—my parents' experience, from which I understood at a very young age that the Holocaust had changed everything; and teenage rebellion. My young rebellious nature was to question Jewish practice, helped along by the inability of most of the rabbis in my yeshiva high school to communicate with American teens. I did not yet appreciate the significance of many of them having been among the students of the Mir Yeshiva who had escaped to Shanghai. My link to staying within the fold was history, particularly Jewish history, and within Jewish history, although every subject interested me, the Holocaust constantly drew me as a magnet and gave me no rest.

My studies and career have been based in Israel and dedicated to studying and teaching the Holocaust. My parents' stories always included the human face of the events they experienced, and I, too, look for the human face in what I research, write, and teach. I work in the hope that I can make a small contribution to helping prevent such things from happening again, with a love for Israel and for Jewish tradition, with a twinkle in my eye every time I speak or hear Yiddish. My wife Bobbie and I are members of a liberal Orthodox synagogue in Jerusalem, and the values with which we raised our now grown children were imbued, for me, by the legacy, memory, and values of my parents. In all of this, God is there, and in accordance with Jewish tradition, I feel free to question and to argue with God, as my parents might have done at many points in their lives. My four children are all interested in their grandparents' personal stories and their broader meanings. Each has studied them in depth and pursued school research projects at one time or another that derived from these stories. Each has been to my father's town in Poland, and all want to visit my mother's in Belarus.

At my youngest son's bar mitzvah, my mother wrote him a moving, legacy-like note in which she related that at one point during the Holocaust, after being long on the run with her elderly mother and all seemed hopeless, she suggested to her mother that they leap into the rushing river below them and end it all. Her mother refused, telling her that she must survive and raise Jewish children. As my mother looked at my son and all her other grandchildren, she said, she was profoundly proud and knew that she had made the right decision.

Life, and Jewish life, is what stays with me from them.

Carol Kahn Strauss

Carol Kahn Strauss is international director of Leo Baeck Institute New York, a research library and archive that documents the history and culture of German-speaking Jewry. She is a former senior editor at the Twentieth Century Fund and the Hudson Institute, and was vice president of the American Federation of Jews from Central Europe and president of Congregation Habonim in New York City. In June 2005, she was honored by German president Horst Köhler with the Order of Merit, First Class, of the Federal Republic of Germany, and in 2009, she received the Ellis Island Medal of Honor.

> "The world in which my values, priorities, and preferences were shaped was German-Jewish, with emphasis on the Jewish."

I have never questioned the Jewish part of my identity. The American part, the German/Central European part—these were not nearly as clear to me as the fact that above all else, I am Jewish. Knowing what my family had been through because of their religion, I have never been confused or uncertain about my Jewish faith, values, or commitment. However, with many summers spent in Switzerland while raised in Manhattan by German-Jewish parents and grandparents who all spoke German to each other and to me, the sense of not being entirely American surfaced often.

In our multigenerational household, I was exposed to recollections of life in Germany at various points in the twentieth century—from the very best to the very worst. My father enlisted in the German army as a teenager in World War I, yet one year after being appointed as a young judge to the court in Dortmund in 1932, he was disbarred. My grandfather had an impressive textile business and was a leading member of the Jewish community until his business was vandalized and his synagogue destroyed.

I was not raised to despise Germans or Germany, but to recognize the great damage Germany did to itself by the terrible atrocities it committed. The Nazis, I understood, were the ruin of a nation, but that nation had much to recommend it.

My father introduced me to German poets, writers, and philosophers. The great German composers were background music for most of my childhood. Books filled with Dürer etchings, shelves lined with Goethe, Heine, Schiller, Kant, and other Germans were everywhere. In our house, German culture was never rejected, nor was the German language.

Although my brother and I were born in the United States and were exposed by our parents to its geography and idiom, the private world in which my values, priorities, and preferences were shaped was German-Jewish, with emphasis on the Jewish.

Friday night dinner concluded with a traditional Hebrew melody. Saturday morning usually found me at Shabbat services at Congregation Habonim—founded by and filled with German Jews and of which I later became president—which kept the traditions of the "liberal" German-Jewish Reform service, with liturgical music by Sulzer and Lewandowski. The religious part of our family life was entirely in the hands of my mother, but the cultural/social/legal heritage was endlessly fascinating to my father. He would explain the genesis of certain prayers to me on Yom Kippur or provide the historical context of certain events or the legal ramifications of certain customs. Judaism was a vibrant and relevant aspect of daily life because my father was able to make a connection between them. Social welfare, minority rights, labor legislation, advocacy for women and children—I learned that these themes were part of both my German-Jewish heritage and the American system.

As a child, the "Holocaust" was not the focus of conversation in our household, and Israel not so much either. Rather, it was the pre-1933 culture of Jews who were steeped in German education, culture, geography, and language that I heard about. My religion and cultural heritage have remained important components of my relationships and my activities. My husband was born in Nuremberg, was sent to England at age eleven, and arrived in the United States at age fourteen. There is nothing in my frame of reference he doesn't get.

In 1995, when I became director of the Leo Baeck Institute, the largest and most comprehensive library and archive documenting the history and culture of German-speaking Jewry, I knew that my appreciation of that culture would serve me well.

Some ambivalence toward Germany was probably inevitable, but in the last twenty years that vestige has all but disappeared. I see no conflict between the American and the German dimensions of my identity. When I was awarded the Ellis Island Medal of Honor for being a proud American who preserves my German-Jewish heritage, it was a truly meaningful moment; when I was honored with the *Bundesverdienstkreuz* from the German president for efforts to preserve our heritage for future generations, I was profoundly moved.

But at the core, the Jewish Carol still trumps all the others, in large part because my mother relied so much on her faith, and my father on the historical texts, to see them through ordeals they never could have imagined. This constant has become mine too, and I am eternally grateful to be so deeply rooted and well grounded in something as extraordinary as the Jewish religion.

Eleonora Bergman

Dr. Eleonora Bergman, a documentalist and researcher of synagogues of the nineteenth and twentieth centuries who received her PhD from Warsaw University, is the former deputy director (1996–1997, 2001–2006) and director (2007–2011) of the Jewish Historical Institute in Warsaw. Awarded the French Legion of Honor in 2012, she is the author and co-author of over twenty case studies on the history and preservation of Polish towns, five books, and about fifty articles. Involved in the preparation of the full edition of the Ringelblum Archive since 2004, Dr. Bergman is the author, co-author, and curator of several versions of an exhibition on the archive that has been shown in Germany, the United States, France, and Spain.

"From the moment—some twenty years ago— that I learned about the secret archive created by Ringelblum and the *Oyneg Shabes* (Joy of Sabbath) group in the Warsaw Ghetto under the worst conditions imaginable, from the time I could see it and touch it, I knew I had to do something to make it better known."

Everybody knows the photograph of the little boy raising his hands during a German roundup of the Jews in the Warsaw Ghetto. Many attempts, none fully successful, have been made to identify the boy. Yet another person in the picture has been identified; the woman standing behind the boy is my mother's older sister, my aunt Golda, who most probably perished in Treblinka together with most of the Jews from the Warsaw Ghetto.

My attention was recently called to an entry about myself in *Wikipedia* that begins with the statement that I was born into a Jewish family. It made me think: what did being Jewish mean to my parents when I was born? They barely remembered the Orthodox Jewish environment in which they were raised in Vilna and Grodno. Already as teenagers, they had both abandoned their religion for Communism, and by moving to the Soviet Union and then condemned to the Gulag, they were spared the fate of those family members who remained in Poland. When my parents returned to Poland, what they carried back with them was Yiddish, the language they spoke, and read, and wrote, and argued in and about.

For much of their lives, my parents lived as citizens of Poland. Aside from a few years in the sixties when my mother worked for the Polish-Yiddish weekly *Folks-Shtime* (People's Voice), she was immersed in research of the history of the Byelorussian national movement. My father worked in publishing, editing the classic Marxist works. Jewish involvement was tenuous. We attended the annual commemorations marking the Warsaw Ghetto uprising, and from time to time a box of oranges would arrive from Haifa, where my father's distant cousins who survived had settled. Some family from Russia stayed with us for a year on their way to Israel, and my mother exchanged letters with the only two surviving members of her family, Golda's sons, in Israel and Australia. My father told me I was Polish, not Jewish, because I didn't speak Yiddish. And I didn't because he didn't allow my mother to teach it to me when I was a child. Yiddish was their secret language, and although I understood some of it, I do not remember a lot.

I studied architecture, and then my work took me to the documentation and conservation of Polish synagogues, and ultimately to their history. This work helped me develop an understanding of Jewish traditions, fragments of which my parents used to reveal from time to time. I tried to learn more Yiddish as an adult, especially after I encountered the work of historian Emanuel Ringelblum (1900–1944) and his legacy. From the moment—some twenty years ago—that I learned about the secret archive created by Ringelblum and the *Oyneg Shabes* (Joy of Sabbath) group in the Warsaw Ghetto under the worst conditions imaginable, from the time I could see it and touch it, I knew I had to do something to make it better known.

The thirty-five thousand pages of the Ringelblum Archive that survive, unearthed in 1946 and 1950, were to me the greatest testimony to Jewish life and intellectual discipline to emerge from the Shoah. The archive's creators, a group of around sixty Jewish teachers, writers, journalists, and rabbis, almost all of whom were murdered, compiled these materials between 1939 and 1943 so that future generations would know the truth about the fate of Polish Jewry.

The archive was supposed to have been published over half a century earlier, by those who had participated in the events it chronicled and had survived. For many reasons, they did not succeed. Subsequently, others started the process again, but they too stopped. I felt that it was my responsibility to carry this project forward, now, here in Warsaw, in the very building where Ringelblum and his group had worked. Nobody appointed me, but people encouraged me when I began to talk about plans for the systematic publishing of the entire collection, some initial funding was raised, and work began. The breakthrough came with a major grant from the Polish government in 2012 and a supplementary grant from the Hanadiv Foundation. I now have the privilege of coordinating a team of some thirty translators and editors, and we hope to complete the publication of all the documents in the archive by 2018. I strongly believe that we can achieve it.

When my father reached his nineties, he once told me that not allowing my mother to teach me Yiddish as a child had been a mistake. But his Polish daughter found her own way to be Jewish.

Rabbi Joseph Potasnik

Rabbi Joseph Potasnik is the former president and presently the executive vice president of the New York Board of Rabbis, the largest interdenominational body of its kind in the world. He is the co-host of *Religion on the Line*, which airs every Sunday morning on WABC Talk Radio, 770 AM. Rabbi Potasnik also serves as a chaplain for the Fire Department of New York, was appointed to the New York City Human Rights Commission by Mayor Michael Bloomberg, and is rabbi emeritus of Congregation Mount Sinai in Brooklyn Heights.

> "Our responsibility is
> not to be silent but to make
> noise in the face of evil."

I am the son of survivors who lost five children during the Shoah.

After my mother died a few years ago, I found a book in her home entitled, *Heroes of the Holocaust: Extraordinary True Accounts of Triumph*. In it is a chapter in which she described how her parents were deported from their Polish hometown of Zdunska

Wolla to the Chelmno death camp, where they were killed; how she herself was taken to the Lodz Ghetto, to Auschwitz, and to a labor camp; how a decent German soldier and a Polish couple enabled her and four friends to survive; and equally important, how she returned to life after the war. Through a cousin in Lodz, she met my father, whom she described as "a kind, gentle man who had known my parents in Zdunska Wolla" and who "proposed marriage and promised me a new life."

Their wedding ceremony, she wrote, "took place in Lodz, under a *chupa* [canopy] made of a patched sheet. It was performed by an old rabbinic-looking Jew, his scraggly beard starting to cover his slender face. No one asked to see his credentials. His prayers and blessings rose to the heavens with clarity and pride."

My parents then settled in Lynn, Massachusetts, where they opened a small grocery. "Our greatest pride," my mother wrote, "came the day that our only son, Joseph, was ordained as a rabbi. For us, this was not only a personal joy, but it reaffirmed that Hitler did not win—*Am Yisrael Chai*! The people of Israel live."[1]

I grew up in a happy home because my parents never thought that they would survive, let alone have a child.

One of the questions I am frequently asked is "Why did you become a rabbi?" I usually respond, "I love the Jewish people." After my parents arrived in Lynn as graduates of Auschwitz, they immediately became members of all three synagogues in town, because they felt the best way to remember those who had died as proud Jews was to live as proud Jews without concern for religious classification. After all, one of the first prayers we recite in the morning liturgy is "Thank you Creator of the universe for making me a Jew."

There is a second compelling reason that inspired me to enter my profession. The Talmud talks of two people traveling in the wilderness with only one flask of water between them. If both drink, they will surely die. If one does, he will live, but only he. After a difficult discourse, the Talmud determines that the owner of the flask is entitled to the water. The reason is predicated on the Jewish principle that "your life takes precedence." You can seek to save another human being but not at the cost of sacrificing your own life. There are limited exceptions to this rule, but they do not apply to the aforementioned scene. I would add that the person who emerges alive has a responsibility to perpetuate the memory of the one who did not have the flask of water. I became a rabbi for two reasons—love for the living Jewish people and loyalty to those who live no more.

Our response as a community during the Shoah was not a proud moment for our people. Perhaps a 1997 letter to the *New York Times* by Bernice S. Tannenbaum, the president of Hadassah, encapsulated the tragedy in these words: "The chief lesson of the Holocaust is that we were silent when we should have shouted."[2] Yes, there were some public protests but not enough. As Rabbi Haskel Lookstein points out in his brilliant book *Were We Our Brothers' Keepers? The Public Response of American Jews to the Holocaust 1938–1944*, "By the end of December 1942, any American Jew who had read the *New York Times* or a Jewish newspaper or periodical knew that two million Jews had been murdered and about four million more were threatened with a similar fate."[3]

On Purim we rabbis tell our people the importance of making noise whenever the name of Haman is uttered. There are those, however, who immediately respond with "shush" as soon as the congregation makes some noise. Tragically, during the Holocaust there were too many "shushers" who were afraid to disturb the status quo, some for fear of increasing the disturbing anti-Semitism that pervaded too many hearts in America at that time, others who were simply apathetic. It seems that so many who could have made a difference were indifferent to the pain of the persecuted. As rabbinic leaders, we are expected to be exemplars of prophetic voice. Challenging the complacency of a community during a period of injustice, some raised their voices, but the decibel level of their outcry was far too low. A Yiddish poet wrote, "Fear not your enemies, for they can only kill you. Fear not your friends, for they can only betray you. Fear only the indifferent who permit the killers and betrayers to walk safely on the earth."

I remember looking through a photo album with my parents and seeing pictures of five children. When I asked them repeatedly who they were, they simply said, "Someday when you are older we will tell you." Unfortunately they died without ever revealing their identities. However, a cousin, also a survivor, admitted to me that four were my father's children with his first wife, and the fifth my mother's child with her first husband—the family I never knew.

All of us, the living, are the descendants of the unknown individual who was fortunate to drink that flask of water.

Jewish tradition teaches us that there are no innocent bystand-ers, only those who did little when they could have done more. Our responsibility is not to be silent but to make noise in the face of evil. If we do, we will bring honor to those of the past and hope to those in the future.

Dr. David N. Kenigsberg

David N. Kenigsberg, MD, FACC, FHRS, is a clinical cardiac electrophysiologist and a founding member of Florida Heart Rhythm Specialists, a practice that pro-vides high-level electrophysiology services to northern Broward County. He is the medical director of the electrophysiology laboratory at Westside Regional Medical Center, clinical assistant professor in the Division of Cardiology at Nova Southeastern University, and voluntary assistant professor of medicine at the University of Miami Miller School of Medicine. He serves on the board of directors of the Florida Chapter of the American College of Cardiology, the Broward County Medical Association, and the Holocaust Documentation and Education Center.

"Learning from our past in order to shape our future is the only way that we will continue to survive as a nation and endure the challenges of tomorrow."

My maternal grandfather, Henryk Ehrlich of Miedzyrzec, Poland, was a survivor of the Holocaust. I always referred to him as *Zeida* Hymie. The lessons he shared with me have been indelibly imprinted into my consciousness and have helped shape me into who I am today.

I am many things to many people. I am a proud observant Jew; a Zionist who stands up for the State of Israel's right to exist and defend herself; a husband; a son to two loving, caring, and nurturing parents; a brother to a younger sister; a father to six inspiring children, who are a breath of fresh air in the hectic life I lead; a friend; a devoted and caring doctor to my patients; a teacher to medical students, residents, and fellows; and forever a student, trying to understand how to be better at all I do. I believe that my *zeida* influenced me to take on all of these roles and responsibilities. Most of all, he encouraged me to live in the moment, a challenge that I struggle with to this very day.

My wife and I are raising our children to be observant and consider ourselves modern Orthodox Jews. This, too, is a result of my *zeida*'s influence. Ever since I was a child, he would pick me up to go to shul on Shabbat and made sure that I sat with him throughout *the entire service* rather than run off and play with my friends. After shul, we would sit together and he would tell me stories of his life as a child before and during the Shoah. I still cherish the times we spent together on Shabbat. I often think that if my *zeida* could have faith in *Hashem* (G-d) despite all that he endured, then I should cling to the mitzvot, the laws of Judaism, and thereby reaffirm my belief and faith in *Hashem* even in my toughest times. It is incumbent on me to pass this important lesson on to each of my children.

My *zeida* always stressed the importance of education, lifelong learning, and the significance of striving for excellence. He was there for me after school during my elementary school years until late in the evening to help me with my Hebrew language and Judaic studies. Excelling in my studies was always of paramount importance to my grandfather. It was obvious that he was a highly intelligent person, as he was mostly self-taught after only being formally educated until the age of fourteen, when the war broke out. I recall that he would read the *Algemeiner Journal* and the *Forward* to me to acquaint me with Yiddish; he taught me how to read my Torah portion and haftorah for my bar mitzvah, and he randomly quizzed me to see if I understood the general concepts of what I was learning. I can still hear him telling me, "They can take everything from you—your house, your clothes, they can starve you—but they cannot take away from you what is in your mind; so study hard and learn as much as you can, as you will always have that no matter what." I am grateful to him for this lesson that has helped to influence and shape my academic accomplishments and achievements.

The Passover Haggadah commands us to teach our history to our children. As I look at my children and lay out in my mind's eye the path I would like to see them follow, I remember the lessons that my *Zeida* Hymie taught me and hope that I will in turn be able to relate to them the wisdom I learned from him. This message, the concept of learning from our past in order to shape our future, is the only way that we will continue to survive as a nation and endure the challenges of tomorrow.

Ilana Weiser-Senesh

Ilana Weiser-Senesh is a writer, playwright, and screenwriter. Born and raised in Israel, she is the daughter of Holocaust survivors from Hungary. Her work explores the artistic sublimation of trauma in Israel's social and political fabric.

"The interrelatedness between life and art, or intertextuality between a writer's biography and literary fiction in this case, bears witness to an inherited and insoluble combat against a sense of an inescapable Apocalypse. In my mind, art is thus harnessed for the benefit of fictitious souls as well as for healing the real, haunted me."

I often confess that when I don't write I become ill. I actually come down with a fever. Writing keeps me sane. When I write, I feel I touch eternity.

My latest novel, *On Tip Toes*, deals with an obsessive character, Daniel. I wrote it five times over long years, during which I wrote many other texts, novels, plays, and scripts. Yet this text in particular haunted me and became itself an object of obsession. More than once I was told to find solace in weaving other plots, but I simply couldn't. Something in Daniel's journey into self-destruction required a bold expression and a closure. I had to find out how his growing up in a post-traumatic Holocaust-surviving family shaped his personality and affected his life. I had to probe into similarities and differences between Daniel's life and mine.

My fiction often succumbs to characters whose childhood was spent in a home where hushed voices of the dead oozed from the walls. Holocaust survivors and their kids spent their days and more so their nights listening to cries of murdered loved ones. Living families could not offer comfort, nor did they serve as a substitute or compensation for all they had lost. And we, children of survivors, were poorly patched up, fragmented reminders of a bereaved past.

If people cannot express their traumatic experiences, symptoms are bound to emerge. Artists are no exception. The struggle between the need to remember and the tendency to forget bears dissociation, which probably will turn into rites of enactment and somatic expressions. With some luck, and because there is no other solution to the unbearable load and sense of suffocation, artistic production will provide both a means of processing and digestion of those raw materials. It will also envelop the artist with a sense of calm and momentary satisfaction from the impingements of her parents' traumas and enable her to better cope with life.

In my novel *An Inner Course*, I further explored the relatedness between life and text, through the work of a writer, Michael, who survived a mother he had not remembered. Michael uses his writing in order to reconstruct an enigmatic, drowned, and forgotten life story. Because he is a child survivor, his trauma is too terrifying to keep back symptoms of mental illness. Nevertheless, despite the lack of a coherent story, he does manage to carve out a life through the numerous plots he concocts. Yet how do Michael's protagonists help his pursuit of a substitute personal story? Furthermore, how do Michael and all my other characters help me negotiate post-Holocaust life?

The interrelatedness between life and art, or intertextuality between a writer's biography and literary fiction in this case, bears witness to an inherited and insoluble combat against a sense of an inescapable Apocalypse. In my mind, art is thus harnessed for the benefit of fictitious souls as well as for healing the real, haunted me.

After reading my first novel, *Double Glazed Windows*, my mother asked me in tears, "Was I such a bad mother to you?" I replied that the book doesn't tell a personal story, but rather is an integrated mapping of a traumatic mental landscape that blends the collective with the personal, something that took place in the life of many people I knew as a child, not necessarily in my own home.

The accompanying witnesses of my artistic journey are both the fictional characters and my real readers. Their presence fills in the void left by the dead. For me, this is the way to heal trauma, or at least free myself from its grasp. My fictional characters have to pay the price in order to enable me to live and write.

Photo: Reikhman Gregory

Ilya Altman

Professor Ilya Altman is co-chair of the Russian Research and Educational Holocaust Center in Moscow and a member of the International Organization Committee for the annual conference "The Holocaust and the Churches." He received his doctorate from the Russian Academy of Sciences and was deputy director of the National Archives in Vladimir and executive officer of the State Archives of the USSR.

"I consider the collecting, archiving, and publishing of letters, diaries, and photographs of Jews from the war to be a personal responsibility of mine."

I am not a religious person, but I took part in the preparation of Russia's first museum of the Holocaust in 1998 in the Memorial Synagogue in Moscow. The museum has become one of the places where I work. I never met my grandparents, who died before I was born—the family of one of them, consisting of seven people, survived the Holocaust in Transnistria. My parents were officers in the Red Army. They met and married during the Second World War. My father told me that he could not believe that by 1944, his entire family had survived, and he went back to his hometown from the front to make sure of this. This is why the history of the war and of the Holocaust became personal for me.

At school I was heavily influenced by the writer Ilya Ehrenburg's memoirs, from which I found out about the *Black Book*—a collection of essays by Soviet writers about the Holocaust in the USSR. The book was destroyed in 1947. Forty years later I managed to find the complete text and notes in the State Archives of the Russian Federation. The preparation for the publication of these materials, which were eventually published in Russia, Lithuania, France, Germany, Italy, the United States, and Spain, and my close collaboration with Yad Vashem resulted in my idea to establish the first Research and Educational Holocaust Center in Eastern Europe. This occurred in 1991. Since June 1993, my work at the center has become my most important professional commitment. It is more likely that it is precisely this occupation as a historian and archivist that has influenced my identity, as none of my relatives died in the Holocaust. The main achievement of my work has been the publication, in 2009 and 2011, of the *Encyclopedia of the Holocaust in the USSR*.

I consider the collecting, archiving, and publishing of letters, diaries, and photographs of Jews from the war to be a personal responsibility of mine. To date, we have collected several thousand such documents, resulting in the publication of three anthologies. I am particularly proud of my involvement in the "Return of Dignity" project created by the Russian Jewish Congress and the Holocaust Center. The project's aim was to erect memorials at sites where Jews had been executed during the Holocaust. One of the first memorials was erected in the small town of Lyubavichi, a town well known to any religious Jew. Perhaps it's symbolic ...

[*Translated from the Russian by Lina Numan*]

Aviva Kempner

Filmmaker Aviva Kempner received a Peabody Award for *The Life and Times of Hank Greenberg*, as well as the 2009 San Francisco Jewish Film Festival's Freedom of Expression Award, a Guggenheim Fellowship, DC Mayor's Art Award, Women of Vision Award, and Media Arts Award from the National Foundation for Jewish Culture. She founded the Washington Jewish Film Festival and writes reviews for numerous publications, including the *Washington Post*, the *Boston Globe*, the *Forward*, and the *Wrap*. She is a voting rights advocate for the District of Columbia.

> "Mother became an abstract expressionist painter and claimed that each one of the strokes in her vibrant works was for one of the six million. I similarly declare that every one of the celluloid frames of my films is in their honor."

The most traumatic memory of my college years was watching the 1965 Oscars and crying hysterically when Lee Marvin's drunken cowboy role in *Cat Ballou* stole the award deserved by Rod Steiger's brilliant performance as a Holocaust survivor in *The Pawnbroker*. I felt personally betrayed as a child of a survivor, and isolated because there was not a single fellow student with whom I could share these feelings.

Steiger's pained portrayal spoke to me, as my own mother, who did not talk much about her experiences in "the war," had not shared her nightmarish memories. Blonde and green-eyed, Hanka Ciesla spoke a non-Yiddish-accented Polish, providing her with valuable weapons of survival. Armed with false passports provided by my grandfather, Mother and two friends passed as non-Jews in a labor camp near Stuttgart, Germany, pretending to recite Catholic prayers.

Her immediate family was deported to Auschwitz, where only my uncle David survived, while my grandparents and aunt were killed. Liberated by the Americans, Hanka married a Lithuanian-born soldier, Chaim Kempner, whose own mother had been murdered by the Nazis. Amid the rubble I was born in a US Army hospital in Berlin, anointed with the Hebrew name Aviva in honor of Jewish survival on German soil.

Instead of family lore, literature and cinema were my entry into Holocaust history. At age thirteen, I learned about the death camps for the first time from Leon Uris's *Exodus*. In high school, John Hersey's *The Wall* taught me about the exterminated Jews of Warsaw. I read Uris's *Mila 18*, about the Warsaw Ghetto uprising, over and over again and imagined being in that heroic struggle.

I attempted to see every film that featured World War II, while shielding Mother from watching any depictions of the Holocaust. *Casablanca*, the classic film romanticizing the French Resistance, became and remains my favorite movie.

I also wanted to be involved in anything that combated fascist tendencies. While in law school, I lobbied against human rights abuses committed by the military regimes in Argentina, Chile, El Salvador, and Iran.

In 1979, thanks to being flunked by the District of Columbia Bar, I changed careers and converted my fantasy of killing Nazis into a full-time profession of defeating them on the screen.

My inaugural attempt was conceiving and producing director Josh Waletzky's *Partisans of Vilna*, a documentary that explores the moral dilemmas Jewish youth faced in joining the resistance led by

Abba Kovner in the Vilna Ghetto and Lithuanian woods. I gloried vicariously in the female couriers' feats, especially Vitka Kempner (no relation) bombing a German troop train.

My directorial debut, *The Life and Times of Hank Greenberg,* was about my father's hero, the Jewish baseball slugger of the 1930s and 1940s who enlisted in the army to fight the Nazis. It was important for me to include Greenberg's son Stephen describing that "every time he would hit a home run, he would feel doubly proud because, as he put it, he would feel he was hitting a home run against Hitler." I am also planning to make a film about the major league catcher Moe Berg, who spied on both the Japanese and the Nazis.

In *Yoo-Hoo Mrs. Goldberg,* I included empathetic scenes radio and television pioneer Gertrude Berg wrote about the Holocaust. In one radio show she crafted a broken window incident during their seder that was broadcast right after *Kristallnacht* in 1938. Berg also composed a sensitive episode about Molly being "so beside myself, we've just received a letter from relations we didn't hear from since before the war." And my documentary about the Jewish philanthropist Julius Rosenwald features the brave Tuskegee airmen who flew heavy bomber escort missions against the Nazis. Even the dramatic feature I co-wrote with Ben West about Larry Casuse, a Navajo activist who was also the product of a marriage between a war bride and a US Army soldier, had a wartime theme. Like me, Casuse's birthright influenced his political activism.

I have still not exhausted exploring World War II topics. I am making a film about Agnieszka Holland, Europe's outstanding female director, whose incredible Holocaust films include *Europa, Europa* and *Angry Harvest.*

Twenty-five years ago, I launched an annual Jewish film festival in Washington, DC, with a fellow child of survivors, Miriam Morsel Nathan, to showcase, among other topics, the best in Holocaust cinema. I have written film reviews about Jewish films with an emphasis on Shoah themes for over thirty years.

Mother became an abstract expressionist painter and claimed that each one of the strokes in her vibrant works was for one of the six million. I similarly declare that every one of the celluloid frames of my films is in their honor.

Like mother, like daughter.

Katrin Tenenbaum

Katrin Tamara Tenenbaum received her PhD from the Sapienza University of Rome in 1972 and was first researcher in theoretical philosophy and then professor of social ethics at La Sapienza for thirty-five years. She is professor of Jewish philosophy in the advanced Jewish study program of the Union of Italian Jewish Communities in Rome. Her teaching and writings have dealt with Immanuel Kant and German Idealism as well as the relationship between modern Jewish culture and experience and philosophical thought, from Moses Mendelssohn to Walter Benjamin and Hannah Arendt.

"The greater our distance from the Holocaust, the more sorrow loses its focus, becoming more diffused and more difficult to grasp."

As far back as I can remember, I have been aware of my parents' story. In my mind, it has always been linked to the overall European history before and during World War II. I grew up with the feeling that theirs was not a particularly dramatic story, given the enormity of the oppression and suffering endured by the Jewish people at the hands of the Nazis and their collaborators in those years.

As foreign Jews living in Italy, my parents were persecuted under the Fascist racial laws that Mussolini introduced in 1938. From 1940 to 1943, they (and then also I, who was born in July 1942) were interned in a small village in Central Italy. The worst came after September 1943, when the Germans occupied Italy and the Jews started to be hunted relentlessly.

My parents hid in the mountains and were fortunate enough to have their baby daughter sheltered in the village by a courageous and big-hearted woman. An entire book could be written about those nine months preceding the liberation of Central Italy in June 1944. The day-by-day fight for survival meant, on the one hand, having to rely on the support and solidarity of the people of the village and, on the other, being exposed to betrayal and denunciation. But more important to me was the fact that my parents were given the opportunity to engage in active resistance against the Germans. They helped, sheltered, and cared for fugitive, often wounded, Allied

POWs who were trying to reach the Allies on the Monte Cassino front. I am stressing this aspect of my parents' experiences because I believe that placing their story in the broader context of not just Nazi-fascist violence, oppression, and anti-Jewish persecution but within the broader picture of World War II as a whole is what has shaped my identity and outlook.

This is the narrative with which I grew up, knowing myself to be a part of it, but not really, since my presence in it was conveyed to me only through my parents' words. That means that for a long time I didn't feel directly and emotionally involved. Instead, I saw myself primarily as a depository and guardian of *their* story. This feeling of being somehow detached may well have initially contributed to shaping my attitudes and perceptions and later oriented the professional choices I made. I studied philosophy and eventually became a university professor in this field. My principal academic interests were in politics, history, and the unresolved puzzle of human behavior. In this context Judaism and my being Jewish represented a historical and cultural belonging, with no religious or metaphysical implications. I belong to a history, which is the history of the Jewish people, and I have also always endeavored to study the way a distinctive Jewish experience has contributed to the general philosophical discourse in modernity.

But there is a second layer, of which I have become gradually aware in recent years and over which I am still contemplating. My family's narrative, in a way almost "harmoniously" embedded in a universal horizon, has revealed another less linear aspect of my identity, one that has gradually emerged after the death of my parents a few years ago. And this concerns *me* in a very direct way and implies the troublesome acceptance of my having been a potential victim. Of the foreign Jews hiding in the mountains during the months of the German occupation, sixteen were deported to Auschwitz and only four survived. A little girl named Naomi, born a couple of weeks before me, didn't.

I have come to realize that the greater our distance from the actual events of the Holocaust, the more sorrow loses its focus, becoming in a way more diffused and, at the same time, more difficult to grasp. For me, this means continuing with the never-ending task of both trying to understand my parents' story that is a part of my past and coming to terms with the hidden internalization of that same story within myself.

Lawrence S. Elbaum

Lawrence S. Elbaum is an attorney with the international law firm Proskauer Rose LLP in New York City. He is a member of 3GNY, a New York City–based group for grandchildren of Holocaust survivors, and also dedicates substantial time to other Holocaust remembrance initiatives. Lawrence also co-chairs the alumni society and serves on the board of trustees of the Golda Och Academy, a Hebrew day school based in West Orange, New Jersey.

> "My desire to recognize ... survivors' legacies ... is why I have become an active member in programming for 3Gs all around the country. In many respects, we are the last living witnesses to the survivors' firsthand accounts of the Shoah."

I am privileged that all four of my grandparents—Fela and David Urman (*z"l*) and Sala and Izak Elbaum (*z"l*)—survived the Shoah. This privilege makes me a member of the third generation, known as 3Gs, and comes with the great responsibility of preserving and transmitting my grandparents' legacies.

As part of a robust Hebrew day school education, I studied the teachings of the Talmudic sage Ben Zoma in *Pirkei Avot*, the Ethics of Our Fathers. The magnitude of his words never made complete sense to me until I began to reflect on my grandparents' lives after they had passed away.

In *Pirkei Avot*, Ben Zoma taught that wise people learn from others, mighty people are slow to anger, rich people are content with their lots in life, and honored people are those that honor others. In the Shoah, the Nazis forced my grandparents into ghettos, deported them to labor and death camps, and murdered virtually their entire families. My grandparents immigrated to the United States several years after liberation and struggled to rebuild their lives.

The process of rebuilding was especially difficult for them because they arrived in the United States with hardly pennies to their names and without more than eighth grade educations. Rebuilding required my grandparents to absorb mentorship on how to "make it" from wherever they could—from family and friends, and from neighbors, bosses, and co-workers. They also had to rebuild against the backdrop of the atrocities they had experienced firsthand in the Shoah. My grandparents could have dwelled on their anger at the Nazis' attempts to exterminate the Jewish people. They could have constantly complained about the hands they were dealt in life. Instead, my grandparents rose above their understandable anger, grief, and trepidation by turning these feelings into a zest for life, with which they showered their family and friends. They had a way of making all with whom they came into contact feel special and loved.

After shedding lots of blood, sweat, and tears, my grandparents built loving families and enjoyed other *nakhes* during the post-war stage of their lives. They managed to recapture and share with their children, grandchildren, and others the warmth and happiness of the youth that had been stolen from them by the Nazis. My grandparents were certainly wise in that they learned from others, mighty in the way they contained their anger, rich in their wholehearted contentment with their new lives and families, and honored because of the respect and love with which they treated others. I can only hope to summon their strengths as I follow in their footsteps.

I was incredibly lucky to grow up knowing three of my grandparents but sadly never got to meet Sala Elbaum, my Nanny Sala, who died in 1978, before I was born. My middle name, Shane, was given to me in her memory. My sister Sala and my cousins Shay and Sarah are named for her as well. We not only proudly bear her name, but we are infused with her spirit and a deep appreciation of her life.

From the age of five, I understood the importance of supporting and participating in Shoah remembrance initiatives. I recall attending Shoah museums and lectures, including programs in which my grandparents told their stories of survival to large audiences. By age fifteen, I was a contributing artist to an anthology of biographies of Shoah survivors, including those of my grandparents.

But since the last of my grandparents passed away in 2009, my desire to recognize their and other survivors' legacies has grown considerably. This is why I have become an active member in programming for 3Gs all around the country. In many respects, we are the last living witnesses to the survivors' firsthand accounts of the Shoah. When we meet, we often reflect on how lucky we are to be able to share our grandparents' stories with each other and with others, and we train ourselves to speak to middle school and high school students about their experiences.

My wife, Melissa, and I will pass on my grandparents' legacy to our daughter Abigail Fela, whose middle name is for my mother's mother. But that is not enough. I recognize that as 3Gs we have a unique obligation to teach—not only our own children, and our children's children, but the whole world—about the Shoah and the critical importance of tolerance. Honoring my grandparents' memory in this way fulfills this obligation, keeps them alive within me, and perhaps, brings me closer to the teachings of Ben Zoma.

Jochi (Jochevet) Ritz-Olewski

Jochi (Jochevet) Ritz-Olewski is the former vice dean of academic studies at the Open University of Israel. She is a board member of the Irgun Sh'erit ha-Pletah Bergen-Belsen Israel, the organization of survivors of Bergen-Belsen in Israel, and serves on the advisory council of the Lower Saxony Memorials Foundation.

"Growing up as a Symbol dictated which path the journey of my life would take. I was in no position to choose."

I am the daughter of Rachel and Rafael Olewski, two survivors of Auschwitz and Bergen-Belsen. I was born stateless, deprived of any nationality, in the Displaced Persons camp of Bergen-Belsen. It took me many years to realize that my parents' personal history of their suffering and survival has powerfully influenced and shaped my identity, my perspectives, and my attitudes to life.

As a child at school, I had to cope with the terrified reaction of my teachers when they asked me where I was born and I answered, "Bergen-Belsen." To them, Bergen-Belsen was only a place of death and not a place of birth.

I was fortunate to grow up in a family where the Shoah was not a hidden or frightening secret. My parents spoke freely about their experiences but always tried to show us that there had been light amid the darkness. When they told us their personal stories, they always emphasized the positive and humane behavior of people they met along the way, even at the worst moments.

My mother, who played the mandolin in the Women's Orchestra at Birkenau, never forgot the glass of milk her friend gave her when she returned crawling to her barrack after recovering from typhus during an epidemic. My father never forgot his friend the barber who saved his life by bribing a *kapo*, who, instead of sending my father to the gas chamber, put a corpse in his place.

My brother and I grew up in a family that was happy, full of laughter and love for life. Yet, I was not just another child. I became a Symbol, with a capital S, of my parents' victory over Nazi Germany, over death, deportation, suffering, humiliation, torture, disease.

I often wondered how my parents were able to live a normal and happy life after all they had been through. In my opinion, what kept my parents alive during the Holocaust and what gave them the amazing strength to rebuild their lives after the war was their optimistic attitude to life. The Holocaust failed to destroy their belief in mankind and in the goodness of human nature.

The ability to look to the future with hope and to always see a "light at the end of the tunnel" enabled my parents to survive. It's impossible to grasp that while in Auschwitz, my father and a friend of his were planning to issue a Yiddish newspaper after the war. And so they did in the Bergen-Belsen DP camp. This same optimism gave my father the spiritual strength to take a prominent part in establishing the Central Committee of Liberated Jews in the British zone of Germany shortly after the liberation.

I inherited this positive attitude to life from my parents. I never take off my "pink lenses." This defines my personality and helps me cope with all hardships. They also taught me to cherish and value friendship.

My parents didn't care for material things. These meant nothing to them after they saw people give away diamonds for a piece of bread. I have inherited this attitude as well. I don't care about breaking or losing material things, but I cannot throw away a piece of stale bread.

My father dedicated his life to commemorating the Shoah and to taking care of the survivors. I find myself doing the same: following his path, walking in his footsteps, I dedicate my time to the Israeli organization of survivors of Bergen-Belsen and the next generations, to remembrance activities, to putting out a newsletter with the same name—*Unzer Sztyme, Our Voice*—as the newspaper my father published in the DP camp. I serve on the advisory council of the Lower Saxony Memorials Foundation, which oversees the Bergen-Belsen Memorial Site.

I try to teach and promote tolerance so as to ensure that what happened to our parents will never be allowed to happen again. At the same time, we in Israel, in addition to our universal message, have to contend with an extra mission: we must go on fighting for our and our children's lives and future in our homeland in the face of continuous threats.

I know that I must fulfill my parents' expectations and pass on their legacy. Growing up as a Symbol dictated which path the journey of my life would take. I was in no position to choose. I've decided that I will carry the Survivors' Torch proudly and lead forward to fulfill this mission.

Jean Bloch Rosensaft

Jean Bloch Rosensaft is assistant vice president for communications and public affairs at Hebrew Union College–Jewish Institute of Religion and director of the HUC-JIR Museum in New York. The author of *Chagall and the Bible*, she serves as vice president of the American Gathering of Jewish Holocaust Survivors and Their Descendants, vice president of Park Avenue Synagogue in New York City, a member of the United States Holocaust Memorial Museum's Collections and Acquisitions Committee, and chair of the Memorial Foundation for Jewish Culture's Panel on Art and Photography, and is a former officer of the Council of American Jewish Museums.

"Artists who are authentic witnesses to the eyewitnesses of the Shoah fulfill a unique role, for their relationship with survivors ... conveys a profound understanding that the victims of the Holocaust did not want to be remembered solely by how they suffered and died, nor do the survivors want to be defined only by their victimization."

The themes of rescue, resistance, and resilience lie at the heart of my family's history during and following the Holocaust: the miraculous rescue of my mother Lilly Czaban and her parents and aunt by an altruistic Polish farmer; the resistance of my partisan father Sam Bloch, who saved his mother and little brother after his father, after whom I am named, was murdered by members of an SS *Einsatzgruppe*; and the resilience of my family in rebuilding their lives in the Bergen-Belsen Displaced Persons camp after their liberation.

My parents' lifelong devotion to the Jewish people and the State of Israel, their capacity for leadership, and their ability to approach the future with optimism continue to be the paradigm for my identity. All that I am and everything that I do are inspired by their example.

They taught my sister Gloria and me, and our children, that the vitality of our Jewish heritage, which had nearly been destroyed during the Shoah, should be cherished. And while charging us with the responsibility to sustain Holocaust remembrance, they also taught us that it was not enough to be introspective or retrospective, that we must not focus on the tragic past to the detriment of the present and the future.

It is this legacy that I seek to transmit as a precious inheritance and call to action to our daughter, Jodi, and our grandchildren and that has forged my commitment to raise the consciousness and conscience of others through the visual arts.

As an art historian, museum director, curator, and educator, it has been my personal and professional mission to illuminate aspects of the Holocaust experience that will ensure an ongoing process of remembrance and education. This mission has taken many forms in venues ranging from the Museum of Modern Art and New York City's Jewish Museum to Hebrew Union College–Jewish Institute of Religion (HUC-JIR) and the United States Holocaust Memorial Museum (USHMM) and has found fulfillment in over one hundred exhibitions to date, in scores of lectures and publications educating about the ultimate consequences of indifference, intolerance, and injustice, and in the empowerment of artists of all generations and backgrounds to embrace this sacred task.

With the current proliferation of Holocaust museums, centers, educational programs, books, films, and popular cultural responses, we too often forget that during the first three decades after the war the prevailing attitude toward the Holocaust, even in the Jewish community, was primarily one of disinterest and that the advanced study of the Holocaust had not yet penetrated educational institutions.

Consequently, as one of the leaders of the second-generation movement during the late 1970s and 1980s, I sought to help "break the
silence" about the Shoah through several pioneering exhibitions that
elevated survivor artists to their rightful place as respected and productive cultural contributors whose work provided visual testimony
to destruction and rebirth. *The Artist as Witness*, presented at the
national gatherings of thousands of survivors and their families in
Washington, DC, in 1983 and Philadelphia in 1985, and *Shadows
of a Lost Childhood*, presented in New York in 1989, were the first
group exhibitions to present the creativity of survivor artists.

For some, clandestinely creating art during the Holocaust was
a crucial form of spiritual resistance or a practical means of survival.
Some of the survivor artists were academically trained but, with
new families to support in a new land, could not afford the luxury
of resuming careers that had been shattered during the war. Other
younger survivors only discovered their artistic talents after the war.

The several hundred paintings, works on paper, and sculpture
in these exhibitions included diverse and highly accomplished reflections by eyewitness artists for whom art was an important means of
assimilating their traumatic past into their new lives. Among them
were David Friedman's powerful charcoal drawings of his ghetto
and concentration camp experiences, Luba Gurdus's images of resistance in the Warsaw Ghetto, Ann Celnik's meditative compositions,
Ari Adler's cubist depictions of pre-war Hasidic shtetl life, and Helen
Ciesla Covensky's life-affirming expressionist paintings. Art-world
professionals who had doubted and even denigrated the aesthetic
quality of art by survivors were amazed by the technical sophisti-
cation and forceful expression of memory, historical experience,
and psychological insight by these eyewitnesses to the Shoah. These
exhibitions helped lead the way to the integration of survivor artists'
works into the permanent collections of Holocaust museums in the
decades that followed.

At the same time, an emerging cohort of children of survivors
was tackling post-Holocaust Jewish identity in their art. *Images of
Identity*, presented at the First International Conference of Children
of Holocaust Survivors in New York in 1984, demonstrated the
transmission of intergenerational memory through powerful works
by young artists who would later become leading figures in the contemporary art world. Tobi Kahn's monumental abstract sculpture

memorializing his parent's murdered family and Rochelle Rubinstein's imaginative mixed-media Torah mantles bespeaking the continuity of tradition despite the rupture of the Shoah conveyed the ethos of an emerging generation whose internalization of the Holocaust was fueling new and unexpected responses to their family legacies. Their diversity of style, mediums, and subject matter—including family relationships, spiritual quests, and search for communal and cultural roots—reflected the individuality, vitality, and complexity of their generation.

My Holocaust-related curatorial work extended beyond art to photo-documentary materials in *Justice in Jerusalem Revisited: The Eichmann Trial 25 Years Later* at the Jewish Museum in 1986. This multimedia exhibition, based on the museum's collection of the complete extant video recordings of the Adolf Eichmann Trial, introduced Israel's prosecution of the Nazi architect of the Final Solution to a new generation and drew record-breaking attendance and extensive coverage in the press. A related panel discussion by leading jurists, including Telford Taylor, the former chief prosecutor at the Nuremberg Trials, focused on present-day international human rights dilemmas.

Prior to the dedication of the USHMM in 1993, I served on the subcommittee of its Collections and Acquisitions Committee that designated public spaces where works by leading American artists would enhance opportunities for reflection in the context of the museum's overwhelming documentation of mass murder. The review of prominent artists' proposals resulted in the commissioning of significant works of art that manifested the inspiration the Holocaust was beginning to have on American artists with no direct personal connection to the subject: Joel Shapiro's broken figure and upended house for the museum's exterior plaza, to introduce the themes of destruction and displacement; Richard Serra's steel stele at the foundation of the Hall of Witness, to message the breach of separations; Ellsworth Kelly's white wall sculptures imagining the inscription of the names of countless anonymous victims; and Sol LeWitt's wall of square black-bordered color fields, each with a gray center evoking the color of ash, expressing infinite loss.

One of my most fulfilling projects was to co-curate the photo-documentary exhibition *Rebirth After the Holocaust: The Bergen-Belsen Displaced Persons Camp, 1945–1950* with my father, who was the youngest member of the Jewish Committee that governed that DP camp. This exhibition was launched in the context of the USHMM's "Life Reborn" conference about the DP camp experience that I helped organize in 2000 as a member of the museum's Second Generation Advisory Group.

In *Rebirth After the Holocaust*, we depicted the survivors' return to life during the five years of the Belsen DP camp's existence, adjacent to the former concentration camp, as the largest autonomous Jewish community in post-Holocaust Europe—complete with a rabbinate, schools, vocational education, health care, a newspaper, the earliest publications documenting the Shoah, sports clubs, an orchestra, a theater that performed throughout Europe, and passionate Zionist activism on behalf of Jewish statehood. After traveling throughout North America, this exhibition is now permanently integrated into the Bergen-Belsen Memorial Museum in Germany, where visitors of all backgrounds can learn not only how Jews died at Belsen, but how Jews returned to life after the Holocaust in the DP camp there.

At a time when the then newly forming Holocaust museums concluded with liberation and jumped to the creation of the State of Israel, the "Life Reborn" conference and this exhibition shed light on a largely unknown chapter of Jewish history. As a co-author in 2001 of the USHMM's Collections Management Policy, the core document that defines the parameters and care of the museum's irreplaceable collections, I successfully argued for the expansion of the scope of the museum's collections to include the immediate post-liberation DP years, resulting in the acquisition of valuable artifacts that otherwise would not have been recognized or preserved for their historical significance. In addition, knowing that future generations would one day want to know how the first generations after the Shoah succeeded in embedding Holocaust memory in the public square, my suggestion to add the documentation of Holocaust memorialization in our own time to the scope of the museum's Collections Management Policy was also adopted.

For the past twenty-five years, my professional life has been at HUC-JIR, where I help strengthen a global institution of higher Jewish learning that ensures spiritual, intellectual, educational, and communal leadership for the Jewish people. A special feature of my work there has been the creation of the HUC-JIR Museum in New

York, which specializes in presenting the creativity of contemporary artists of all faiths exploring Jewish identity, values, history, culture, and experience and circulates the largest traveling Jewish exhibition program in North America.

Art expressing Holocaust remembrance and the sanctity of human life have been intrinsic to these efforts, including Natan Nuchi's pixilated Shoah-inspired images, the first digital drawings to be acquired by the Metropolitan Museum, and Mirta Kuperminc's vivid graphic art imbued with the themes of uprootedness, exodus, legacy, memory, and continuity (whose work is featured on the cover of this book).

Faced with both the current abundance of scholarly research into the destruction of European Jewry and the ubiquitous exploitation, trivialization, commodification, and universalization of the Holocaust, I continue to seek out artists who embody Elie Wiesel's admonition about the difference between knowledge and understanding. Artists who are authentic witnesses to the eyewitnesses of the Shoah fulfill a unique role, for their relationship with survivors transcends mere knowledge of historical data and conveys a profound understanding that the victims of the Holocaust did not want to be remembered solely by how they suffered and died, nor do the survivors want to be defined only by their victimization. Through the power of art, we can challenge others to remember their extraordinary will to live and the values they hoped to pass on to future generations.

Today, my grandchildren represent the next chapter in our family's narrative. As the fourth generation in the chain of Jewish memory after the Shoah, I pray that Hallie and Jacob will grow up to be proud Jews, inspired by the indestructible Jewish spirit of their extraordinary great-grandparents who emerged from death to embrace life. May they and their children in turn be committed to the continuity of our heritage as the ultimate expression of *Am Yisrael Chai*—the Jewish people lives.

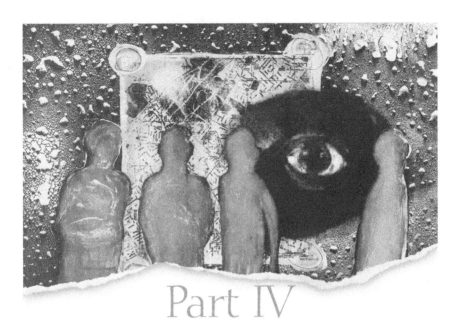

Part IV

Tikkun Olam

Changing the World
for the Better

"We must take sides. Neutrality helps the oppressor,
never the victim. Silence encourages the tormentor,
never the tormented. Sometimes we must
interfere. When human lives are endangered, when
human dignity is in jeopardy, national borders and
sensitivities become irrelevant. Wherever men
and women are persecuted because of their race,
religion, or political views, that place must—at that
moment—become the center of the universe."

—Elie Wiesel[1]

Rabbi Judith Schindler

For the past decade, Rabbi Judith Schindler has been senior rabbi of Temple Beth El, the largest synagogue in the Carolinas, with eleven hundred families. Ordained by Hebrew Union College–Jewish Institute of Religion, Rabbi Schindler was named Charlotte's Woman of the Year in 2011 and is a past co-chair of the Women's Rabbinic Network, an international organization of women Reform rabbis. She is known for her activism and responsible for creating three educational and social justice documentaries on diversity, education, and affordable housing.

"When I hear of rhetoric or legislation built upon racism, anti-Semitism, homophobia, Islamophobia, xenophobia, or any other bigotry, I cannot be silent. Even in the face of those who seek to intimidate and threaten me, my past enjoins me to act. My grandfather's voice does not allow me to look the other way when inequities permeate our society and prejudiced voices echo in the air. Acting with moral courage is the message I teach, preach, and aspire to fulfill."

The Talmud teaches that when we quote someone who has died, their lips whisper from the grave. The memory of my family members who died in the Holocaust and the voices of those who survived motivate my everyday actions. Their voices continually speak to me as I share the messages of their lives and deaths with the world.

First and foremost, I hear the voice of my grandfather, Eliezer Schindler, a Yiddish poet and activist who lived in Munich, Germany. Even though he died nine years before I was born, I inherited his fearlessness in speaking out against hatred and evil. It has become the most prominent pillar of my professional and personal life.

In the early 1930s, my grandfather read *Mein Kampf*, foresaw the evil that Hitler threatened to unleash upon the world, and warned his community in an underground Yiddish newspaper for which he regularly wrote. On the night of March 4, 1933, as Hitler moved to solidify his dictatorial powers by introducing legislation that would override Germany's parliamentary process, my grandfather left home and slept at a Jewish hospital. Hours later, the Nazi forces arrived at his residence to arrest him as an opponent of the Nazi Party. The next day, my grandfather fled Germany, first to Austria and then Switzerland, never to return.

My grandfather's voice calls to me, saying, "Never be complacent. Be vigilant about hatred. Speak out against injustice, no matter what the cost." When I hear of rhetoric or legislation built upon racism, anti-Semitism, homophobia, Islamophobia, xenophobia, or any other bigotry, I cannot be silent. Even in the face of those who seek to intimidate and threaten me, my past enjoins me to act. My grandfather's voice does not allow me to look the other way when inequities permeate our society and prejudiced voices echo in the air. Acting with moral courage is the message I teach, preach, and aspire to fulfill.

The call of our biblical prophets such as Amos to bring righteousness and justice to the world is a primary Jewish legacy I choose to embrace. My role as a rabbi is to comfort the disturbed, to disturb the comfortable, and to bring God's vision for justice to the world. The Holocaust taught us that human good is not a given. Free will demands that when free will fails humanity, we must act.

As the memories of the Holocaust shape my soul, I also hear my father's powerful voice. My dad lost his childhood to Hitler's reign. He was just eight years old when his father fled Nazi persecution. My grandmother Sali was a successful businesswoman who ran one of Germany's largest mail-order companies. For five years, she smuggled funds to my grandfather abroad.

As the only Jewish child to remain enrolled in his school in Munich, my father suffered not physical abuse but emotional abuse. He was an outsider, with not one friend. When the class said their pledge of allegiance, they would complete it by saying, "in the name of Jesus, whom the Jews killed," and stare contemptuously at my father. Anti-Semitism was woven into the curriculum. "If you have ten Jews and kill three, how many are left?" my father's elementary school teacher would ask.

The threat of my father being beaten up after school was too great for my grandmother to allow him to play with his peers. Instead, each afternoon my father was tutored by university professors who had lost their jobs as a result of Nazi anti-Jewish legislation. On June 9, 1938, after Hitler had publicly ordered the destruction of Munich's magnificent Great Synagogue, my grandfather sent a message to my grandmother, "This is the last train out." My grandmother arranged for my dad's and his sister Eva's final departure.

My father left Germany with just a simple suitcase packed for what he thought was another Swiss vacation to visit his dad. When the great Hasidic rabbi Dov Ber, the Maggid of Mezeritch, was asked why he lived with barely a piece of furniture in his home, he replied that he was "just a traveler" in this world—he was "just passing through." It was only when one reaches one's final destination, the Maggid explained, that one needs furniture. Living in the shadow of the Holocaust makes me well aware that material possessions can be lost, stolen, or destroyed and that it is not the material but the spiritual that sustains you.

After an elaborate and heroic escape by my grandmother via Hungary, my father's family was reunited in Switzerland and ultimately immigrated to the United States to become chicken farmers in New Jersey. Upon completing his high school requirements, my father joined the US Army's Tenth Mountain Division and fought Hitler's forces in World War II. He was wounded in Italy, earning a Purple Heart and Bronze Star.

Fighting tirelessly for Jewish survival and acting with creativity to ensure its continuity is the legacy I have been blessed to receive from my dad, Rabbi Alexander Schindler. He committed his life to the survival of Judaism, first as a congregational rabbi, then as president of the Union of American Hebrew Congregations (now the Union for Reform Judaism) for twenty-three years, and also as chairman of the Conference of Presidents of Major American Jewish Organizations. Outreach was his greatest legacy. He believed that Judaism must adapt to remain strong even as it remains rooted in our rich past. While controversial and breaking from rabbinic tradition, my father's vision for the future of the Jewish people— welcoming the non-Jew married to the Jew into our midst and encouraging the couple to raise Jewish children, inviting conversion of the "unchurched," and acknowledging patrilineal descent—was strongly rooted in the tradition of Torah.

As a refugee from Germany, my father became a rabbi to ensure Jewish survival. My mission as a rabbi is the same. Creating and nurturing a thriving Jewish community drives my daily actions. At my congregation, we have a thousand children under the age of eighteen connected to Jewish life, a hundred teens who teach younger students, annual congregational trips to Israel, a *chevra kadisha* that prepares the deceased for burial with only a few hours' notice, a caring community that makes meals for those who are sick for weeks, months, and sometimes years, dozens of students studying for conversion, and one hundred young retirees studying Torah and engaging in actions that bring about social justice. As a congregational rabbi, I strive to fulfill the Jewish philosopher Emil Fackenheim's teaching that the Holocaust reveals to us a 614th commandment: not to give Hitler a posthumous victory and to keep Judaism alive. My goal is to nurture a community that lives its Judaism fully. My task is to transmit the melodies of Judaism and the teachings of Torah to the next generation so that the song of our faith will never die.

I aspire to nurture a Jewish community that not only lifts the lives of Jews but also has an impact on society. To be a Jew is to fulfill Isaiah's vision of being an *or lagoyim*, "a light to the nations." As my father put it, "The wisdom we glean from the fearsome experience of the Holocaust is twofold: first, our determination to secure the future of the Jew and to achieve the creative continuity of the Jewish people as we try to give rebirth; and second, to understand that we are not the only ones to have suffering. We have to learn to be compassionate and understanding and respond to suffering wherever and whenever it occurs."[1]

As the Holocaust has seared an indelible mark upon my memory, I hear the voice of my great-aunt Judith, for whom I was named. Only when I became pregnant with my oldest son and was exploring the family tree to find names and souls whom I could honor did I learn about this woman. By then, my parents already had seven grandchildren. My siblings, in naming their children, had already honored the memories of all our close relatives. I reached out to a cousin, the family historian, who pulled one of my grandfather's books off the shelf. In the front pages, he had written about his entire family: his parents, my great-grandparents, Avraham Yitzchak and Nechama, perished in Theresienstadt; his sister, Chaya, perished in Warsaw with her husband and children; another sister, Kayla Chana, and her husband, Yehezkil, perished in Auschwitz; and another sister, Judith, for whom I was named, was a *rebbetzin*, a rabbi's wife. It was not until I was thirty-three years old that I learned that the woman for whom I was named lived a religious life and a life of leadership and commitment to the Jewish community. She and her husband, Elezar Steinberg Rotenau, met the same fate as the others in Auschwitz. As my great-aunt devoted herself to the Jewish people, so do I. Her voice calls to me saying, "Teach and live Judaism in life. Teach and live Judaism even in the face of death."

I hear the voices of several famous survivors whose mandates replay tirelessly in my mind. There is Pastor Martin Niemöller, whose famous words "First they came for the Communists, and I did not speak out—because I was not a Communist ..." reprimand us for the sin of silence. I hear the poetic writings of Rabbi Abraham Joshua Heschel, who transformed his past of enduring Nazi persecution into a future of fighting for African American civil rights. In calling upon us to shatter the walls of segregation, Heschel wrote, "The tragedy of Pharaoh was the failure to realize that the Exodus from slavery could have spelled redemption for both Israel and Egypt. Would that Pharaoh and the Egyptians had joined the Israelites in the desert and together stood at the foot of Sinai!"[2] Heschel teaches us that oppression of any people is oppressive not only to the victim but also to the oppressor and the bystander. It stains our souls, constrains our spirituality, and destroys our sense of peace. The lives and lessons of Niemöller and Heschel teach me the imperative of forging alliances. Interfaith work is a primary pillar of my rabbinate. Engaging in interfaith dialogues, leading interfaith trips to Israel, serving on interfaith councils for our public schools and community, and Martin Luther King pulpit exchanges are an important part of my professional path.

Finally, I hear the instruction of Elie Wiesel, who when meeting with me and other clergy in Charlotte, told us to use our words to create change. Speaking out, standing up for others, preaching, and writing are the tools I use to transform the voices of my family's past into a more hopeful future.

I do not sleep much. The voices of the Holocaust often keep me awake at night. Occasionally, I have nightmares of anti-Semitism that casts my family from the shelter of safety and democracy and freedom we know. I create educational documentaries on diversity and inclusion that are used in schools, businesses, congregations, and communities across our country so that all minorities are safe, and so that we, as Jews, also, are safe. The voices of the Holocaust keep me alert in the day. My family tree filled with lives murdered by Nazi evil does not allow me the luxury of silence and complicity in the face of hatred.

I'd love to sleep soundly, but I can't. I pray that I can use my extra hours to honor the memories of those who died by creating a society that honors diversity and by tending to the altar of my people in order to keep the flames of Judaism and Torah vibrant so that they can forever warm and bring light to our world. As I hear the echoes of the six million Jews massacred, among them the one and a half million children, I offer the *Kaddish*, "*Yitgadal v'yitkadash sh'mei rabba*—May God's great name be exalted and sanctified." And I add, "May every soul in God's image be uplifted."

Photo: Lynda Shenkman Curtis/IRC

The Right Honourable David Miliband

The Right Honourable David Miliband is president and CEO of the International Rescue Committee. He was a member of Parliament in the United Kingdom from 2001 to 2013 and secretary of state for foreign and commonwealth affairs from 2007 to 2010.

"As the chain of memory is broken by the passing of time and generations, so history and its lessons become more important. And the biggest lesson I draw is that when we are asked, 'Whose responsibility is it to save a life?' the answer must be 'Ours.'"

Every family story is unique, but each one will find echoes, parallels, and intersections with the experience of others. This is my family's story—or at least part of it.

My father and grandfather found their own way to the United Kingdom after the Germans invaded Belgium in 1940. They were helped by many people along the way. Then they did what refugees and immigrants have done down the ages: they put something back. My grandfather spent the war clearing out bombed buildings. My dad studied and then joined the Royal Navy. Fortunately my grandmother and aunt, left behind in Belgium, were in the latter years of the war sheltered by a Catholic farming family. They were eventually allowed into the United Kingdom in the 1950s (having been turned down after the war by the home secretary of the time, who was, ironically, one of my predecessors as member of Parliament for South Shields; talk about a small world).

My mother was not so lucky as to escape Poland before 1940. She spent the war in hiding before being brought to the United Kingdom by Rabbi Solomon Shonfeld in 1946, where she was looked after by British families before going to university and making her own career and family.

These stories were the background music to my childhood. After all, I was born only twenty years after the Holocaust. Now I am part of a transitional generation, born early enough to have met survivors, but part of a generation destined to outlive them, and required in years to come to take up their story and its lessons without the benefit of their living testimony.

The Holocaust was the memory of our parents, but it is history taught to our children. As time moves on and the number of survivors declines, the responsibility of remembrance grows heavier still on this generation and those not yet born.

Those who saved lives during the darkest years believed that in each person there burned a moral flame that if nurtured could defeat the darkness. Many of those who survived and those who saved them have spent the years since telling their stories, educating Jews and non-Jews about the dangers of intolerance and the need to respect the dignity of difference. In doing so they make a great affirmation of life. That is one reason that efforts by foundations and trusts to archive and explain are so important.

The Wiener Library in London has the slogan "If we do not save our history it will perish." History and memory—two different words, so closely related that in Hebrew (I am not a speaker), they are the same: *zachor*.

What is the difference between history and memory? Consider the powerful words of former United Kingdom Chief Rabbi, Professor

Lord Sacks, in *The Chief Rabbi's Haggadah*: "History is *his* story—an event that happened sometime else to someone else. Memory is *my* story—something that happened to me and is a part of who I am. History is information. Memory, by contrast, is part of identity."[1]

As the chain of memory is broken by the passing of time and generations, so history and its lessons become more important. And the biggest lesson I draw is that when we are asked, "Whose responsibility is it to save a life?" the answer must be "Ours." When I asked the Catholic farmer in Belgium why he put himself in danger to save my aunt and grandmother, his answer was simple: "One must."

As president of the International Rescue Committee, founded by Albert Einstein when he found refuge in the United States in 1933 and now a global charity helping the victims of civil conflict and natural disaster around the world, I feel in a small way I am repaying a personal debt to those who helped my parents.

Unlike some others contributing to this volume, I was raised in a secular household. But I know the injunction "He who saves one single life it is as if he has saved an entire world." That is the spirit of those who helped my family. It is the spirit I try to honor. And it is the spirit we need to keep alive tomorrow.

Justice Rosalie Silberman Abella

Justice Rosalie Silberman Abella was appointed to the Supreme Court of Canada in 2004 after serving on the Ontario Court of Appeal for twelve years. She is the first Jewish woman appointed to the Supreme Court. Justice Abella is married to Canadian historian Irving Abella, and they have two sons, Jacob and Zachary, both lawyers.

"My generation is the generation that has a particular duty to promise our *children that we will do everything possible to keep the world safer for them than it was for their grandparents."*

There are times in our history of such irreversible images that they enter the soul of history and cry out through the generations not to be forgotten. The Holocaust was such a time.

It was one of those unforgivable times when, tragically, the world forgot to be tolerant, to be compassionate, or even to care. France, anxious to appease the Germans, cooperated in Jewish extinction mercilessly; other countries expressed horror but opened their doors only creakingly to the victims; and Canada, as the book *None Is Too Many* so eloquently describes, in one of her most shameful hours, put the arguments of national unity, economic viability, and anti-Semitism over humanity.

The Jews of Europe begged the world to be released from their horrible victimization, begged for entry to be released from their dehumanization, and begged for refuge to be released from destruction. We now know the world's answer—it was an echo of neglect that reverberated throughout history, a dispassionate litany of rules, regulations, and priorities whose message was clear: victims you have been, victims you are, victims you will remain.

The Holocaust is the legacy of this neglect. Six million innocent people, who happened to be Jewish, no longer laugh, weep, love, think, or create. The world lost, and lost cruelly, not only the minds and hearts of millions who died in utter despair at the inconceivable indifference that permitted their loss, it lost the right ever to expect a single Jew to stand silently at the sight of an injustice.

This, I think, is the real lesson of the Holocaust. Our experience in those unspeakable years left a searing imprint in our collective consciences. Where were our friends, who were our friends, and why were we so alone? We may with time come to better understand why the world was indifferent, but we will never come to accept it. And if there are those who urge us to permit time to wipe away the horrors and forget the crimes of the past, they must be told with equal urgency that to forget the indignities and horrors of the past is to permit their recurrence.

History is a teacher. It trains us for the future by reminding us of what we came from. History does not exaggerate. It can be placed in context, but it can never be undone. And in its explication of what was, history shows us what should never be again. How can you ask an entire people for tolerance when our very annihilation was itself tolerated?

The Holocaust left those who survived dumbfounded by its inception, stunned by its continuance, shaken by its acceptance, and decimated by its completion. How can we be expected ever to forget the sheer horror of being denied the very right to exist? Of course it was arbitrary, of course it was immoral, and of course it was uncivilized. But it was also unforgivable, and we ought not to waste the tiniest ounce of energy on persuading anyone of the need to remember with tenacity and vigor this cornerstone of our history this century.

We in turn need ask no one to forgive us this preoccupation. It has taught us much. It has taught us that we can never value anything more than justice; that we can never put economies over dignity; that we can never appease bigotry; and that we can never sacrifice morality to expedience. We can never be indifferent. We belong to the generation that saw and survived the Holocaust. We must therefore be the generation, as Jews and non-Jews, that rails most vigilantly against the intolerance that produced it. The banality of evil must never blur our capacity to see it. And having seen it, to identify it, fight it, and extinguish it. What can we leave our children if not an intense loyalty to humanity and a passionate commitment to its civilized expansion? Each of us, in our own ways, in our own fields, and in our own families must face the future proudly, wearing the sadness of our past as a shield, and bearing the lessons of our history as weapons against an indifferent present. We must be proud of who and what we are, courageous in our uniqueness, and generous in our willingness to fight for what we cherish. We cannot undo history, but we can, as people humbled by its awesome power, contribute to a powerful momentum against its repetition.

In addition to its universal lessons for humanity, the Holocaust has had powerful impacts of a more private kind for me. In July 1946, the month the prosecution summed up its case in the Major War Criminals Trial at Nuremberg, I was born in a Displaced Persons camp in Germany to parents who had married in Poland on September 3, 1939—the day World War II started—spent almost four years in concentration camps, and lost everything and everyone, including a two-year-old son. Then, in an act that seems to me almost incomprehensible in its breathtaking optimism, they transcended the inhumanity they had experienced and, like thousands of other survivors, decided to have more children.

My father was thirty-five when the war ended; my mother was twenty-eight. As I reached each of these ages, I tried to imagine how they felt when they faced an unknown future as survivors of an unimaginable past. And as each of my sons reached the age my brother had been when he was killed, I tried to imagine my parents' pain at losing their two-year-old son. I couldn't.

In fact, I have never been able to comprehend what happened to my parents. Or how they managed to survive. Or how, having survived, they were able to create such resolutely normal lives for themselves and their two children, let alone encourage us to embrace optimism so unreservedly. But they did, and so did thousands of other survivors who rebuked the indignity and barbaric humiliation they had suffered as Jews, by living and creating lives of dignity and pride in who they were.

I have always considered it a great privilege to be the daughter of my father and mother. All my values I learned from them; all my optimism I learned from watching the hope and courage with which they overcame events which would have overwhelmed me. For me, as a woman deeply marked by her family's past and as one who holds her parents and other survivors in awe for their persistence in rebuilding healthy lives, I am shaped in two fundamental ways. The first is that I feel an obligation to repay them for the efforts they made to reconstruct their lives and to prove that it was worth their effort. Most survivors derived the energy and sustenance to carry on from their hope of guaranteeing for their children a life free from pain. They succeeded and we are a spoiled generation—our lives have not been horribly uprooted, nor did we have to bear witness to parents, children, and spouses dying cruelly and unnaturally.

But as people free from this experience, we must repay our parents' love by drawing from it the strength to contribute our energies and talents to society generally and to the Jewish community of which we are an integral part. With strength comes a capacity for generosity, and we must generously return in our various communities the investment our parents made—by insisting on vigorous regard for the rights of others, by living our lives proud of our Jewishness, and by keeping alive the memories of those who themselves never had the chance to fulfill their potential. We have the gift of survivorship, and it both enables and obliges us to live our lives to the fullest limit of our abilities. We have undoubtedly the right to live private lives, but we also have a fundamental sense that we must make, too, a public contribution in whatever ways our capacities direct us.

The second major influence I have felt is that I cannot take anything or anyone for granted. One comes away from the history of the Holocaust with a driving urgency for life—having watched a whole generation intolerably interrupted in mid-life, one learns to appreciate intensely the fragility and temporal limitations of our own lives. There is, as a result, a compelling need to make the most of the opportunities you are given and to value, cherish, and nurture the people you love.

It is not an unbridled drive—it is firmly circumscribed by the values one equally strenuously embraces. If anything, the sense of fairness and decency rooted in Jewish tradition is heightened in those of us who feel the weight of history. We live not only for ourselves, but to honor our ancestors by living with courage, integrity, and compassion. There is no competition with others; the competition is with time.

Our lives as individuals and particularly as Jewish individuals have been permanently shaped by World War II, and we have a duty to ourselves as Jews and to the wider community never to forget who we are and where we come from. And we must constantly remind others who we are and where we come from, and to demand respect for our right to grieve forever the irretrievable losses of the Holocaust. The memory must never die, and we and our children and our children's children must do everything in our power to keep it alive as a source of personal inspiration, of commitment to justice, and of pride in who we are.

My life started in a country where there had been no democracy, no rights, no tolerance, no justice. No one with this history does not feel lucky to be alive and free. No one with this history can take anything for granted. My generation grew up in the shadow of the worst injustice and inhumanity the world had ever known, an injustice perpetrated because of our identity as Jews. That means, to me, that my generation is the generation that has a particular duty to promise *our* children that we will do everything possible to keep the world safer for them than it was for their grandparents. And that means a world where *all* children, regardless of race, religion, or gender, can wear their identities with pride, in dignity, and in peace.

Senator Ron Wyden

Ronald Wyden is the United States senator from Oregon, serving since 1996, and became chairman of the Senate Finance Committee in February 2014. He previously served in the United States House of Representatives from 1981 to 1996.

"Like my great-great-grandfather, who sat on the Berlin City Council around the turn of the last century, I've chosen to serve my neighbors and my country in government."

Lately, I have been giving a lot of thought to *tikkun olam*. It is a concept that has had many meanings over the centuries and is often internalized uniquely by each individual. At its heart, however, is a simple idea: heal the world. There are many ways to have an impact on the world around us. Like my great-great-grandfather, who sat on the Berlin City Council around the turn of the last century, I've chosen to serve my neighbors and my country in government. Others, like my father, an award-winning journalist, recognized the importance of uncovering truths to help us all better understand—and change—the world around us.

I count my family to be very lucky. With the exception of one elderly aunt, my entire family escaped Nazi Germany before the *Kristallnacht* pogrom of November 9–10, 1938. However, they did not escape the fear of those years. They could not escape the injustice of having livelihoods taken from them—of their way of life irreparably changed. If it hadn't been for distant family in the United States, our history may have been very different.

It is hard, then, to think about what it means to heal the world, as *tikkun olam* emphasizes. It is hard, with the memory of that time still imprinted on future generations of my family, to think about creating a perfect world. Inspiration to do so comes to me precisely from my family history.

As a member of the Berlin City Council, my great-great-grandfather fought against the entrenched interests of the public utilities. He worked for years to fight corruption and bring the necessities of modern life to his neighbors. In my own career, I have seen the need to stand up to those who seek to maintain the status quo at the expense of those less fortunate and have taken stands similar in spirit to those of my great-great grandfather more than one hundred years ago.

My father, Peter, asked questions. From a young age, Peter sought to understand the world around him and to use that knowledge to stand against injustices. He was one of only two Jewish boys in his Berlin school prior to the war. One day, as a young boy, he decided not to give the fascist salute when prompted to during class. For that, he was beaten by his own young classmates.

He came to America in 1937, knowing little English, but within a few years he was writing stories for local newspapers. He was no less a public servant than I; he simply carried a notebook and not an election certificate. His life was spent in the service of the truth, and he taught me lessons about seeking answers to tough questions and how citizenship requires vigilance.

The tough questions he asked sometimes led to hard truths, but without the discovery of a problem, there can be no solution—no *tikkun olam*. He taught me the value of holding those who work in the public trust accountable and the importance of maintaining my own accountability as I seek to earn that trust. It's an invaluable lesson for any public servant to learn, and it has in no small way contributed to *tikkun olam*.

I have recently been given the opportunity and responsibility of chairing a powerful Senate committee. In my new role, I am better positioned to impact the country and the world than I have ever been in my career. Now is the perfect time to be reminded of the importance of *tikkun olam*. In the last few decades a rift has grown in America. It exceeds party or ideology and resides in the inherent inequality between those who have the means to live the American dream and those who no longer do. We've seen a contracting of the middle class to the point where the next generation of Americans doubts that it will have it better than the previous generation. It is hard to see *tikkun olam* at work in this scenario, and I want to use my position as chair of the Senate Finance Committee to work for bipartisan ways to forward the spirit of *tikkun olam*.

Like my family members before me, I ask tough questions and work to remove entrenched obstacles to the public good. It's not easy, but where there is a coalition of those willing to seek change and work hard for it, it's possible to heal the world.

MK Merav Michaeli

Merav Michaeli, a member of the Knesset, the Israeli parliament, from the Labor Party, is chair of the Caucus for Female Knesset Members and is a member of the Foreign Affairs and Defense Committee. Prior to entering politics, she was known as one of Israel's most prominent journalists, an op-ed writer for the *Ha'aretz* newspaper, and the producer and star of her own prime-time, documentary, and current affairs television and radio programs. She has taught university classes and lectured extensively on the topics of feminism, media, and communications and is a longtime advocate for women's and minority rights. This essay is adapted from her inaugural speech in the Knesset on February 27, 2013.

"We cannot remain just the victims of the Holocaust. Because the discourse of victimhood cannot be a constructive one. Nothing can grow from it. I came here in order to change that discourse into one of empowerment, of mutual aid, of acceptance of the other."

On Wednesday morning, July 3, 1944, a Zionist Jew in a suit stood in Adolf Eichmann's Budapest office. "Your nerves seem tattered," said Eichmann to the man. "Maybe I'll send you on vacation in Auschwitz." The Zionist Jew who stood before Eichmann was unfazed. As a gesture demonstrating he was no inferior in front of this interlocutor, he removed a case from his pocket and lit a cigarette.

That man was Dr. Israel (Reszo) Kasztner. The reason why he was in the room was to negotiate with Eichmann and other Nazi officers, thereby saving tens of thousands of Jews from extermination. Later, he came to Israel and ran for the Knesset. Rezso Kasztner was my grandfather. I am privileged to be part of consecutive generations dedicated to this project that is the State of Israel and to the way it provides a home for those people who were a Diaspora, with the understanding that there is no other place for us.

This is also the place from which my critique of Israeli society emerges. On the one hand, I'm part of a founding dynasty; on the other, I'm a woman. A privileged woman, a woman who is "the granddaughter of," but still a woman. A woman who is still part of a minority in a masculine and military society where the "machismo of the sabra" is still a supreme value. That's the place from which my critique emerges, and this is a sensitivity with which I come to this Parliament.

I certainly do not come as a victim. If there is anything I have learned from the story of my grandfather, it is not to be a victim. Even when he was cast into the role of the ultimate victim—Jew versus exterminator-in-chief—he managed to take his fate and that of his community into his own hands.

We, feminist women, don't come as victims. We come as equals, to take our fate in our hands and to shape the reality we live in. But not only the reality of our lives as women. There's no such thing as "women" separate from men, or from work, from society, economy, security, army, and war. Yes, despite your determined efforts to exclude us from decisions—on war, on peace, on how we define "security" and how to achieve it—yet, we are still part of this conversation. Because we pay the price on the home front when you decide to open a war front. We pay the price when children are killed and wounded because there is no peace. We pay the price when you invest one-fifth of our national budget on a security budget that does not deliver security.

The problem of exclusion of women in Israel does not start or end in military ceremonies and seats on buses. Women are excluded here, in the Knesset, where we're still barely one-quarter of the members. Women are excluded in the cabinet, in key economic positions, in academia, in the army.

As a feminist who has devoted long years to feminist activism, I do not aim to work only on behalf of women. I'm not here to beg on behalf of the minority I represent. I'm here as a feminist because I believe that feminism and feminist thinking can change the entire way we think about society and state. And as a feminist I not only focus on how we, as a society, can save underprivileged women, but ask how we, as women, can save our society.

Because the exclusion of women is just a symptom for the exclusion of other sectors. In exactly the same way, I see how Israel excludes *Mizrahim* (Jews from Arab countries), Ethiopians, Arabs, Russians, the disabled, the elderly, foreigners, and non-Jews. They're excluded from access to resources, from access to justice, from access to active citizenship. The weakened are excluded from the basic human right to housing and to a dignified existence.

Israel as a state also does not take responsibility for its strong and privileged position vis-à-vis our neighbors-cum-enemies, the Palestinians, as the strong and rich state, the one that exists. Instead of grasping this advantage and offering real peace, based on trust and cooperation, Israel hunkers down in a defensive-aggressive posture. Instead of extending a hand to our neighbors—who have lived for so long in extremely difficult conditions, due to their own fault and ours—and helping them build a future that will benefit all of us, Israel the strong continues to fight the Palestinians for the title of victim.

It's understandable, of course, why we're in this position of victimhood. Few are the peoples with a national trauma like the Holocaust in their pasts. But our renewal is already here and has been for quite a while now. We must internalize that revival. We cannot remain just the victims of the Holocaust.

Because the discourse of victimhood cannot be a constructive one. Nothing can grow from it. I came here in order to change that discourse into one of empowerment, of mutual aid, of acceptance of the other. An authentic and deep acceptance. A discourse that replaces shrillness with cooperation and the nurturing of a safe place. A safe space is a place where I have a secure job, earn a living wage, can walk the streets secure that I won't be spat at, beaten, harassed, and excluded. Not because I'm a woman or dark-skinned. Not because I'm Jewish or non-Jewish, Israeli or non-Israeli.

My grandfather saved tens of thousands of Jews in the Holocaust, and he was murdered here, in the State of Israel, before becoming a member of Knesset, because he saved them through negotiations with their Nazi exterminators. He was murdered despite saving Jews, because he did so in a way that some thought wrong, not Jewish enough, not Zionist enough. I come from a founding dynasty, but also from one not entirely in the mainstream, not consensual. A dynasty of doing things differently.

The position of wanting *tikkun olam* is often one of weakness. Identification with the distress of others makes one vulnerable. Concern for the rights of "the other," those not on "your side" or exactly like you, can make you seem eccentric, unreliable, suspected of bleeding-heart tendencies, a self-hater. In Israel, any criticism of the state and its doings is often received as nothing less than an act of treason.

But the truth is that this criticism comes from a commitment to the State of Israel, an identification with it. It comes from a desire to make this place the best place for us to live in. The safest place. The most empowering. The most pleasant. The most worthy. That's what I'm here for.

Moreover, the ability to embrace the differences in the other is the ability to embrace our own differences and live in peace with ourselves. Only when we stop repressing those parts of society that we have labeled not-us, not part of us, will we become a whole and healthy society. Only when we allow all parts of our society to be fully present, to fully participate, will we really become a prosperous society, a strong society. That's where we should be headed. That's what we need to work on. That's what I'm here for.

Michael Ashley Stein

Photo: Juliet Bowler

Michael Ashley Stein is executive director of the Harvard Law School Project on Disability and visiting professor at Harvard Law School. An internationally recognized expert on disability law and policy, he participated in the drafting of the United Nations Convention on the Rights of Persons with Disabilities, works with disabled persons organizations around the world, actively consults with governments on their disability laws and policies, and advises a number of UN bodies. He has received numerous awards for his work, most recently the inaugural Henry Viscardi Achievement Award and the inaugural Morton E. Ruderman Prize for Inclusion, and was appointed by President Obama to the United States Holocaust Memorial Council.

"Advocating for disability-based human rights and combating the modern avatars of the Shoah are linked in my mind by the common thread of enabling people to see the full breadth of humanity, and beauty, and Godliness within each other."

Through a series of fortunate circumstances, persistence, and strategic positioning, I am privileged to spend my professional life advocating for disability-based human rights. It may be apparent that as a person with a visible disability (specifically, a wheelchair user), I have a personal stake in such work. More so, that my academic career has followed an arc that began with creating theory around and advocating for disability rights in the United States toward expanding those concepts internationally through the United Nations and in some forty countries on the ground. Perhaps less apparent, but clear to me, is the connection of this human rights work to the dark shadow cast over my generation by the Shoah.

My mother and her family's experiences were framed in terms of "the War." The murderous pogrom by their very willing neighbors in Panevežys (known in Yiddish as Ponevezh), Lithuania, absent Nazi intervention and prior to the arrival of Soviet troops; subsequent exile, starvation, and death in Siberia; displacement and eventual relocation to the United States—all were, in the brief descriptions afforded me, parallel to but separate from the Shoah. And yet those events have deep-seated effects for those of us comprising the second generation, even when we were children. One frequent and very earnest game played by two dear cousins and myself was "Who will hide us?" Another one involved strategies for hoarding food and munitions. Both those cousins became psychologists, and I became a human rights lawyer. I doubt those choices arose merely by coincidence.

At fourteen, I transmogrified from a "normal" childhood to the circumstance of being a young adult with a severe physical disability and all its attendant social and stigmatic implications. A few friends and most family members were resolute and life-affirming, but most "friends" and some family disappeared, my beloved yeshiva day school did not want me to return, and my life, put simply, was turned upside down (although enriched in other ways). Common to the negative experiences, and to many others that I would experience later in life—both personally and through the work I perform for others with disabilities—is the notion that people with disabilities do not belong in "normal" society because somehow our differences make us less than human.

Often this idea remains unstated and is implied in cold reluctance to engage with disabled persons, but sometimes it is stated overtly. For instance, when the rabbi of an Orthodox shul denied my request to lead a minyan so I could say *Kaddish* on my mother's *yahrzeit* on the grounds that I was "half a man." Or the assurances of a then minister of health of a South Asian country that "of course people with mental and intellectual disabilities need to be kept behind bars." On occasion this notion is rationalized and justified, as when two Jewish philosophers (one by choice, and one the descendant of a Shoah victim) argued, respectively, that persons with intellectual disabilities are less than fully human and that those with profound disabilities are suitable for euthanasia. Each of those views trumpets loudly and tragically a failure to grasp the full assault on humanity that the Holocaust represented.

Advocating for disability-based human rights and combating the modern avatars of the Shoah are linked in my mind by the common thread of enabling people to see the full breadth of humanity, and beauty, and Godliness within each other. Each, in my view, mandates an embrace of what another person offers and the value that we each inevitably contribute to the world. Such a mandate requires us to question why children and adults with certain disabilities are conspicuously missing from societies, to demand an end to forced conditions such as "population centers" in North Korea or "social care institutions" in much of Central and Eastern Europe, and to advocate against notions that anyone can be viewed as "excess population" or lack inherent worth. Ironically, but not lost on me, the Nazi authorities would have wanted to kill me as a disabled person even before they would have murdered me as a Jew.

Tali Nates

Tali Nates, director of the Johannesburg Holocaust & Genocide Centre, has lectured internationally about Holocaust education, genocide prevention, reconciliation, and human rights. In 2010, she was chosen as one of the top one hundred newsworthy and noteworthy women in South Africa (*Mail & Guardian Book of South African Women*). She acts as a scholar and leader of many Holocaust education missions to Eastern Europe as well as educational missions in South Africa and Rwanda.

"After the Holocaust, the survivors truly believed that when the 'world' saw what had happened to them, surely it would never happen again. But it did.... In Rwanda ... hundreds of thousands of Tutsis were murdered."

"I am alive because of a German who was a member of the National Socialist Party," my father used to say to me. "And so are you." My father, Moses (Marion) Turner, was saved by Oskar Schindler. Together with his brother Chanoch (Henryk), they were part of what we now know as "Schindler's List"; both appear on page ten of this list. Throughout my childhood I learned from my father that one should not generalize and pass sweeping judgements about people. He believed that "not all Germans were bad." He used to say, "Look at Schindler. He was a German." My father taught me that people have choices, always, every day of their lives. This lesson shapes my identity and, in some way, forms the way I see the world today.

My father was fourteen years old when he was forcefully removed from his town of Nowy Targ in the Tatra Mountains of southwestern Poland, to work and suffer in four different labor and concentration camps (Zakopane, Płaszów, Gross-Rosen, and Brünnlitz). When he was seventeen years old and a prisoner at Płaszów, he was beaten severely because potatoes were found hidden on him when he returned to the camp from forced labor. In 1944, when the Nazis wanted to destroy the evidence of the mass graves in the camp, they ordered Jews, among them my father, to dig up the bodies and burn them. He had nightmares about it until the day he died.

My grandmother Leah and two aunts Helen and Cela, twelve and sixteen years old at the time, were murdered in the gas chambers of the Belzec killing center in August 1942. Taken away from his town early in the war, my father never saw his mother and sisters again. More than five hundred thousand men, women, and children were murdered in Belzec in the ten months of its existence (March to December 1942). There were only a very few known survivors. One of them, Rudolf Reder, provided the only eyewitness account of the mass murder at Belzec. Reading his testimony years ago allowed me to have a glimpse into the horrific fate of my family.

I was born to the story of the Holocaust. Like most other children of Holocaust survivors, I was named after my family member who was murdered. I was the "memorial candle" Israeli psychologist Dina Wardi refers to.[1] My father named me after his sister Helen. I was the second-born child, but the first daughter of a survivor who had lost all female members of his family. Only the boys survived. Born years after the end of the war, I have never even seen a picture of Helen. All I knew was that she had been murdered in the Belzec gas chambers. However, Helen was my second name; my parents decided to give me an Israeli first name, Tali (*tal* means "morning dew," earthy and fresh), as the attitude in Israel in the 1960s was to cut off the Diaspora and bond with the earth and the Land of Israel. By giving me an Israeli name, my parents felt they gave me a new identity and a fresh start in life. Yet this was not an easy decision. They had to reach a compromise, giving me a second name and telling me always what that name meant to my father. The name became both a gift and a burden. It is always there as a reminder and a force behind my work in Holocaust and genocide memory and education. It is there as a marker to the life I was born to and the path that I have to go on, no matter the difficulties and the challenges. Yet at times the name is a great burden; I have to carry the name and memory of Helen, the young teenager who never had a chance to really live.

Many children of survivors I spoke to often have difficulties developing a positive sense of Jewish identity, because they associate being Jewish with being killed. Many of the survivors I am close to have ambivalence to religion and "an account" with God. My father came from a religious background but lost his faith in the camps. From a very young age, he used to tell me that "luckily, I did not look Jewish." I had blond hair and blue eyes, and for him, that was a blessing, because "if it happens again," I would survive. Despite my deep involvement in many aspects of Jewish history and community and my pride in my Jewish identity, I found myself whispering the same words when my youngest son was born with blond hair and blue eyes. I thought immediately that "he does not look Jewish" and felt a great sense of relief and joy.

My relationship with God and the Jewish faith remained a complicated one throughout my life. A defining moment I will never forget was my first trip as a scholar to Auschwitz, where I saw prayer shawls on display. I felt an immense sense of anger at God and at the Jewish men who naively believed that they were going to live and pray in a place where God could not be present. Yet, when I lead groups to the sites of life and death in Poland, in each site I direct the group to recite the Jewish prayers in honor of the dead, *Kaddish* and *El Maleh Rachamim.* Anger and prayer live side by side in my heart.

The Holocaust shaped many other aspects of my identity. Like many children of Holocaust survivors, I also grew up without an extended family. It was completely natural not to have many uncles, aunts, and cousins on my father's side of the family. Growing up in Israel in the 1960s, there were very few children in my school who had grandparents. Dinners were held with our immediate family or other friends of the family who were adopted to replace the huge void. I grew up with Uncle Moshe and Uncle Elimelech, even though they were not real blood relatives, but survivor friends of my father. This was the reality, and it seemed normal.

Throughout my life, the Holocaust always penetrated my world, and my father's past affected my thoughts and dreams in varying degrees. I was dreaming for years of escaping ghettos, camps, forests, and Nazis. I always managed to survive, many times with the help of a good man or woman, usually German, very much like the real-life Schindler who saved my father. I became interested in discussions and dialogues with second-generation perpetrator or bystander Germans. I wanted to understand their past and the reality they had to live with. A chance meeting in 2004 in Johannesburg with a fellow educator, Thomas Hagspihl, whose father was a member of the Hitler Youth, started a dialogue between us. We researched our fathers' history and reflected on how it influenced us and the lessons we learned from it. We looked at connections to our lives in post-apartheid South Africa, a country that went through its TRC (Truth and Reconciliation Commission) process, imperfect as it was, and could not but think that Germans and Jews never had a TRC. Speaking with him at conferences and writing about our dialogue was an important experience for both of us. The attitude of many survivors and second generation toward Germany and Germans is a complex issue. In South Africa, many survivors would not buy a German car, for example. In my family's case, perhaps because a German saved my father, he chose to work in a VW car agency in the 1960s; my brother still owns this agency to this day.

My father did not talk much about his experiences during the war. My uncle did not stop talking about it. He spoke about his Holocaust experiences to me all the time and wrote a memoir and moving poetry about it too. He felt guilty until his death about the loss of his family and his own survival. It was very important to him that I was interested, that I listened and chose to work in this field. Before one of my many trips to Poland, he told me for the hundredth time about the selection and the separation from his mother and sisters in the soccer stadium of the town. How he never said good-bye to them, never told them that he loved them. He begged me to try and get a picture of his mother. "I have nothing left of her," he said. "I want a picture that I can kiss good night before I go to sleep." Sadly, I did not find a picture, as nothing had survived. I wonder if I am trying to say that evasive "good-bye and I love you" to my murdered family through my work. After the genocide in Rwanda in 1994, I started working with survivors of that genocide. On one of my trips to Rwanda I encountered the testimony of sixteen-year-old Bernard, who said, "I don't have any photos of my family." I felt again my uncle's pain and helplessness and wondered if it will always stay there with me as unresolved as it was for him.

I feel driven to continue the work I do in the Holocaust and genocide fields. A picture that will stay with me is from a visit to one of the churches in Rwanda, in Ntarama, where 4,000 men, women, and children were murdered. I was sitting with Cocous, a sweet young man with a huge machete scar on his skull. He was visibly upset, as that morning we started our day at the Kigali Memorial Centre, the last resting place of 250,000 people, all in mass graves, and where Cocous's parents were buried. I shared with him my family's story, how they were also murdered in another genocide many years ago, that this genocide happened in Europe, that my grand-mother, aunts, and many other members of the family were whites, and that they were murdered by other whites who looked very much like them. Cocous's eyes opened wide in disbelief, learning that geno-cide had happened before and yet had happened to him, too. In the background was a sign with the words "Never Again."

The words "Never Again" always make me very upset. They are hollow words without any meaning. After the Holocaust, the survivors truly believed that when the "world" saw what had hap-pened to them, surely it would never happen again. But it did. In April 1994, at the same time that South Africa was celebrating its freedom from apartheid and I was standing proudly in queues for hours to vote, in Rwanda, just three and a half hours flight away from where I was, hundreds of thousands of Tutsis were murdered. So there is much work to be done by all of us to make those words a reality.

The Holocaust and my father's and uncle's experiences have a constant influence on me, on my thoughts and beliefs. The most important lesson I learned is to try and act every day for *tikkun olam*, that is, mending the world. Holocaust scholar Michael Berenbaum tells of a veteran prisoner in the Sachsenhausen concentration camp who told new prisoners honestly and directly about the rules of the concentration camp, of the difficulties they would experience, of the horror that awaited them. His honest warning ended with these con-cluding words: "I have told you this story not to weaken you. But to strengthen you. Now it is up to you!" I always felt that in some way, as a second-generation Holocaust survivor, these words were directed at me—that it is also up to me.

Dr. Richard Prasquier

Dr. Richard Prasquier served as president of the Conseil Représentatif des Institutions juives de France (the Representative Council of French Jewish Institutions) from 2007 to 2013. A cardiologist by profession, he is president of the Keren Hayessod (United Israel Appeal) of France, vice president of the Fondation pour la Mémoire de la Shoah, and a member of the International Auschwitz Committee.

> "I helped to bring public awareness to the many righteous French Christians thanks to whom a large part of the French-Jewish community was not annihilated."

I was born in Gdansk, Poland, in 1945 at a time when there were almost no Jewish babies in the country. We immigrated to France the following year. My mother tongue was Polish, and almost all my parents' friends had also left Poland after the war. My parents and their friends did not speak to their children about what had happened to them. I knew, of course, that Hitler had wanted to kill all our families, but it seemed that what had happened to the Jews during World War II was not important enough to be included in the history we were being taught at school.

We strongly supported the young State of Israel, which is what I spoke about at my bar mitzvah, one year after I was circumcised. The anguish of possibly having to confront another Auschwitz that overwhelmed us in May of 1967 when Nasser threatened Israel's very existence never left me. But the attitude toward the Shoah was different. For a long time it was a largely black hole into which most of my family had disappeared, without leaving behind any photographs, or histories, or virtually any names.

I remember precisely the moment when I realize that this crime, which was not then known by a name—I had heard speak of deportations, of deaths, but not of a Shoah, nor of a Holocaust, nor even of exterminations—continued to gnaw at my father every day. It was in June of 1960 and we heard television reports that Argentinian president Arturo Frondizi was protesting against

Israel's abduction of a Nazi named Adolf Eichmann. I said that I understood this reaction, since there had been a violation of Argentinian sovereignty. My father became livid and for the only time in his life spoke to me in anger. "When one doesn't know what one is talking about," he rebuked me, "one keeps quiet. You have no idea who Eichmann was!"

My father died suddenly in 1986 during my son's bar mitzvah. He had always kept his distance from the organized Jewish establishment, afraid that they would make *Judenrat*-like compromises. But to make sense of his death, I began my Jewish communal activities. In 2007, I became the president of the Conseil Répresentatif des Institutions juives en France (CRIF), the French-Jewish umbrella organization that represents the Jewish community in the political arena.

In contrast to the large majority of French-Jewish descendants of survivors, my background was not linked to France, and I was not involved in the efforts that slowly brought about public recognition of the Vichy government's responsibility for the crimes that were committed in France during the Holocaust. After 1995, however, as president of the French Committee for Yad Vashem, I helped to bring public awareness to the many righteous French Christians thanks to whom a large part of the French-Jewish community was not annihilated and whose very existence belies any generalizations regarding the supposed anti-Semitic character of an entire nation.

Poland was another story. For my father, it, too, was a black hole. He had forbidden me to return there. But slowly, that country also changed. The *Solidarnosc* movement and Pope John Paul II imbued me with a sort of national pride that made me reexamine the relationship between Jews and Christians as well as the realities of Polish anti-Semitism, which should neither be denied nor considered immutable and eternal.

I started dealing with the history of the Shoah and the history of Poland. Although I have not been able so far to confront my own family history, I have frequently visited the Nazi extermination sites, notably in the company of Father Patrick Desbois, the founder of the "Holocaust by Bullets," project who is also our institutional partner in the Jewish–Catholic dialogue. We brought Cardinal Jean-Marie Lustiger to the site of the so-called "Red House," just outside the Birkenau perimeter, which I had bought and donated to the Auschwitz Museum. It was there that the first Jewish mass gassings, including the cardinal's mother, took place in 1942. This gave me the opportunity to participate personally in the work of remembrance that my generation owes to our murdered people.

I consider this work inseparable from the critical need for interfaith dialogue and the imperative of supporting the State of Israel and fighting the growing resurgence of anti-Semitism and neo-Nazism in different parts of Europe. We have an obligation to confront both our past and our present.

[*Translated from the French by Menachem Z. Rosensaft*]

Dr. Yaffa Singer

Dr. Yaffa Singer, who was born in the Displaced Persons camp of Bergen-Belsen, is an Israeli clinical psychologist whose major field is psychic trauma. She received her PhD in psychology from Bar Ilan University and was for many years the head of the Post Traumatic Central Clinic in the Israeli Military Mental Health Department. She has vast experience in the treatment of patients with post-traumatic stress disorder (PTSD), mostly soldiers and Holocaust survivors, and she has lectured and written extensively on PTSD-related issues in Israel and abroad.

> "It is possible for wounded human beings to create a coherent chain of life events that contain the horrors of the past, but also revive cherished aspirations and dreams that give a specific purpose to their lives."

Psychological consequences of traumatic events are well known across cultures and people. Psychiatrist Judith Herman has written that trauma "robs the victims of a sense of power and control.... It destroys the sustaining bonds between individual and community."[1] In therapy, the repeated exposure to trauma material is distressful for the patients and sometimes for the therapists as well. In this setting, one of the therapist's tasks is to help his or her patients build new lives.

I am a clinical psychologist whose primary field is psychic trauma. For seventeen years, I was the head of the Post Traumatic Central Clinic in the Israel Defense Forces. We treated mostly Israeli soldiers who were emotionally wounded on the battlefield and in captivity. In addition, I have worked with Holocaust survivors and with victims of other traumatic events.

Being a daughter of Holocaust survivors exposed me from an early age to my parents' experiences during World War II. When I started my professional career and chose to work with trauma survivors, I understood that my special personal history would be an invaluable resource for my therapeutic work and would give me the necessary strength and confidence to believe that these harmed patients would be able to build a future for themselves.

I learned from my parents' experiences—especially those that occurred after their liberation, immediately after the traumatic events had ended—how to help trauma patients develop a belief that it was possible for them to resume a normal life, a life with hope and meaning. I would like to share this experience with my readers.

My parents were liberated in the Bergen-Belsen concentration camp on April 15, 1945. After liberation, the survivors were gathered together in a Displaced Persons camp that had been set up in nearby German military barracks. During their first days of freedom, while still behind barbed-wire fences and battling against the spread of typhus, and before burying the dead, a group of young survivors, including my parents, organized themselves under the Hebrew term *Sh'erit ha-Pletah*, meaning the "Surviving Remnant." Their goal was to return to normality, to rebuild life for their fellow survivors as well as for themselves. They instinctively understood, as Judith Herman would write decades afterward, that the fundamental stages of recovery for trauma survivors are establishing safety, reconstructing the trauma story, and restoring the connection between survivors and their community.[2]

Historian Hagit Lavsky describes this group of active survivors as having been quick to organize, to take charge and establish a multidimensional committee. She explains that already two weeks after their liberation, these young people, many of whom had belonged to Zionist youth movements before the war, understood that they had the ability to organize and inspire the sick, broken survivors and were ready to start a new life. As Lavsky puts it, "They had a real goal, they were full of hope, and their strong Zionist belief and enthusiasm transmitted itself to others."[3]

This organized group of young motivated survivors provided the Jewish DPs of Bergen-Belsen with food, clothing, health services, schools, vocational courses, theater, a newspaper, jobs, and a vast array of social and cultural activities. In this organized environment, the survivors could feel safe to start a new chapter in security and with a sense of stability.

After years of captivity and humiliation, the former concentration camp inmates were able to attribute value and meaning to their lives. They were able to regain a feeling of belonging and rebuild their identities as human beings.

As their society consisted only of survivors, there were thousands who shared both their pre-Holocaust years and their Holocaust experiences. Unlike Holocaust survivors who started life in alien surroundings and were subjected to skepticism in their attempts to return to normalcy, the new lives of the DPs in Bergen-Belsen crystallized in a most receptive environment, where their stories "made sense." Because of their shared fate and circumstances, these survivors were able to confront the good and the bad of their recent past with others who understood what they were going through. They had a whole community of listeners and friends who gave them and their feelings legitimacy and enabled them to reconstruct their sufferings into a coherent and meaningful narrative. As a result, there was probably less need of denial and repression among them.

Their friends, who were witnesses to what they had experienced, gave them strength and support, which also made telling their stories to their families and to the outside world much easier. This was a spontaneous support system that lasted for many years after they left the DP camp.

In his book *Man's Search for Meaning*, Viktor Frankl wrote that even in the most seemingly hopeless situations, one should remind oneself of one's past. "What you have experienced," he explained, citing a German poet, "no power on earth can take from you."[4] Frankl believed that searching for and finding value and meaning within oneself made traumatic events more bearable, enhancing the eventual ability to adjust and rebuild one's future.

The story of the Bergen-Belsen DPs that was transmitted to me by my parents and other survivors was a fulfillment of Frankl's hypothesis. The most important insight that I gained from my personal history and have been able to apply to my professional philosophy is the concept that it is possible to help trauma patients regain a positive image of themselves and find meaning in their past as well as in the present. This legacy has been a source of emotional support for me. It has helped me develop the conviction that it is possible for wounded human beings to create a coherent chain of life events that contain the horrors of the past but also revive cherished aspirations and dreams that give a specific purpose to their lives.

Robert Singer

Robert Singer is the CEO and executive vice president of the World Jewish Congress. Before assuming his present position, he served for fourteen years as the London-based director general and CEO of World ORT, the largest Jewish education and vocational training non-governmental organization in the world. As a senior official in the Israeli Prime Minister's Office from 1987 to 1999, he was instrumental in developing diplomatic relations and negotiating agreements with governments in the countries of the former Soviet Union.

> "Thus, the impulse to rescue those Jews who could be rescued, regardless of the risks and cost involved, has been the guiding imperative of my professional life, especially because in the back of my mind I always felt that a disaster could happen again and that I needed to do anything and everything in my power to prevent it from happening again."

My mother was born in Alexandreni, a predominantly Jewish village near the Moldovan city of Balti, known as Beltsy in Russian. In the summer of 1941, as the Fascist government of Romanian dictator Ion Antonescu, an ally of Nazi Germany, was taking control over that part of the historical region of Bessarabia and began forcing Jews into ghettos, my mother's parents, Reiza and Shulem

Prizement, took their seven daughters and several grandchildren in a drawn cart and headed east, toward Soviet-occupied territory. When they reached the Dniester River, it was clear to my grandmother that the horse was not strong enough to continue pulling all of them, and so she decided to divide the family. She gave the horse and cart to my mother and three of her sisters, two of whom had children of their own, and told them to continue across the Dniester, while their parents and other siblings would follow somehow. It was the last time my mother saw her parents.

My grandparents and their children who stayed behind were murdered together with thousands upon thousands of Ukrainian, Moldovan, and Russian Jews in what proved to be the beginning of the murderous phase of the Holocaust.

My mother and her three sisters continued to Samara (former Kuybyshev) in southeastern Russia and from there to Kirgizstan, but my mother's young daughter and one of my mother's sisters died in the course of this arduous journey. My mother's first husband had enlisted in the Red Army and was killed in battle. After the war, my mother returned to Ukraine and met and married my father in Czernowitz, where I was born in 1956.

Our family was affirmatively Jewish, and in 1972, when I was fifteen, we made aliyah. We arrived in Israel with $200 to our name and three suitcases, and we settled in the northern development town of Karmiel. My father pushed me on an intense academic path—I skipped four classes in my agricultural boarding school and graduated from Tel Aviv University with a BA in political science and international relations.

In the Israeli army, I became an officer, rising to chief education officer of the Southern Command before becoming the youngest of my immigration wave to attain the rank of lieutenant colonel. I then entered the diplomatic service and helped open Israeli embassies and cultural centers throughout the former Soviet Union. The Prime Minister's Office also sent me to North America to be the liaison between the Israeli and US and Canadian governments on issues concerning Jews in the countries of the former USSR and elsewhere in Eastern Europe.

In 1999, I left Israeli government service for the arena of international Jewish public service. I spent fourteen years as director general and CEO of World ORT, the largest Jewish educational and vocational training organization in the world, and in 2013, I became the CEO and executive vice president of the World Jewish Congress.

The Holocaust as such has not been a prominent part of my mind-set. My parents rarely spoke about the war years, and I never found out the details about how my grandparents and other members of my family were killed. I never pressed my parents on this topic. It was far too painful for them.

And yet, in retrospect it is clear to me that that moment many years before I was born when my grandmother made the decision to send my mother and her sisters across the Dniester into the unknown, so as to save at least some members of our family, made me who I became and am.

Growing up in Ukraine, I experienced anti-Semitism firsthand, especially during the years after the June 1967 Six-Day War when we were waiting for permission to emigrate. I know how precarious Jewish existence in the Diaspora can be. But unlike during the years of the Shoah, we now had a haven—the State of Israel—whose doors were open to us. More than anything else, I wish that no Jewish parent or grandparent should ever again be confronted with a horrendous life-and-death predicament such as the one into which my grandmother was thrown on the banks of the Dniester.

Thus, the impulse to rescue those Jews who could be rescued, regardless of the risks and cost involved, has been the guiding imperative of my professional life, especially because in the back of my mind I always felt that a disaster could happen again and that I needed to do anything and everything in my power to prevent it from happening again—to my family or to any Jews anywhere in the world.

Dr. Stephen L. Comite

Stephen L. Comite, MD, FAAD, is an Ivy League–trained dermatologist who maintains a private practice in Manhattan, where he treats both general dermatology and cosmetic patients. He is an assistant clinical professor of dermatology at the Mount Sinai Department of Dermatology. He has written or co-authored over fifteen peer-reviewed original journal articles and book chapters.

"I chose dermatology partly as a response to the suffering my parents endured during World War II. They had such a miserable quality of life under some of the worst conditions mankind has ever inflicted and perpetrated that I now want to alleviate the misery of others as best I can."

Parents, of course, have an enormous influence over their offspring, but children of survivors are especially affected in myriad and often unique ways by parents who had lived through the Holocaust. Being a child of survivors carries burdens but also potential aspirations and high motivations to succeed.

Growing up, my older twin sisters and I knew only bits and pieces of our parents' histories. They both refused for the most part to talk about their experience. Still, we understood that they had endured indescribable pain along with substantial psychological distress.

My father, the late Morris Comite, came from Krakow, Poland. When Nazi Germany and the USSR simultaneously invaded Poland in 1939, he escaped to Soviet-occupied territory but was quickly arrested and imprisoned by the NKVD, the forerunner to the KGB. He was then sent to a Soviet prison camp, where the prisoners were forced to perform meaningless labor under horrific conditions. After the Germans attacked the Soviet Union, many Poles, including my father, were freed, and he spent much of the remainder of the war in Uzbekistan. My paternal grandparents were both murdered by the Nazis.

After the Germans invaded Hungary in March 1944, my mother and her family hid in the forest near their village of Velke Rakovice in Subcarpathian Ruthenia (today in western Ukraine) for six weeks before they were betrayed by a neighbor, captured, and deported to Auschwitz-Birkenau. When they arrived there, my mother's parents and her grandmother were sent directly into a gas chamber. In October 1944, my mother was taken to a labor sub-camp of the Gross-Rosen concentration camp near a village called Kleinschönau (now Sieniawka, Poland), where she was liberated by Soviet troops on May 7, 1945.

After World War II, my parents lived for a while in Displaced Persons camps in Germany before immigrating to New York City, where they met and married. Despite my parents' limited education, they managed not only to survive but to actually thrive in a new country. I am often astounded by how many survivors and children of survivors have become so successful in their careers and professions.

My father had been a skilled hat maker in Poland, and he became the foreman of a hat-making factory in the United States. When hats went out of fashion in the 1960s and my father lost his job, he was forced to reinvent himself, purchased a taxi medallion, and drove a cab. My mother was initially a homemaker, and after their children were in elementary school, she began working in real estate.

My parents raised three accomplished Ivy League–trained physicians. My sisters Harriet and Florence both attended Yale Medical School. After attending the University of Pennsylvania as an undergraduate, I attended that university's School of Medicine, completed an internship in internal medicine at the University of Michigan Affiliated Hospitals, and received my dermatology residency training at NYU. I maintain a private practice in Manhattan and teach at the Mount Sinai Department of Dermatology.

My choice of medicine as a profession may well have come at least partly in response to my parents' travails—being a doctor is very mobile, as the knowledge is all in your brain, and if political troubles arise in your home country, a physician can usually find a career elsewhere.

My parents also gave us a thorough Jewish education, and I attended a yeshiva through ninth grade. My wife, Anita, and I have in turn passed on the importance of being Jewishly knowledgeable to our three children, Matthew, Elliot, and Alison, all of whom have had many years of Jewish day school education, Jewish summer camps, and trips to Israel.

I love being a dermatologist. It is truly a privilege to be able to care for my patients, to listen to and understand them, and to help them through many stressful, intimate, difficult, confidential, and anxiety-provoking moments of their lives.

I am proud to have written or co-authored over fifteen peer-reviewed original journal articles and book chapters. The subjects I have written about include methods to minimize pain when performing skin surgery. Could this need to lessen pain be a reaction to my parents' suffering? Perhaps.

When HIV was first discovered, some health-care professionals did not wish to take care of such patients. I was far from alone in trying to help patients with HIV, but early in the infancy of the disease, I treated many patients with HIV who suffered from dermatological disease.

As a dermatologist, I treat patients with life-altering illnesses such as skin cancers. I have had the privilege of saving many lives or at least extending them—and that is infinitely gratifying.

Dermatologists also have the unique privilege of doing much to maintain a patient's quality of life. It is extraordinarily gratifying as well for me to ease the anxieties and fears of a patient who might be upset, depressed, frustrated, or even near suicidal about his or her condition.

I would speculate that I chose dermatology partly as a response to the suffering my parents endured during World War II. They had such a miserable quality of life under some of the worst conditions mankind has ever inflicted and perpetrated that I now want to alleviate the misery of others as best I can.

Florence Shapiro

Florence Shapiro is recognized as a national leader in education reform, having served for nine years as chair of the Texas Senate Education Committee concluding her distinguished nineteen-year career as a state senator and Republican caucus chair. Prior to the Senate, she spent six terms on the Plano City Council and served as mayor and president of the Texas Municipal League. A public policy consultant, she was appointed by President George W. Bush to the United States Holocaust Memorial Council and today serves as president of Texans for Education Reform and vice president of the Dallas Holocaust Museum for Tolerance and Education.

> "I believe G-d put me on this earth
> to be the bridge between my parents
> and their past and my children/
> grandchildren and their future."

April 9, 2005—I am the governor of the State of Texas ... even though only for a day! As I look down from the dais, I see a chamber filled with hundreds of spectators. As I look to my left, I see my parents, Holocaust survivors, with tears in their eyes. How in the world did I get here? And better still, how did they get here?

Everyone has a "family history." But mine was spotty, at best. World War II and the Nazi regime's effect on my immediate family were devastating. I had no heritage to look back upon except through short vignettes, told by my father. Always the same stories, always on the High Holy Days, and always with the caveat, "What can I say, there was nothing we could do." The pain burning inside my father was apparent ... a furrowed brow, a pensive stare, and very few new clues with which to build a family tree. My mother never spoke of her past. Her tears would begin, and the pain was unbearable. She would stop in midsentence, never to return to those horrific days.

As the eldest child of Holocaust survivors, I often played the role of the adult. I took control of the Americanization of our small close-knit family. I began teaching American culture, American values and mores. All along, I knew these were Jewish values, Jewish lessons taught by them, lest we forget their grief or sorrow. My parents taught us a sustainable, robust value system that kept us going throughout our adult life. "Treat others with respect and they will in turn respect you." "Maintain strong ties with family ... remember there are so few of us left, we must remain strong together." They were committed to maintaining a strong viable unit around which everything flowed. My core value system stemmed from their roots. Today, I invest this belief in my own children.

I was loud and demonstrative at a young age, becoming a cheerleader, class officer, and class favorite. My father was the person in my life who moved me forward. He was proud of everything I did, and I always wanted to please him.

One of the highlights of my life occurred in 1984 with the surprise announcement at a chamber of commerce banquet that I was selected "Citizen of the Year" in Plano, Texas. The joy I felt was expressed in my acceptance speech: "You will never know the significance of this honor. My parents, Holocaust survivors from Berlin, Germany, were stripped of their citizenship in the 1930s. Today, you honor me and my entire family who perished under Hitler and for this I thank you." It was my "coming out." I wore this title, "Citizen of the Year," proudly my entire career as an elected official. As city council member, mayor, and Texas state senator, my past was now my present, and I was the heir to my parents' heritage. It was now possible for me to learn from their past and give credibility to my children's future.

Throughout my thirty years of public service, I used the values my parents instilled in me to make the best decisions representing my constituents in a most honorable and humble way—lessons learned by their everyday teachings that America truly was the land of opportunity and that I was the poster child for this democracy. My elections, seventeen of them to be exact, punctuated the affirmation of my family's crossing over from devastation in Germany to validation in America. My patriotism has always bolstered my service. I fly the American flag in the front of our home *every* day, not just on holidays.

So, what lessons have I learned? What is *my* legacy? The very fiber of my being is Jewish. My husband, Howard, and I share great pride that our three children, Lisa, Todd, and Staci, have all married within the Jewish faith, and we have been blessed with twelve grandchildren. Always remembering those days, my heritage now gives me strength for the future.

I have probably given thousands of speeches, and at the conclusion I have been known to say, "I believe G-d put me on this earth to be the bridge between my parents and their past and my children/grandchildren and their future." I pen this essay today in memory of my family—those I knew and those I never met—and for my children and grandchildren, in the hope that they, too, will carry on this legacy.

David Harris

David Harris has led the American Jewish Committee (AJC) as its executive director since 1990. Described by Israeli president Shimon Peres as the "foreign minister of the Jewish people," he has been honored a total of fourteen times by the governments of Azerbaijan, Belgium, Bulgaria, France, Germany, Italy, Latvia, Poland, Spain, and Ukraine for his international efforts in defense of human rights, advancement of the transatlantic partnership, and dedication to the Jewish people.

> "Achieving Jewish well-being also meant fighting for societies devoted to the full protection of human dignity and democratic values."

It would be no exaggeration to say that the Holocaust has shaped the trajectory of my entire life.

I was born four years after the end of World War II. It didn't take me very long to figure out that my family had a rather complicated history because of what happened from 1933 to 1945.

It's not as if they dwelled at length on their difficult wartime experiences, or, in my father's case, his heroic deeds against the Nazis, or, for that matter, that they shouted from the rooftops that I was the first person in the extended family to be born in the United States.

Rather, it became clear because I was curious to know, from an early age, where they came from, why they had lived in so many different European countries, and why they spoke such an array of languages—often, by the way, in the very same sentence.

Having most of my family within easy walking distance helped. My Russian-born maternal grandparents lived literally in the next apartment to ours. My paternal grandparents, from Poland and Hungary, were a few blocks away, as were my Polish-born aunt and Russian-born uncle.

I saw them all the time, so I had ample opportunity to hear the discussions, ask questions, and begin to pick up what otherwise might have been obscure references to seemingly strange places, people, and events.

I was inexplicably drawn into a world I could hardly begin to imagine, starting to feel an intimate connection to it. As a result, I experienced a growing need both to help protect those within that world and to ensure their story would never be forgotten. Sounds a bit like a cliché, I know, but true nonetheless.

And various experiences along the way only strengthened the link.

Unexpectedly, my parents and I moved to Munich when I was in the seventh grade, just fifteen years after the war's end. I witnessed my mother and father coping with an unsought situation and over-heard whispered conversations between them as they eyed adult Germans and wondered what their wartime role might have been. Surely, there must be better ways to shape a child's outlook on life, but these were rather unusual circumstances, to say the least.

I recall reading Arthur Morse's *While Six Million Died* at university and being totally shocked by the author's account of American indifference to the plight of European Jewry. How could this be, I asked, when my own family couldn't find enough ways to express their love for America, the country that had allowed them to start over?

I remember my first trip to Israel and the sight of a Haifa bus passenger in a short-sleeved shirt with a number on his forearm. It's not that I hadn't seen the number before. But seeing it in Israel made me ask myself what it must have felt like for this man to find a home in a sovereign Jewish state—a state that, had it existed in 1938, might have saved countless Jews still able to leave but with nowhere to go.

I will never forget visiting Mauthausen, the first Nazi camp I ever saw. Suddenly, I found myself between the gas chamber and the crematoria and broke down in fear, anger, and shock as I sought a quick exit.

And then came perhaps the most decisive experience in my young life—several months spent in the USSR on a government-to-government exchange. There, I became deeply involved with Soviet Jews determined to emigrate, but too often prevented from doing so by a ruthlessly totalitarian regime.

It began to dawn on me that this was the challenge of my post-war generation.

In other words, it was terribly important, yes, to remember and proclaim, "Never Again," to read the compelling accounts of Elie Wiesel and Primo Levi, and to guard against Holocaust denial or trivialization. And it was essential to honor the legacies of those who perished, those who survived, those who rescued, and those who liberated.

But, still, this was insufficient.

To truly embrace the meaning of the Holocaust and the abyss into which the world descended, I concluded, meant to do a course correction—to steer away from my initial hope of becoming an American diplomat or UN official and instead devote my life to helping ensure that all Jews everywhere would have the chance to live in freedom and safety.

And this in turn became inextricably coupled with a belief that achieving Jewish well-being also meant fighting for societies devoted to the full protection of human dignity and democratic values.

I made that course correction in 1975, at the age of twenty-five. Nearly forty years later, I'm still on it.

I could never have imagined a life of such meaning, purpose, and fulfillment. But it wouldn't have happened had it not been for the insatiable curiosity of a young child on New York's West Side wanting to understand the journey of his family—a journey, alas, defined by the most tragic events of the twentieth century.

Mathew S. Nosanchuk

Mathew S. Nosanchuk, an attorney in Washington, DC, currently works in the White House as director for outreach on the National Security Council and is also an adjunct professor of law at Georgetown University School of Law. He previously served as associate director and Jewish liaison in the White House Office of Public Engagement; as senior counselor to the assistant attorney general for the Civil Rights Division at the Department of Justice; as associate general counsel at the Department of Homeland Security; and as counsel for Senator Bill Nelson (D-FL). He attended college and law school at Stanford, where he was a Truman Scholar, and is the recipient of the American Bar Association's inaugural Stonewall Award and the Attorney General's Award for Distinguished Service at the Department of Justice.

> "I have often asked myself how I can honor the memory of my family and the millions of others who perished during the darkest period in the entirety of Jewish history. What does it mean to proclaim, 'Never Forget' and 'Never Again'? How do we make those admonitions more than mere words?"

My family's Holocaust nightmare is captured for posterity in my great-uncle Michael's letter, sent to his older brother, Boris—my grandfather—after the war. It's become the foundational narrative in my family and one of the few written accounts of what happened in the Belarusian towns near what is now the border with Ukraine. Imagine receiving such a letter from a brother, not knowing until it arrived whether or not he had survived. Yes, Michael wrote, he had survived, barely escaping death over and over again—first, when the Germans descended on the shtetl—Rubel—in September 1941 to kill all the Jewish men there. Fifty-three Jewish men were killed in one day. The fifty-fourth Jewish man in the town—my great-uncle—survived because he had left town to go fishing and then hid on a small island under the protection of a gentile father and son.

Afterwards, my great-uncle found refuge with his family in the ghetto of the nearby town of Stolin. One year later on *Erev* Rosh Hashanah in 1942, which happened to be September 11, the Jews of that ghetto were marched out to a field on the outskirts of town called Stasino and murdered—seven thousand of them, including Michael's parents (my great-grandparents) and the rest of his immediate family who had still been living there. Once again, Michael survived. Over his objection, Michael's parents admonished him to flee—and he did, first hiding in a cellar for eighteen days before escaping the ghetto to return to the island to be sheltered by the same father and son who had hid him a year earlier. Eventually, Michael joined the partisans and marched into Berlin with the Soviet army as the war ended.

My grandfather died on my second birthday, but Michael lived until I was nineteen. He was a kind, loving, and generous soul—and a surrogate grandfather for me growing up. Like so many survivors, Michael did not talk about what happened, and that reticence disconnected those of us in the second and third generations from his—our—dark past. Which is, of course, exactly what Michael and so many others intended. They were protective—of themselves and their children and grandchildren. The lives Michael and so many others rebuilt in North America were so different and so far removed from the lives they left behind. It is no wonder they would have wanted to bury the horror in the deepest recesses of memory.

During those decades after the war when so many survivors lived, their very presence on this earth meant that there were countless untold eyewitness accounts available to provide a link to the past. Now, most of the survivors are gone. What remains are the memories they left behind, and we are the custodians of that memory. Michael's letter, published in the Yiddish *Forward* at the time my grandfather received it, can easily be found in a Google search. Every time I read it, I cannot believe this is what happened to my family and to the Jews of Europe during my parents' lifetime.

To further connect myself to my family's story, I traveled in 2002—around the time of the sixtieth anniversary of the massacre in Stolin—to modern-day Belarus to visit the towns Michael wrote about in his letter. I walked through my great-grandparents' house—it looks exactly the same on the outside as it did when my family lived there, but inside it had become a police station. The killing field outside of town had become a mass grave, and as I began to walk across it, the gray sky unleashed crashes of thunder and sheets of rain—the elements and seven thousand Jewish souls were crying with us.

After returning from that trip to Belarus, I have often asked myself how I can honor the memory of my family and the millions of others who perished during the darkest period in the entirety of Jewish history. What does it mean to proclaim, "Never Forget" and "Never Again"? How do we make those admonitions more than mere words?

In my own life, I have tried to put my energy and effort into work that is meaningful and consequential. From working at the US Department of Justice to implement a federal hate crimes law that, for the first time, covers sexual orientation and gender identity, to challenging unconstitutional laws—like the Defense of Marriage Act—that sought to legitimize discrimination by codifying it, I have tried to rectify injustice and reinforce human dignity and to honor in that way the memory and legacy of my own family and the six million Jewish souls who perished with them.

Photo: David Roth

Jeffrey S. Wiesenfeld

Jeffrey S. Wiesenfeld is a principal at Bernstein Global Wealth Management. He has served on numerous public and non-profit boards throughout his adult career. His transition to Bernstein followed twenty years of government service, including positions as a senior aide to New York State governor George Pataki, US senator Alfonse D'Amato, and New York City mayor Ed Koch.

"I idolized strong Jews and was shamed by weak, apologetic Jews."

Perhaps the stories were related to me too soon. I was about eight years old, and as I would inquire of my Romanian mother and Polish father regarding the paucity of our extended family, their overprotectiveness, and the relatively poor conditions under which we lived in the South Bronx in the early and mid-1960s, they would tell me strange stories thoroughly incompatible with the lives of my peers.

Barracks, extreme cold, starvation, forced marches through icy mud, enforced traipsing over half-dead, still-breathing humans, shootings, beheadings, hard labor, selections, *Appels*, rock-hard bread, wormed potato peels, slime-water soup ...

Where did I come from? From whom did they emerge? What kind of people were their families and fellow Jews that they merited such degradation, torture, and murder? They must have been truly bad. Why else would the people of Europe have joined our German tormentors in trying to finish us off with such sadism and glee?

As the years went by, I would come to divide American Jews and Holocaust survivors into distinct categories.

There were what I came to call the "Mayflower Jews"—who were in America prior to the Holocaust—and their descendants on the one hand and Holocaust survivors and their descendants on the other. The survivors and their families, meanwhile, were divided into those who overcame their trauma and became wealthy and success-ful and those (where my brother and I fit in) who never overcame the trauma and remained mired in near-poverty.

As our section of the Bronx became depleted of most Cauca-sians, let alone Jews, my brother and I became mired in a world of cultural isolation, a ghetto, if you will. Hoodlums and muggers made it unsafe to get to and from public school, let alone play in the streets. My junior high school, by 1969 one of the worst in the city, was more like a prison camp than a school, with all manner of violent and deviant behavior. It would not be until 1973, long after anyone we had known was long gone from the area that, with mea-ger resources, we finally made our way to Queens.

In Rego Park and Forest Hills, my world opened up a bit. I com-pleted my high school years at the prestigious Bronx High School of Science, which had literally saved my life in our last year in East Tremont, commuting between Queens and the South Bronx on three subway trains.

So why would the years following Queens College of the City University of New York lead me to the FBI Academy, five years in the FBI, and fifteen additional years of government service in the Koch and Pataki administrations and with Senator D'Amato, as well as numerous other government assignments, and public and non-profit boards? Why would I spend twenty years in government before going on to make a living as a wealth manager?

In the first place, the breakdown of the rule of law during my parents' generation and the lawlessness I experienced growing up made me something of a conservative law-and-order type. Jewish powerlessness through the ages strengthened my conviction that Jewish involvement in government was essential, and my idols became Ze'ev Jabotinsky; Ben Hecht and the Bergson group; the heroes of the Six-Day War; Yonatan Netanyahu, Menachem Begin, and Meir Kahane. In short, I idolized strong Jews and was shamed by weak, apologetic Jews.

While I certainly believed then and continue to believe today that the Jewish people should perform positive deeds and be exemplars for the world, I am astonished by those Jews who, I am convinced, work against Jewish interests and the State of Israel. Let me be clear: I believe that the demise of Israel would be the end of the Jewish people, period.

Many of the Mayflower Jews had arrived in the era of pogrom-laden Eastern Europe and came to believe that socialism, communism, and other leftist movements would be their salvation. The Holocaust survivors who came much later, many of whom mocked the "naiveté" of the Mayflower Jews, saw that these movements were no more protective of them than fascism and other right-wing political manifestations.

On top of this ideological mess, some American-Jewish religious movements would constantly expand egalitarianism and add all variety of options to the *tikkun olam* menu. As far as I am concerned, this brief phrase in the *Aleinu* prayer, generally recited three times daily, refers simply to the promotion of God's sovereignty through the elimination of idolatry.

I believe that the limitless expansion of any faux *tikkun olam* philosophy, promoted over the last two generations, to include all manner of causes, many of them valid, but having nothing to do with the *Aleinu*'s injunction—including social justice, gay rights, abortion rights, Palestinian rights, whale rights, Aboriginal rights, boycott/divestment/sanction rights, anti-Judea-Samaria rights, and all manner of make-it-up-as-you-go rights—has resulted in historic communal division and possible irreparable harm to Jewish communal unity.

As a son of Holocaust survivors, I further believe that we, as a Jewish nation, must commence a national debate and nurture a movement to bring Jews back to an authenticity of basic principles essential for Jewish survival. I don't necessarily mean this from a religiously ritualistic perspective. I believe that we must oppose the idea of Jews utilizing expansive precepts constructed out of whole cloth to permit themselves to partner with enemies of the Jewish people and the State of Israel, many of whom exhibit every desire to make Jews the first victims of their ill designs should they ultimately get their chance. This, to me, is at least as important as Israel's security and Jewish continuity.

Many will see harshness in this view, a darkened view of the world in which human nature has in fact been harsh on the Jews. I wish I could see the future more positively. It is said that the bottom must be touched before one's fortunes rise.

Let the Holocaust be the last of all bottoms for the Jewish people.

Sam Sokol

Sam Sokol is the Jewish world correspondent at the *Jerusalem Post*, covering Jewish life around the globe. He is the former business editor of *18 Magazine*, a bohemian Tel Aviv quarterly. He lives in Beit Shemesh, Israel, with his wife, Chava, and four children.

"As a journalist I have continuously endangered myself in order to warn my people of threats to their well-being. My ability to overcome my stress and to report from the front lines is the legacy bequeathed me by my grandparents and their revenge against those who sought our destruction."

I am the only Jew in a room full of neo-Nazis, right where I want to be.

My heart pounds as I gaze at the Svoboda banners hanging limply from the gallery, the yellow hand against a blue field flashing its eternal victory sign burning deeply into my soul. Standing in the center of the grand plenum chamber of Kiev's Stalinist Gothic city council building, young men in combat boots and army helmets jostling around me, I feel intensely alone. Yet at the same time, I suddenly feel closer to my grandparents than I ever have before.

As the maternal grandson of survivors, the Holocaust has played an outsized role in charting the course of my life, both personally and professionally. Both my grandparents are from Poland, and both escaped to the Soviet Union, where my grandfather supported his parents and siblings through black-market dealings and my grandmother was impressed into virtual serfdom as a worker in a Siberian mine. They met, married, and had my mother in a Displaced Persons camp in Germany after the war.

As a child, my grandfather would tell me stories of his adventures during the war, largely omitting the carnage, death, and hunger and instead regaling me with tales of his underground exploits, escaping the law on horseback as bullets flew all around, and how his mother would use the proceeds of his sales to help feed fellow Jews. However, as I got a bit older, he began to tell me more of the horror, although sanitized for my young ears.

As a child, though I had not yet seen the pictures of the walking skeletons, the corpse pits, or the children's bodies left to decay on the sidewalks of the ghetto, the Holocaust was constantly with me. My mother told me of her persistent childhood dreams of Nazis standing at her window, watching her as she slept, and in due course, these dreams began to haunt me as well. I can't recall ever telling my parents, but in my nightmares the helmeted Gestapo thugs stalked Manhattan's Upper West Side searching for me.

My mother was somewhat high-strung, a typical West Side Jew with more than a passing similarity to Woody Allen's nebbishy screen persona. As I grew up, her natural anxiety, enhanced by her upbringing as a second-generation survivor, infected me as well.

I am a supremely anxious person, always worried about my finances, stressed out by the slightest task, and paralyzed by anything but the shortest to-do list. However, despite my own neuroses, the reality of being a third-generation survivor also pushes me to take risks that I would otherwise not have taken. Personally meek, professionally bold.

When I was a teenager, my grandfather recalled when the great Zionist leader Ze'ev Jabotinsky came to his shtetl and entreated the

Hasidic and other Jewish locals to liquidate the exile and immigrate to Palestine.

"We should have listened to him," he declared regretfully.

It is this conviction, passed down to me by my parents and grandparents, that the Holocaust cannot be allowed to happen again that led to me dropping out of Yeshiva University in my junior year to enlist in the Israel Defense Forces.

"I can't read the news about terror attacks and violence and not do something," I told a friend after my decision. "I can't stand by."

Later on, as a journalist, I began to take on assignments that I believed would enable me to help prevent the recurrence of what had befallen my family in Europe.

From meeting with prominent figures from Hamas's political wing in Jerusalem to dodging missiles in Sderot during Operation Pillar of Defense, I have striven to report on the threats to Jewish life and continuity.

Lately, that has meant covering the rise of the ultra-nationalist right in Europe. Once again the European Jew feels endangered, and I suddenly feel the weight of history, both national and familial, bearing down on me, demanding that I do something.

That is how I found myself in the midst of the Kiev, covering the political upheavals wracking the city in the aftermath of the subsequently ousted President Viktor Yanukovich's late 2013 rejection of tighter European integration. With the anti-Semitic Svoboda party, which at the time held 36 out of 450 Parliamentary seats, having such a prominent presence in the streets, I felt I had to be there to tell the world what was happening.

While I may be a sad parody of Woody Allen in my personal life, as a journalist I have continuously endangered myself in order to warn my people of threats to their well-being. My ability to overcome my stress and to report from the front lines is the legacy bequeathed me by my grandparents and their revenge against those who sought our destruction.

Ghita Schwarz

Ghita Schwarz is an attorney at the Center for Constitutional Rights in New York City and the author of a novel, *Displaced Persons*.

"To work in the civil rights field is to have a constant awareness that the pictures Americans see of ourselves are often framed by partial truths, even lies, about our freedoms and our welcoming spirit."

In the black-and-white photograph of my father just a few moments after disembarking from the ship that had carried him from Hamburg, Germany, into the New York Harbor, he is almost entirely covered: hat, long coat, and gloves carrying a satchel. He looks to the side, perhaps unaware his brother is taking his picture, and his slim face looks both serious and distracted. The year is not 1946, when a tiny number of Jewish refugees began trickling into the United States, nor 1948, when Congress passed its most sweeping Displaced Persons Act, nor 1952, when all but two of the Displaced Persons camps in Germany had closed. It is 1957. Despite numerous efforts to join his surviving family in New York, he was prevented for years by a post-war injury and a quirk of US immigration law that marked him as a potential "public charge," a potential burden on the country that sometimes, not always, prides itself as a "nation of immigrants."

It is that experience—the rejection by the world, the loneliness of rebuilding alone—that I think about most when I consider the legacy of the Holocaust in my own life. Born into safety and security more than a decade after my father arrived in the United States, I don't claim particular insight into the experience of the Holocaust because of my Polish-born parents' experiences in Europe during the war. But perhaps an awareness of the isolation of survivors and refugees—and the arbitrariness and cruelty of US immigration laws—resonated with me enough to draw me to civil rights law.

To work in the civil rights field is to have a constant awareness that the pictures Americans see of ourselves are often framed by partial truths, even lies, about our freedoms and our welcoming spirit. The contemporary immigrant experience is far more challenging than it was for my parents, who came to a country experiencing economic growth and who did not face a government policy of systematically punishing immigrants already here. Today, tens of thousands of immigrants are held every day in detention facilities without ever being charged with a crime, and hundreds of thousands of immigrants each year are picked up for minor infractions or, often, nothing at all and deported, leaving their families torn apart and their US-born children motherless or fatherless. I try to play a small part in struggling for change, and I credit my parents' willingness to talk about their experiences, during the war and its aftermath, for my own desire to look critically at American social policy and history.

Despite my civil rights work, I was well into adulthood before I began to question similar stories of Israeli history. Viewed through the lens of immigration, the creation and unwavering support of Israel makes perfect sense to someone who grew up in a reflexively Zionist family, well aware that once the camps were liberated, Jewish refugees, desperate to flee deeply anti-Semitic local populations, had few doors open to them. But decades after hundreds of thousands of refugees resettled, it is harder for me to see Israeli policies as justified. My youthful fear of betraying family and community allowed me to obscure, to myself, the segregation and collective punishment of Palestinians in the occupied territories, the destruction of the homes and mosques of Israeli Arabs for minor permit violations, and the reluctance to punish settler violence. These practices are not just isolated acts that now, like many American Jews, I oppose—they are systematic policies that to me echo the worst parts of American history and undermine the images I once had of Israel as a refuge. That Israeli politicians often use the Holocaust or the possibility of another one to justify the oppression of another group sometimes makes me question the benefits of so much Holocaust legacy.

These thoughts might disturb the man who stepped off the boat to start a new life in a cramped apartment in Jackson Heights, Queens. He likely wouldn't have imagined a time when Holocaust survivors would be esteemed as models of immigrant success or when Asians and Africans would move to Israel for the economic opportunity. But when I think of him in the photograph, eyes glancing sideways, not acknowledging the camera, I interpret a willingness to look off-center, to view his new world with both optimism and ambivalence.

Photo: Peter Eastway

Eddy Neumann

Eddy Neumann is the eldest of six children of the late Ludwig and Kola Neumann, both Shoah survivors who migrated from Germany to Australia in 1951. He grew up in Sydney, New South Wales, and has been a practicing lawyer for over forty years. While a law student at the University of Sydney, he became involved in the struggle of the Aboriginal people of Australia for recognition of their rights and received the 1999 Law Society Pro Bono People's Choice Award for his work with indigenous people.

> "To me and to so many other Jews in Australia, the Shoah meant that we could not turn a blind eye to or be neutral on [the Aboriginal rights] issue; we had to become involved and be active in whichever way we could."

I was born in Leipzig, Germany, two years after World War II ended and the Jews were liberated from the Nazi death machine. My father survived the Lodz Ghetto in Poland, and my mother's life was saved first by a Christian Ukrainian in her hometown of Podhajce (then in Poland and now in Ukraine) and thereafter by continually fleeing to the east.

My family migrated as refugees to Australia when I was three years old. My parents would probably never have met and married, and certainly we would never have come to Australia, except for the Shoah. My father's reason for bringing his family to Australia was that that was the farthest place from Europe that he could migrate to.

As it has turned out, Australia has a Jewish community with the highest percentage of Shoah survivors of any Jewish community in the Diaspora. Furthermore, just as Europe had racism in the form of anti-Semitism at the core of its basic fabric, even in progressive Germany, I came to learn that Australia also had racism as a core belief, but Australia's form of racism was directed at the Aboriginal people, the continent's original inhabitants.

The British settlers regarded the Aborigines as subhuman. The Aboriginal race was subjected to massacre, extermination, displacement, and dispossession of their homes and property, they were prevented from practicing their culture and speaking their language, and they were only able to save themselves if they were offered and then accepted conversion to Christianity.

As a result of what I, at the time, considered a series of coincidences, I and other Australian Jews became an integral part of the fight by the Aboriginal people over the past fifty years to be accorded basic civil rights, to be able to protect themselves from police harassment, to be able to have access to medical services, to be able to have access to education, to have their culture accorded respect, and to be recognized to be the original owners of and to be given rights to their own land.

My personal journey in this struggle commenced in 1969 when I became involved in the vanguard of the pursuit of justice for the Aboriginal people. I took part in protests for Aboriginal justice and self-determination, including the Aboriginal Tent Embassy; in the setting up and running of the first Indigenous legal service controlled by Aboriginal people, the first Indigenous medical service controlled by Aboriginal people, the first Indigenous corporations controlled by Aboriginal people to provide adequate housing to Aboriginal people, and Aboriginal cultural centers and preschool services controlled by Aborigines; and in the fight for recognition of Aboriginal sovereignty.

To me and to so many other Jews in Australia, the Shoah meant that we could not turn a blind eye to or be neutral on this issue; we had to become involved and be active in whichever way we could.

What I and other Jews in Australia did not know until close to the turn of the twentieth century was that Aboriginal people in Australia had refused to be silent in the face of *Kristallnacht* and the reports that came from Germany. In 1938, a deputation of Aboriginals led by the late William Cooper, representing the Australian Aborigines League, passed a resolution that stated, "On behalf of the Aborigines of Australia, we strongly protest the cruel persecution of the Jewish people by the Nazis government of Germany, and ask that this persecution be brought to an end."

When the Aboriginal deputation then went to the German consulate in Melbourne to convey that resolution, they were refused admittance but left a letter containing the resolution with the German consul, with a request that it be forwarded to his government.

William Cooper and his deputation of Aboriginal people were all themselves disenfranchised, on the other side of the world, still fighting for recognition of the rights of their own people in Australia without success and regarded as powerless and of no importance in Australia. And yet, they did what was in their power to do on behalf of persecuted Jews in Europe by leading a protest when in effect the rest of the world stood silent.

The fight for Aboriginal rights in Australia continues to this day, with significant involvement and championing by descendants of the survivors of the Shoah.

Rabbi Abie Ingber

Rabbi Abie Ingber is the executive director of the Center for Interfaith Community Engagement at Xavier University in Cincinnati, Ohio. He also serves as visiting associate professor of theology and special assistant to President Michael Graham, SJ. Prior to his position at Xavier, Ingber served as the executive director and rabbi of the Hillel Jewish Student Center at the University of Cincinnati and adjunct lecturer in homiletics at Hebrew Union College–Jewish Institute of Religion.

> "Only when we can reach the point of celebrating the other will dialogue and bridge building work. The road to merely tolerance is a road to failure."

We are all born before we are born. This understanding allows parents, grandparents, and other significant elders in the family to really have a part in a child's birth and in his or her formation. So, even though I was born in 1950, I feel that I was birthed in the events that are called the Holocaust. Every story my parents, Wolfe and Fania (Paszt) Ingber, shared came to be part of my story. I didn't know it in the first moments of life, but it didn't take very long until I figured that out. I was raised in an immigrant home in Montreal, Canada. We were very, very poor. I may have missed out on some comforts, but I was not devoid of my parents' commitment to education, my parents' commitment to faith, or my parents' commitment to love and embracement of the world community. I have had a charmed life.

Among the great teachers in my life was Rabbi Shlomo Carlebach. He once famously said, "If I had two hearts like I have two legs and two arms, I could love with one and hate with the other, but God gave me just one heart and I choose to use it for love." My parents, with everything that they had seen, with the tragedies in their lives, with their independent journeys through the lands of the Holocaust, chose to use their lives for love. My parents met in a Displaced Persons camp in Germany, decided to marry, and in the greatest testament of faith in God, they chose to bring children into this world. Two Jews who had seen and experienced what they had experienced stood up and said, "God, if you don't mind, we'd like to bring Jewish children into this world." This testament to faith in God was also a prayer that humanity might yet continue and find its grace and compassion. I doubled my parents' "production." I brought four daughters into the world. If I wanted my four daughters to be in a place that was safe but at the same time challenged them to live life with their eyes wide open, then I had to do the same. I've pursued a life where I felt that I could be a teacher to my daughters, as my parents had been to me. An adage by which I try to live is "The purpose of life is a life of purpose." If the rest of the world, so to speak, wanted to look on, I was very amenable to that.

My life has been defined by service to three universities—the University of Cincinnati, Hebrew Union College–Jewish Institute of Religion, and Xavier University. The last has been my home since 2008, and it is the most cherished as I pursue an initiative to bring people from tolerance to celebration. How a rabbi ends up in service to a Jesuit Catholic college is worthy of explanation.

Catholics and Ingbers have been interrelated for centuries. My father, when asked about the experience of being a Jew in a little Polish shtetl where the majority was Catholic, said, "At the best of times, it was intolerable." And yet, my grandfather, whom I never knew, had a unique relationship with the Catholic priest who served the church on the other side of the street from where my father lived. They would speak across the stone wall of the church courtyard about the Bible. My grandmother was allowed to go into that courtyard to draw water from its well so as not to have to go into the central part of town. So, while "the best of times was intolerable," the Ingbers somehow found a relationship with those who were leaders, people of faith within the church.

My mother's own story is harrowing. She was literally the last survivor of a ghetto on the border between Poland and Ukraine, a city called Lutzk (in Polish, Łuck). For the next three days after she escaped, the 17,500 Jews who remained were taken out of town and machine-gunned to death. My mother was left naked, without any human being to save her life. Six righteous Christians, one after another, appeared miraculously to save her life. She did not need one Oscar Schindler; she needed six to survive.

I was raised in Catholic French-speaking Montreal; the anti-Semitism was palpable. Just as my father, grandfather, and great-grandfather had been chased through the streets and called a dirty Jew and a Christ killer, I was chased through the streets and beaten up and called a dirty Jew. I thought, "That's what life is; this is what it means to be a Jew in a Christian world." But I also had these other stories of my grandfather discussing biblical texts with a priest, of my mother's life being saved by righteous Christians, and the experience of colleagues on every campus who have embraced me and my Judaism.

I knew psychologically that I was eager for the presence of a righteous Christian in my own life. I knew that I would never feel secure until I was satisfied that someone would open a door in the middle of the night for me and my daughters. I found that first righteous Christian in the Methodist minister at the University of Cincinnati. I boldly even told him so. But that night as I lay in bed ready for peacefulness in my sleep, I began to wonder who in the community knew that they could knock on my door in the middle of the night, knowing that I would give them shelter. It was in that moment that I recognized the gentle hand of God and my most significant calling. I define that calling by my devotion to the value of healing the world—the world that was the legacy given to me by my parents.

At the end of the twentieth century, each of our institutions, civic, commercial, or philanthropic, aspired to the same goal—in a world of increasing awareness of diversity, we aspired to "tolerance." That was it—tolerance. We wanted to tolerate the other. Tolerate them? We need to celebrate them. Only when we can reach the point of celebrating the other will dialogue and bridge building work. The road to merely tolerance is a road to failure.

My work in bridge building across faith traditions, cultures, and geography affirms my own foundational belief that every person is a child of God, created in God's image. Whether it has been in Darfur refugee camps or with Muslims in Cameroon, whether on American Jesuit campuses or in Israel, I have not only brought back stories, I have been emboldened in my own story to find hope across the generations, to find God in every human being, to feel the holiness in each person—our shared human mission. In a sense then, we are Jews because we are master bridge builders—bridges through history, bridges with every culture on the face of the earth, and bridges between heaven and earth.

We live in a critical time—it's called the present. We are trapped between the past and the future. Whatever we do is shaped by what we have done in the past, shaped by what we have experienced and learned from the past. And whatever we do has an impact on the future, on our own children and on our community.

My feet emotionally took their first steps in the Polish homes of my parents—they have been solidly anchored in the past. My arms, enfolding my own daughters and those young people who have become like family, have been outstretched to embrace the present. My eyes, with the benefit of every teacher and visionary who has taught me, have been boldly looking to a vision of the Jewish future.

My God, the God of my parents, has been very generous.

Rabbi Kinneret Shiryon

Rabbi Kinneret Shiryon is the first woman to function as a rabbi in the history of the State of Israel. Ordained by Hebrew Union College–Jewish Institute of Religion in New York in 1981, she is the founding rabbi and leader of the community of YOZMA—a progressive synagogue, community center, early childhood educational center, and elementary school in the city of Modi'in, Israel. She is the granddaughter of Dora Swiczman Goldman (1904–1961).

"Building a life in Israel was my conscious choice to make as a commitment to my bubbe and to the memory of her family. It is also my statement to the world that the Jewish people deserves a nation of its own."

I have a beautiful simple wood rolling pin in the utility drawer of our kitchen. I do not use it often, but I like to run my fingers over the smooth surface and recall the childhood distant memory of my *bubbe* ("grandmother" in Yiddish) down on her hands and knees on the kitchen floor in her upstairs apartment in Queens Village, New York. I remember her rolling out the dough on what we lovingly called one of her *shmates* ("rags" in Yiddish). Perhaps it was a long cotton towel—I do not quite remember. I do remember her sprinkling nuts and sugar across the dough and smiling at me. I do not have many memories of my *bubbe*. She died when I was a young child, of just five years. To this day I also have an affinity for wooden clothespins. They remind me of the ones I played with in *Bubbe* and *Zayde*'s home.

My *bubbe* and *zayde*'s photographs peer down at me every day from my hallway at home. I sometimes pause in the middle of my hectic life to stare into their faces. *Bubbe* stands tall; her excellent posture makes me feel that I am in the presence of an aristocratic figure. I look at her and wonder how she found the strength to continue her life after every member of her family had been murdered by the Nazis and their collaborators. How did she manage to bring four children into the world and raise them in a foreign country, without grandparents, aunts, or uncles to dote on them and offer her their support? Frankly, I wonder how she rose every morning and moved forward, given the pain and sorrow she suffered after losing those who gave her life and nurtured her. I marvel that she had the strength to travel alone across the ocean to meet her *shidduch* ("match" in Yiddish) in America.

I do not know the backstory of why she was sent from Poland to America, but I do know that she refused the *shidduch*, and that gives me some insight into the kind of woman that she was. I love the fact that she had the backbone to refuse the match that had been made for her and instead chose my *zayde*.

We know very little about my *bubbe*'s family from Poland. When I asked my mother about her mother's family, she told me that her mother refused to speak about them. My *bubbe* is a survivor not only because she escaped the fate of the rest of her family by leaving Poland before the Nazi death machine caught her, but also because somehow she found the strength to continue in spite of her horrific loss. I understand that people deal with loss and emotional suffering in various ways. My *bubbe* shut down that part of her life in order to build a new one. My mother often told me that she believes that if *Bubbe* had lived a longer life and had the chance to know me as a young adult, she would have opened up to me and would have shared stories from her past. We will never know, because she died at the young age of fifty-seven.

The only glimpses of her past we ever had came at two different times in my life. The first glimpse came just after I was born. My mother had medical complications after my birth and had to stay in the hospital for a few weeks to recover. While she was in the hospital, my *bubbe* came to visit her and extracted a promise from her. She demanded that my mother change my name. *Bubbe* told her that she had a dream (her very own *Fiddler on the Roof* episode), and in the dream her father came to her with a request. He told her that his soul was wandering and had no peace and needed a place to settle. My mother was attentive and anxious, trying for the first time to learn something about her mother's family! Only then did my mother learn that her *zayde*'s name was Yaakov. She tried to probe deeper by asking *Bubbe* to share something about *Zayde* Yaakov's personality in order to better understand the namesake that she would be passing on to her daughter, but *Bubbe* refused to add any information regarding her father, except for his name.

I use my name Yaakova for the most precious religious moments in my life. I use it when I am called up to the Torah or when a *Mi She-berakh* (a blessing for well-being) is given on my behalf. On my rabbinical ordination certificate my name appears as "Rabbi Yaakova Kinneret Shiryon." My great-grandfather's name not only graces the high points of my religious life, it also ties me to a past that was intentionally and viciously destroyed simply because my relatives were Jews. My namesake, Yaakov, also planted in me a desire to build my life as a committed Jew in the State of Israel. When I was thirteen years old, I made a decision in the deepest place of my heart that I wanted to be part of the renaissance of the Jewish people in their homeland. My strong Jewish identity was a gift from my parents passed down from generation to generation. I had no doubts about the pride I had for my Jewish heritage and knew that I would pass it down to the next generation even if I stayed in the United States; yet, somehow I knew that I needed to honor the memory of those whom I did not know and never would know by moving to Israel, where Jewish life is as natural as breathing. In Israel I felt their lives would somehow be resuscitated.

The second glimpse of my *bubbe*'s family came approximately fifty years after my birth. On a visit to her younger brother's apartment in New York, my mother came across a box filled with old postcards and photos. My uncle brought the box with him from their parents' home in Queens Village. When my mother began looking through the photos on the postcards, she felt a lump in her throat and her heartbeat increased. On the reverse side of the postcards there was correspondence in Polish and Yiddish. She decided to bring the box to Israel. She placed the box on the table in my home and said there was something she wanted to share with me. I took the postcards into my hands, and tears welled up in my eyes as I stared into the faces of young women who all looked like my *bubbe*. I knew immediately that I was looking at the photos of my *bubbe*'s sisters and their families. My *bubbe* was one of eight sisters and a brother. This treasure was the first tangible peek we had been given into my *bubbe*'s life before she immigrated to America. We had the messages in Polish and Yiddish translated. The postcards were filled with brief greetings to my *bubbe* from her family, asking how she was and saying that they miss her. There were no real revelations, but we did learn two of the sisters' names and two others' initials. Perhaps the most chilling message was a simple note that said, "I am sending you a keepsake—remember us forever." It was one of the only remnants my *bubbe* ever had of her parental family.

Building a life in Israel was my conscious choice to make as a commitment to my *bubbe* and to the memory of her family. It is also my statement to the world that the Jewish people deserves a nation of its own where they can not only shelter their loved ones from the cruelty of other nations but serve as a source of Jewish values and as a wellspring of Jewish creative living. It is here that I wish to impact the future of Jewish life. It is here, in the State of Israel, that I also hope to influence a new generation to build a just society where respect for minorities and outreach to those on the margins of society are foremost on the agenda.

I am doing my part in rebuilding Jewish community life in the independent State of Israel today. As the first woman to function as a congregational rabbi in the State of Israel, I have the honor to be among the pioneers, building Reform Jewish communal life in Israel. I established a Reform Jewish synagogue and community center in the city of Modi'in seventeen years ago, which I named YOZMA. The word *yozma* means "initiative" in Hebrew. I bring to an Israeli-Jewish population that defines itself as secular the tools for them to take initiative for exploring their religious Jewish identity beyond their cultural and national identity. *YOZMA* is also a Hebrew acronym for "Judaism of Today, Heritage of the People." Just as Hillel the elder was asked to define Judaism while standing on one foot, this is my definition of Reform Judaism while standing on one foot. I am proud of the six preschool classes of our early childhood education center, where children learn about Jewish traditions and the blessings and joy of Jewish life in an open and accepting environment. The students in the twelve classes of YOZMA's public Reform elementary Jewish day school know the significance of prayer in the life of a community. They study classical Jewish texts as a part of their daily education. Our outreach to children with special needs is recognized as a model for replication. The YOZMA synagogue and community center have been awarded prizes of excellence in the meaningful work they do with underprivileged and marginalized communities. Out of the ashes of my *bubbe*'s families, and those of the millions of other Jewish families who perished in the fires of hate, new Jewish life has been born in Israel.

Each time I hold my granddaughter, Ora, in my arms and introduce her to all the faces of her ancestors that grace our hallway, I feel the spirit of my *bubbe* and her family embracing her. As Ora smiles and shines her generous heart toward their images, their memories live on and thus their deaths were not in vain.

Hannah Rosenthal

Hannah Rosenthal has dedicated her life to the Jewish values taught to her by her father, a Holocaust survivor, and her mother, who helped the Jewish immigrants on the US side. She has headed the Jewish Council for Public Affairs, the Milwaukee Jewish Federation, and several women's rights organizations, served as midwest regional director of the US Department of Health and Human Services, and been an education director at a synagogue. She recently served as President Obama's special envoy to monitor and combat anti-Semitism at the US State Department.

"I have doubted my faith too often and theology too much…. But what I am sure about is my personal responsibility … to mourn, to remember, to honor life, and to both teach the particular and universal lessons of the Holocaust and demand that these lessons be heeded."

Mourning

We look at the empty chairs at family reunions, we listen to the family stories of survival, of loss. We think of the millions in unmarked graves. We focus on the permanent presence of their absence. We say *Kaddish*. We cry.

As a child of a Holocaust survivor, this is profoundly personal for me. My father was a rabbi in Mannheim, Germany, who on *Kristallnacht* watched his synagogue burned to the ground and his congregants' homes and businesses destroyed. He himself was taken to Buchenwald—away from his beloved congregation and without being able to say good-bye to his family, who were living in Beuthen, then part of Germany. Dad was the only survivor of his entire family. I grew up in a home where the Holocaust was at our dinner table every night. It was in my every thought, in my DNA. The Holocaust has informed all that I have done, all that I do. Like the Jewish values with which I was raised, the realities and messages of the Holocaust define who I am.

The summer of 2012, my sister Debbie and I went to Germany and Poland to visit Mannheim, where Dad had served the Jewish community, and Beuthen—now Bytom, Poland—where his father, grandfather, and great-grandfather had served their communities.

In Mannheim, Debbie and I were presented with a *Stolperstein*, a bronze cobblestone piece of art that would be placed in the ground to remember and mourn the city's destroyed Jewish community. In a way, the city was looking for ways to mourn, to say *Kaddish*, to sob.

Our heaviest mourning was in Bytom, the city where Dad played, studied, went to shul, sang, became a bar mitzvah, and was raised by his loving family. On May 28, 1942, the city's Jewish population was liquidated—the Nazi word for emptied and annihilated. No trace of Jewish life remains. One "prayer room," never used, with a scarred and burned Torah in its makeshift ark. One plaque where the synagogue once stood, now an old Soviet-styled apartment building. Nothing else. Even the marks of old mezuzot have disappeared from the doorposts.

The Jewish cemetery, overgrown and untended, is all that is left of the city's once vibrant Jewish community. Among the dilapidated gravestones we could still find eighteen Rosenthal graves. We were the only mourners there.

From Bytom, we went to Auschwitz-Birkenau. This is where my father's parents were murdered in one of the death camp's gas chambers. As I told a group of imams when I brought them to Auschwitz, this is my family cemetery.

As Jewish professionals who have dedicated ourselves to the future of Jewish life, we were struck by how hard it is to appropriately mourn the profound loss of life, the loss of potential, the loss of future generations, the loss of our grandparents, aunts, uncles, cousins. So we mourn, daily.

Memory

When we celebrate Pesach, we recite, "In each generation it is incumbent on each of us to see ourselves as if we had come out of Egypt."

And then we approach Shavuot and are taught that we must act as if we too were at Sinai. Both teach us that we, the living, are really the continuity of history. Remembering the Shoah, we stand at Auschwitz, or Buchenwald, or the other thirty-five thousand camps and ghettos now known to have been developed to kill our families, our people—and remember and recount the darkest chapter of history. We preserve the memory of the Holocaust and loss by lighting candles, telling stories, building museums and memorials—transferring the memory is the solemn obligation and urgent mission of our generation. It is a critical part of our precious inheritance, as we bridge two distinct worlds—remembering the past and looking toward the future.

We hold essay contests to engage generations removed from the Holocaust. We listen for declarations of memory from leaders around the world. We make and watch movies and plays about the Holocaust, hoping the arts will make the history more accessible and understood. We build and use social media and websites to inform. We support universities and institutions in their academic pursuit to translate memory and history. We also continue to demand accountability—there are still perpetrators who have not been tried, archives still unopened, and collaborators trying to rewrite history. And there are also individuals dedicated to literally unearthing truth, like Father Patrick Desbois, who continues to find previously unknown mass graves of murdered Jews in Ukraine and Belarus.

Despite our desire to preserve and learn from the past, we grow further from it each passing day. Time is not on our side.

Honor

We must honor not only the dead but the living. We honor the survivors who faced indescribable horror, clinging to life amid agony and death. Some of them survived camps and ghettos. Some were rescued by brave righteous people who risked their lives to save them. Some hid—in basements, in forests, in churches in Poland, in Albanian mosques, even a few in embassies. After the Shoah, they embraced life, had families, told and tell their stories, showed their tattoos, built businesses, and helped ensure a Jewish future. We honor their memories, their courage, their inner strength, their ability not to wallow in anguish or despair or bitterness, their commitment to find and create joy in the world.

Lessons

The Holocaust teaches us what is possible. The Holocaust teaches us what can happen when hatred goes unanswered, when people of otherwise good conscience look the other way, when governments, including ours, slow the rescue of the doomed. The Holocaust teaches us the power of propaganda, that a history of hatred preached from pulpits and told in fairy tales can turn ordinary family-centered people into murderers.

There are universal lessons. Wherever there is evil—mass injustice, killings, genocide—we must call it out and do everything possible to stop it. And the last thing we should ever participate in is competing victimhoods.

But, we must also at all times remind and emphasize that Jews—not some anonymous, amorphous group—were the subject of the Final Solution. Much of the world has not yet absorbed that particular lesson of the Holocaust.

When I had the great honor to serve as special envoy to monitor and combat anti-Semitism for the US State Department, I had to deal with people—from prime ministers to civil society members—who would state that anti-Semitism ended when Hitler killed himself. They ignore the somber reality that anti-Semitism increased significantly in over seventy-five countries in 2013 alone.

The old czarist forgery *The Protocols of the Elders of Zion*, which falsely purports to chronicle a nonexistent Jewish conspiracy to control the world, is still a best seller in many countries. It is taught in Saudi Arabian schools as a textbook. It is sold in establishment bookstores throughout Europe and Asia. It is truly the lie that will not die.

The medieval blood libel accusation is still being included in some Spanish churches. Recently, an elected official in Hungary stood on the floor of the Parliament and warned others that Pesach/Easter is the time Jews kidnap Christian children to use their blood to bake matzah—and no one condemned him until we complained! There are still places were Nazis are glorified—parades honor Waffen SS veterans in Latvia and Estonia.

There are religious leaders in Europe and the Middle East who call for another Holocaust "to finish the job." There are those who deny that the Holocaust ever occurred—including the former president of Iran, heralded leaders of some Catholic renegade groups, and resurgent neo-Nazi movements in Hungary, Greece, Ukraine, and elsewhere. Most schools in the Middle East refuse to teach about the Holocaust "because it will confuse the children" and "we're not sure it really happened."

And then there are those who seek to minimize or relativize the Holocaust, who say that it couldn't really have been six million or that Hitler did some good in unifying Germany.

These are not isolated incidents being advanced by a few crazy people. Like the contemporary genocidal language and atrocities in Africa, the Middle East, Asia, or Europe, we must treat these manifestations as serious warning signals of unchecked hatred. Seventy years after the end of the Shoah, anti-Semitism is alive and well.

I am unable to apply all this to my faith and my theology. I have doubted my faith too often and theology too much. It is an ever-changing challenge in my life. But what I am sure about is my personal responsibility, as a citizen of the world, as a mother, and of course as my father's daughter, to use whatever platform I am given—personally or professionally—to mourn, to remember, to honor life, and to both teach the particular and universal lessons of the Holocaust and demand that these lessons be heeded. My charge as a Jew in 2015 and in the future is to ensure that "Never Again" has meaning and becomes reality.

Acknowledgments

From the moment we came up with the concept for *God, Faith & Identity from the Ashes*, through the process of identifying and reaching out to potential contributors, compiling and editing the essays, and all the other substantive, aesthetic, and technical stages it took to make this book a reality, Stuart M. Matlins, founder and editor in chief of Jewish Lights Publishing, has been a true friend, an always constructive advisor, and, on numerous occasions, a much-needed reality check. I shall be forever grateful for and have benefited greatly from his guidance, wisdom, structural suggestions, insights too numerous to list, and, not least, his good-humored forbearance.

Romy Golan, my outstanding and incredibly efficient editorial and administrative right hand from the outset of this project, managed to keep track of the status of each contribution to this volume from the moment I first reached out to a potential contributor until each essay was edited and finalized and all the contributors' bios and photos were duly received, and she was invaluable in first formatting each individual essay and then the entire manuscript, as well as producing the glossary. Many thanks also to Emily Wichland, vice president of Editorial and Production at Jewish Lights, who patiently, enthusiastically, judiciously, and meticulously managed the final production stage of this book; and to Tim Holtz, Barbara Heise, Leah Brewer, and the entire staff at Jewish Lights for their critical "back office" support in turning the submitted manuscript into the hopefully meaningful volume you now hold in your hands.

Most importantly, my heartfelt thanks to each of the contributors who put their thoughts, views, and emotions on paper, often for the first time, to enable us collectively to create a book that indeed tells both the world and future generations who we are and what we stand for. My one profound regret is the absence in the book of my late friend Elan Steinberg's irrepressible voice in defense of memory and on behalf of justice for survivors.

My teacher and mentor Professor Elie Wiesel most graciously gave of his time and shared his wisdom with me throughout the compilation and editing of this book. His guidance and friendship over more than five decades have been one of the most important influences in my life and career. His prologue, for which I am most thankful, encapsulates how he has inspired and motivated the generations born after the Shoah to its survivors.

I am deeply grateful to Ambassador Ronald S. Lauder, the president of the World Jewish Congress (WJC), the WJC's CEO and executive vice president Robert Singer, the WJC's secretary general emeritus Michael Schneider, and WJC chief program officer Sonia Gomes de Mesquita for their encouragement and for understanding the importance of this book to Jews, Jewish communities, and others across the globe.

I am also most appreciative to Rabbi Elliot Cosgrove of Park Avenue Synagogue in New York City for inviting me to give the guest sermon there on the Shabbat between Rosh Hashanah and Yom Kippur in 2013, and to my friend and colleague Claudio Epelman, the executive director of the Latin American Jewish Congress, for bringing my attempt to discover God's presence in the horrors of the Shoah to the attention of Pope Francis. That sermon and Pope Francis's unexpected and remarkable reaction to it were the catalysts that sparked the concept for this book.

Many people shared their ideas as to who might be invited to participate in this project, enabled me to make contact with specific contributors, and generously offered suggestions and advice. In particular, I am indebted to Canadian member of Parliament and former minister of justice Irwin Cotler, Philippe Allouche, Chen Arieli, Rabbi Elliot Cosgrove, Roger Cukierman, Claudio Epelman, Steven Friedman (on our Shabbat walks home from shul), Sonia Gomes de Mesquita, Robert Goot, Sam Grundwerg, Rabbi Jan Caryl Kaufman, Rabbi Naamah Kelman, Aviva Kempner, Annette Lévy-Willard, Daniel Mariaschin, Rabbi Michael Marmur, Leslie Meyers, Jean Bloch Rosensaft, Jodi Rosensaft, Michael Rosensaft, Dr. David Sekons, Mervyn Smith, Irwin Tenenbaum, Jerzy Warman, Dov Weissglas, Fred Zeidman, Marjoleine Zieck, and Rabbi Neil Zuckerman of Park Avenue Synagogue, who also graciously reviewed and commented on the religion-based glossary entries.

Rabbi Peretz Rodman masterfully translated three of the essays from their original Hebrew into English.

Mirta Kupferminc, a daughter of survivors and one of the most original and most talented contemporary artists of the post-Holocaust generation, graciously allowed us to feature her graphic work *Spilt on Another Map*, on the cover of this book and the opening page of each section. Other examples of her powerful art can be seen at www.mirtakupferminc.net. Hers is the last of the photographs on the page facing the title page.

My thanks also to Jonathan Safran Foer, Stephan Kramer, Samuel Norich, Rabbi Marc Schneier, and Annette Wieviorka for their interest in the book.

I owe a special debt of gratitude to Robert Fagenson, my best friend ever since I came to the United States from Switzerland at the age of ten, and his wife, Margaret, for their gracious hospitality, which enabled me to work on this book at their homes in St. Thomas and on the New Jersey shore, and for their unfailing friendship.

Above all, this book would not have been possible without Jeanie—Jean Bloch Rosensaft—my love, my inspiration, my sounding board, and my partner in everything I have ever accomplished. Jeanie, our daughter Jodi, our son-in-law—really our son—Mike, and our grandchildren, Jacob and Hallie, have been at the forefront of my thoughts throughout the creation of this volume, as they are each and every day. Their unconditional love and enthusiastic support are the fuel that keeps me going.

Glossary

Akedah: Hebrew; lit. "binding," as in the binding of Isaac in the book of Genesis.

Aktion: German; mass assembly of Jews in Nazi ghettos for deportation to death and concentration camps.

Aleinu: Hebrew; the closing prayer of daily services that signifies the Jewish people's faith and dedication to God.

Aliyah: Hebrew; lit. "ascent," term used to describe immigration of Jews to Israel.

Am Yisrael: Hebrew; the people of Israel.

Am Yisrael Chai: Hebrew; lit. "The people of Israel lives," slogan that denotes Jewish survival.

Amidah: Hebrew; central prayer of Jewish liturgy, said silently while standing during the three daily prayer services.

Appel: German; roll call.

Avinu Malkeinu: Hebrew; lit. "Our Father, Our King." Name of the prayer recited on Rosh Hashanah, Yom Kippur, and during other major Jewish services.

Baba: Yiddish; grandmother.

Baruch shekivanti: Hebrew; a Talmudic expression meaning "It is to be praised that I had the same intention as a previous scholar."

Bildung: German; lit. "education," term for German tradition of self-cultivation.

Bracha: Hebrew; blessing.

Bubbe: Yiddish; grandmother.

Chevra kadisha: Aramaic; lit. "sacred society." An organized group of usually unpaid Jewish men and, among the non-Orthodox, women who see to it that the bodies of deceased Jews are prepared for burial in accordance with Jewish laws and traditions.

Chupa: Hebrew; lit. "canopy," canopy under which a Jewish couple stands during their wedding ceremony that symbolizes the home the couple will build together.

Dafka: Hebrew; despite expectations to the contrary; term often said with a slightly amused or ironic connotation.

Daven: Yiddish; to pray.

Durchgangslager: German; transit camp.

Eicha: Hebrew; the book of Lamentations.

Einsatzgruppen, sing. *Einsatzgruppe*: German; SS mobile killing squads that followed the German army in the invasion of the Soviet Union in June 1941 and systematically murdered perceived racial and political enemies of the Third Reich, primarily Jews and Communist officials.

El Maleh Rachamim: Hebrew; "God full of mercy," prayer for the souls of the dead.

Erev: Hebrew, evening; term for the eve or onset of a Jewish religious day, as in *Erev Shabbes* for Friday night, or *Erev Rosh Hashanah* for the evening marking the beginning of the Jewish New Year.

Freilich: Yiddish; happy, joyous.

Frum: Yiddish; religious, observant.

Goldene medine: Yiddish; lit. golden country, expression used in reference to the United States.

Gottenyu: Yiddish; affectionate, personal term for God.

Hachnasat kallah: Hebrew; lit. attending the bride. Jewish religious and traditional mitzvah, or obligation, of assisting orphaned or impoverished brides of the community to get married.

Haftorah: Hebrew; one of the biblical selections from the books of the Prophets read after the Torah portion during prayer services.

Haganah: Hebrew; lit. "defense," Zionist paramilitary organization in Palestine from 1920 to 1948.

Haggadah: Hebrew; Jewish text that is read during the Passover seder.

Halakhah: Hebrew; Jewish law; adj.: **Halakhic**.

Halal: Arabic; permissible.

Haram: Arabic; sinful.

Haredim: Hebrew; ultra-Orthodox Jews; adj.: **Haredi**.

Haroset: Hebrew; a sweet delicacy made of fruit, nuts, and wine eaten during the Passover seder, which is supposed to signify mortar the Israelites used while enslaved in ancient Egypt.

Hashem: Hebrew; lit. "the Name," manner in which many Orthodox Jews refer to God.

"Hatikva": Hebrew; lit. "The Hope," the Israeli national anthem.

Hazzan: Hebrew; cantor.

Hesed: Hebrew; loving-kindness.

Imma: Hebrew; mother.

Judenrat: German; Jewish councils and municipal authorities established in September 1939 to implement Nazi policies and maintain order in the ghettos.

Kaddish: Hebrew; prayer of praise to God, recited as principal mourner's prayer.

Kapo: German; an inmate in a Nazi concentration assigned to carry out certain administrative tasks.

Kindertransport: German; a series of rescue efforts that brought thousands of refugee Jewish children out of Nazi Germany and into Great Britain between 1938 and 1940.

Kippa, pl. *Kippot:* Hebrew; skullcap.

Kol Nidre: Aramaic; lit., "all vows." Solemn and hauntingly beautiful declaration chanted before the beginning of the synagogue service on the eve of Yom Kippur; also used to refer to this service as a whole.

Kristallnacht: German; lit. "Night of Broken Glass," wave of anti-Jewish pogroms on November 9–10, 1938, throughout Germany, Austria, and German-occupied Czechoslovakia.

Kultur: German; pre–Third Reich Germanic intellectual concept, defined by Princeton University professor of art Frank Jewett Mather Jr. as "the organized efficiency of a nation in the broadest sense—its successful achievement in civil and military administration, industry, commerce, finance, and in a quite secondary way in scholarship, letters, and art" ("Culture vs Kultur," *New York Times,* November 8, 1914, p. 30).

Lagerführer: German; lit. "camp leader," the head SS officer assigned to a particular concentration camp, serving as the commander of the camp.

Landsman: Yiddish; person from the old neighborhood or country.

Mameloshn: Yiddish; lit. "mother tongue," referring to Yiddish.

Marror: Hebrew; bitter herbs eaten during Passover seder.

Mezuzah, pl. *Mezuzot:* Hebrew; encased strip of parchment inscribed with two passages from the Torah and hung on the right doorpost of a house or room.

Mi Sheberakh: Hebrew; a prayer for recovery; a blessing for well-being.

Mincha: Hebrew; afternoon prayer service.

Minyan: Hebrew; traditionally a quorum of ten Jewish male adults at least thirteen years of age (in progressive Judaism today, ten Jewish male or female adults) needed for certain religious prayer services and traditions.

Mir zeinen do: Yiddish; "We are here," closing phrase of the song *Zog Nit Keynmol az Du Geyst dem Letzten Veg* (Never say that you are going the last road), composed in 1943 by Hirsh Glick in the Vilna Ghetto, also known as the Partisan's Song, which has become the anthem of the survivors.

Mishpacha: Hebrew; family.

Mit di takhríkhim: Yiddish; [buried] in shrouds.

Mitzvah, pl. Mitzvot: Hebrew; commandment, obligation, or more colloquially, good deed.

Mizrahim: Hebrew; Jews from Arab countries.

Nakhes: Yiddish; pride, pleasure.

Niggun, pl. *Niggunim*: Hebrew; melody.

Nu: Yiddish; exclamation, most akin to "So," but with an inflection denoting mild impatience tinged with resigned inevitability, as in "*Nu*, speak already, I don't have all day."

Oeuvre de Secours aux Enfants (OSE): French; lit. "Organization to Save the Children"; French-Jewish organization that saved the lives of hundreds of children during World War II and then, after the end of the war, took care of orphaned Jewish children, many of whom had survived Nazi concentration camps.

Oyneg Shabes: Yiddish; lit. "Joy of the Sabbath"; code name of documentary group in the Warsaw Ghetto that kept diaries and collected testimonies and other documentation.

Pirkei Avot: Hebrew; the Ethics of Our Fathers; segment of the Talmud that deals with ethical and moral principles.

Rav: Hebrew; rabbi.

Rebbe: Yiddish, derived from the Hebrew for rabbi; used to refer to Hasidic rabbis, as in the Lubavitcher Rebbe, the Satmar Rebbe, or the Kotzker Rebbe.

Rebbetzin: Yiddish; the wife of a rabbi.

Rebono shel olam: Hebrew; Master of the universe; God.

Saba: Hebrew; grandfather.

Sabra: Hebrew; Jew born in Israel.

Sephardi: Hebrew; Jews of Spanish or Portuguese origin.

Shabbat Shuva: Hebrew; the Shabbat between Rosh Hashanah and Yom Kippur.

Shabbes: Yiddish for the Hebrew Shabbat.

Shekhina: Hebrew; mystical divine spark that characterizes Jewish faith.

Sheol: Hebrew; biblical term for the final resting place of the dead.

Sh'erit ha-Pletah: Hebrew; lit. "the Surviving Remnant," term by which the Jewish survivors of the Holocaust referred to themselves collectively after the end of the war.

Shidduch: Yiddish; an arranged marriage; lit. "a match."

Shmates: Yiddish; dress or garment; rags.

Shtetl: Yiddish; small town in pre-Holocaust Europe with a large Jewish population.

Shul: Yiddish; synagogue.

Shulchan Aruch: Hebrew; the ultimate code of Jewish law.

Smichah: Hebrew; rabbinic ordination.

Solidarnosc: Polish; Solidarity, name of anti-Communist political and social movement in Poland credited with a major role in the collapse of the Communist regime in that country.

Sonderkommando: German; a detail of Jewish prisoners in Nazi death camps whose task was to dispose of bodies from gas chambers.

Stolperstein: German; a bronze monument placed in pavement that commemorates a victim of the Holocaust.

Sukkot: Hebrew; Feast of Tabernacles.

Tal: Hebrew; lit. "dew"; also prayer for dew recited on the first day of Passover.

Tallit, Hebrew; or *Tallis,* Yiddish: Jewish prayer shawl, worn over the outer clothes during prayer services.

Talmud: Two multi-tractate compendia of legal opinions and rulings, Rabbinic commentaries, and legends constituting the most authoritative source and exegesis of Jewish law. The more prominent of the two, the Babylonian Talmud, is described in the *Encyclopaedia Judaica* as "a literary work of monumental proportions (5,894 folio pages in the standard printed editions) which draws upon the totality of the spiritual, intellectual, ethical, historical and legal traditions produced in rabbinic circles from the time of the destruction of the Second Temple in the first century of the Common Era until the Muslim conquest at the beginning of the seventh century" (2nd ed., vol. 19, p. 470). The earlier Jerusalem or Palestinian Talmud was completed in the fourth century.

Talmud Torah: Hebrew; Jewish learning; also a communal school for the teaching of Hebrew, Bible, and the basics of the Jewish religion to children.

T'fillin: Hebrew; small square black leather boxes that contain parchments inscribed with verses from the Torah, worn on the forehead and upper left arm during weekday morning prayer services.

Tikkun olam: Hebrew; a concept that means to heal or repair the world.

Tishah B'Av: Hebrew; lit. the ninth day of the Hebrew month of Av; a fast day that commemorates the destruction of the First and Second Temples in Jerusalem and the subsequent exile of the Jews from Israel and other tragic events in Jewish history.

Traif: Hebrew; non-kosher food.

Tzedakah: Hebrew; charity; righteousness.

Yahrzeit: Yiddish; anniversary of someone's death.

Yiddishkeit: Yiddish; Jewish character or quality; Jewish way of life.

Yizkor: Hebrew; memorial prayer.

Yom HaShoah: Hebrew; lit., "Day of the Holocaust." Official day of remembrance for the victims of the Holocaust set by the Knesset, the Israeli Parliament, for the twenty-seventh day of the Hebrew month of Nissan, coinciding with the beginning of the Warsaw Ghetto uprising and falling a week after the end of the Passover holiday.

Yom Tov: Hebrew; lit., "good day." Hebrew and Yiddish term for a Jewish holiday.

Zachor: Hebrew; remember.

Zayde or **Zeida**: Yiddish; grandfather.

Z"l: Hebrew; abbreviation for *zichrono* [or *zichrona*] *livracha*, Hebrew for "may his [or her] memory be for a blessing," placed after someone's name to indicate that the individual has passed away.

Zone Libre: French; lit. "Free Zone"; southern half of France during World War II, which remained unoccupied by the Germans until November 1942 but was run by the collaborationist Vichy government.

Index of Contributors

Credits

The prologue by Elie Wiesel is excerpted from his "To Our Children," *Against Silence: The Voice and Vision of Elie Wiesel* (Irving Abrahamson, editor, Holocaust Library, 1985), vol. 3, p. 319.

Parts of the introduction by Menachem Z. Rosensaft were originally published in "Transferring Memory: The Task of Children and Grandchildren of Holocaust Survivors," *Midstream*, Spring 2011, and in "A Message from Pope Francis to a Son of Holocaust Survivors," *The Jewish Week*, October 25, 2013.

"Falling in Love in Cologne" by Lily Brett was originally published as "Was möglich ist," in *Die Zeit*, August 8, 2013.

"My grandmother is now a lake ..." by Amichai Lau-Lavie was originally published on August 28, 2011, on the author's website at http://amichai.me/bitter-herbs.html.

Merav Michaeli's inaugural speech in the Knesset was previously published in full on the website Israelseen.com on March 7, 2013, at http://israelseen.com/2013/03/07/merav-michaeli-new-labor-mk-my-inaugural-speech-i-mean-every-word.

"If God was at Treblinka ..." by Menachem Z. Rosensaft was originally published as "The Days of Awe and the Years of Terror" on the *Washington Post*'s religion blog, *On Faith*, on September 11, 2013, at http://www.washingtonpost.com/blogs/on-faith/wp/2013/09/11/the-days-of-awe-and-the-years-of-horror/.

Notes

Prologue, by Elie Wiesel
1. Elie Wiesel, "To Our Children," *Against Silence: The Voice and Vision of Elie Wiesel*, ed. Irving Abrahamson (New York: Holocaust Library, 1985), vol. 3, p. 319.

Introduction, by Menachem Z. Rosensaft
1. Hadassah Rosensaft, *Yesterday: My Story* (New York and Jerusalem: Yad Vashem, 2005), p. 27.
2. Elie Wiesel, "To Our Children," p. 321.
3. Ibid., p. 323.

Part I: God and Faith
1. Elie Wiesel, Address, 49th General Assembly of the Union of American Hebrew Congregations, November 1967, in *Against Silence: The Voice and Vision of Elie Wiesel*, ed. Irving Abrahamson (New York: Holocaust Library, 1985), vol. 1, p. 235.

Yossi Klein Halevi
1. Jacob Glatstein, *I Keep Recalling: The Holocaust Poems of Jacob Glatstein*, trans. Barnett Zumoff (New York: Ktav, 1993), p. 92.

Rabbi Moshe Waldoks
1. Abraham Joshua Heschel, *The Earth Is the Lord's* (New York: Harper Torchbooks, 1966), p. 107.
2. Joseph Berger, "Man in the News; Witness to Evil: Eliezer Wiesel," *New York Times*, October 15, 1986.

Rabbi Lilly Kaufman
1. "It is to be praised that I had the same intention as a previous scholar." This is an exclamation said by students of Talmud, who anticipated an idea that they later find expressed by a rabbi in the text.

Rabbi Michael Marmur
1. Emil L. Fackenheim, *God's Presence in History: Jewish Affirmations and Philosophical Reflections* (New York: Harper & Row, 1970), pp. 97–98.
2. Peter Berger, *Redeeming Laughter: The Comic Dimension of Human Experience* (Berlin: Walter de Gruyter, 1997).
3. Abraham Joshua Heschel, *God in Search of Man—A Philosophy of Judaism* (New York: Farrar, Straus & Cudahy, 1955), p. 426.

Eric Nelson

1. For this characterization of the *Tal* prayer, I am indebted to a sermon delivered by Rabbi Elliot Cosgrove at Park Avenue Synagogue in New York City in 2013.

Shimon Koffler Fogel

1. Rabbi Israel Meir Kagan (1838–1933), influential Lithuanian rabbinic scholar, popularly known by the title of his first book, *Chofetz Chaim* (Desirer of Life).

Menachem Z. Rosensaft

1. Hadassah Rosensaft, *Yesterday: My Story* (New York and Jerusalem: Yad Vashem, 2005), p. 39.
2. Eliezer Berkovits, *Faith after the Holocaust* (New York: Ktav, 1973), pp. 4–5.
3. "Lubavitcher Rebbe Rejects Assertion That Holocaust Was Divine Punishment," JTA, December 31, 1990, www.jta.org/1990/12/31/archive/lubavitcher-rebbe-rejects-assertion-that-holocaust-was-divine-punishment#ixzz2dEqx7XRW.
4. Dovid Dubov Nissan, "Belief after the Holocaust," http://www.chabad.org/library/article_cdo/aid/108398/jewish/Belief-After-the-Holocaust.htm.
5. David Weiss Halivni, *The Book and the Sword: A Life of Learning in the Shadow of Destruction* (New York: Farrar, Straus & Giroux, 1996), p. 154.
6. Yehuda Bauer, "God as Surgeon," *Haaretz*, June 1, 2007, www.haaretz.com/print-edition/opinion/god-as-surgeon-1.221983.
7. David Weiss Halivni, *Breaking the Tablets: Jewish Theology after the Shoah* (Lanham, MD: Rowman & Littlefield, 2007), p. 107.
8. Roger A. Ritvo and Diane M. Plotkin, *Sisters in Sorrow: Voices of Care in the Holocaust* (College Station, TX: Texas A&M University Press, 1998), pp. 181–182.
9. Rosensaft, *Yesterday*, pp. 43–44.

Part II: Identity

1. Elie Wiesel, "Against Despair," First Annual Louis H. Pincus Memorial Lecture, United Jewish Appeal, 1973, p. 5.

Josef Joffe

1. Yuri Slezkine, *The Jewish Century* (Princeton, NJ: Princeton University Press, 2004), p. 1.

Rabbi Benny Lau

1. Joseph B. Soloveitchik, *Fate and Destiny: From Holocaust to the State of Israel* (New York: Ktav, 2000), p. 25.

André Singer

1. Barack Obama, *Dreams from My Father, A Story of Race and Inheritance* (New York: Three Rivers Press, 2004), p. 111.

Part III: A Legacy of Memory
1. Elie Wiesel, Preface to the new translation of *Night* (New York: Hill & Wang, 2006), p. xv.

Rabbi Joseph Potasnik
1. Arnold Geier, *Heroes of the Holocaust: Extraordinary True Accounts of Triumph* (New York: Berkley Books, 1998), p. 194.
2. *New York Times*, November 13, 1977, Section 4, p. 16.
3. Haskel Lookstein, *Were We Our Brothers' Keepers? The Public Response of American Jews to the Holocaust 1939–1944* (New York: Hartmore House, 1985), p. 208.

Part IV: *Tikkun Olam*: Changing the World for the Better
1. Elie Wiesel, Nobel acceptance speech, Oslo, December 10, 1986.

Rabbi Judith Schindler
1. Alexander Schindler, USC Shoah Foundation, Visual History Archive, interview 45311, September 2, 1998.
2. Abraham Joshua Heschel, *The Insecurity of Freedom, Essays on Human Existence* (New York: Noonday Press, 1967), p. 103.

The Right Honourable David Miliband
1. Jonathan Sacks, *The Chief Rabbi's Haggadah* (London: HarperCollins, 2003), p. 29.

Tali Nates
1. Dina Wardi, *Memorial Candles: Children of the Holocaust* (London & New York: Routledge, 1992).

Dr. Yaffa Singer
1. Judith Herman, *Trauma and Recovery* (New York: Basic Books, 1992), p. 159.
2. Ibid., p. 4.
3. Hagit Lavsky, *New Beginnings: Holocaust Survivors in Bergen-Belsen and the British Zone in Germany, 1945–1950* (Detroit, MI: Wayne State University Press, 2002), p. 66.
4. Viktor E. Frankl, *Man's Search for Meaning* (Boston: Beacon Press, 1959/2006), p. 82.

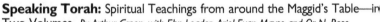

Bible Study / Midrash

Passing Life's Tests: Spiritual Reflections on the Trial of Abraham, the Binding of Isaac *By Rabbi Bradley Shavit Artson, DHL*
Invites us to use this powerful tale as a tool for our own soul wrestling, to confront our existential sacrifices and enable us to face—and surmount—life's tests
6 x 9, 176 pp, Quality PB, 978-1-58023-631-7 **$18.99**

Speaking Torah: Spiritual Teachings from around the Maggid's Table—in Two Volumes *By Arthur Green, with Ebn Leader, Ariel Evan Mayse and Or N. Rose*
The most powerful Hasidic teachings made accessible—from some of the world's preeminent authorities on Jewish thought and spirituality.
Volume 1—6 x 9, 512 pp, HC, 978-1-58023-668-3 **$34.99**
Volume 2—6 x 9, 448 pp, HC, 978-1-58023-694-2 **$34.99**

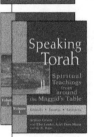

A Partner in Holiness: Deepening Mindfulness, Practicing Compassion and Enriching Our Lives through the Wisdom of R. Levi Yitzhak of Berdichev's *Kedushat Levi*
By Rabbi Jonathan P. Slater, DMin; Foreword by Arthur Green; Preface by Rabby Nancy Flam
Contemporary mindfulness and classical Hasidic spirituality are brought together to inspire a satisfying spiritual life of practice.
Volume 1— 6 x 9, 336 pp, HC, 978-1-58023-794-9 **$35.00**
Volume 2— 6 x 9, 288 pp, HC, 978-1-58023-795-6 **$35.00**

The Genesis of Leadership: What the Bible Teaches Us about Vision, Values and   Leading Change *By Rabbi Nathan Laufer; Foreword by Senator Joseph I. Lieberman*
6 x 9, 288 pp, Quality PB, 978-1-58023-352-1 **$18.99**

Hineini in Our Lives
Learning How to Respond to Others through 14 Biblical Texts and Personal Stories
By Dr. Norman J. Cohen 6 x 9, 240 pp, Quality PB, 978-1-58023-274-6 **$18.99**

Masking and Unmasking Ourselves: Interpreting Biblical Texts on Clothing & Identity *By Dr. Norman J. Cohen* 6 x 9, 224 pp, HC, 978-1-58023-461-0 **$24.99**

The Messiah and the Jews: Three Thousand Years of Tradition, Belief and Hope
By Rabbi Elaine Rose Glickman; Foreword by Rabbi Neil Gillman, PhD
Preface by Rabbi Judith Z. Abrams, PhD 6 x 9, 192 pp, Quality PB, 978-1-58023-690-4 **$16.99**

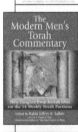

The Modern Men's Torah Commentary: New Insights from Jewish Men on the 54 Weekly Torah Portions *Edited by Rabbi Jeffrey K. Salkin*
6 x 9, 368 pp, HC, 978-1-58023-395-8 **$24.99**

Moses and the Journey to Leadership: Timeless Lessons of Effective Management from the Bible and Today's Leaders *By Dr. Norman J. Cohen*
6 x 9, 240 pp, Quality PB, 978-1-58023-351-4 **$18.99**; HC, 978-1-58023-227-2 **$21.99**

The Other Talmud—The *Yerushalmi*: Unlocking the Secrets of *The Talmud of Israel* for Judaism Today *By Rabbi Judith Z. Abrams, PhD*
6 x 9, 256 pp, HC, 978-1-58023-463-4 **$24.99**

Sage Tales: Wisdom and Wonder from the Rabbis of the Talmud
By Rabbi Burton L. Visotzky
6 x 9, 256 pp, Quality PB, 978-1-58023-791-8 **$19.99**; HC, 978-1-58023-456-6 **$24.99**

The Torah Revolution: Fourteen Truths That Changed the World
By Rabbi Reuven Hammer, PhD 6 x 9, 240 pp, Quality PB, 978-1-58023-789-5 **$18.99**
HC, 978-1-58023-457-3 **$24.99**

The Wisdom of Judaism: An Introduction to the Values of the Talmud
By Rabbi Dov Peretz Elkins 6 x 9, 192 pp, Quality PB, 978-1-58023-327-9 **$16.99**

Or phone, mail or email to: JEWISH LIGHTS Publishing
An imprint of Turner Publishing Company
4507 Charlotte Avenue • Suite 100 • Nashville, Tennessee 37209
Tel: (615) 255-2665 • www.jewishlights.com
Prices subject to change.

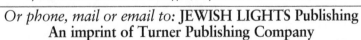

Bar / Bat Mitzvah

The Mitzvah Project Book
Making Mitzvah Part of Your Bar/Bat Mitzvah ... and Your Life
By Liz Suneby and Diane Heiman; Foreword by Rabbi Jeffrey K. Salkin; Preface by Rabbi Sharon Brous
The go-to source for Jewish young adults and their families looking to make the world a better place through good deeds—big or small.
6 x 9, 224 pp, Quality PB, 978-1-58023-458-0 **$16.99** *For ages 11–13*

The Bar/Bat Mitzvah Memory Book, 2nd Edition: An Album for Treasuring the Spiritual Celebration *By Rabbi Jeffrey K. Salkin and Nina Salkin*
8 x 10, 48 pp, 2-color text, Deluxe HC, ribbon marker, 978-1-58023-263-0 **$19.99**

For Kids—Putting God on Your Guest List, 2nd Edition: How to Claim the Spiritual Meaning of Your Bar or Bat Mitzvah *By Rabbi Jeffrey K. Salkin*
6 x 9, 144 pp, Quality PB, 978-1-58023-308-8 **$15.99** *For ages 11–13*

The Jewish Prophet: Visionary Words from Moses and Miriam to Henrietta Szold and A. J. Heschel *By Rabbi Dr. Michael J. Shire*
6½ x 8½, 128 pp, 123 full-color illus., HC, 978-1-58023-168-8 **$14.95**

Putting God on the Guest List, 3rd Edition: How to Reclaim the Spiritual Meaning of Your Child's Bar or Bat Mitzvah *By Rabbi Jeffrey K. Salkin*
6 x 9, 224 pp, Quality PB, 978-1-58023-222-7 **$18.99**
    Teacher's Guide: 8½ x 11, 48 pp, PB, 978-1-58023-226-5 **$8.99**

Teens / Young Adults

Text Messages: A Torah Commentary for Teens
Edited by Rabbi Jeffrey K. Salkin
Shows today's teens how each Torah portion contains worlds of meaning for them, for what they are going through in their lives, and how they can shape their Jewish identity as they enter adulthood.
6 x 9, 304 pp, HC, 978-1-58023-507-5 **$24.99**

Hannah Senesh: Her Life and Diary, the First Complete Edition
By Hannah Senesh; Foreword by Marge Piercy; Preface by Eitan Senesh; Afterword by Roberta Grossman
6 x 9, 368 pp, b/w photos, Quality PB, 978-1-58023-342-2 **$19.99**

I Am Jewish: Personal Reflections Inspired by the Last Words of Daniel Pearl
Edited by Judea and Ruth Pearl 6 x 9, 304 pp, Deluxe PB w/ flaps, 978-1-58023-259-3 **$19.99**
Download a free copy of the *I Am Jewish Teacher's Guide* at www.jewishlights.com.

The JGirl's Guide: The Young Jewish Woman's Handbook for Coming of Age
By Penina Adelman, Ali Feldman and Dr. Shulamit Reinharz
6 x 9, 240 pp, Quality PB, 978-1-58023-215-9 **$16.99** *For ages 11 & up*
    Teacher's & Parent's Guide: 8½ x 11, 56 pp, PB, 978-1-58023-225-8 **$8.99**

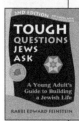

The JGuy's Guide: The GPS for Jewish Teen Guys
By Rabbi Joseph B. Meszler, Dr. Shulamit Reinharz, Liz Suneby and Diane Heiman
6 x 9, 208 pp, Quality PB, 978-1-58023-721-5 **$16.99**
    Teacher's Guide: 8½ x 11, 30pp, PB, 978-1-58023-773-4 **$8.99**

Tough Questions Jews Ask, 2nd Edition: A Young Adult's Guide to Building a Jewish Life *By Rabbi Edward Feinstein*
6 x 9, 160 pp, Quality PB, 978-1-58023-454-2 **$16.99** *For ages 11 & up*
    Teacher's Guide: 8½ x 11, 72 pp, PB, 978-1-58023-187-9 **$8.95**

Pre-Teens

Be Like God: God's To-Do List for Kids
By Dr. Ron Wolfson
Encourages kids ages eight through twelve to use their God-given superpowers to find the many ways they can make a difference in the lives of others and find meaning and purpose for their own.
7 x 9, 144 pp, Quality PB, 978-1-58023-510-5 **$15.99** *For ages 8–12*

The Book of Miracles: A Young Person's Guide to Jewish Spiritual Awareness
By Lawrence Kushner, with all-new illustrations by the author
6 x 9, 96 pp, 2-color illus., HC, 978-1-879045-78-1 **$16.95** *For ages 9–13*

Children's Books by Sandy Eisenberg Sasso

The *Shema* in the Mezuzah
Listening to Each Other
Introduces children ages 3 to 6 to the words of the *Shema* and the custom of putting up the mezuzah. Winner, National Jewish Book Award.
9 x 12, 32 pp, Full-color illus., HC, 978-1-58023-506-8 **$18.99** *For ages 3–6*

Adam & Eve's First Sunset
God's New Day
Explores fear and hope, faith and gratitude in ways that will delight kids and adults—inspiring us to bless each of God's days and nights.
9 x 12, 32 pp, Full-color illus., HC, 978-1-58023-177-0 **$17.95** *For ages 4 & up*

Also Available as a Board Book: **Adam and Eve's New Day**
5 x 5, 24 pp, Full-color illus., Board Book, 978-1-59473-205-8 **$7.99*** *For ages 1–4*

But God Remembered
Stories of Women from Creation to the Promised Land
Four different stories of women—Lilith, Serach, Bityah and the Daughters of Z—teach us important values through their faith and actions.
9 x 12, 32 pp, Full-color illus., Quality PB, 978-1-58023-372-9 **$8.99** *For ages 8 & up*

For Heaven's Sake
Heaven is often found where you least expect it.
9 x 12, 32 pp, Full-color illus., HC, 978-1-58023-054-4 **$16.95** *For ages 4 & up*

God Said Amen
An inspiring story about hearing the answers to our prayers.
9 x 12, 32 pp, Full-color illus., HC, 978-1-58023-080-3 **$16.95** *For ages 4 & up*

God's Paintbrush: Special 10th Anniversary Edition
Wonderfully interactive, invites children of all faiths and backgrounds to encounter God through moments in their own lives. Provides questions adult and child can explore together. 11 x 8¼, 32 pp, Full-color illus., HC, 978-1-58023-195-4 **$18.99** *For ages 4 & up*

Also Available as a Board Book: **I Am God's Paintbrush**
5 x 5, 24 pp, Full-color illus., Board Book, 978-1-59473-265-2 **$7.99*** *For ages 1–4*

Also Available: **God's Paintbrush Teacher's Guide**
8½ x 11, 32 pp, PB, 978-1-879045-57-6 **$8.95**

God's Paintbrush Celebration Kit:
A Spiritual Activity Kit for Teachers and Students of All Faiths, All Backgrounds
9½ x 12, 40 Full-color Activity Sheets & Teacher Folder w/ complete instructions
HC, 978-1-58023-050-6 **$21.95**
8-Student Activity Sheet Pack (40 sheets/5 sessions), 978-1-58023-058-2 **$19.95**
Single-Student Activity Sheet Pack (5 sessions), 978-1-58023-059-9 **$3.95**

In God's Name
Like an ancient myth in its poetic text and vibrant illustrations, this award-winning modern fable about the search for God's name celebrates the diversity and, at the same time, the unity of all people.
9 x 12, 32 pp, Full-color illus., HC, 978-1-879045-26-2 **$18.99** *For ages 4 & up*

Also Available as a Board Book: **What Is God's Name?**
5 x 5, 24 pp, Full-color illus., Board Book, 978-1-893361-10-2 **$8.99*** *For ages 1–4*
Also Available in Spanish: **El nombre de Dios**
9 x 12, 32 pp, Full-color illus., HC, 978-1-893361-63-8 **$16.95** *For ages 4 & up*

Noah's Wife
The Story of Naamah
When God tells Noah to bring the animals of the world onto the ark, God also calls on Naamah, Noah's wife, to save each plant on earth.
9 x 12, 32 pp, Full-color illus., HC, 978-1-58023-134-3 **$16.95** *For ages 4 & up*

Also Available as a Board Book: **Naamah, Noah's Wife**
5 x 5, 24 pp, Full-color illus., Board Book, 978-1-893361-56-0 **$7.95*** *For ages 1–4*

**A book from SkyLight Paths, Jewish Lights' sister imprint*

Children's Books

Lullaby
By Debbie Friedman; Full-color illus. by Lorraine Bubar
A charming adaptation of beloved singer-songwriter Debbie Friedman's best-selling song *Lullaby*, this timeless bedtime picture book will help children know that God will keep them safe throughout the night.
9 x 12, 32 pp, Full-color illus., w/ a CD of original music & lyrics by Debbie Friedman
HC, 978-1-58023-807-6 **$18.99** For ages 3–6

Around the World in One Shabbat
Jewish People Celebrate the Sabbath Together
By Durga Yael Bernhard
Takes your child on a colorful adventure to share the many ways Jewish people celebrate Shabbat around the world.
11 x 8½, 32 pp, Full-color illus., HC, 978-1-58023-433-7 **$18.99** For ages 3–6

It's a ... It's a ... It's a Mitzvah
By Liz Suneby and Diane Heiman; Full-color illus. by Laurel Molk
Join Mitzvah Meerkat and friends as they introduce children to the everyday kindnesses that mark the beginning of a Jewish journey and a lifetime commitment to *tikkun olam* (repairing the world).
9 x 12, 32 pp, Full-color illus., HC, 978-1-58023-509-9 **$18.99** For ages 3–6
Also available as a Board Book: **That's a Mitzvah**
5 x 5, 24 pp, Full-color illus., Board Book, 978-1-58023-804-5 **$8.99** For ages 1–4

What You Will See Inside a Synagogue
By Rabbi Lawrence A. Hoffman, PhD, and Dr. Ron Wolfson; Full-color photos by Bill Aron
A colorful, fun-to-read introduction that explains the ways and whys of Jewish worship and religious life.
8½ x 10½, 32 pp, Full-color photos, Quality PB, 978-1-59473-256-0 **$8.99*** For ages 6 & up

Because Nothing Looks Like God
By Lawrence Kushner and Karen Kushner
Invites parents and children to explore, together, the questions we all have about God.
11 x 8½, 32 pp, Full-color illus., HC, 978-1-58023-092-6 **$18.99** For ages 4 & up

In God's Hands By Lawrence Kushner and Gary Schmidt
Each of us has the power to make the world a better place—working ordinary miracles with our everyday deeds.
9 x 12, 32 pp, Full-color illus., HC, 978-1-58023-224-1 **$16.99** For ages 5 & up

What Makes Someone a Jew? By Lauren Seidman
Reflects the changing face of American Judaism. Helps preschoolers and young readers (ages 3–6) understand that you don't have to look a certain way to be Jewish.
10 x 8½, 32 pp, Full-color photos, Quality PB, 978-1-58023-321-7 **$8.99** For ages 3–6

In Our Image: God's First Creatures
By Nancy Sohn Swartz God asks all of nature to offer gifts to humankind—with a promise that the humans would care for creation in return.
Full-color illus., eBook, 978-1-58023-520-4 **$16.95** For ages 5 & up
Animated app available on Apple App Store and the Google Play Marketplace **$9.99**

The Book of Miracles: A Young Person's Guide to Jewish Spiritual Awareness
Written and illus. by Lawrence Kushner
6 x 9, 96 pp, 2-color illus., HC, 978-1-879045-78-1 **$16.95** For ages 9–13

The Jewish Family Fun Book, 2nd Edition: Holiday Projects, Everyday
Activities, and Travel Ideas with Jewish Themes By Danielle Dardashti and Roni Sarig
6 x 9, 304 pp, w/ 70+ b/w illus., Quality PB, 978-1-58023-333-0 **$18.99**

When a Grandparent Dies: A Kid's Own Remembering Workbook for
Dealing with Shiva and the Year Beyond By Nechama Liss-Levinson
8 x 10, 48 pp, 2-color text, HC, 978-1-879045-44-6 **$15.95** For ages 7–13

*A book from SkyLight Paths, Jewish Lights' sister imprint

Congregation Resources

Relational Judaism: Using the Power of Relationships to Transform the Jewish Community *By Dr. Ron Wolfson* How to transform the model of twentieth-century Jewish institutions into twenty-first-century relational communities offering meaning and purpose, belonging and blessing.
6 x 9, 288 pp, HC, 978-1-58023-666-9 **$24.99**

The Spirituality of Welcoming: How to Transform Your Congregation into a Sacred Community *By Dr. Ron Wolfson*
Shows crucial hospitality is for congregational survival and dives into the practicalities of cultivating openness. 6 x 9, 224 pp, Quality PB, 978-1-58023-244-9 **$19.99**

Jewish Megatrends: Charting the Course of the American Jewish Future
By Rabbi Sidney Schwarz; Foreword by Ambassador Stuart E. Eizenstat
Visionary solutions for a community ripe for transformational change—from fourteen leading innovators of Jewish life. 6 x 9, 288 pp, HC, 978-1-58023-667-6 **$24.99**

Inspired Jewish Leadership: Practical Approaches to Building Strong Communities *By Dr. Erica Brown*
Develop your leadership skills and dialogue with others about issues like conflict resolution and effective succession planning.
6 x 9, 256 pp, HC, 978-1-58023-361-3 **$27.99**

Building a Successful Volunteer Culture: Finding Meaning in Service in the Jewish Community *By Rabbi Charles Simon; Foreword by Shelley Lindauer; Preface by Dr. Ron Wolfson*
6 x 9, 192 pp, Quality PB, 978-1-58023-408-5 **$16.99**

The Case for Jewish Peoplehood: Can We Be One?
By Dr. Erica Brown and Dr. Misha Galperin; Foreword by Rabbi Joseph Telushkin
6 x 9, 224 pp, HC, 978-1-58023-401-6 **$21.99**

Empowered Judaism: What Independent Minyanim Can Teach Us about Building Vibrant Jewish Communities *By Rabbi Elie Kaunfer; Foreword by Prof. Jonathan D. Sarna*
6 x 9, 224 pp, Quality PB, 978-1-58023-412-2 **$18.99**

Finding a Spiritual Home: How a New Generation of Jews Can Transform the American Synagogue *By Rabbi Sidney Schwarz*
6 x 9, 352 pp, Quality PB, 978-1-58023-185-5 **$19.95**

Judaism and Health: A Handbook of Practical, Professional and Scholarly Resources
Edited by Jeff Levin, PhD, MPH, and Michele F. Prince, LCSW, MAJCS
Foreword by Rabbi Elliot N. Dorff, PhD
6 x 9, 448 pp, HC, 978-1-58023-714-7 **$50.00**

Jewish Pastoral Care, 2nd Edition: A Practical Handbook from Traditional & Contemporary Sources *Edited by Rabbi Dayle A. Friedman, MSW, MAJCS, BCC*
6 x 9, 528 pp, Quality PB, 978-1-58023-427-6 **$35.00**

Jewish Spiritual Direction: An Innovative Guide from Traditional and Contemporary Sources *Edited by Rabbi Howard A. Addison, PhD, and Barbara Eve Breitman, MSW*
6 x 9, 368 pp, HC, 978-1-58023-230-2 **$30.00**

A Practical Guide to Rabbinic Counseling
Edited by Rabbi Yisrael N. Levitz, PhD, and Rabbi Abraham J. Twerski, MD
6 x 9, 432 pp, HC, 978-1-58023-562-4 **$40.00**

Professional Spiritual & Pastoral Care: A Practical Clergy and Chaplain's Handbook
Edited by Rabbi Stephen B. Roberts, MBA, MHL, BCJC
6 x 9, 480 pp, HC, 978-1-59473-312-3 **$50.00***

Reimagining Leadership in Jewish Organizations: Ten Practical Lessons to Help You Implement Change and Achieve Your Goals
By Dr. Misha Galperin 6 x 9, 192 pp, Quality PB, 978-1-58023-492-4 **$16.99**

Rethinking Synagogues: A New Vocabulary for Congregational Life
By Rabbi Lawrence A. Hoffman, PhD 6 x 9, 240 pp, Quality PB, 978-1-58023-248-7 **$19.99**

Revolution of Jewish Spirit: How to Revive Ruakh in Your Spiritual Life, Transform Your Synagogue & Inspire Your Jewish Community
By Rabbi Baruch HaLevi, DMin, and Ellen Frankel, LCSW; Foreword by Dr. Ron Wolfson
6 x 9, 224 pp, Quality PB, 978-1-58023-625-6 **$19.99**

*A book from SkyLight Paths, Jewish Lights' sister imprint

Holidays / Holy Days

Prayers of Awe Series

An exciting new series that examines the High Holy Day liturgy to enrich the praying experience of everyone—whether experienced worshipers or guests who encounter Jewish prayer for the very first time. *Edited by Rabbi Lawrence A. Hoffman, PhD*

Who by Fire, Who by Water—Un'taneh Tokef
6 x 9, 272 pp, Quality PB, 978-1-58023-672-0 **$19.99**; HC, 978-1-58023-424-5 **$24.99**

All These Vows—Kol Nidre
6 x 9, 288 pp, HC, 978-1-58023-430-6 **$24.99**

We Have Sinned—Sin and Confession in Judaism: *Ashamnu* and *Al Chet*
6 x 9, 304 pp, HC, 978-1-58023-612-6 **$24.99**

May God Remember: Memory and Memorializing in Judaism—*Yizkor*
6 x 9, 304 pp, HC, 978-1-58023-689-8 **$24.99**

All the World: Universalism, Particularism and the High Holy Days
Combines the particularistic concern for Israel as a People called by God with the universalistic proclamation that Israel is called for universal ends.
6 x 9, 288 pp, HC, 978-1-58023-783-3 **$24.99**

Rosh Hashanah Readings: Inspiration, Information and Contemplation
Yom Kippur Readings: Inspiration, Information and Contemplation
Edited by Rabbi Dov Peretz Elkins; Section Introductions from Arthur Green's These Are the Words
Rosh Hashanah: 6 x 9, 400 pp, Quality PB, 978-1-58023-437-5 **$19.99**
Yom Kippur: 6 x 9, 368 pp, Quality PB, 978-1-58023-438-2 **$19.99**; HC, 978-1-58023-271-5 **$24.99**

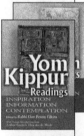

Reclaiming Judaism as a Spiritual Practice: Holy Days and Shabbat
By Rabbi Goldie Milgram 7 x 9, 272 pp, Quality PB, 978-1-58023-205-0 **$19.99**

The Sabbath Soul: Mystical Reflections on the Transformative Power of Holy Time
Selection, Translation and Commentary by Eitan Fishbane, PhD
6 x 9, 208 pp, Quality PB, 978-1-58023-459-7 **$18.99**

Shabbat, 2nd Edition: The Family Guide to Preparing for and Celebrating the Sabbath
By Dr. Ron Wolfson 7 x 9, 320 pp, Illus., Quality PB, 978-1-58023-164-0 **$21.99**

Hanukkah, 2nd Edition: The Family Guide to Spiritual Celebration
By Dr. Ron Wolfson 7 x 9, 240 pp, Illus., Quality PB, 978-1-58023-122-0 **$18.95**

Passover

My People's Passover Haggadah
Traditional Texts, Modern Commentaries
Edited by Rabbi Lawrence A. Hoffman, PhD, and David Arnow, PhD
A diverse and exciting collection of commentaries on the traditional Passover Haggadah—in two volumes!
Vol. 1: 7 x 10, 304 pp, HC, 978-1-58023-354-5 **$24.99**
Vol. 2: 7 x 10, 320 pp, HC, 978-1-58023-346-0 **$24.99**

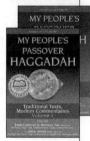

Creating Lively Passover Seders, 2nd Edition: A Sourcebook of Engaging Tales, Texts & Activities *By David Arnow, PhD* 7 x 9, 464 pp, Quality PB, 978-1-58023-444-3 **$24.99**

Freedom Journeys: The Tale of Exodus and Wilderness across Millennia
By Rabbi Arthur O. Waskow and Rabbi Phyllis O. Berman
6 x 9, 288 pp, HC, 978-1-58023-445-0 **$24.99**

Leading the Passover Journey: The Seder's Meaning Revealed, the Haggadah's Story Retold *By Rabbi Nathan Laufer*
6 x 9, 224 pp, Quality PB, 978-1-58023-399-6 **$18.99**

Passover, 2nd Edition: The Family Guide to Spiritual Celebration
By Dr. Ron Wolfson with Joel Lurie Grishaver 7 x 9, 416 pp, Quality PB, 978-1-58023-174-9 **$19.95**

The Women's Passover Companion: Women's Reflections on the Festival of Freedom
Edited by Rabbi Sharon Cohen Anisfeld, Tara Mohr and Catherine Spector
Foreword by Paula E. Hyman
6 x 9, 352 pp, Quality PB, 978-1-58023-231-9 **$19.99**; HC, 978-1-58023-128-2 **$24.95**

The Women's Seder Sourcebook: Rituals & Readings for Use at the Passover Seder
Edited by Rabbi Sharon Cohen Anisfeld, Tara Mohr and Catherine Spector
6 x 9, 384 pp, Quality PB, 978-1-58023-232-6 **$19.99**

Ecology / Environment

A Wild Faith: Jewish Ways into Wilderness, Wilderness Ways into Judaism
By Rabbi Mike Comins; Foreword by Nigel Savage
6 x 9, 240 pp, Quality PB, 978-1-58023-316-3 **$18.99**

Ecology & the Jewish Spirit: Where Nature & the Sacred Meet
Edited by Ellen Bernstein 6 x 9, 288 pp, Quality PB, 978-1-58023-082-7 **$18.99**

Torah of the Earth: Exploring 4,000 Years of Ecology in Jewish Thought
Vol. 1: Biblical Israel & Rabbinic Judaism; Vol. 2: Zionism & Eco-Judaism
Edited by Rabbi Arthur Waskow Vol. 1: 6 x 9, 272 pp, Quality PB, 978-1-58023-086-5 **$19.95**
Vol. 2: 6 x 9, 336 pp, Quality PB, 978-1-58023-087-2 **$19.95**

The Way Into Judaism and the Environment *By Jeremy Benstein, PhD*
6 x 9, 288 pp, Quality PB, 978-1-58023-368-2 **$18.99**; HC, 978-1-58023-268-5 **$24.99**

Graphic Novels / Graphic History

The Adventures of Rabbi Harvey: A Graphic Novel of Jewish Wisdom and Wit in the
Wild West *By Steve Sheinkin*
6 x 9, 144 pp, Full-color illus., Quality PB, 978-1-58023-310-1 **$16.99**

Rabbi Harvey Rides Again: A Graphic Novel of Jewish Folktales Let Loose in the
Wild West *By Steve Sheinkin*
6 x 9, 144 pp, Full-color illus., Quality PB, 978-1-58023-347-7 **$16.99**

Rabbi Harvey vs. the Wisdom Kid: A Graphic Novel of Dueling Jewish Folktales in
the Wild West *By Steve Sheinkin*
6 x 9, 144 pp, Full-color illus., Quality PB, 978-1-58023-422-1 **$16.99**

The Story of the Jews: A 4,000-Year Adventure—A Graphic History Book
By Stan Mack 6 x 9, 304 pp, Illus., Quality PB, 978-1-58023-155-8 **$16.99**

Grief / Healing

Facing Illness, Finding God: How Judaism Can Help You and Caregivers Cope
When Body or Spirit Fails *By Rabbi Joseph B. Meszler*
6 x 9, 208 pp, Quality PB, 978-1-58023-423-8 **$16.99**

Grief in Our Seasons: A Mourner's Kaddish Companion *By Rabbi Kerry M. Olitzky*
4½ x 6½, 448 pp, Quality PB, 978-1-879045-55-2 **$18.99**

Healing and the Jewish Imagination: Spiritual and Practical Perspectives on
Judaism and Health *Edited by Rabbi William Cutter, PhD*
6 x 9, 240 pp, Quality PB, 978-1-58023-373-6 **$19.99**

Healing from Despair: Choosing Wholeness in a Broken World
By Rabbi Elie Kaplan Spitz with Erica Shapiro Taylor; Foreword by Abraham J. Twerski, MD
5½ x 8½, 208 pp, Quality PB, 978-1-58023-436-8 **$16.99**

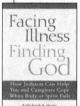

Healing of Soul, Healing of Body: Spiritual Leaders Unfold the Strength & Solace
in Psalms *Edited by Rabbi Simkha Y. Weintraub, LCSW*
6 x 9, 128 pp, 2-color illus. text, Quality PB, 978-1-879045-31-6 **$16.99**

Judaism and Health: A Handbook of Practical, Professional and Scholarly Resources
Edited by Jeff Levin, PhD, MPH, and Michele F. Prince, LCSW, MAJCS
Foreword by Rabbi Elliot N. Dorff, PhD 6 x 9, 448 pp, HC, 978-1-58023-714-7 **$50.00**

Midrash & Medicine: Healing Body and Soul in the Jewish Interpretive Tradition
Edited by Rabbi William Cutter, PhD; Foreword by Michele F. Prince, LCSW, MAJCS
6 x 9, 352 pp, Quality PB, 978-1-58023-484-9 **$21.99**

Mourning & Mitzvah, 2nd Edition: A Guided Journal for Walking the Mourner's
Path through Grief to Healing *By Rabbi Anne Brener, LCSW*
7½ x 9, 304 pp, Quality PB, 978-1-58023-113-8 **$19.99**

Tears of Sorrow, Seeds of Hope, 2nd Edition: A Jewish Spiritual Companion
for Infertility and Pregnancy Loss *By Rabbi Nina Beth Cardin*
6 x 9, 208 pp, Quality PB, 978-1-58023-233-3 **$18.99**

A Time to Mourn, a Time to Comfort, 2nd Edition
A Guide to Jewish Bereavement *By Dr. Ron Wolfson; Foreword by Rabbi David J. Wolpe*
7 x 9, 384 pp, Quality PB, 978-1-58023-253-1 **$21.99**

When a Grandparent Dies: A Kid's Own Remembering Workbook for Dealing
with Shiva and the Year Beyond *By Nechama Liss-Levinson, PhD*
8 x 10, 48 pp, 2-color text, HC, 978-1-879045-44-6 **$15.95** *For ages 7–13*

Life Cycle
Marriage / Parenting / Family / Aging

The New Jewish Baby Album: Creating and Celebrating the Beginning of a Spiritual Life—A Jewish Lights Companion
By the Editors at Jewish Lights; Foreword by Anita Diamant; Preface by Rabbi Sandy Eisenberg Sasso
A spiritual keepsake that will be treasured for generations. More than just a memory book, shows you how—and why it's important—to create a Jewish home and a Jewish life. 8 x 10, 64 pp, Deluxe Padded HC, Full-color illus., 978-1-58023-138-1 **$19.95**

The Jewish Pregnancy Book: A Resource for the Soul, Body & Mind during Pregnancy, Birth & the First Three Months *By Sandy Falk, MD, and Rabbi Daniel Judson, with Steven A. Rapp* Medical information, prayers and rituals for each stage of pregnancy. 7 x 10, 208 pp, b/w photos, Quality PB, 978-1-58023-178-7 **$16.95**

Parenting Jewish Teens: A Guide for the Perplexed
By Joanne Doades Explores the questions and issues that shape the world in which today's Jewish teenagers live and offers constructive advice to parents.
6 x 9, 176 pp, Quality PB, 978-1-58023-305-7 **$16.99**

Celebrating Your New Jewish Daughter: Creating Jewish Ways to Welcome Baby Girls into the Covenant—New and Traditional Ceremonies *By Debra Nussbaum Cohen*
Foreword by Rabbi Sandy Eisenberg Sasso 6 x 9, 272 pp, Quality PB, 978-1-58023-090-2 **$18.95**

The New Jewish Baby Book, 2nd Edition: Names, Ceremonies & Customs—A Guide for Today's Families *By Anita Diamant* 6 x 9, 320 pp, Quality PB, 978-1-58023-251-7 **$19.99**

Secrets of a Soulful Marriage: Creating & Sustaining

a Loving, Sacred Relationship *By Jim Sharon, EdD, and Ruth Sharon, MS*
Useful perspectives, tools and practices for cultivating a relationship; with insights from psychology, the wisdom of spiritual traditions and the experiences of many kinds of committed couples. 6 x 9, 192 pp, Quality PB, 978-1-59473-554-7 **$16.99***

The Creative Jewish Wedding Book, 2nd Edition: A Hands-On Guide to New & Old Traditions, Ceremonies & Celebrations *By Gabrielle Kaplan-Mayer*
9 x 9, 288 pp, b/w photos, Quality PB, 978-1-58023-398-9 **$19.99**

Divorce Is a Mitzvah: A Practical Guide to Finding Wholeness and Holiness When Your Marriage Dies *By Rabbi Perry Netter; Afterword by Rabbi Laura Geller*
6 x 9, 224 pp, Quality PB, 978-1-58023-172-5 **$18.99**

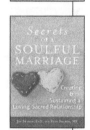

Embracing the Covenant: Converts to Judaism Talk About Why & How
By Rabbi Allan Berkowitz and Patti Moskovitz 6 x 9, 192 pp, Quality PB, 978-1-879045-50-7 **$16.95**

Introducing My Faith and My Community: The Jewish Outreach Institute Guide for the Christian in a Jewish Interfaith Relationship
By Rabbi Kerry M. Olitzky 6 x 9, 176 pp, Quality PB, 978-1-58023-192-3 **$16.99**

Jewish Visions for Aging: A Professional Guide for Fostering Wholeness
By Rabbi Dale A. Friedman, MSW, MAJCS, BCC; Foreword by Thomas R. Cole, PhD
Preface by Dr. Eugene B. Borowitz
6 x 9, 272 pp, HC, 978-1-58023-348-4 **$24.99**

Making a Successful Jewish Interfaith Marriage: The Jewish Outreach Institute Guide to Opportunities, Challenges and Resources
By Rabbi Kerry M. Olitzky with Joan Peterson Littman
6 x 9, 176 pp, Quality PB, 978-1-58023-170-1 **$16.95**

A Man's Responsibility: A Jewish Guide to Being a Son, a Partner in Marriage, a Father and a Community Leader *By Rabbi Joseph B. Meszler*
6 x 9, 192 pp, Quality PB, 978-1-58023-435-1 **$16.99**

So That Your Values Live On: Ethical Wills and How to Prepare Them
Edited by Rabbi Jack Riemer and Rabbi Nathaniel Stampfer
6 x 9, 272 pp, Quality PB, 978-1-879045-34-7 **$18.99**

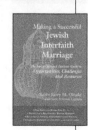

*A book from SkyLight Paths, Jewish Lights' sister imprint

Social Justice

Where Justice Dwells
A Hands-On Guide to Doing Social Justice in Your Jewish Community
By Rabbi Jill Jacobs; Foreword by Rabbi David Saperstein
Provides ways to envision and act on your own ideals of social justice.
7 x 9, 288 pp, Quality PB, 978-1-58023-453-5 **$24.99**

There Shall Be No Needy
Pursuing Social Justice through Jewish Law and Tradition
By Rabbi Jill Jacobs; Foreword by Rabbi Elliot N. Dorff, PhD; Preface by Simon Greer
Confronts the most pressing issues of twenty-first-century America from a deeply
Jewish perspective. 6 x 9, 288 pp, Quality PB, 978-1-58023-425-2 **$16.99**
There Shall Be No Needy Teacher's Guide 8½ x 11, 56 pp, PB, 978-1-58023-429-0 **$8.99**

Conscience
The Duty to Obey and the Duty to Disobey
By Rabbi Harold M. Schulweis
Examines the idea of conscience and the role conscience plays in our relationships
to government, law, ethics, religion, human nature, God—and to each other.
6 x 9, 160 pp, Quality PB, 978-1-58023-419-1 **$16.99**; HC, 978-1-58023-375-0 **$19.99**

Judaism and Justice: The Jewish Passion to Repair the World
By Rabbi Sidney Schwarz; Foreword by Ruth Messinger
6 x 9, 352 pp, Quality PB, 978-1-58023-353-8 **$19.99**

Spirituality / Women's Interest

Embracing the Divine Feminine: Finding God through the Ecstasy of
Physical Love—The Song of Songs Annotated & Explained
Annotation and Translation by Rabbi Rami Shapiro; Foreword by Rev. Cynthia Bourgeault, PhD
Restores the Song of Songs' eroticism and interprets it as a celebration of the love
between the Divine Feminine and the contemporary spiritual seeker.
5½ x 8½, 176 pp, Quality PB, 978-1-59473-575-2 **$16.99***

The Women's Haftarah Commentary
New Insights from Women Rabbis on the 54 Weekly Haftarah Portions,
the 5 Megillot & Special Shabbatot
Edited by Rabbi Elyse Goldstein
Illuminates the historical significance of female portrayals in the Haftarah and the
Five Megillot. 6 x 9, 560 pp, Quality PB, 978-1-58023-371-2 **$19.99**

The Women's Torah Commentary
New Insights from Women Rabbis on the 54 Weekly Torah Portions
Edited by Rabbi Elyse Goldstein
Over fifty women rabbis offer inspiring insights on the Torah, in a week-by-week format.
6 x 9, 496 pp, Quality PB, 978-1-58023-370-5 **$19.99**; HC, 978-1-58023-076-6 **$34.95**

The Divine Feminine in Biblical Wisdom Literature
Selections Annotated & Explained *Translation & Annotation by Rabbi Rami Shapiro*
Foreword by Rev. Cynthia Bourgeault, PhD
5½ x 8½, 240 pp, Quality PB, 978-1-59473-109-9 **$18.99***

New Jewish Feminism: Probing the Past, Forging the Future
Edited by Rabbi Elyse Goldstein; Foreword by Anita Diamant
6 x 9, 480 pp, HC, 978-1-58023-359-0 **$24.99**

The Quotable Jewish Woman
Wisdom, Inspiration & Humor from the Mind & Heart
Edited by Elaine Bernstein Partnow
6 x 9, 496 pp, Quality PB, 978-1-58023-236-4 **$19.99**

See Passover for *The Women's Passover Companion: Women's Reflections on
the Festival of Freedom* and *The Women's Seder Sourcebook: Rituals &
Readings for Use at the Passover Seder.*

*A book from SkyLight Paths, Jewish Lights' sister imprint

Spirituality

Amazing Chesed: Living a Grace-Filled Judaism
By Rabbi Rami Shapiro Drawing from ancient and contemporary, traditional and non-traditional Jewish wisdom, reclaims the idea of grace in Judaism.
6 x 9, 176 pp, Quality PB, 978-1-58023-624-9 **$16.99**

Jewish with Feeling: A Guide to Meaningful Jewish Practice
By Rabbi Zalman Schachter-Shalomi (z"l) with Joel Segel
Takes off from basic questions like "Why be Jewish?" and whether the word *God* still speaks to us today and lays out a vision for a whole-person Judaism.
5½ x 8½, 288 pp, Quality PB, 978-1-58023-691-1 **$19.99**

Perennial Wisdom for the Spiritually Independent: Sacred Teachings— Annotated & Explained *Annotation by Rabbi Rami Shapiro; Foreword by Richard Rohr*
Weaves sacred texts and teachings from the world's major religions into a coherent exploration of the five core questions at the heart of every religion's search.
5½ x 8½, 336 pp, Quality PB, 978-1-59473-515-8 **$16.99**

A Book of Life: Embracing Judaism as a Spiritual Practice
By Rabbi Michael Strassfeld 6 x 9, 544 pp, Quality PB, 978-1-58023-247-0 **$24.99**

Bringing the Psalms to Life: How to Understand and Use the Book of Psalms
By Rabbi Daniel F. Polish, PhD 6 x 9, 208 pp, Quality PB, 978-1-58023-157-2 **$18.99**

Does the Soul Survive? A Jewish Journey to Belief in Afterlife, Past Lives & Living with Purpose *By Rabbi Elie Kaplan Spitz; Foreword by Brian L. Weiss, MD*
6 x 9, 288 pp, Quality PB, 978-1-58023-165-7 **$18.99**

Entering the Temple of Dreams: Jewish Prayers, Movements and Meditations for the End of the Day *By Tamar Frankiel, PhD, and Judy Greenfeld*
7 x 10, 192 pp, illus., Quality PB, 978-1-58023-079-7 **$16.95**

First Steps to a New Jewish Spirit: Reb Zalman's Guide to Recapturing the Intimacy & Ecstasy in Your Relationship with God
By Rabbi Zalman Schachter-Shalomi (z"l) with Donald Gropman
6 x 9, 144 pp, Quality PB, 978-1-58023-182-4 **$16.95**

Foundations of Sephardic Spirituality: The Inner Life of Jews of the Ottoman Empire
By Rabbi Marc D. Angel, PhD 6 x 9, 224 pp, Quality PB, 978-1-58023-341-5 **$18.99**

God & the Big Bang: Discovering Harmony between Science & Spirituality
By Dr. Daniel C. Matt 6 x 9, 216 pp, Quality PB, 978-1-879045-89-7 **$18.99**

God in Our Relationships: Spirituality between People from the Teachings of Martin Buber
By Rabbi Dennis S. Ross 5½ x 8¼, 160 pp, Quality PB, 978-1-58023-147-3 **$16.95**

The God Upgrade: Finding Your 21st-Century Spirituality in Judaism's 5,000-Year-Old Tradition *By Rabbi Jamie Korngold; Foreword by Rabbi Harold M. Schulweis*
6 x 9, 176 pp, Quality PB, 978-1-58023-443-6 **$15.99**

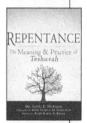

The Jewish Lights Spirituality Handbook: A Guide to Understanding, Exploring & Living a Spiritual Life *Edited by Stuart M. Matlins*
6 x 9, 456 pp, Quality PB, 978-1-58023-093-3 **$19.99**

Judaism, Physics and God: Searching for Sacred Metaphors in a Post-Einstein World
By Rabbi David W. Nelson 6 x 9, 352 pp, Quality PB, inc. reader's discussion guide
978-1-58023-306-4 **$18.99**; HC, 352 pp, 978-1-58023-252-4 **$24.99**

Repentance: The Meaning and Practice of Teshuvah
By Dr. Louis E. Newman; Foreword by Rabbi Harold M. Schulweis; Preface by Rabbi Karyn D. Kedar
6 x 9, 256 pp, HC, 978-1-58023-426-9 **$24.99**; Quality PB, 978-1-58023-718-5 **$18.99**

The Sabbath Soul: Mystical Reflections on the Transformative Power of Holy Time
Selection, Translation and Commentary by Eitan Fishbane, PhD
6 x 9, 208 pp, Quality PB, 978-1-58023-459-7 **$18.99**

Tanya, the Masterpiece of Hasidic Wisdom: Selections Annotated & Explained
Translation & Annotation by Rabbi Rami Shapiro; Foreword by Rabbi Zalman Schachter-Shalomi (z"l)
5½ x 8½, 240 pp, Quality PB, 978-1-59473-275-1 **$18.99**

These Are the Words, 2nd Edition: A Vocabulary of Jewish Spiritual Life
By Rabbi Arthur Green, PhD
6 x 9, 320 pp, Quality PB, 978-1-58023-494-8 **$19.99**

Spirituality / Prayer

Davening: A Guide to Meaningful Jewish Prayer
By Rabbi Zalman Schachter-Shalomi (z"l) with Joel Segel; Foreword by Rabbi Lawrence Kushner
A fresh approach to prayer for all who wish to appreciate the power of prayer's poetry, song and ritual, and to join the age-old conversation that Jews have had with God. 6 x 9, 240 pp, Quality PB, 978-1-58023-627-0 **$18.99**

Jewish Men Pray: Words of Yearning, Praise, Petition, Gratitude and Wonder from Traditional and Contemporary Sources
Edited by Rabbi Kerry M. Olitzky and Stuart M. Matlins; Foreword by Rabbi Bradley Shavit Artson, DHL
A celebration of Jewish men's voices in prayer—to strengthen, heal, comfort, and inspire—from the ancient world up to our own day.
5 x 7¼, 400 pp, HC, 978-1-58023-628-7 **$19.99**

Making Prayer Real: Leading Jewish Spiritual Voices on Why Prayer Is Difficult and What to Do about It *By Rabbi Mike Comins* 6 x 9, 320 pp, Quality PB, 978-1-58023-417-7 **$18.99**

Witnesses to the One: The Spiritual History of the *Sh'ma*
By Rabbi Joseph B. Meszler; Foreword by Rabbi Elyse Goldstein
6 x 9, 176 pp, Quality PB, 978-1-58023-400-9 **$16.99**; HC, 978-1-58023-309-5 **$19.99**

My People's Prayer Book Series: Traditional Prayers, Modern Commentaries *Edited by Rabbi Lawrence A. Hoffman, PhD*
Provides diverse and exciting commentary to the traditional liturgy. Will help you find new wisdom in Jewish prayer, and bring liturgy into your life. Each book includes Hebrew text, modern translations and commentaries from all perspectives of the Jewish world.

Vol. 1—The *Sh'ma* and Its Blessings
  7 x 10, 168 pp, HC, 978-1-879045-79-8 **$29.99**
Vol. 2—The *Amidah* 7 x 10, 240 pp, HC, 978-1-879045-80-4 **$29.99**
Vol. 3—*P'sukei D'zimrah* (Morning Psalms)
  7 x 10, 240 pp, HC, 978-1-879045-81-1 **$29.99**
Vol. 4—*Seder K'riat Hatorah* (The Torah Service)
  7 x 10, 264 pp, HC, 978-1-879045-82-8 **$29.99**
Vol. 5—*Birkhot Hashachar* (Morning Blessings)
  7 x 10, 240 pp, HC, 978-1-879045-83-5 **$24.95**
Vol. 6—*Tachanun* and Concluding Prayers
  7 x 10, 240 pp, HC, 978-1-879045-84-2 **$24.95**
Vol. 7—Shabbat at Home 7 x 10, 240 pp, HC, 978-1-879045-85-9 **$29.99**
Vol. 8—*Kabbalat Shabbat* (Welcoming Shabbat in the Synagogue)
  7 x 10, 240 pp, HC, 978-1-58023-121-3 **$24.99**
Vol. 9—Welcoming the Night: *Minchah* and *Ma'ariv* (Afternoon and Evening Prayer) 7 x 10, 272 pp, HC, 978-1-58023-262-3 **$24.99**
Vol. 10—Shabbat Morning: *Shacharit* and *Musaf* (Morning and Additional Services) 7 x 10, 240 pp, HC, 978-1-58023-240-1 **$29.99**

Spirituality / Lawrence Kushner

I'm God; You're Not: Observations on Organized Religion & Other Disguises of the Ego
6 x 9, 256 pp, Quality PB, 978-1-58023-513-6 **$18.99**; HC, 978-1-58023-441-2 **$21.99**

The Book of Letters: A Mystical Hebrew Alphabet
Popular HC Edition, 6 x 9, 80 pp, 2-color text, 978-1-879045-00-2 **$24.95**
Collector's Limited Edition, 9 x 12, 80 pp, gold-foil-embossed pages, w/ limited-edition silkscreened print, 978-1-879045-04-0 **$349.00**

The Book of Miracles: A Young Person's Guide to Jewish Spiritual Awareness
6 x 9, 96 pp, 2-color illus., HC, 978-1-879045-78-1 **$16.95** *For ages 9–13*

God Was in This Place & I, i Did Not Know: Finding Self, Spirituality and Ultimate Meaning 6 x 9, 192 pp, Quality PB, 978-1-879045-33-0 **$16.95**

Honey from the Rock: An Introduction to Jewish Mysticism
6 x 9, 176 pp, Quality PB, 978-1-58023-073-5 **$18.99**

Invisible Lines of Connection: Sacred Stories of the Ordinary
5½ x 8½, 160 pp, Quality PB, 978-1-879045-98-9 **$16.99**

The Way Into Jewish Mystical Tradition
6 x 9, 224 pp, Quality PB, 978-1-58023-200-5 **$18.99**

Inspiration

The Chutzpah Imperative: Empowering Today's Jews for a Life
That Matters *By Rabbi Edward Feinstein; Foreword by Rabbi Laura Geller*
A new view of chutzpah as Jewish self-empowerment to be God's partner and
repair the world. Reveals Judaism's ancient message, its deepest purpose and most
precious treasures. 6 x 9, 192 pp, HC, 978-1-58023-792-5 **$21.99**

Judaism's Ten Best Ideas: A Brief Guide for Seekers
By Rabbi Arthur Green, PhD A highly accessible introduction to Judaism's greatest contributions to civilization, drawing on Jewish mystical tradition and the
author's experience. 4½ x 6½, 112 pp, Quality PB, 978-1-58023-803-8 **$9.99**

Into the Fullness of the Void: A Spiritual Autobiography *By Dov Elbaum*
One of Israel's leading cultural figures provides insights and guidance for all of us.
6 x 9, 304 pp, Quality PB, 978-1-58023-715-4 **$18.99**

The Bridge to Forgiveness: Stories and Prayers for Finding God and Restoring Wholeness
By Rabbi Karyn D. Kedar 6 x 9, 176 pp, Quality PB, 978-1-58023-451-1 **$16.99**

The Empty Chair: Finding Hope and Joy—Timeless Wisdom from a Hasidic Master,
Rebbe Nachman of Breslov *Adapted by Moshe Mykoff and the Breslov Research Institute*
4 x 6, 128 pp, Deluxe PB w/ flaps, 978-1-879045-67-5 **$9.99**

The Gentle Weapon: Prayers for Everyday and Not-So-Everyday Moments—
Timeless Wisdom from the Teachings of the Hasidic Master Rebbe Nachman of Breslov
Adapted by Moshe Mykoff and S. C. Mizrahi, together with the Breslov Research Institute
4 x 6, 144 pp, Deluxe PB w/ flaps, 978-1-58023-022-3 **$9.99**

God Whispers: Stories of the Soul, Lessons of the Heart *By Rabbi Karyn D. Kedar*
6 x 9, 176 pp, Quality PB, 978-1-58023-088-9 **$16.99**

God's To-Do List: 103 Ways to Be an Angel and Do God's Work on Earth
By Dr. Ron Wolfson 6 x 9, 144 pp, Quality PB, 978-1-58023-301-9 **$16.99**

Happiness and the Human Spirit: The Spirituality of Becoming the Best You Can Be
By Rabbi Abraham J. Twerski, MD
6 x 9, 176 pp, Quality PB, 978-1-58023-404-7 **$16.99**; HC, 978-1-58023-343-9 **$19.99**

Life's Daily Blessings: Inspiring Reflections on Gratitude and Joy for Every Day, Based
on Jewish Wisdom *By Rabbi Kerry M. Olitzky* 4½ x 6½, 368 pp, Quality PB, 978-1-58023-396-5 **$16.99**

Restful Reflections: Nighttime Inspiration to Calm the Soul, Based on Jewish Wisdom
By Rabbi Kerry M. Olitzky and Rabbi Lori Forman-Jacobi
4½ x 6½, 448 pp, Quality PB, 978-1-58023-091-9 **$16.99**

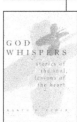

Sacred Intentions: Morning Inspiration to Strengthen the Spirit, Based on Jewish Wisdom
By Rabbi Kerry M. Olitzky and Rabbi Lori Forman-Jacobi
4½ x 6½, 448 pp, Quality PB, 978-1-58023-061-2 **$16.99**

Saying No and Letting Go: Jewish Wisdom on Making Room for What Matters Most
By Rabbi Edwin Goldberg, DHL; Foreword by Rabbi Naomi Levy
6 x 9, 192 pp, Quality PB, 978-1-58023-670-6 **$16.99**

The Seven Questions You're Asked in Heaven: Reviewing and Renewing Your
Life on Earth *By Dr. Ron Wolfson* 6 x 9, 176 pp, Quality PB, 978-1-58023-407-8 **$16.99**

Kabbalah / Mysticism

Ehyeh: A Kabbalah for Tomorrow
By Rabbi Arthur Green, PhD 6 x 9, 224 pp, Quality PB, 978-1-58023-213-5 **$18.99**

The Gift of Kabbalah: Discovering the Secrets of Heaven, Renewing Your Life on Earth
By Tamar Frankiel, PhD 6 x 9, 256 pp, Quality PB, 978-1-58023-141-1 **$18.99**

Jewish Mysticism and the Spiritual Life: Classical Texts, Contemporary
Reflections *Edited by Dr. Lawrence Fine, Dr. Eitan Fishbane and Rabbi Or N. Rose*
6 x 9, 256 pp, HC, 978-1-58023-434-4 **$24.99**; Quality PB, 978-1-58023-719-2 **$18.99**

Seek My Face: A Jewish Mystical Theology *By Rabbi Arthur Green, PhD*
6 x 9, 304 pp, Quality PB, 978-1-58023-130-5 **$19.95**

Zohar: Annotated & Explained *Translation & Annotation by Dr. Daniel C. Matt*
Foreword by Andrew Harvey 5½ x 8½, 176 pp, Quality PB, 978-1-893361-51-5 **$18.99**
(A book from SkyLight Paths, Jewish Lights' sister imprint)

See also *The Way Into Jewish Mystical Tradition* in The Way Into... Series

Theology / Philosophy / The Way Into... Serie

The Way Into... series offers an accessible and highly usable "guide tour" of the Jewish faith, people, history and beliefs—in total, a introduction to Judaism that will enable you to understand and interac with the sacred texts of the Jewish tradition. Each volume is writte by a leading contemporary scholar and teacher, and explores one ke aspect of Judaism. The Way Into... series enables all readers to achieve a real sense of Jewish cultural literacy through guided study.

The Way Into Encountering God in Judaism
By Rabbi Neil Gillman, PhD
For everyone who wants to understand how Jews have encountered Go throughout history and today.
6 x 9, 240 pp, Quality PB, 978-1-58023-199-2 **$18.99**; HC, 978-1-58023-025-4 **$21.95**
Also Available: **The Jewish Approach to God:** A Brief Introduction for Christian
By Rabbi Neil Gillman, PhD
5½ x 8½, 192 pp, Quality PB, 978-1-58023-190-9 **$16.95**

The Way Into Jewish Mystical Tradition
By Rabbi Lawrence Kushner
Allows readers to interact directly with the sacred mystical texts of the Jewish tradition An accessible introduction to the concepts of Jewish mysticism, their religious an spiritual significance, and how they relate to life today.
6 x 9, 224 pp, Quality PB, 978-1-58023-200-5 **$18.99**

The Way Into Jewish Prayer
By Rabbi Lawrence A. Hoffman, PhD
Opens the door to 3,000 years of Jewish prayer, making anyone feel at hom in the Jewish way of communicating with God.
6 x 9, 208 pp, Quality PB, 978-1-58023-201-2 **$18.99**

The Way Into Jewish Prayer Teacher's Guide
By Rabbi Jennifer Ossakow Goldsmith
8½ x 11, 42 pp, PB, 978-1-58023-345-3 **$8.99**
Download a free copy at www.jewishlights.com.

The Way Into Judaism and the Environment
By Jeremy Benstein, PhD
Explores the ways in which Judaism contributes to contemporary social-environmenta issues, the extent to which Judaism is part of the problem and how it can be par of the solution.
6 x 9, 288 pp, Quality PB, 978-1-58023-368-2 **$18.99**; HC, 978-1-58023-268-5 **$24.99**

The Way Into *Tikkun Olam* (Repairing the World)
By Rabbi Elliot N. Dorff, PhD
An accessible introduction to the Jewish concept of the individual's responsi bility to care for others and repair the world.
6 x 9, 304 pp, Quality PB, 978-1-58023-328-6 **$18.99**

The Way Into Torah
By Rabbi Norman J. Cohen, PhD
Helps guide you in the exploration of the origins and development of Torah explains why it should be studied and how to do it.
6 x 9, 176 pp, Quality PB, 978-1-58023-198-5 **$16.99**

The Way Into the Varieties of Jewishness
By Sylvia Barack Fishman, PhD
Explores the religious and historical understanding of what it has meant to b Jewish from ancient times to the present controversy over "Who is a Jew?"
6 x 9, 288 pp, Quality PB, 978-1-58023-367-5 **$18.99**; HC, 978-1-58023-030-8 **$24.99**

Theology / Philosophy

Believing and Its Tensions: A Personal Conversation about God, Torah, Suffering and Death in Jewish Thought
By Rabbi Neil Gillman, PhD Explores the changing nature of belief and the complexities of reconciling the intellectual, emotional and moral questions of Gillman's own searching mind and soul. 5½ x 8½, 144 pp, HC, 978-1-58023-669-0 **$19.99**

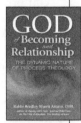

God of Becoming and Relationship: The Dynamic Nature of Process Theology *By Rabbi Bradley Shavit Artson, DHL* Explains how Process Theology breaks us free from the strictures of ancient Greek and medieval European philosophy, allowing us to see all creation as related patterns of energy through which we connect to everything. 6 x 9, 208 pp, HC, 978-1-58023-713-0 **$24.99**

The Way of Man: According to Hasidic Teaching
By Martin Buber; New Translation and Introduction by Rabbi Bernard H. Mehlman and Dr. Gabriel E. Padawer; Foreword by Paul Mendes-Flohr
An accessible and engaging new translation of Buber's classic work—*available as an eBook only.* eBook, 978-1-58023-601-0 Digital List Price **$14.99**

The Death of Death: Resurrection and Immortality in Jewish Thought
By Rabbi Neil Gillman, PhD 6 x 9, 336 pp, Quality PB, 978-1-58023-081-0 **$19.99**

Doing Jewish Theology: God, Torah & Israel in Modern Judaism *By Rabbi Neil Gillman, PhD*
6 x 9, 304 pp, Quality PB, 978-1-58023-439-9 **$18.99**; HC, 978-1-58023-322-4 **$24.99**

From Defender to Critic: The Search for a New Jewish Self
By Dr. David Hartman 6 x 9, 336 pp, HC, 978-1-58023-515-0 **$35.00**

The God Who Hates Lies: Confronting & Rethinking Jewish Tradition
By Dr. David Hartman with Charlie Buckholtz 6 x 9, 208 pp, Quality PB, 978-1-58023-790-1 **$19.99**

A Heart of Many Rooms: Celebrating the Many Voices within Judaism
By Dr. David Hartman 6 x 9, 352 pp, Quality PB, 978-1-58023-156-5 **$19.95**

Jewish Theology in Our Time: A New Generation Explores the Foundations and Future of Jewish Belief *Edited by Rabbi Elliot J. Cosgrove, PhD; Foreword by Rabbi David J. Wolpe Preface by Rabbi Carole B. Balin, PhD*
6 x 9, 240 pp, Quality PB, 978-1-58023-630-0 **$19.99**; HC, 978-1-58023-413-9 **$24.99**

Maimonides—Essential Teachings on Jewish Faith & Ethics: The Book of Knowledge & the Thirteen Principles of Faith—Annotated & Explained
Translation and Annotation by Rabbi Marc D. Angel, PhD
5½ x 8½, 224 pp, Quality PB, 978-1-59473-311-6 **$18.99***

Maimonides, Spinoza and Us: Toward an Intellectually Vibrant Judaism
By Rabbi Marc D. Angel, PhD 6 x 9, 224 pp, HC, 978-1-58023-411-5 **$24.99**

Our Religious Brains: What Cognitive Science Reveals about Belief, Morality, Community and Our Relationship with God
By Rabbi Ralph D. Mecklenburger; Foreword by Dr. Howard Kelfer; Preface by Dr. Neil Gillman
6 x 9, 224 pp, HC, 978-1-58023-508-2 **$24.99**

Your Word Is Fire: The Hasidic Masters on Contemplative Prayer
Edited and translated by Rabbi Arthur Green, PhD, and Barry W. Holtz
6 x 9, 160 pp, Quality PB, 978-1-879045-25-5 **$16.99**

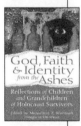

God, Faith & Identity from the Ashes
Reflections of Children and Grandchildren of Holocaust Survivors
Almost 90 Contributors from sixteen countries inform, challenge and inspire people of all faiths and backgrounds. *Edited by Menachem Z. Rosensaft; Prologue by Elie Wiesel*
6 x 9, 352 pp, HC, 978-1-58023-805-2 **$25.00**

I Am Jewish
Personal Reflections Inspired by the Last Words of Daniel Pearl
Almost 150 Jews—both famous and not—from all walks of life, from all around the world, write about many aspects of their Judaism.
Edited by Judea and Ruth Pearl 6 x 9, 304 pp, Deluxe PB w/ flaps, 978-1-58023-259-3 **$19.99**
Download a free copy of the *I Am Jewish Teacher's Guide* at www.jewishlights.com.

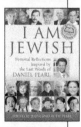

*A book from SkyLight Paths, Jewish Lights' sister imprint

About Jewish Lights

People of all faiths and backgrounds yearn for books that attract, engage, educate, and spiritually inspire.

Our principal goal is to stimulate thought and help all people learn about who the Jewish People are, where they come from, and what the future can be made to hold. While people of our diverse Jewish heritage are the primary audience, our books speak to people in the Christian world as well and will broaden their understanding of Judaism and the roots of their own faith.

We bring to you authors who are at the forefront of spiritual thought and experience. While each has something different to say, they all say it in a voice that you can hear.

Our books are designed to welcome you and then to engage, stimulate, and inspire. We judge our success not only by whether or not our books are beautiful and commercially successful, but by whether or not they make a difference in your life.

For your information and convenience, at the back of this book we have provided a list of other Jewish Lights books you might find interesting and useful. They cover all the categories of your life:

Bar/Bat Mitzvah	Life Cycle
Bible Study / Midrash	Meditation
Children's Books	Men's Interest
Congregation Resources	Parenting
Current Events / History	Prayer / Ritual / Sacred Practice
Ecology / Environment	Social Justice
Fiction: Mystery, Science Fiction	Spirituality
Grief / Healing	Theology / Philosophy
Holidays / Holy Days	Travel
Inspiration	Twelve Steps
Kabbalah / Mysticism / Enneagram	Women's Interest

Stuart M. Matlins, Publisher

Or phone, mail or email to: **JEWISH LIGHTS Publishing**
An imprint of Turner Publishing Company
4507 Charlotte Avenue • Suite 100 • Nashville, Tennessee 37209
Tel: (615) 255-2665 • www.jewishlights.com
Prices subject to change.

Printed in the USA
CPSIA information can be obtained
at www.ICGtesting.com
JSHW022206140824
68134JS00018B/900

9 781683 360933